THE

RISE OF CHRISTENDOM.

BY

EDWIN JOHNSON, M.A.

"Quis nescit primam esse historiæ legem ne quid falsi dicere audeat, deinde ne quid veri non audeat: ne quæ suspicio gratiæ sit in scribendo? ne qua simultatis?"—Cic. de Or. ii. 15

LONDON

KEGAN PAUL, TRENCH, TRÜBNER, & CO., Lᵗᵈ

1890.

TO THE RIGHT HONOURABLE

SIR JOHN LUBBOCK, Bart.

LL.D., D.C.L., F.R.S.,

MEMBER OF PARLIAMENT FOR THE UNIVERSITY OF LONDON,

IN

SINCERE ESTEEM FOR HIS CHARACTER AND HIS MANY SERVICES

TO HUMANITY AND SCIENCE,

This Volume

PREFATORY NOTE.

WHILE engaged in the revision of the following pages, I have examined some further branches of evidence relating to the subject, and have confirmed myself in the general conclusions which I have laid before the reader. About four hundred years ago the schools of England and of the West were ruled by the Black Monks, with their allies the Black, the White, the Grey, the Austin Friars, and other religious orders They had formed an orthodox system of education. Its principle was theological; it was derived from a peculiar interpretation of the Jewish Scriptures. From it was deduced an orthodox geography and chronology, an orthodox physiology and anthropology, and an orthodox astronomy.

Every one of these orthodox doctrines has been superseded in the course of experience. In the light of orthodox geography the dream of Columbus was absurd, but the discovery of Columbus—the fourth anniversary of which we shall soon be commemorating —converted the orthodox geography into an absurdity. The orthodox chronology has been shown to be as artificial as other mediæval chronologies. The proceedings of Galileo were absurd in the opinion of the orthodox astronomers; and so was the philosophy of Bacon. Yet we hear nothing now of the orthodox astronomy, nor do men now seek to arrive at facts by dreaming first and observing later. We do not now seek to deduce our facts from our theories, as our early teachers persistently did. As for the orthodox physiology and anthropology, these subjects have passed so completely into the lumber-room of obsolete lore that most educated persons would be astounded if they knew what was the teaching on these subjects in our schools about a century before the time of Bacon.

The Church history of the monks has not altogether escaped the fate of the rest of their teaching. An Anglican clergyman in the seventeenth century made a most damaging attack upon a part of it; and late in the same age a Catholic clergyman exposed the system of it, with severer invectives against the literary monks than have ever fallen from the pen of layman or Protestant. It would be long to explain how it is that in this respect the monks of the West have so long retained their hold upon our imagination, and how it comes to pass that our scholars continue to edit as genuine representations of our past what are little more than a series of fables agreed upon, deduced from dogma, and published to the world as a means of ruling the world.

In the present day it is well understood that history is the task of the solitary student; and the notion of an university or other corporation conspiring and collaborating in the production of a dogmatic theory of the world in the form of story appears absurd. In the present day it appears to be conceded that no university or other learned body·should rest upon a dogmatic principle which sets finality to any kind of knowledge and excludes inquiry. Our schools were founded on the opposite principle, and every thoughtful student of our history is aware of the great injuries to our spiritual and social life that have flowed from it. A chasm deep and impassable separates us from the Middle Age and clerical theory of education.

I have shown in this work, with as much of succinctness and brevity as it seemed to me the subject admitted, that orthodoxy in historical study leads to results in sharp contradiction with the facts of the past as they may still in their outline be known. Christianism is the system of a corporation; it is the theory of the primitive monks. No other primitive Christians are to be ascertained. With regard to the epoch when the primitive Order appeared, I have endeavoured to approximate towards the fact, hoping that I may be enabled in some future work to do something more for the elucidation of this obscure question. I have written, though with the sense of great imperfections, for the best audience of my time, and especially for those who are aware with me of the need for solving this long-vexed historical problem; because upon the solution of it great consequences in reference to our system of education, and to our common civility and culture, depend.

CONTENTS.

CHAPTER I.

THE OBJECT OF THE INQUIRY.

CHAPTER II

THE ROMAN EMPIRE AND CHRISTENDOM.

CHAPTER III.

GLIMPSES OF MEDIÆVAL ROME AND ITALY.

CONTENTS.

CHAPTER VII.

THE TRADITIONS OF THE MOSQUE—Continued.

CHAPTER VIII.

THE RISE OF HEBREW LITERATURE.

CHAPTER IX.

THE SYSTEM OF CHURCH LITERATURE.

CHAPTER X.

EARLY FORMS OF THE CHRISTIAN LEGEND

CHAPTER XI.

THE INTERPOLATIONS IN THE LITERATURE OF THE ROMAN EMPIRE.

CHAPTER XII

SUMMARY AND CONCLUSION.

THE RISE OF CHRISTENDOM.

INTRODUCTION.

I⊤ is now about one hundred and twenty-five years since Edward Gibbon stood musing amidst the ruins of the Capitol of Rome, "while the bare-footed friars were singing vespers in the Temple of Jupiter," and the idea of writing the story of the Decline and Fall of the City first occurred to his mind. The reader may, however, search in vain through the pages of his elaborate and splendid composition for any clear and intelligible account of the course of events which brought the Franciscan friars to the Capitol, where they had been from about the year 1250. It is said that the Benedictines had occupied the Capitol before them; but if so, the Benedictines could not have been there much earlier than the end of the twelfth century. The very site of the Temple of Jupiter, and the history of the transition from the old Roman to the Mediæval worship, remain wrapped in profound obscurity.

Had Gibbon, while he meditated the rise of the Christian Church, remained still in thought upon the Capitol until he could discern the figure of the first monk ascending that sacred hill, he would have been led to very different conclusions from those which he adopted in his famous work. He might have waited

A

until he could hear the monks proclaiming how the
Emperor Augustus had, after a visit to the Pythian
priestess at Delphi, been converted to belief in the
power of a Hebrew Boy, the Ruler of Olympus, and
how he had raised an altar on the Capitol to the First-
Begotten of God. Had Gibbon determined the age
of that legend, he would not have erred so widely from
the true epoch of the origin of the Church. He has
laid his finger upon the word " organisation," as indi-
cating one of the secondary causes of the spread of
Christianity, yet he has nowhere pointed out the nature
of that organisation, nor how and where it was founded.

Gibbon has acquired the repute of the first of ecclesiastical historians ; yet he has not been able to trace
the rise of the Church in accordance with the laws of
reason and experience. An enthusiasm for Oriental
ideas appears suddenly to take possession of the popular mind. Monotheism sets in. The tolerance of the
Empire is violated, first for the persecution of the Christians, then for the persecution of all who are not
Christians. The emperors become theological madmen,
either in their attachment or their enmity to this new
religious system, which gradually becomes an establishment of the Empire. Gibbon should have observed,
I think, that the Church historians delight in representing the story as from the first incredible and contrary to human reason. He should have taken the
warning, and have made a more searching examination
of his original sources.

He has explained to us how he used his materials.
He was guided by great Church collectors, as Tille-
mont ; he verified the references given him ; he detected
and exposed some falsehoods, but the rest he treated
as genuine narrative. In short, he wrote too much on

Cordova is one of the most suitable places in our world from which the rise of Christendom may be surveyed. There, about two hundred years after the erection of the mosque, the Rabbins, teachers of another and much smaller clan or caste of the children of Israel, began to read a somewhat different version of the Biblical tradition, and to give the preference to the younger son of Ibrahim (Abraham) as their ancestor. They leaned on the Arabian tradition; they passed for Muslim in the world, but in secret they dreamed the dreams and saw the visions of an imaginary regal and rabbinical past. Gradually, during the next two hundred years, they formed a new people, and another great dogma was launched, that of the Prophetical Succession, stretching from Moses, whom they honoured in common with the Arabians, to Moses Maimonides of Cordova and Cairo. Here again the dogma of history is one thing, the facts are another, separated from the dogma by an impassable chasm. Again, but for historic circumstances, we might have been converted to the observance of the Sabbath, and synagogues of Moorish architecture might have been thickly studded over the lands of the West. As Friday is followed by Saturday, so the Synagogue succeeds the Mosque. Yet another branch of the children of Israel, settled at Nablus in Syria, had their theory of a priestly succession from Aaron, and a rival Law and Chronicle. These are the so-called Samaritans.

In the time of that great revenge of the West upon the East, those Oriental wars we call the Crusades, a third religious corporation arose, and once more asserted a dogma of history absolutely irreconcilable with the facts. The literary members of the two primitive Orders of St. Basil and St. Benedict, once united, laid down the basis on which all Church literature was to

be contrived and constructed. It was the theory that
the Holy Catholic Church or Holy Roman Empire
began with the reign of the Emperor Augustus, and
that, according to an early legend I have already cited,
Augustus was himself a Christian. These clerics looked
with envious eye upon the prosperity of the Jews
and the confederation of synagogues. They were bent
upon crushing them, as their warlike allies were bent
upon crushing the servants of Allah and his Apostle in
the East. They directed in concert a malignant invective against the whole people, whom they call Judæi.
They represented them as cast off from the mercy of the
Eternal their God, and the Christians a sect from them,
as having succeeded to their religious status and privileges. Sunday becomes the new day of worship.

It was necessary, in support of this dogma, to invent
a mass of fables respecting the Judæi, which still disgrace
the pages of the writers under Imperial Rome, who were
innocent of any knowledge of that Oriental caste. It
was the greatest misdeed, I believe, that wielders of
the pen had ever perpetrated ; and it is time that by
wielders of the pen in this happier age it should be
exposed and denounced. I write simply as an Englishman of Northern extraction. I do not enjoy the acquaintance of many members of the Synagogue. But I am
sure there are now many admirable critical scholars of
Jewish extraction who do not desire that the history of
the people should any longer be darkened by fables
which are injurious to our common culture. They may
confirm or they may correct my views, but at least they
will not be displeased with my intention, which is to do
their respected community a long-delayed justice. I
am in sympathy with those who are weary of hearing of
the faults of the Jews, and who prefer to contemplate

what is exemplary in their life; who think, with Jules Michelet, that their vices are mainly of our own creation, while their virtues are all their own.

I have endeavoured in the present work to deal with the masses of evidence relating to the rise of Christendom, and to define the effect which they produce upon the mind of one who desires to be an impartial observer and critic. Until the masses have been surveyed, no study of the details will bring us nearer to the objects of our research. We are concerned with four classes of witnesses. First of all, with the Imperial writers, who cease soon after the time of the Emperor Justinian. These are our best witnesses, not only as the earliest, but as the highest in character. They were, as a rule, men of rank; they wrote—as Englishmen should write now—in freedom and independence, yet with loyalty to the Empire which they served. They wrote to give information, not to promote a religious dogma nor to deceive the world. To their testimony may be added the unconscious testimony of inscriptions and other monuments. Next come the clergy of Islam, who are responsible for the Koran and all the explanatory literature connected with the Koran, down to the late Arabian chroniclers of the thirteenth century. Their testimony, of an importance still more massive, has hitherto been neglected or carelessly misunderstood. The Spanish Rabbins, from Samuel the Nagid to Maimonides, follow. Lastly, the Benedictines and Basilians of Monte Cassino and Grotta Ferrata, of Cluny and Citeaux, and many other cloisters, followed by the Franciscans and Dominicans, the Augustinians and the Carmelites, clamour to be heard. I have listened to the substance of what these various dogmatists had to say to the

world through the universities, and I have drawn my
own conclusions. They are such, I believe, as might
have been drawn by a scholar at the court of Frederic
II. during the first half of the thirteenth century ;
they are such as might have been drawn by Laurence
Valla or by Poggio, had they persevered in their
critical inquiries.

They are such conclusions as Prebendary Thomas
Fuller, the keen satirist of the monks and their Church
history of Britain, would have drawn, had he traced the
monks to the earliest cloisters. Gibbon himself, had
he felt the full force of what he wrote about Valla,
and the discovery of the imaginary foundations of the
Church, would have been led to similar conclusions.
Macaulay, who, fresh from India, was in Rome some
fifty and more years agone, wondering at what he called
the Brahmanical government of the city, had he addressed himself to the question, might have given to it
the most masterly elucidation.   It is with regret one reflects upon the names of other English men of letters who
have adorned our time, and who might have done much
for the enlightenment of the public on these matters.

Still more deplorable is it to reflect that the interest
of the clergy cannot be in favour of free historical
inquiry, and that a large number of the best-educated
men of the time are where they are for the purpose of
resisting inquiry. Bishop Sprat, in writing of Cowley,
alluded to a prevalent opinion of his time that Christianity was "the interest of a profession."   Dr. Robert
South, that master of the science of human nature,
remarked that *sometimes* Providence casts things so
that truth and interest lie the same way, but that it
is incredible to consider how interest outweighs truth.
Interest turns the doubtful into the probable, or the

truth into the doubtful or the downright false. He goes so far as to hint that when divines are unanimous on a disputed point, their opinion depends on interested considerations. Interest, he says, casts the balance; interest is the grand wheel and spring that moves the whole universe. In the next age, the Bishop of Durham is complaining that the educated classes treat Christianity as no longer a subject even of inquiry; as if it were discovered to be fictitious. In a perplexed work, he undertakes to show that it is not so clear a case that there is nothing in it. The same strong contrast of the ecclesiastical with the secular mind still obtains in England. How pathetic a record is to be found in Mr. Thomas Mozley's Reminiscences of the Oxford movement, of noble spirits whose force has been squandered in the effort to uphold the Mediæval tradition, while leading Englishmen in politics and letters are said to have rejected it!

I write myself in the interest of teachers who feel that it is a great inconvenience not to understand the past of the world, or to understand that it has been misrepresented, and not freely to say so. The monks who first visited these islands had no such interest. Their object was to bring us under their yoke, and they succeeded in establishing credulity towards them and their theories as the first principle of education. They never earned even our confidence; their works have long been condemned; yet slowly, very slowly, are we recovering the intellectual freedom of which they deprived us. They have left certain fixed ideas about history on our minds which are destined to be unfixed and to pass away, as fixed ideas about astronomy have passed away.

To be useful to others, we must write out of painful

experience; and the reader will discover that there have been painful experiences behind what I have written. The result of these studies has forced me to withdraw from beloved avocations, wherein I have spent some of the happiest years of life. Could I have found an answer to my own arguments, I would gladly have done so, because interest—in more than one sense of the word—has not in my case lain the same way with truth. If the fact lends any indirect corroboration to my arguments, any weight to my conclusions, I shall perhaps be justified in having mentioned it.

I have to thank many friends at home for their intelligent sympathy, also several professors of letters in Holland, France, and Germany for their civility in the reception of my former essay. Especially I am under deep debt to Dr. A. D. Loman of Amsterdam for the bright example of gentleness, truthfulness, and humanity which he has set in his writings, for the cordial friendship he has extended to me, and the great pains he has taken to assist me in the endeavour to solve this great historical problem. I may name also Dr. W. C. van Manen of Leyden, the late Professor Ernest Havet of Paris, Professor Jean Réville, Dr. Harnack, and Dr. Lünemann; their suggestions have received my respectful attention. The lamented Dr. Hatch of Oxford maintained in a recent essay that many so-called "primitive" institutions of Christianity were in reality Mediæval. It will be observed that I give a great extension to that proposition.

Curiously, my esteemed critics have complained of me for omitting the New Testament from the sources, although I was required by the conditions of the question to do so. It is no part of my present undertaking to investigate in detail the New Testament. A great advance has been made in this direction by the *Verisi-milia* of Professors Pierson and Naber (1886), with whose results my own coincided at many points. But I may simply say in this place that it is clear the books once called the *Apostle*, the *Book of the Gospels*, and the *Acts of the Apostles* must be studied in relation to the Missal if a genuine New Testament criticism is ever to begin. These books do not contain the history of the causes; they are themselves parts of the effects of Christendom. They show the great Orders of Religious already formed, and represent in symbolic and allegoric forms their ideals, their canons, their dogmata, their visions and aspirations; the enthusiasms of a mode of life which is remote from ours.

The same principle must be applied to the Arabian and the Jewish Scriptures. They also are the effects, not the causes, of organisations. Nor will our knowledge of this subject be improved until from other sources than these oracular books we have ascertained the epoch of the rise of those organisations.

Will the kindly reader indulge me to some extent in the license of repetition? Although I am stating a series of commonplaces, they will appear so novel to the mass of readers, that I am forced to remind them again and again of the leading and decisive points in the evidence. Moreover, the nature of the subject renders repetition desirable, because we are forced to return again and again to the same ground. Each part of the evidence throws a gleam of light on the position of the Church in time. But again the mists of fable gather from other quarters, and the truth already won is apt, without reiteration, to be forgotten. My friend Dr. Loman says that my motto appears to be *Frappez vite, frappez fort, mais frappez toujours.* I would modify another motto, and say it must be with me *De l'emphase, encore de l'emphase, et toujours de l'emphase*, until I have succeeded in impressing my points upon the reader. I have done little more than play the part of pioneer, which circumstances have forced upon me, into an ill-explored field of inquiry. If I have explained the causes of our long ignorance by laying bare the nature of our literary sources, if I have defined more clearly the epoch at which the Church arose in our world, and the nature of its earliest teaching than my predecessors, I shall have accomplished all that I intended in this work.

In meditating on this great subject, it recently occurred to me to glance again at Cardinal Newman's *Grammar of Assent*, which I was reading in the summer of 1871, and which I had scarcely opened since. On p. 289, Newman refers to the opinion of the paradoxical Father Hardouin, that most of our Latin classics were forgeries of the monks of the thirteenth or fourteenth centuries. I have never been distressed by that suspicion. I have never thought that Horace singing Lalage is in fact a monk singing the praises of the Church, or that the Æneid is allegorical of the journey of St. Peter to Rome. Father Hardouin's discovery of wholesale Benedictine frauds during the thirteenth and following ages appears to have filled his mind with almost universal suspicion towards the Latin literature. The suspicion was well grounded; even his favourite, Pliny, has not escaped interpolation. But that the monks could produce the finest classical quality of writing, even in the age of Petrarch, few will believe. Moreover, the motive must have been wanting.

But the Cardinal, in discussing the opinion, pertinently observes, "That all knowledge of the Latin classics comes to us from the Mediæval copies of them, and they who transcribed them had the opportunity of forging or garbling them. We are simply at their mercy. . . . The existing copies, whenever made, are to us the autographic originals. . . . The numerous religious bodies then existing over the face of Europe had leisure enough, in the course of a century, to compose not only all the classics, but all the Fathers too."

I was led by these remarks to consult the works of Father Hardouin. To my surprise, I found that in his posthumous *Ad Censuram Veterum Scriptorum Prolegomena* (1766) he had anticipated the substance of what I have had to say in these pages concerning the Basilian and Benedictine literature by some two hundred years. He denounces the ecclesiastical histories and the Fathers and Councils as a system of fable. He reveals to us the forgers sitting down in their *scriptoria*, with sixth, seventh, eighth, ninth, or tenth century ink and parchments, and with corresponding alphabets, to write works in the names of imaginary authors. He designates the producers of the first Church literature a conspiracy, a wicked and impious crew of atheists, whose virus had infected the Missal even, and the Breviary. He was aware that he was attacking the Benedictines of the thirteenth century, and he pointedly says that he bears no ill-will to the Benedictines of his own day.

He maintained, as he was bound to do, the genuineness of the canonical literature, but his great object was to emancipate the Church from dependence on book tradition, with the exception of the Vulgate, and to found her on "oral tradition." He thought that he might thus beat the weapons out of the hands of the Jansenists and the Protestants in general, who appealed to "Pseudo-Augustine" and other so-called Fathers. The polemical objects of this extraordinary scholar do not, however, concern me here. What Father Hardouin had as a literary critic destroyed, he was bound as a priest in some sort to try to build again; but in construction he certainly failed.

The fact remains that, as a critic of the Church literature of vast experience, he has never been refuted, and that his critique in effect cuts at the roots of the claim to antiquity on behalf of the Church. It leaves her a purely Mediæval institution, without either literary or oral links with the past. For if the Patristic literature be cancelled, which contains no slightest proof of the existence of an oral tradition, but merely the pretension to it, the oral tradition is simply a baseless figment. I have been somewhat more conservative than Father Hardouin, because I have admitted that the military organisation against the Semites, which began the Crusades, may during the latter half of the twelfth century have been transforming itself into a spiritual organisation, and that there may possibly have been literary as well as military abbots before that century closed.

Many a reader will thank me for calling attention to this fascinating work of the great Jesuit scholar. It appears to have been written in 1725–26, when he was about eighty years of age, some three years before his death. Nothing can be more impressive than to see the aged priest firmly persisting in opinions which he had long ago been required to retract by his superiors, and supporting them by all the weight of experience derived from a long life spent among books. The Benedictine literary historians of 1754 have treated his memory with respect, and have described a most entertaining scene which passed between him and one of their Order in Paris in the year 1711. In the *Bibliothèque* of Jesuit writers (1872), edited by A. De Backer, there is an inadequate account of these *Prolegomena*, which the writer can hardly have perused, and which he speaks of as "refuted." Hardouin's arguments in reference to the late origin of Patristic literature cannot be refuted ; they will receive increasing confirmation from all critical students of the Middle Ages.

The *Prolegomena* form the like useful introduction to the Benedictine mythology that the *Prolegomena* of C. O. Muller form to the old Greek mythology ; in which relation there are some valuable remarks on the last chapter of Mr. Grote's first volume of the *History of Greece;* also in the sixth chapter of Mr. Buckle's *History of Civilisation.* We shall never understand our own English mythology until we understand the habit of mind of the Benedictines, who, under the influence of Jewish and Mohammedan teaching, sat down to trace the descent of King Alfred and the Bishop of London from Noah and from Abraham.

All that I have written is intended merely as an introduction to the epoch of Church beginnings. I hope that I have dealt with what is material in the evidence ; nor can it be desirable that I should discharge into my pages more of the distasteful fictions which it has been my business to expose than is absolutely necessary. The waste of labour over this subject has been enormous, and the most useful thing one can do is to prevent it from going on. I have done my best to report faithfully upon the evidence ; but further, let me suggest to the serious student a method by following

B

which he will be enabled either to confirm or to correct
my conclusions. Let him, then, take up the Ecclesiastical
History ascribed to Nicephorus Callistus, and said to have
been written early in the fourteenth century. Let him
compare with it the first Ecclesiastical History ascribed
to Eusebius Pamphili ; he will convince himself of the
absurdity of supposing that an interval of one thousand
years elapsed between the two productions. They were
written very nearly at the same time, and they represent
the first effort at making out a Church theory of the
past. Let the student then ascertain what Dante, Petrarch, and Boccaccio knew of the origin of the Church.
He will find it extremely difficult, by the aid of any
indications in those writers, to grope his way upward
through the preceding age, and to ascertain what had
actually been done in Church organisation at the time
of the death of the great Jewish legislator. He will
find that the literature must be used with the greatest
caution, and with constant glances of circumspection
at the state of an ignorant world.

For my own part, I am forced to think of the earliest
homes of the Church in the Campagna, at Subiaco,
Frascati, Anagni, Aquino, Monte Cassino ; and her
cradle-period as the latter half of the twelfth century.
But I cannot trust what profess to be contemporary
sources ; while the admissions in the Papal annals of
the obstinate resistance of the magistrates and people of
Rome to Church invasions, together with the fact of the
flight to Avignon, are strong evidences of the struggling
condition of the monkish confederacy during the thirteenth century. It has never yet been ascertained at
what period the Bishop of Rome contrived to subordinate the Præfect of the city to himself, nor what was
the part played in the movement by the families of the

its own origin and refer itself to divine authorship, then the Roman people, so glorious in war, may refer its parentage to Mars without offending the tribes of men which endure the Roman Empire.

It certainly never entered the heart of Livy to conceive that a manifestation of the Divine in human form was near at hand, and that a great theological empire was to be founded within the heart of the old order, destined to be the source of all prosperity to the Romans, and to supersede their Empire. But such was the theory of the first Church mythographers. Let the reader's thought move swiftly on to the time after the first Crusades, when that Roman people, who had never forgotten their traditions, were sternly resisting, amidst riot and bloodshed, the efforts of the monks to set up the *cathedra* of a high priest as ruler of the city and the world. Then, looking back, he will see how deep and dark and how impassable is the chasm which sunders the old Roman tradition from that of the Holy Roman Empire, which was the shadow and the faint imitation of its predecessor.

What was the theory of the Holy Romanists? Let the dates in their mythographic structure be for the moment neglected, and the mere theory be the object of attention. An Eastern bishop is supposed to be addressing a Roman emperor :—

Theory of Holy Romanism

"Our philosophy formerly flourished among barbarians, but it flowered out among your nations about the great reign of Augustus, your ancestor, and became in the highest degree to your Empire a fortunate blessing. For from that time the might of the Romans increased to that great splendour, of which you have become the desired successor, and will be, along with your son, if you preserve the philosophy which was nursed in the same cradle with the Empire and began with Augustus; which also your ancestors honoured, in addition to the other cults."

The given names of the emperor and the bishop signify nothing. The fable is audacious, and one of a mass of the most audacious fables relating to the old Roman emperors, which disappear from the theatre of genuine history in the light of the known facts of the Empire. Another fable, relating to perhaps the most glorious period of the Roman Empire, is the following :—

"There went on" (amidst slanders, persecutions, the constant pullulation of heresies), "there went on, increasing in greatness, ever alike and the same, the splendour of the UNIVERSAL AND ONLY TRUE CHURCH, distilling the solemnity, the sincerity and freedom, the temperance and piety, of the inspired policy and philosophy, upon every race of Greeks and Barbarians. With the course of time the accusation against the Dogma has died out; and there has remained alone, prevailing, and confessed for the most part to excel in majesty and temperance, and in divine philosophic dogmata—our teaching."

Here then stands revealed, at whatever epoch, the Catholic Church in her majesty and boundless pretensions to empire, such as they remain to this very day. It was at the same epoch that another monk of the same primitive Order put forth the dictum :—

"*The beginning of all things is the Catholic and Holy Church.*"

The style of the monk is somewhat swollen and
The Programme of the First Ecclesiastical History. ventose. In simpler language may be stated what he proposes in his preface to do for the elucidation of the obscure past of the Church. He will record—

loss, it may be, will be felt, or rather imagined, as objects once thought to be real pass into the world of the ideal. Yet if our earthly horizon only opens the more widely, if our glance at the commonplace of existence becomes unfettered, if we learn to see the continuity of human life through all the ages the more distinctly, the gain will be great. Science and imagination are each enriched by the discipline which separates their respective provinces. The fidelity of the poet is distinct from that of the historian ; and the facts which claim the attention of the historian are not to be confounded with the impassioned dreams of the mystic. The historian, according to any sound definition of his office at any time, is bound not to impose upon the world representations of what was not as if they were reflections of what was, nor to treat the things that were as if they had not been.

These are but broad rules, but they have been utterly disregarded by the first historian of the Church, Not that he was the only offender. Before him there had been Orientals who, with the muscular activity of imagination characteristic of their race, had bounded over thousands of years as if they had been but days, had planted themselves at the creation, and had thence deduced the scheme of the world to their own times. In the Middle Ages it may have been impossible for any corporation to rule mankind except by means of theological fables. There lies in part a certain apology for what the first Churchmen did. But their literary deeds have proved a deep injury to our conscience and our culture, and we consent to that injury and prolong it, if we refuse to submit their writings to the closest scrutiny, and to correct their erroneous representations of the past.

And now to resume. It will be shown in the following pages that the whole system of Church ideas originated in the Middle Ages, at an epoch when every effort was being made to redress the balance of power between Europe and Asia, and to resist the great domination of the Orientals. The first Church literature was solely the product of the two great primitive Orders, who were united in this enterprise.

Programme of the Present Work.

The old Roman Empire had long run its course, exhausted in its struggles with its foes in the East and in the West. It had been replaced in Syria, Egypt, Africa, Sicily, Spain by the empire of Islam, and by the Teutonic kingdoms in the West. But down to the end of the reign of Justinian, when our contemporary sources fail, the faith and the ideas of the Romans had remained substantially what they had been in the days of Augustus. The Romans had never forgotten their sacred legends of Æneas and Romulus, had never ceased to cherish the lore of poets who sung of Roman virtue, and of philosophers who strove to lead them in the path of wisdom. There was not a Roman in the time of Justinian who dreamed that the city or the Empire was to become the seat of an Oriental or semi-Oriental propaganda, or that the memory of Roman gods and heroes, seers and lawgivers, was to be eclipsed by that of Arabian prophets and apostles.

It is because the literature of the Empire has come to our hands from those of monachic editors, who have added to and taken from the text in the interest of their great dogma, that an illusion in this regard has obtained, ever since the opening of the universities, in the educated world.

During the period 800–900, the building of mosques,

the foundation of schools of Arabian learning, was no doubt going rapidly forward throughout the empire of Islam, from Bagdad to Cordova. The Koran had probably assumed the form in which we now possess it during that period, and it was completed early in the tenth century by the great Chronicle of Al Tabari the Persian, which yields us a clearer view of that great dogma of the prophetical and apostolical succession from Adam to Mohammed which is characteristic of Islam.

Towards the close of the same century a people akin to the Arabs formed themselves into a new religious organisation in the land which they called Sepharad or Spain, under the protection of their Muslim masters. The first Sephardim in the field of letters, *i.e.*, the Spanish Rabbins, were known by Arabic names, and probably passed outwardly for Muslim. Their early school was Cordova; others were found at Seville, Malaga, Toledo. Their literary activity was at first secret, and they based it on the traditions of the Arabians. They claimed, like the Muslim, to be children of Israel, and they deduced their origin from the younger, as the Arabians deduced theirs from the elder son of Abraham.

The Spanish Rabbins had, as a matter of course, a theory of a great Rabbinical Succession and of a Great Synagogue, which served to lead imagination into a high ideal past. But this theory proves, on examination, to fall under mythological law, abundantly illustrated in the old Greek legends. It may be safely assumed that nothing definite was known of the people or of their priesthood until the foundation of the synagogues in Spain. Their buildings show a Moorish parentage, as their sacred language is the daughter of the Arabic.

It may be said that the foundation of the whole synagogue system dates from the period between Rabbi Samuel the Nagid of Cordova and R. Moses Maimonides, also a Spaniard, who settled at Cairo, and became the great lawgiver and dogmatist of his people. The period in round numbers is 1000–1200.

From Spain the Rabbins went on their missionary errands, and founded schools in Africa, Syria, and Persia, in South and West France, Germany, and the Crimea. If there was ever a period during which the teachers of the Mishna travelled over sea and land to make proselytes, it must have been during that period, when their hearts beat high in the hope of realising the ideal kingdom of David and establishing another ecclesiastical empire in the world. They suffered a terrible blow at the time of the first Crusade. The records of a previous persecution at Granada are faint and indistinct, and those referring to the Crusade relate to the German synagogues. It is probable, however, that they all suffered; and one of their feasts, with the explanatory legend in an allegorical form, bears witness to their belief that at some epoch a great conspiracy was formed with the object of extirpating them from the world. It is to no other time that we can refer the origin of this belief.

They recovered from that blow; and though they had to travel through a long valley of Baca, the woeful plaints from which are familiar in all our ears, they prospered under the peculiar conditions of the times. The twelfth century is the great age of early Rabbindom. It was then that their most celebrated scholars flourished; then that Messiahs were often appearing to restore the kingdom of David; then that they began to encounter the abbots at the head of their spiritual militia, the monks; then that the canon of the Old Testament was completed and the New Testament was begun; then that the Christian system was founded on a theory both of the great antiquity of the Jewish people, and of the Christiani as an offshoot from them.

Here the root is touched of those fixed ideas and illusions which have long proved so injurious to our intellectual and moral culture. Had scholars taken their stand at the time of Maimonides, and strictly confined themselves to the question how much did he and his compeers know of the origins of his people, the question about the Jews would long ago have received an analogous solution to that which we have arrived at in the case of the Greeks and the Romans. It would have been seen that the dreams of a rising people about its past are one thing, its actual appearance in history another. But the monks exaggerated the Rabbinical claim to antiquity to a pitch of the greatest absurdity. The Bible is in greater debt to the Latin and the Greek than is commonly known; and yet it has been pretended that the Hebrews were the elders of the Greeks, and that Moses was the teacher of Plato. Hebrew is one of the most vigorous but least cultivated of dialects, the reflex of minds of great energy but narrow education; while Greek is the most magnificent monument of highly endowed, deeply cultivated, and long labouring genius that exists in the world.

The illusion in respect to the antiquity of the Jews in Syria is destined to disappear the moment that Jewish critical scholars, of whom there are many in the present day, refuse all complicity with the dreams of the Rabbins, and still more of the monks of St. Basil and St. Benedict. We have some particulars of the Rabbi Jehuda Halevy, and his enthusiastic journey from Spain to Syria about the middle of the twelfth century—a journey that seems to have ended in a cloud of disappointment. We have particulars so late as 1267 of R. Nachmanides, who is securing some ruined buildings near Jerusalem for a synagogue of some dozen of his people. The settlement at Tiberias may date from the twelfth century, but probably not earlier. During the preceding four centuries and more, the land was holy to its Muslim occupiers, the true authors of the tradition about David and Solomon.

But not to enter here into further details, the figure of Maimonides is the great landmark in the history of the Synagogue. His people say of him that "between Moses and Moses there is not another Moses." Since the Moses of the ideal time is derived from the Moses of the Arabs, the later Moses of the Jews is their true lawgiver. He is believed to have passed away about the year 1205. He had stereotyped the creed of Judaism. In his time the Scripture lessons for the synagogue had doubtless been completed; the Mishna had been begun.

A new world begins to appear from that time, whether we glance at the seats of Judaism, of Islam, or of Christianism in East and West. In Rome our glance falls on the figure of Innocent III., who is epochal in Church legend. The great monastery of the Benedictines at Monte Cassino, and all the cloisters of the two Orders connected with it, are said to be in the full tide of activity, and the foundations of that great system of mixed ideas under which we have so long lived have been laid. Glancing forward a little distance, we encounter the Emperor Frederick II., the favourer of the Muslim in Sicily and South Italy. It is said that he listened to advocates of the three religions, and gave the preference to the Orientals over the Christians. If we may venture to divine his thoughts, he must have been well aware that Islam was the parent of the other two.

It will tend to steady our attention and to fix it upon the proper objects, if we imagine ourselves to be students living at the court of that Emperor, and busying ourselves in the work of critical examination of the rival traditions of the Mosque, the Synagogue, and the Church. It will be found, on attentive inspection of the evidence, that at the Emperor's death the schools of the Mosque had been some four hundred years in existence, those of the Synagogue some two hundred years, while those of the Church were in their infancy. His reign witnessed the rise of the great mendicant Order of St. Francis and the preaching Order of St. Dominic, by whose agency the popular influence of the Church was greatly extended, and dissenters of Oriental persuasions were cruelly suppressed. The advance of this second great line of the Church army is another landmark of history. Some of the most fervid passages in the Epistles and the Gospels resume the spirit and the life which they have long lost so soon as they are carried into the light of the legends of the Franciscans concerning their ideal saint. The spirit of enthusiasm, so fatal both for good and ill, has been aroused in the breasts of the mass of the people.

But to return for a moment to the question with which we began this chapter, the relation of the Church to the old Roman Empire. It was long after the reign of Frederick that an Augustinian produced a celebrated work on the new City or Church of God, which, as we

The Augustinian on the Divine State.

shall show, has been antedated into an earlier age.
He follows in this work the general lines laid down
by the first ecclesiastical historian, but his composition is of a far more elaborate and finished character.
He expands the theme of the Church's relation to
old Roman times. He pretends that the Erythræan
Sibyl wrote certain manifest prophecies concerning
the Christ, that he had read in some poor Latin verses.
He produces them, and they form an acrostic on the
words Ἰησοῦς Χρειστὸς Θεοῦ υἱὸς σωτήρ. He points out
that the first letters of these words form the word
ἰχθύς, that is, fish, by which name Christ is mystically understood, because in this abyss of mortality,
as in the depth of waters, He could live—that is, be
without sin.

He produces also a pretended prophecy of the Passion from the same Sibylline source, and adds that
there are some who place the Sibyl not in the time of
Romulus, but of the Trojan war. He deduces the
Nativity at Bethlehem wholly from the Hebrew prophet.
Christ is declared to be "man manifest from a human
virgin, God occult from God the Father." His first
miracle is His birth, His last the Ascension. The whole
proof is drawn from an à priori, a metaphysical necessity, and from literature allegorically and mystically
understood. Should the Sibylline verses, he says, prove
to be forgeries, still the Psalms and Prophets suffice
for the establishment of the theory.

He proceeds to unfold his view of Roman history
from similar foregone conclusions. There must have
been ten persecutions, because there had been ten
plagues in Egypt. But he is embarrassed by the fact
that more than ten persecutions have been discovered
in Roman history.

He draws a parallel and a contrast between Romulus and Christ. The belief in the deity of Romulus was imbibed by the Romans with their mother's milk. The nations ruled by Rome became also imbued by this idea. Not that they believed the dogma, but they professed it for fear of offending Rome. Rome herself believed, not from love of error, but from error of love. The new state, on the other hand, that is, the Holy Roman or Christian Empire, did not believe in Christ, her celestial and eternal Founder, because she was founded by Him, but because she believed, she must be founded. Rome, already built and dedicated, worshipped her founder in a temple as a god; but the New Jerusalem placed on the foundation of faith her Founder, Christ-God, so that she might be built and dedicated.

Old Rome loved Romulus, and believed him to be a god, but the new state believed in the deity of Christ, and then loved Him. Old Rome was led into error by love, but by right faith the divine state is to be led into truth. We hear of Romulus what he did, not what was prophesied of him; we hear that men believed in his deification, but we do not know that he was actually deified. Moreover, men confessed the deity of Romulus from fear, but men overcame fear and suffering in their eagerness to confess the deity of Christ. The belief in Romulus produced no martyrs.

This curious argumentation from theories to facts is not the eccentricity of an individual; it is the consentaneous and organised argumentation of the servants of the Christian Empire. They never depart from it. They are aware that they have no facts, either in mass or in fragments, to which they can point in confirmation of it. They announce a dogma evolved out of their mystical consciousness; they demand a blind assent to it; they call that blind assent faith. They read the dogma into writings where it is not to be found; they forge oracles which re-echo it. In obedience to a theory, they call an army of martyrs into existence, treat them as real persons, and ascribe to them sufferings in defence of the theory of which the martyrs themselves were the offspring.

It is a mistake to suppose that the Middle Ages were wholly subject to unhappy dreams and hallucinations. The Church theory of history was firmly laid down by men the most shrewd and clear-headed, keen observers of the condition of the world. It was a theory that fell in with the militant and ambitious passions of the time, and was therefore accepted by a large, interested class. It came to be believed in that sense in which men say they believe whatever they wish to act upon. To a certain extent the saying of Tacitus, *Fingunt simul creduntque*, was made good. A great confluence of motives—fear, self-interest, love, hope—brought about that state of passive acquiescence in the dogma which the Churchmen call faith.

But to the modern student belief means an intelligent state of mind produced by the knowledge of the facts. It will be shown in the following pages that the proud theory of a State or Church of God, a Christian Empire, founded in the reign of Augustus and destined to survive all other empires, the theory so long and so massively supported by the great sacerdotal Orders, is a theory not merely unsupported by facts, but massively refuted by them.

CHAPTER II

THE ROMAN EMPIRE AND CHRISTENDOM.

I HAVE briefly to show in the following pages that the Roman Empire, from its rise to its decline, from the time of Augustus to that of Heraclius, was entirely unconscious of any such revolution in religious affairs as was implied by the introduction of Christianity.

The greatest effort was made during the Crusades by the Basilian and Benedictine monks to make the facts appear otherwise. The consequence has been that the literary monuments of the Empire have come down to us in a fearfully garbled, corrupted, and interpolated condition, so that every branch of the evidence needs to be examined with circumspection, that we may distinguish in this great palimpsest the old Roman Scripture from the monkish over-scribble. Gratitude is sometimes expressed towards the monks because they preserved and handed down to us the classical letters. To borrow one of their own illustrations, the gratitude we owe them is of the kind that one feels towards the robber, who takes our purse and leaves us our bare subsistence. They have abstracted part of the literature of the Empire; they have foisted their own theory of the world upon the remainder. They have contrived a great imaginative screen which has hidden from us the old Roman world, and which has at the same time offered to us dream-pictures of a world as they wished it had been.

It may need a steady and a studious gaze to dispel the illusions they have created. But to those who seek it, the truth is still plainly visible. The monuments of the Empire, carefully reperused, not only reveal entire ignorance of the Christian movement, but they supply a mass of evidence condemnatory of those who strove to pervert and distort their testimony, and to wring from them false and dubious voices. Down to that great epoch, the rise of Islam, neither the inscriptions, the history of architecture, the history of religious rites, neither the laws nor the literature of the Empire, afford the slightest evidence of any religious revolution having taken place in the Roman state. The Empire was and remained neutral amidst a great variety of creeds and cults. There was no toleration because there was no persecution.

I. *The Evidence from Inscriptions.*

The inscriptions—I allude especially to the sepulchral inscriptions—have a still and ghostly tale to tell. They offer the criticism of the silent dead upon all those flourishing legends of the origin and sufferings of the Christians by which we have been so long deceived. These pathetic memorials of old culture have a weighty burden to deliver. They are devoid of polemical passion; they have been less open to the meddling hand of fraud, and the massive effect of their meaning admits of no contradiction.

What have they to tell us concerning the rise of the Catholic Church? Had the tales of the monks been even approximately true, the inscriptions should supply powerful confirmation of the idea that Christians had been swarming everywhere in the Roman world from the beginning of the second century of our era. But the first fact that arrests attention is the utter paucity of any pretended Christian inscriptions, and the next fact is that the pretended Christian inscriptions are not Christian at all.

These pretended Christian antiquities of the Catacombs were a discovery of the fifteenth century : they were a discovery, in fact, in the sense of an invention. Those collected by De Rossi, Le Blant, and others, form a mere driblet amidst a great mass of antique inscriptions which show beyond dispute that the religion which had been recognised in the first century continued to be recognised as long as any ancient traditions of Rome lingered in the hearts of the people. Tombs and altars continued to be dedicated *Dis Manibus*, to the deified spirits of the departed ; and there is no reason to suppose that the beautiful and pious rites of the Parentalia and Feralia described by Ovid were not still annually practised by the majority of Romans at the close of the sixth century.[1] The greater gods of Rome, Jove Optimus Maximus, Mars, Apollo, and other deities continued to receive reverential recognition to the end.

Oriental deities also claim a considerable share of the inscriptions. Mithras, the Sol Invictus, to whose legends and rites the early apologists of the Church make reference in so pointed and sensitive a manner—

---

[1] "Est honor et tumulis · animas placate paternas,
Parvaque in extructas munera ferte pyras
Parva petunt Manes : pietas pro divite grata est
Munere ; non avida Styx habet ima deos."
—*Fasti* ii. 533.

Cf. the remains of the treatise of Jo Lydus of the sixth century. Late in the Middle Ages, the Fasti of Ovid continued to be a study of delight to those who described the *Mirabilia*, or wonders of the golden city. Cf. also Agathias of the sixth century, v. 2.

Mithras, whose birthday feast on the 25th December was destined to give way to the feast of the Nativity, very frequently occurs. So do Isis and Osiris. There are, moreover, numerous inscriptions relating to the ministers of the old religions—to the priests and priestesses, the sacerdotes, the antistites, the flamines and the flaminicæ. The only Pontifices Maximi are the emperors themselves, who were wont to wear the official Pontifical garb in time of peace.[1] With the exception of something spurious, relating to the notorious "Damasus," there is no hint or trace to be found of any papa or pontiff in the Catholic acceptation of the words.

It is impossible to resist the massive and overwhelming contradiction which is thus given to the notorious boasts of the apologists concerning the universal diffusion of the Christian name during the Roman Empire. No student whose attention has been once steadily fixed upon this subject can rise from the examination of the volumes edited by Theodor Mommsen and others without the conviction that our traditional views of the origin of the Christians have been steeped in illusion. It is but one of many experiences, which brand upon the mind the ineffaceable impression that the monks have not only not told us the truth, but that they have actually smothered it beneath mountains of fable.

But this is not all. De Rossi, Le Blant, and others have hastily assumed as Christian inscriptions all in which the monogram ☒ occurs. No doubt in the notorious Eusebian story of Constantine and the vision of the Labarum it is claimed

The Monogram, the Sign of Victoria.

---

[1] See the description of the insignia of Augustus in time of peace in Jo. Lydus, *De Magistrat.*, ii 4, who knows of no other *pontiffs*. Cf. the list of emperors as pontiffs in *Corpus Inscr. Lat.*, Berol. 1873, vol. iii. part ii. pp. 1108 seq. Julian is the last *named* Imperial pontiff in this connection.

as the *Christian* sign of victory; but the character of the writer and of the miraculous story ought to have aroused suspicion. We have nothing here but one of the numerous attempts on the part of the Churchmen to fabricate evidence where it was not forthcoming, or to pervert extant evidence in favour of their own views.

The monogram is notoriously of most antique origin. It occurs, for example, in monuments of Isis and of Pallas.[1] It appears on coins of emperors of the fourth century—for example, on those of Jovian—who must have known what its real significance was, but who have been falsely claimed, partly on this ground, as Christians.

This is not the place wherein to examine the archæology of the monogram and of the related sign of the cross. Perhaps it may be said that the "cross" is one of the oldest objects in the lore of Egypt and of the West as a sign propulsive of evil spirits, and hence pointing, as a sign of weal, salvation, victory. Certainly in the times of the Empire the cross was associated with Victoria, and golden victorioles were probably as common in temples as in the time of Cicero.[2]

The Egyptian Tau or Crux Ansata, the handled cross, seen so constantly in the hands of Egyptian deities, had perhaps a more directly religious signification. The Basilian monks have endeavoured, though clumsily, to turn it to account in their argument for the antiquity of Christianity, and they say that it symbolised the life

[1] Eckhel, *Doct. Numm.*, ii. 210   For Isis, I have found, but have been unable to verify, a reference to Franz, *C. I. Gr.*, 4713b.   The date is given B.C. 137~138.

[2] See the story in *N. D.*, iii. 34.   Suetonius tells of a Victoria carried at the funeral of Augustus.   Cf. Justin, xxxix. 2.

to come.[1] It seems probable that the monogram or the cross on sepulchral Roman monuments had the meaning of victory over death.[2] Other sepulchral signs—the dove, the fish, the palm, the olive-branch, the anchor —imply no religious revolution, and may be probably explained from popular ideas concerning death and the life to come, that are as old as the world of thought and sentiment.

The letters BM denote simply *Bene Merenti*, "to the well-deserving," a mark of respect to the departed. Yet an enormous fraud has here been perpetrated by ecclesiastics. The letters have been interpreted to signify *Beato Martyro*, and in this way scores and hundreds of imaginary martyrs have been called into being. So late as the seventeenth century Bonfante was thus discovering three hundred martyrs in the inscriptions of Sardinia, and Piacenza was allowed to share in the precious boon.[3]

But we need not dwell upon these follies. The Churchmen have made massive representations of the prevalence of the Christian name in the early times, and we are bound to demand massive confirmations. Instead of this, we find that the famous monogram has nothing whatever to do with the crucifix or with Chris-

---

[1] Sozom, *H. E.*, v. 17, on its connection with the worship of Serapis. The student will find similar things in the Basilian monk Cedrenus, probably of the fourteenth century, *Compend*, p. 325 P., also in J' Pollux, *Chron.*, p. 366, probably of the same age, to which may also be referred the Latin tracts ascribed to Tertullian, *Apology*, and M. Felix, *Octavius*.

[2] It is needless to observe that the monogram ☧ had nothing whatever to do with such words as χριστός, or χρειστός, or χρηστός It is often found in the reversed form ☧. In the form ℞ and ℞ we seem to recognise a transition.

[3] See Bonfante's *Triumph of the Saints of the Kingdom of Sardinia*, 1635, and Ciampi's *History of the Church of Piacenza*. Cf. Muratori, *Diss.* 58. Similarly, DM has been made to signify *Deo Maximo!* *Elementary History of Art*, by N. D'Anvers, p. 55.

tianity, and the sepulchres of the Romans remain utterly unconscious of the presence of any new body of religionists, or of a body of martyrs, whose horrible sufferings for unintelligible reasons, occupied the crudely artistic pens of the monasteries.

The ordinary oblong cross, supported by the winged figure which we see on Imperial coins, is also the sign of Victoria, of Triumph, as the monks in their efforts at adaptation very well knew.

The Cross as Sign of Victory.

The monk of Aquileia,[1] who expounds the creed, is here a good witness; and the same triumphal, by no means ignominious associations, inspire the prayers on the annual feast of the Exaltation of the Holy Cross, September 14. It is in the light of these old feasts that we can understand the enthusiasm kindled by the elevation of the cross in the year 1096. It expressed alike the sentiments of revenge and of hope on the part of the men of the West in their struggle against the Oriental invader. We see already in the Plenary Missals, which date perhaps from the thirteenth century, that the sentiment of enthusiasm for the cross has been fused with the idea of the Crucifixion. Much obscurity has hence arisen; and it is important, for the sake of historical clearness, to observe that the martial sentiment of the Crusaders for the old sign was inherited from the times of the Empire, and could have nothing to do with the Church legends concerning the ignominious death of God. Pride in the cross implied antipathy to the Oriental conquerors. It did not imply from the first that *theological* antipathy to the systems of the Jew and the Turk and the infidel which was born and bred in the cloisters of the Orders of St. Basil and St. Benedict.

[1] Rufinus, *De Symbolo.*

It has never yet been ascertained at what time the
crucifix or the representative of the Passion of
Christ began to appear.   No Catacomb picture
nor sculpture on sarcophagus reveals it.   The Paschal
victim was originally the lamb ; and the acts of a pseudo-
synod only are cited to prove that in 692 the figure of
Christus Deus was substituted for the lamb.   But in
truth it is entirely unsafe to assume that Church art
of any kind had begun a century before Giotto.   The
whole myth of Veronica or Beronice and her handkerchief points both to the poor quality and the late
date of all stories of early Church art.[1]

The Crucifix.

Moreover, when the Crucified One does appear, He
is arrayed in a tunic and diadem, or He is in glory
above the cross.   Nothing is more important, therefore,
than to distinguish the associations of the old world
cross, the exhibition of which puts demons or foes to
flight, from those of the Passionary cross or crucifix, which especially denotes hatred of the Jews, and
from those of the stigmata or marks of the sacred
wounds.

It has cost us but a few paragraphs to state with
brevity the blankly negative result of our examination
of this branch of the evidence as to the existence of the
Church or of Christians during the period of the Empire.   The candid reader will naturally not be content,
in a matter of so much moment, with our assurances.
But if he imbues his mind with the sense and significance of the inscriptions, as they lie before him in any
of the miscellaneous collections, he will discern that he
is still in the old Roman world, and that nothing but
the ingenious and easily-detected device of appropriat-

---

[1] Gregorovius, *Gesch. d. Stadt Rom*, ii. 188, 212 ; Milman, *Lat. Christianity*, iv. c. 4 ; Baronius on the Trullan Synod, xii. 119.

ing to the Christians an old sign of victory and glory has given any colour to the loud assertions that multitudes of them had been put to death in horrible tortures of fiendish ingenuity, and for unexplained reasons, by emperors and rulers of Roman provinces.

Let us, though late, the more thoroughly make amends to the spirits of the mighty dead. The debt of our culture is heavy to the men and the institutions of the Roman Empire. If we cherish any longer the Mediæval misrepresentations on this subject, we do deep wrong to our friends in the world of the departed, and we wilfully obscure the lustre of the Roman majesty.[1]

II. *The Evidence from Coins.*

We pass on to the closely-related evidence from coins. In important particulars the coins of the emperors flatly contradict the statements of the ecclesiastical historians. For example, the latter claim Philip (244–249) as the first Christian emperor,[2] although one of their number frankly explains that this has been done on the usual *à priori* principle. The year 247 was the thousandth year of the city of Rome; therefore Philip must be a Christian, in order that that year "*might be dedicated to Christ rather than to idols.*"[3] This statement, together with the conventional story of Philip's submission to clerical domination in Eusebius, is suffi-

---

[1] On the monogram see the learned discussions of Letronne, and Raoul Rochette, *Mém. de l'Acad. des Inscr.*, xvi. 284, and the articles in Herzog, 1882 (G. F. Piper), in Martigny, in Smith and Wace's Dictionary. It is to be hoped that some scholar will attempt a careful historical analysis of the inscriptions, and show from them what was the real condition of religious affairs in the Empire before the rise of Islam.

[2] Eus., *H. E.*, vi. 34; Orosius, vii. 20, 2.

[3] Exc. Vales., sec. 33.

cient self-refutation. But a coin of Philip with the inscription *Ex oraculo Apollinis* clearly proves that he was an adherent of the old cults.[1]

The coins of Jovian (363), who, as Ammian relates, practised extispicium in the camp, and who was, like his glorious predecessor Julian, an old Roman, show the signs of Victoria, the monogram of the cross.[2]

About the middle of the fifth century, the simple oblong cross with the figure of Victoria begins to appear on the Imperial coins. We still have before us the symbols of unconquered Rome. There is no Oriental or sectarian allusion whatever in the emblem.[3]

At length we arrive at the period in which, as we have seen, the crucifix has been said, and falsely, to have first appeared, in the seventh century. There are coins of Justinian II., horribly nicknamed Rhinometus, sole emperor (685–711). They bear the inscription—

Dominus Justinianus Servus Christi.

In a standing attitude, the emperor grasps the cross, which rests on a step, presumably of an altar. Or we see a globe surmounted by a cross, and inscribed *Pax*. Or the right hand of Christ, as King of Kings, is raised in the act of blessing. A book is also seen, doubtless intended for the Book of the Gospels. This

---

[1] Eckhel, vii. 321. Cf. Waddington and Liebas, *Inscr.*, iii. 2075–2076. The father of Philip is a god (θεός), and himself, as usual, Pontifex Maximus. Cf. *Inscr. Africæ Lat.*, 1881, ii. p. 1049

[2] Eckhel, viii. 147. Cf. Ammian, xxv. 6, 1. We shall have separately to speak of the glaring interpolations in the *Res Gestæ* which make Julian an apostate, and the dissipated Jovian a zealot for the Christian law, xxv. 10, 15. In Rufinus, *H. E.*, ii. 1, see the absurd story of his sudden conversion, with that of his army.

[3] See the coins of Valentinian III., of Pulcheria, Majorian, Libius Severus, of the period 425–465.

is the beginning of a new epigraphy and type frequent afterwards on coins.[1]

On the coins of Leo. IV. and Constantine VI. (775–780, 780–797) appears the inscription :—

IHΣTS XPIΣTTS NICA.

Were these coins genuine, they would enable us to fix an important epoch, the beginning of Catholic influence at the Roman court. These coins, however, are undoubtedly frauds, as will appear on a fuller consideration of the evidence.

Pope Hadrian I., according to the Church tradition, sat in the chair of Peter 772–795. We ought to be more certain of his coins than of those Papal Coins. of the Eastern emperor. Yet the critical history of Papal coins has brought genuine coins down to a very late date indeed. Cinagli rejects as spurious all coins prior to Hadrian I., but offers no evidence of the genuineness of the latter. A review of far later coins teaches us decisively to reject them. From about 984 occurs a vast gap in the Papal coins. There are two ascribed to Leo. IX. (1049–1055) and Paschalis II. (1099–1118). There is a spurious coin of John XVI. (982) in Cinagli. An absurdity of the seventh century is produced in Maffei's *Verona Illustrata.* Under such conditions of evidence we may applaud the prudence of Buonanni, who appeared to hold that no coins before Boniface VIII. (1291) can be trusted, and who begins his collection from Martin V. (1415). It may now be assumed that none are genuine before the latter date.

From this standpoint let us glance for a moment at

---

[1] Eckhel, viii. 228, 479, 685 ; Ducange, *Dissert. de Infra Ævi Numm*, sec. 43.

the notorious legend of the conversion of Constantine and the apparition of the "Labarum" or victorious sign in the sky. In connection with the evidence already adduced and hereafter to be supported, it is impossible to date the genesis of that legend earlier than the time of the Crusades. It was the time when military men came under monkish influence, and when the monks themselves constituted a fierce spiritual militia ; when the soldiers of the Orders of St. James and St. John girt on the sword in the form of the cross, and when the contemplative men of the cloisters dreamed of great defenders of the faith in the past. The anterior world of Church story is an ideal world. In point of fact, there is as much and as little to be said for the conversion of Constantine as for the conversion of Clovis, which closely resembles it. The picture in the "Triclinium" of Leo III., which represents Charlemagne with the Labarum and the Pope with the keys of St. Peter, is not less and not more authentic than the picture of the alliance of Constantine with Sylvester. Ecclesiastical ideas repeated themselves in proleptic, mythic, duplicated representations, not of what the past had been, but of what the artists considered it ought to have been.

The Legend of the Labarum

In this light again we should reconsider the tales penned by writers in the *scriptoria* of Western monasteries concerning the downfall of "Paganism," and the removal of the figure of Victoria from the Senate-house. These writers may place their productions under the august patronage of an "Ambrose" or a "Prudentius," illustrious names of their own invention ; but they could not have penned down those tales until the monastic system and the monastic literary confederacy had been finally established. All

Legend of Victoria.

talk of Pagans, in the ecclesiastical sense of the word, is a sheer anachronism until deep in the Middle Ages, when the old popular rites had been driven to their rural strongholds.   There were no Pagans, except in the old and respected Roman sense of the word, during the fourth or fifth century of our era.   Nor was Paganism overthrown, because it did not exist.   No Victoria could have been removed from the Senate-house by Christian emperors in the fourth century, if there were no Christian emperors to give the order.   The obvious tendency of these tales is to detach the cross from its old Roman association with the idea of victory, that they may confuse it with the new idea of the crucifix.

The reader may peruse again, in the light of what we have advanced, the somewhat unfortunate chapters[1] in which Gibbon deals with the "splendid and brittle mass" of fable relating to the vision of Constantine and the sign of the cross.   He speaks fallaciously of "the rapid fall of Paganism," and he has been corrected by Milman.   The system of old Roman customs could not and did not dissolve in any sudden and miraculous way.   Nothing is more tenacious of life than old religious custom.   Temples and the images remained wherever there was shelter from the iconoclastic blast from the desert of Arabia; nor can we, by any direct evidence, ascertain at what epoch the crucifix replaced the cross on the Capitol, in the Forum, or the Pantheon.   Gibbon should have seen that his sources of information on this subject were all late, interested, and dishonest.   Had he returned in thought to his station on the Capitol, and watched the first party of Crusaders who passed through Rome, he might have convinced himself that at that epoch—a century and a

[1] Chaps. xx., xxviii.

half before the coming of the Franciscans—the cross inspired men's breasts with ardour who as yet knew little or naught of the meaning of the crucifix.

This contrast between the military and the theological sign—the labarum and the crucifix, the symbol of triumph and that of shame—is of extreme historical interest. It helps us to measure the profound chasm in point of time and in point of sentiment which opens between old Romanism and Mediæval Romanism. Victory and weakness, triumph and humiliation, are ideas that do not readily blend in the image of the same person. Yet the Churchmen have laboured to unite them. By a multitude of fantastic similes they contrive to find the reflection of the cross in every object of nature and of human art. Armies are constantly routed by the mere exhibition of it in the hands of a St. Martin or other heroes of the cloister. But there is no such connection of cause and effect in the case of the crucifix, which speaks of defeat, ignominy, death. It cannot be denied that it is a great poetic effort which represents that God in human form voluntarily submitted to a shameful death that He might ascend to the supremest throne and receive the homage of the universe.[1]

III. *The Feasts of the Sacred Year.*

The origin of annual popular feasts is obviously one of the strongest clues to the origin of institutions connected with them. Could we fix the epoch at which the Epiphany began to be celebrated in any part of the old Roman world, we should be very near to the beginning of the Church itself. She could have made

[1] John xii. ; Phil. ii.

no great way among the people until Christ had replaced Sol, the new sun who is born afresh at the winter solstice, and until the feast which commemorated the days of good King Saturn had acquired a new theological colouring.   When did the natal days of gods, heroes, or emperors give place to those of confessors, martyrs, and saints?

The change was immense, and could have been but very gradually effected.   The old Roman customs which we find described in the *Fasti* of Ovid, in the *Noctes Atticæ* of Aulus Gellius of the second century, and the *Saturnalia* of Macrobius of the fifth century, in the treatise *On Months* of Joannes Lydus of the sixth century, continued, there is no reason to doubt, in Rome, as long as any old Roman form of life remained. The last of those writers, one of the latest of the Empire, has no suspicion of any coming change.

The ecclesiastics, however, *i.e.*, the Benedictines, offer us two presumed antique calendars, the former ascribed to D. Philocalus, and the year Supposed Church 354.   Here the 25th December is marked as Calendars the natal day of Sol Invictus.   But certain black or unlucky days in each month are marked, not as *dies posteri* or *dies nefasti*,[1] but as Ægyptiac days.   The term is ecclesiastical and Mediæval,[2] and, for the fourth century, an anachronism.

The next calendar we have is that ascribed to Ptolomæus Silvius (A.D. 448--449).   It is not wholly Christian, but in this interval of about a century some Christian feasts are supposed to have been introduced. What are they?

January 6.—The Epiphany.   The star was seen

[1] A. Gellius, v. 17; Macrob, S., 1. 16.
[2] See the Augustinian on Galatians iv. 10; Ambrose, Ep. 23, n. 4.

which announced our Lord. The water was made wine, and the Saviour was baptized in the river Jordan.

February 22.—The birthday of St. Vincent the martyr.

March 25.—The Crucimission of the Gentiles. Christ suffered on this day.

March 27.—Lavation. Resurrection.

August 1.—The martyrdom of the Maccabees.

August 10.—The birthday of St. Laurence the martyr.

August 12.—The birthday of Hyppolytus the martyr.

December 25.—The birthday of the Lord in the body.

December 26.—The birthday of St. Stephen the martyr.

These data must have been inserted from some early Missal, and it is needless to observe that there was no Missal in the fifth century. But that these particulars are wholly anachronistic is shown by the remains of John the Lydian's writings. He was a state official under Justinian I., and was well acquainted with the whole administration of the Empire. It is sufficient to peruse his work *De Mensibus* to see that the old feasts were being celebrated much as in the time of Ovid, while his treatise on Magistrates shows that he had no knowledge of any ecclesiastical Pontiff or any *Catholics*, except the fiscal officers, who bore that name under the Empire, who were called in Latin *Rationales*, ministers of the Imperial exchequer. These calendars, then, are not genuine. The term "Ægyptiac days" is to be found in other calendars of the Middle Ages produced by Muratori. We have simply before us another attempt, and a clumsy one, to represent that during the most famous period claimed, and claimed falsely, for Church literature—from the middle of the fourth to the middle of the fifth century—the feasts of the Nativity, the Passion, and the Resurrection were coming into observance. That the monks of East and West, who introduced so great a mass of martyrologies of saints during the Middle Ages, have forged nothing better than these calendars in support of them is a great weakness.

Apart from the massive confutation of the genuineness of these calendars in the old Roman monuments, they are condemned by the inconsistency of the forgers themselves. The Churchmen do not pretend that the new era from the Incarnation was recognised till the sixth century. And yet they dare to tell us that the Emperor Julian, though secretly an unbeliever, pretended, for the sake of popularity, in the year 360 at Vienne, to adhere to the Christian cult; that he went to church on the feast of the Epiphany in January.[1]

The reason why at first they fixed on the 6th January for Christmas was that the Second Adam might appear on the same day with the first. The calendar is, in short, deduced from the dogma, and then antedated into a time which anticipates the existence of the Church by many long ages. It is part of the same system by which monks of the thirteenth century make a retrospective bound over more than eight centuries, and point to one "Rufinus of Aquileia" as the authority for the Apostles' Creed; or by which they, who have just become acquainted with the customs of the synagogue, pretend that the question of the Passover was a burning one so early as the fourth century.

In this branch of the evidence, then, again the pretensions of the Church to antiquity meet on all sides

[1] Ammian, R. G., xxi. 2, 4, one of the numerous flagrant interpolations in that work.

with a crushing denial—from the records of the Arabians, the Jews, no less than of the old Romans, and their own self-contradictory writers.

IV. *The Evidence from Roman Laws.*

Among the dubious honours which have been showered by the monks upon the names of certain Roman emperors, and the calumnies with which other Roman emperors have been assailed, it is noticeable that Justinian has been singled out as a Church legislator and as a church builder. His consort, Theodora, has been made the object of perhaps the vilest lampoon that has ever disgraced the pages of literature.

We have here briefly to show that the Emperor Justinian was never guilty of the horrible persecuting legislation "in the name of our Lord Jesus Christ" which has been ascribed to him.

The Monk of Gemblours, Sigebert, who is said to have lived in the eleventh and twelfth centuries, is one of the first to enrol Justinian in the list of ecclesiastical writers, on the ground of his having composed a code of laws in favour of the Church. The genuineness of this code is, however, decisively disproved by the contents of the Institutions and the Digests, no less than by the whole weight of evidence that can be collected relative to the actual condition of the Roman Empire. The whole history, indeed, of the pretended efforts of this emperor in legislation is one so self-contradictory and absurd, that it ought long ago to have excited the attention of critics. It belongs probably to the thirteenth century, to the period when legal study was reviving in Italy, and when the notorious Canons of Gratian were fabricated.

Now the Imperial Institutions—that hornbook of Roman jurisprudence, as Mr. Austin has styled it—clearly lay down the law in respect to religious affairs.   Under the text *De Rebus Nullius*[1] we read that of this quality are :—

Sacred Things.

Religious Things.

Sanct Things.

What is of divine right, says the text, cannot be the property of any one.

" Sacred things are those which have been duly consecrated to God (or a god) through the Pontiff, such as sacred buildings, and gifts (*donaria*) which have been duly dedicated for the ministry of God, which things by our constitution we forbid to be alienated and obligated, except for the sake of the redemption of captives. If any one by his own authority has constituted a thing sacred to himself, it is not sacred, but profane.   But the place in which sacred buildings have been built, even though the building has been destroyed, remains sacred, as Papinianus has written."

There is not a word here which points not to old Roman ideas and usages, such as we find illustrated in Roman men of letters, from Virgil and Ovid down to Macrobius.

Again, under the text "On Religious Things," we read :—" Any one may make a place *religious* by his own will, by the burial of a dead body in his place," &c.

The passage is important, because it reminds us of the fact that with the Romans, as indeed with the Eastern peoples, the idea of religion was intimately connected with their reverence for the departed.   The tomb is indeed ever the centre of all popular religious observance,

[1] Lib. ii. tit. i.

as it signifies the continuity of human life, and knits the departed to the living in one great communion.[1]

Finally, the text " On Sanct Things " says, more vaguely, that they are such as the walls and gates of a city. Walls are sanct because the penalty is capital against those who have been guilty of any delinquency against them. The prototypical myth of Romulus slaying Remus is a reflection of these ideas. We are in the old Roman world, and there is no recognition whatever of any special privileges enjoyed by any church or religious community.

Again, had any church or universitas been recognised and established by the state from the time of Constantine, we should have found traces of it in those authentic compilations of Roman law. There is no trace of anything of the kind. The property of a university is defined as distinct from that of individuals, and the examples given are " theatres, stadia, and the like," or anything that is common property of cities.

Universities.

The slight manner in which religious affairs are dealt with in the laws only goes to confirm the knowledge we have from other sources of the perfect tolerance, or rather the indifferent equity and ignorance of the very principle of intolerance, under the Empire.

We open the pretended Codex, and plunge at once into an atmosphere of the greatest ferocity against all sects which dispute the pretensions of the Catholic Church. It is needless to do more than point out the strange illusion under which

The False Codex of Justinian.

---

[1] The ancient temple rose above the tomb, and all our great Mediæval churches, following the same law, derived their venerable character from the martyrs' bones beneath the altar. The tales of the discovery or the transference of the bones of saints are the forms under which the monks announced the building of new churches, and the multiplication of churches necessitated the multiplication of those profitable tales.

we have laboured in accepting this Code. So acute a mind as that of Montesquieu observed that in the course of a few years under Justinian, jurisprudence varied more than during three hundred years of the French monarchy. Yet, accustomed to think of the Church as a maddening influence, he did not draw the true inference from such representations.

The Codex Theodosianus is another ecclesiastical fabrication. It is falsely dated into the reign of the second Theodosius, and makes a still more frightful exhibition of the persecuting The "Codex Theodosi- anus" spirit against "Jews, Manichees, and Pagans." They are to be harried out of house and goods, to be exiled or cast to the flames. And yet the emperors are represented as so fickle and uncertain of their own minds in respect to the Jews, that within a few months they issue contradictory edicts, now protecting and now menacing that unfortunate people. We know not whether any part of this Code contains genuine documents, but most certainly all that relates to Christians and their rivals is an anachronism. The one criticism which kills the whole representation is this : there were no such Oriental sects known throughout the Roman Empire at that time. And one can well picture the astonishment of the Præfect Macrobius, or any Roman gentleman of the fifth century, had they heard that they were "Pagans," and liable as such to the penalties of the law ! One wearies of the mere absurdity of such contemplations.

Another attempt to drag in the Jews and their Mishna occurs in the false *Novellæ* ascribed to Jus- tinian, wherein also there is much concern- The Novellæ. ing church-building and the privileges of monasteries. These allusions are also utterly anachronistic, and they deserve no other criticism.

I lay my hand calmly upon the genuine monuments of Roman law, believing that they witness on the whole to the wise and enlightened spirit of a great people, and that they silently protest against the injurious thoughts we have been taught to cherish against a succession of emperors who wore the purple worthily, and were entangled in no such theological frenzy as the monastic fancy has been pleased to ascribe to them. The people looked upon these men as on their way to the gods, and if they themselves did not always feel godlike, they were never suffered to forget the duties of civility, and still more of that clemency which was an imitation of Heaven.[1]

Under the Roman Empire it was the crimes of high treason, of conspiracy, of adultery, and illicit arts that were most severely punished. And had such a great *thiasos* or confederacy as the Catholic Church been detected at any period, we should have heard of the sufferings of its members, not as martyrs to monotheism, but as traitors to the purple and the person of the emperor in setting up a rival system to that which he represented. There is no trace of such events in the historians of the Empire, or of any such rebellion against the authority of the Imperial Pontiff. It is only when we imagine the lapse of many ages, and the revolution introduced by the zealous theocrats from the East, that we can at all realise how the old Roman customs could have been suspended in any part of the Empire. Let us honour Justinian as one who, like the glorious Julian, knew the value of our Western culture,

---

[1] I may cursorily allude to other Mediæval Codes, such as the Visigothic Code, the Burgundian Code, and that ascribed to Charlemagne, which proceeded from the clerical imagination, and for which no other historical basis can be found. They may be referred to the period of the rise of the universities.

and did his utmost to stem the inroads of barbarism ; who was not guilty of establishing a Holy Inquisition, and of sanctioning by his example the cruelties of the thirteenth century.

V. *The Evidence from Architecture.*

There have been ascribed to Procopius, the historian of Justinian's time, works of which he was quite guiltless, viz., a treatise on Building and that foul *Historia Arcana* to which we have already adverted. It is time that we should no longer confound the true Procopius with the monks, who utter their inventions and their basenesses from behind his mask.

The figure of Belisarius, a genuine old Roman, and the commander of an army of true Romans—Belisarius, the deliverer of Carthage, Rome, and Ravenna—adorns this reign. There is not the slightest reason to suppose that the morale of the court was lowered in tone from what it had been in the time of Claudian. The philosophers were still teaching, and the people were still receiving those lessons of virtue which had made the Romans great. The severest efforts and sacrifices were being made to preserve the Empire from the inroads of Goths and Vandals in the West, and Persians in the East. And yet, in our indolent credulity, we have allowed ourselves to believe that in such a time as this 'the emperor was seized with a frenzy for extravagant expense, for rapine and extortion, and for the building of churches, while the awful dignity of his purple was sullied by his alliance with the most abandoned of harlots.[1]

---

[1] The *Historia Arcana*, discovered by Alemanni, was written by a monk, and perhaps designed obliquely to strike at another lady Theodora.

It has cost the author of the treatise on Building nothing but some strokes of the pen to call Imaginary Churches of Justinian. into existence a number of churches founded by the Emperor Justinian. They have never yet been discovered to have existed except on paper. They are more imaginary than ancient Troy or Tiryns. Nay, strain our eyes as we will through the darkness and the mist from Thorney by the Thames to Ælia or to Constantinople, it is not until more than six hundred years have elapsed from the time of Justinian that we can begin to discern the slowly rising pile of a Christian church.

The monks of St. Basil, in their so-called Church histories, vaguely speak of the places of worship of the Christians as oratories, houses of prayer, or Lord's houses. They speak also of *Hyperoa*,[1] or upper rooms, a term to be found in the canonical writings. They speak of the Jewish places of prayer by the seashore as *Proseuchæ*, and of their own as *Proseukteria*. If the eleventh century of our era is the earliest age in which we can think of the Rabbins as venturing to gather their flocks in public synagogues under the eyes of their Arabian masters, we can understand the faintness of the allusions to buildings in the Basilians of a later age. They refer also to *cemeteries*, which, as private and religious ground by Roman law, probably offered shelter to forming confederacies and sects. Under the Empire, temples were not seldom the haunts of conspirators. For example, in the reign of Constantius and Julian,[2] a political conspiracy was detected in the temple of the god Besas in Egypt, and severely punished. And it is a curious circumstance

---

[1] Bingham, *Ant.*, chap. viii.
[2] Ammian, xix. 12, 3.

that the first ecclesiastical historian, writing, as we have probably shown, in the thirteenth or fourteenth century, has actually ventured to claim Besas as a martyr or soldier of God.[1]   The monks appear to have used the terrible details of Imperial prosecution of political criminals in the fourth century in the contrivance of their martyrologies.

In the *Acts of St. Justin*,[2] Justin is supposed to tell a Præfect of the city of Rome that he has a lodging at the Tridentine Bath over one Martin, and that he knows of no other meeting of the Christians.   In all the mass of the Church literature referred to early times, it is impossible to fix in the mind's eye upon a single public building consecrated to a new worship.   And this, in spite of a series of passages inserted in the literature of the Empire which speaks of bishops, priests, and deacons, of monks and nuns, constantly appearing in the most unexpected places, and under the most unexpected circumstances. Once in Ammian a pretender to the purple is said to have been slain at Cologne on his way to a "conventicle of the Christian rite."   The false *Novellæ* still speak of houses of prayer (*eukterioi oikoi*), rather than of basilicæ or ecclesiæ.

In the course of our search for authentic particulars of churches in Rome before the twelfth century, we come upon strange and clumsy descriptions of an imaginary Rome.   Thus Zacharias, a Churchman referred to Justinian's time, talks of two magnificent basilicæ, "in which the Emperor dwells, and the Senators meet daily before him."   He talks also of twenty-four churches of the Apostles, also of eighty golden statues of the gods, sixty-six ivory ones,

An Imaginary Rome.

[1] Eus , *H. E* , vi. 41, 16.   [2] Sect. 3.

bronze statues of emperors and other Duces, 3785;
twenty-five bronze statues relating to Abraham, Sara,
and kings of the stock of David, which Vespasian had
brought to Rome after the destruction of Jerusalem.
There were also thirty-one theatres and eleven amphi-
theatres.[1]

If the story of Justinian's church-building activity
is a baseless fable, still more so is that concerning
Constantine and Sylvester.   Could we know the date
at which the feast of the dedication of the Church of
our Saviour on the Lateran (November 9th) began to
be celebrated and was inscribed in the Missal, we
should not be far from the actual date of the foundation.   It could not have been held till late in the
twelfth century, for we do not hear of the first St. Peter's
or St. John's until 1180.   But the whole history of the
Lateran Palace, from the time of Constantine and
Fausta until that late age, is wrapped in obscurity.

[1] Cardinal A. Mai, *Script. Vett.*, x. p. xii   These Hebrew references
point to the thirteenth century or later.   The tales about Titus' Arch and
the candlestick spring from some similar source.

CHAPTER III.

GLIMPSES OF MEDIÆVAL ROME AND ITALY.

I⊤ is possible from extant sources, which have not been hopelessly garbled in the Church interest, to *Rome from* obtain glimpses of the Eternal City during *the Fourth to the Twelfth* the Middle Ages, and to satisfy ourselves that *Century.* its charm ever was for the traveller as it is now, in those monuments of a genuine and glorious antiquity, which acted like a magnet upon the civilised world, as in the days of Seneca.

We may in fancy visit Rome in the company of the Emperor Constantius, and his friend the *The Fourth* Persian Prince Hormisdas, about the middle *Century.* of the fourth century (A.D. 356). The city was then "the home of empire and of all virtues." The Forum brought back recollections of primeval greatness. It was densely crowded with the miracles of art. The nobility assembled in the Curia, and the Emperor sojourned in the palace of the Cæsars. The temple of Tarpeian Jove was eminent in divine splendour. The Pantheon was adorned with statues of princes and consuls; and among other things of beauty were the Temple of the City, the Forum of Peace, the Theatre of Pompey, the Odeum and the Stadium. Above all, the Forum of Trajan filled the spectator with astonishment, in the atrium of which stood the horse of that emperor, so magnificently stabled. Hormisdas said that he was pleased (or displeased) to learn that even in Rome men died.[1]

Let us now open our earliest guide-book, the *Notitia* *Urbis*. The city, we find, is divided into fourteen regions; and nothing of the ecclesiastical division into seven diaconates is known. Several large basilicæ meet the eye,[2] but they are not basilicæ in the ecclesiastical sense of the word. They are buildings devoted to commerce, and to the administration of justice, as were all the antique basilic.. Some of them may be described as bazaars, each devoted to a particular merchandise, as their descriptions, *Floscularia*, *Argentaria*, *Vascularia*, show. We come upon several temples devoted to the cult of Isis and Serapis, and upon multitudes of *ædiculæ* or open-air chapels, each furnished with its image and its lamp. The city is still old Roman in its externals, in its customs, in its religion. Such Oriental rites as it knows are the ancient Egyptian. It has not been touched by any form of Christianism, whether Jewish, Samaritan, Arabian, or Catholic. It has heard nothing of parochiæ, of bishops, nor of deacons. Pagani are known, but not in any but the old sense of members of Pagi in the city. And the local business, both civil and religious, is probably in the hands of the officers called Vicomagistri.

We may inform the reader that our guide-book knows nothing of a Basilica of Sicininus, where the massacre under Pope Damasus is said to have occurred about the year 367. And indeed, as we linger in the city, and dwell on the scene it presents, the story vanishes

The *Notitia* *Urbis*.

---

[1] Ammian. xvi. 10.

[2] The Basilica Pauli was a monument of the Æmilian family. Tacit. *Ann.* iii. 72.

from our thoughts as a crude and wild anachronism.[1] Nor is there any reason to believe that a century later the aspect of the city had undergone any substantial change. Letronne found, to his surprise, that about 453, and later, the cult of Isis and Serapis was flourishing in Egypt, with no hint of its illicit character.[2] Doubtless it continued also in Rome. No monastery had been heard of, no atrium had been converted into a church, no peristyle into cloisters, exhedra into chapter-house, triclinium into refectory, or bath into baptistery.

The Fifth Century.

We have the *Itinerary* of Rutilius, an ex-præfect of the city, who fervidly describes its glories; but though there is an absurd interpolation in his poem, describing monks as swarming in the Isle of Capraria, and another about Jews,[3] he is not made to refer to either Jews or monks in Rome. He is thoroughly old Roman in thought and sentiment, like his contemporaries Claudian and Macrobius, who was also a prefect. To such men the view of Rome reflected in the *De Civitate Dei* was as utterly unknown as they themselves are distant from the time of the cloisters. We must leave their society and pass over an interval of many ages, during which the remains wrapped in darkness and hidden from our exact knowledge, before we arrive at the time when men were actually sitting down in the cloisters that might envelop the city in a dense mist of Papal fables.

---

[1] See the valuable work of H. Jordan, *Die Topogr. d. St. Rom im Alterthum*, ii. 216; Zestermann, *De Basilicis*, p. 64; Mommsen, *Abh d. sächs. Gesell. d. Wissensch.*, ii. 601, dates the *Notitia* before, and the *Curiosum Urbis Romæ* after A.D. 357. Cf. Grævius, *Thes.*, iii. 300.

[2] *Matériaux*, &c., Paris, 1833, p. 63. Pachomius, destined to name a saint, is here a prophet of Isis.

[3] *Vide* 384, 446. These passages may be traced to Ambrose, *Hexæmeron*, iii. 5, 23

Let us take the step across a chasm of some seven hundred years and more, from the time of Justinian to the time following the first Crusades, when the Roman Empire had long been reduced to a name, and when Orientals were swarming everywhere in the lands of the Mediterranean. How have the long troubles and changes affected the state of the city of the Cæsars? Our new informants are chiefly monks of the Order of St. Benedict, but it is clear that Rome is still neither Orientalised nor Catholicised. Never did she exert a greater charm over men's spirit than now, when the forms of the Republic are still preserved, and her monuments recall the times of liberty in contrast to Oriental despotism.

An Anonymus of Einsiedeln, who probably writes in the thirteenth century, gives a dry list of monuments and inscriptions in Rome, which is said to be the first of its kind before the fifteenth century. Antique Rome is the object of his interest. His references to themes of Church legend, as to a palace of Pilate near St. Maria Major, are dubious and indistinct. He says nothing of the Leonine city.[1] Another Anonymus of the Order relates the curious folk-tale of the seventy bronze statues of all nations set up by the old Romans on the Capitol. Each bore on its breast the name of a people, and had a bell about its neck. Day and night the priests kept watch over them. If a province rebelled, the statue moved, the bell sounded, and the priests reported the occurrence to the Emperor. The statues had been carried to Byzantium and clothed in silk by Alexander, son of the Emperor Basil. St. Peter had appeared to him by night, saying in wrath, "I am the Prince of the Romans!" In the morning he was found to be dead.

The Thirteenth Century.

---

[1] Mabillon, *Vet. Analecta,* 364.

Another Anonymus, of Salzburg, of about the same age, professes to give notices of churches built in the eighth century, which are entirely baseless and impossible.[1] Mosque-building in Spain, and during the following age in Sicily, is beginning. The Capitol remained inviolate, the first miracle of the world.[2] In the Pantheon, Mary had not supplanted Cybele so long as the tale was current that the Præfect Agrippa had Mediæval built that temple after an apparition to him Guide-Books, of the mother of the gods. The Mediæval guide-books —the *Graphia* and the *Mirabilia*—to golden Rome, mingle references to Noah, Japhet, Nimrod, with the names of Janus, Saturn, and Jupiter in the genealogy of Rome's founders, after the fashion of the thirteenth century. The confusion of Semitic ideas with old Roman reminiscences, which is so distasteful in the *Gesta Romanorum*, now begins to set in.

Meantime the old divisions of the city remain unaltered. Twelve civil regions are still counted ; there is no sign of the ecclesiastical division into the seven diaconates. On the Palatine stood the remains of the palace of the Cæsars, replete with memorials of ancient art. The Septemzonium of Severus was called the Templum Septem Solia Major. Apparently it came into the possession of the Benedictine cloister of San Gregorio, in the thirteenth century.[3] If the Benedictines occupied the cloister of Ara Cœli before the

---

[1] *Notit. Eccles. U. R.*, in Opp. Alcuini, ed. Froben, ii. 597.

[2] *Codd. Vatican.*, 1984, 2037, fol. 170 in Gregorovius, *Gesch. d. Stadt*, iii. 535.

[3] The charters, as with many of the cloisters, begin with the eighth century (754), and reach to 1559. But the editors complain of the "caliginous tenth century" and the absence of material. Mittarelli and Cortadoni, *Annal. Camald. Ord. S. Benedicti*, 1755-1773, I. App. 41, p. 96, anno 975.

Franciscans, their settlement cannot be dated before
the closing decades of the twelfth century, or the
opening of the thirteenth. It is needless to add that
the altar which links them with the time of Augustus
has never been, and never will be, discovered. A
transition from old to Mediæval Rome is curiously
marked in the name of St. Bacchus, patron of the
church on the site of the Temple of Concord, where
Cicero's eloquence had been heard; also of St. Achilles
and St. Hermes. To about the same epoch belongs
the Benedictine settlement near the Circus Maximus.
There was a dispute between them and the priests of
St. Eustachius about the little churches of St. Maria,
St. Benedict, and St. Salvator.

A web of retrospective fiction connects this saint with
the Emperor Trajan and his friend Placidus.
Legend
of St.
Eustachius. The latter, after a miraculous conversion,
changed his name to Eustachius, and finally
suffered martyrdom, with miraculous consequences.
His name also figures in a poetic genealogy—characteristic of the revival of holy Romanism—by which the
Frangipani and other noble houses are traced up to
a Placidus, scholar of St. Benedict himself. As we
ascend this line, we come to the Octavian family, and
rest at last upon the name of Octavius Mamilius, who
fell in the battle of Lake Regillus!

In like manner the Benedictines strove to connect
their Gregory I. with the Anician gens of old Rome.
The same facts are impressed upon us everywhere in
perusing the meagre notices of the guide-books or the
graceful festoons of Church romance by which their
baldness is decorated. In the thirteenth century the
servants of the Christian Empire are striving, alike in
stone and in literary structure, to found the new system

upon the old foundations and the glorious memories of the Cæsars.   Not otherwise could the Bishop of the Eternal City have grasped the reins of power than by conciliating the affections and dreams of the peoples of the West, who, recovering from the long terror of the Orientals, never looked back with more joy and pride upon the divine Roman past than when they saw the last of the Saracens disappear from the Campagna. The Papal militia of monks seized the moment when Rome lifted her head again and breathed freely, to proclaim that their system had been founded by an incarnation at the very beginning of the old Empire.

Not earlier than the closing years of the twelfth century, the canon Petrus Mallius is writing a fable concerning the Basilica of St. Peter's, St Peter's. going back to Constantine and the donation, and dwelling, of course, with fondness upon Charlemagne and *his* assumed donation of temporalities.   The object of this ecclesiastic is, as usual, to make good the rights of his church by a string of notices of such matters. It is only from the fifteenth century that the literature of St. Peter's acquires a formidable bulk.   A canon of the Lateran Church, John Deacon, supplies contemporaneously his story of that basilica.[1]   Not without interest to us Englishmen is the fact that about the same epoch the Abbot of Rievaulx is writing of Edward the Confessor and the Abbey Church of St. Peter's at Westminster.

This account of the rise of church architecture should remind us that a correct historic view of the rise of Christianity itself cannot be secured until we draw a line between the fictions and the facts of the great Benedictine order; and this line can only be drawn

[1] Gregorovius, iv. 614.

at the time they began their literature. That literature
is founded upon the Arabian and Jewish literature,
and it is hardly conceivable that they should have been
acquainted with the legends of the Koran or of Al
Tabari, much less of the Old Testament, until the
thirteenth century. Here one line may be roughly
drawn. Again, by the end of the twelfth century an
effort in church-building may have been beginning, one
of the results of the stimulus supplied by the Crusades.
The Norman architecture, in its dependence on the
architecture of Islam, bears witness in the most indis-
putable manner to the priority of Islam. If, as Mr.
Owen Jones has remarked, the Gothic architecture
reflects the Bible, as the Alhambra the Koran, it is
but to admit that the Koran is the earlier form of the
book.

The oldest Mediæval Schola of strangers in Rome
appears to be that of the Jews in the Traste-
vere. Its history is quite dark until about
the middle of the twelfth century. I shall
have subsequently to point out that all those
strange notices which run through the Roman literature
from Cicero concerning the *Judæi* and their great influence in Rome form part of the system of monkish interpolation. Such Jews are purely imaginary, entirely
unknown to their own literary records. The dates in
those records are very uncertain, and it is doubtful
whether at the time of the first Crusade many Jews were
to be found in Rome. But for the twelfth century we
find a convergence of various lines of evidence. There
is the curious notice of R. Benjamin of Tudela, which
describes Rabbins as forming part of the suite of the
Pope, the head of the "Edomites." There are the
notices of the Jewish Leoni family, who give an occu-

The Roman Guilds: Schola of the Jews.

pant to the chair of St. Peter.   Finally, it is the Benedictine records which first mention the Schola or Synagogue of the Jews[1] in that age.

The ritual book called the "Graphia of Golden
Rome" describes the Emperor—probably one of the
Ottos is intended—ascending the Capitol amidst faust
acclamations in the Hebrew, Greek, and Latin tongues.
This scene is, however, probably artistic rather than
mechanically photographic.   Great liberties have been
taken with the names of the Ottos, as of earlier emperors, in monastic fiction.   There was also a Schola of
Greeks in Rome.   But even the Book of the Popes
does not mention either Schola in the time of Charlemagne.

That Pontifical book does, however, refer to the time
of Karl the Scholæ of Franks, of Frisians, of Saxons,
and of Lombards.   That is to say, the first hint of
these guilds is to be found in the writer who pens the
notice of Pope Leo III.   For the sake of clearness, it
may be well again to remind the reader of the epoch
of Innocent III., with whom the *continuous* registers
of the Popes begin.   We shall hereafter show it to be
probable that the Book of the Popes, beginning with
St. Peter, was not commenced until some time in the
thirteenth century.   The biographer of Leo III. is
another of those proleptic writers who refer the beginning of rising institutions into earlier ages.

The history of the guild of Anglo-Saxons must be
of peculiar interest to us Englishmen.   Its
origin has been referred to King Ina, who is
said to have arrived in Rome in the year 727; to have
founded a school of Catholic instruction for the princes
and clergy of England; also to have built a church for

Anglo-
Saxons.

---

[1] *Ordo Romanus*, xii., in Mabillon, *Mus. Ital.* ii. 195.

English pilgrims, where they might be buried should they decease from life in Rome. Further, that his foundations might be maintained, Ina is said to have ordained the Romescot, or donation from each house in Wessex of the denarius to St. Peter. The institute is said to have been strengthened by Offa of Mercia, who arrived in Rome in 794 to atone for blood-guilt.

A steady attention to the nature of our sources for English history must dispel these interested fables. Neither the work ascribed to Gildas nor the works ascribed to the Venerable Bede could possibly have been written before the Norman conquest. These writers are acquainted with the Biblical writings, and the Biblical writings could not have been known until the Rabbins had made themselves felt in Spain, South Italy, Provence, Normandy, and England. There was not a Jew in this island until the coming of the Normans; not a Rabbin known until R. Ben Ezra in London in the twelfth century. The Abbots, with their spiritual battalions, ever followed in the wake of the Rabbins.

The root of the legend of the Anglo-Saxons is to be found in the ambitions of the Order of St. Benedict. It is writers in that service, as William of Malmesbury, and his correspondents and contemporaries through all the West, who delight in converting at pleasure, by a mere stroke of the pen, rude princes, of whom they knew nought but the mere names, into ecclesiastics and repentant pilgrims to Rome.[1] It is a writer of the same confederacy who, to impart false notoriety to pilgrimage, slanders the character of our countrywomen, by pretending that there was scarce a town in Lom-

[1] Cf. Mabillon, *Act. SS. O. S. B.*, iii. 465; *Acta SS.*, Bolland., February, vol. i. p. 913.

bardy, France, or Gaul which was not disgraced by the presence of some English lady who found in pilgrimage a pretext for loose living.[1]

But from Matthew of Westminster we learn that the *xenodochium* or *hospice* connected with the aforesaid church of Ina was founded about 1204, the date of the institution of the Order of San Spirito. Here then we appear to touch the root and springing-point of the fables about Ina. It was necessary to dignify the *hospice* and the Order with a semblance of high antiquity. We may conclude that the Anglo-Saxons were known in Rome not long before the time of Innocent III.

Similarly, it was in the thirteenth century that the Guild Churchmen of the Frisians conceived the happy thought of ascribing their founda- The Frisians. tion to Charlemagne and Leo IV.[2] The Guild Church of the Franks is named in a Bull of Leo IX., Franks. dated 1053. The document is equally doubtful Lombards. with other deeds ascribed to this Pope. That of the Lombards is uncertainly alluded to in the Book of the Popes.

When we carry this dubious question into the light of the general facts concerning church-building, it will appear a safe conclusion that none of these guilds were known until the latter decades of the twelfth century, the period of the first Church of St. Peter's in the Vatican, where these guilds were settled. At some time as yet undetermined, the quarter of the Vatican came to be called the Leonine City. The legend The Leonine in the Book of the Popes relates that it was City. founded about the middle of the ninth century, after Rome had been invaded by the Saracens. The criti-

[1] S. Bonifacii, *Ep. Cuthberto Archiep.*
[2] This Pope was half a century later than Charlemagne in the tradition.

cism on this story is that the Arab and Greek writers say nothing about any such violation of Rome by the Hagarenes. Nor is the rhetorical life of Pope Leo IV. of such a quality as to invite our credence in the event. The fortification of the Vatican probably began from the Norman time.

Perhaps these particulars will suffice to show in what ignorance we are as to the actual state of Rome from the time of the rise of Islam. Such knowledge as we may glean, however, from the Mediæval guide-books enables us to call up the image of that antique and august city of the Cæsars, which still kindled emotions of wonder and delight in strangers alike from the East and the West. There is no reason to suppose that its monuments had suffered much, unless from its own turbulent nobles and riotous mobs. Temples were beginning to be converted into churches, and the city to assume a partly Mediæval appearance not earlier than that century to which these inquiries have compelled us again and again to return.

If we inquire into the state of the Campagna, the earliest territory of that league of nobles and priests who formed the nucleus of the Church, our sources are always retrospective and fabulous. The monk never describes—perhaps dares not describe—what is passing around him in any direct manner. His stories of distant times may often be understood as allegorical of events within his experience. They offer, in this sense, astounding revelations of violence and of depravity past shame, in the lives of the Abbots and the devoted band of slaves whom they commanded. They hint the rise, under false pretences, of a kingdom entirely of this world. But it is impossible to extract from all the monastic chronicles together any clear account of the state of the Church at the time when Dante was a boy and beginning to grope about in a world not yet realised.

Let us transfer our attention to a spot which has been called the Sinai of the New Dispensa- The Cloister tion, and which had more to do with the rise of Monte of Christendom than Rome itself.   We refer Cassino. to the great Benedictine cloister of Monte Cassino in Campania, where the "Abbat of abbats" reigned.

Every such cloister has, by the necessity of the theories of the Order, a suitable legend of Legends of origin.   The traditional date of the dedica- Origin. tion of the church is October 1, 1071.   From that epoch we look back upon a variety of fanciful vicissitudes experienced by the brethren of the Order.   They talk of destructions by the Saracens and of restorations in previous ages.   They say they were at Capua and Teano, where in 889 the autograph of the Benedictine rules had been burned.   Monte Cassino had suffered destruction some five years before.   From that time a new flight of retrospection begins, and they strain their gaze athwart 360 long years, until they rest it upon the figure of St. Benedict himself.   In 529 the old philosophers are supposed to vanish with more than dramatic suddenness off the stage of spiritual activity, to make room for the new philosophers, of whom the coryphæus is that saint.

And who was St. Benedict? Like Gregory, he is traced up to an old Roman *gens*.   Through their spiritual telescope the good monks espy him in that far distant time busily breaking down a temple of Apollo at the spot now called Monte Cassino, that he may erect there a monastery.   A dæmon, perhaps the spirit of Apollo himself, sits on a column, and would hinder the work. Whence had the Saint come thither? From Castrum Sublacum or Subiaco, on the Anio, where he had erected twelve small cloisters, and, cheered by the society of the pious St. Scholastica, had composed the rules of the Order. Roman senators, an Equitius and a Tertullus, had sent their sons to him, and the saint had trained them for apostles to Gaul or to Sicily. The jealousy of the neighbouring priests had been aroused. Seven beautiful girls had arrived to tempt his young disciples to break their vows. The saint himself, who had already armed himself against feminine blandishments by rolling naked among thorns and nettles, quitted Subiaco, and came in the society of three ravens, guided by angels, to Monte Cassino.

Such particulars we derive from the *Dialogues of Gregory the Great*, a Benedictine work perhaps of the thirteenth century, to which age the roll of the illustrious literates of Monte Cassino belongs. They occurred to Benedictine invention at the time when Sicily was becoming their Paradise, and when they were daring enough to assert that the aforesaid Tertullus endowed St. Benedict with Messina and Palermo, and with 7000 slaves.[1] This was the time of the Normans.

Father Montfaucon has produced a MS., supposed of the eleventh century, from Monte Cassino, which gives figures of St. Benedict and of the old costume of the Order.[2] It may indeed date from the next century, but it is certain that little or nothing had been done in literature on Monte Cassino until there was talk of Abbot Desiderius, dated 1087. The history of this abbey has been attempted by Father Tosti, of course within ecclesiastical lines. But should a thoroughly critical examination of its archives be made, it would

[1] Pirro, *Sicilia Sacra*, 1155.   [2] *Diar. Ital*, 323.

throw a flood of light upon the origin of the Church itself. Here we content ourselves with a few further observations.

Subiaco, as parent of Monte Cassino, should yield us some earlier information about the Bene- dictines. We find here in the Sagro Speco Subiaco. frescoes of the thirteenth century, and no hint of a high architectural antiquity. In the annals of the Order we find tales and tales. The cloister was destroyed by the Langobards in 601, and the monks fled to S. Erasmo on Monte Cœlio. Subiaco is deserted till a restoration by John VII. (706). A second destruc- tion by the Saracens occurs in 840.[1] It is restored by Abbot Peter the First, and falls to the Saracens again in 936.

It is obvious that here again proleptic fiction has been busily at work. And we would insist again upon the point of criticism so much neglected by our prede- cessors, that monasteries could not have been built till the monks knew what they were going to do in them, and that they had practically little to do until they had the Jewish writings in some shape in their hands. It is impossible to date either of the cloisters earlier than the time of the Crusades.

And if so, noted writers who hail from Monte Cassino must have persistently antedated their productions. Thus John the Deacon is referred to about the year 882. Even if he had lived at that epoch, what could he have known of Gregory the First, whose life he pretends to write; who, with the aid of the Archangel

---

[1] Mabillon, *Annal. Bened.*, xix. 23, and Gregorovius, iii. 274, who gives the references to Papal Bulls and to the Chartary of Subiaco, but adds that the cloister *has not a history*, and that Jannuccelli's *Memoirs*, 1856, have no scientific value.

Michael, secures the retirement of the Langobards from the city in the sixth century; who, by the exhibition of the coat of the Evangelist John before the door of the Lateran, produces fair weather or rain? Neither St. Michael nor St. John could have been heard of in that age. In like manner, Paul the Deacon takes upon himself to paint another Gregory, the defender of images. He is another Monte Cassino monk. A third tells a story, already disputed, of the invasion of Rome by Saracens in 846. It is men of the same confederacy who paint the Admiral Popes Leo. IV. and John VIII., and who see their prototypes in Peter and Paul delivered from the waters and from shipwreck. Others ascend higher up the stream of time and concoct fables about Constantine. In short, Monte Cassino was a great factory of fables, which have too long passed for fact, but which were not heard of in the world until the epoch of the Crusades.

The modern pilgrim to Monte Cassino will recall the adjacent towns of Roccasecca and Aquino, associated with the name of St. Thomas, the Angelic Doctor, another of the luminaries connected with the famous cloister, and the author of an attack upon human reason, from which, perhaps, human reason has not yet fully recovered. Thomas Aquinas stands yet in the dawn of the Catholic Church.

Let us revert to another Benedictine cloister, that of Farfa. Its chronicle, as usual, relates strange stories of origins.[1] We are told that it was besieged seven years (890–897) by the Saracens, then deserted. The Saracens spared it, but Christian robbers set it in flames. A splendid picture of its early glories is drawn. The Abbot manned a ship, which entered

Farfa.

[1] Mon. Germ., xi. 532; Chron. Farf., p. 387; Vatican. Regest. Farf., 285.

the royal harbours toll-free. Charters can of course be produced granting the abbey immunities from the time of Charlemagne, and confirmatory Bulls of the Popes. At the time when a Benedictine, Leo VII. (933), is said to have sat in the chair of Peter, and the rule of the beautiful Marozia was on the wane, Farfa was rebuilt by the Abbot Raffred, who was murdered by his monks in 936. Campo, one of the murderers, obtains from King Hugo, husband of Marozia, the abbacy, and lives along with Hildebrand, the other murderer, in riotous pleasure. Both have concubines. Campo has seven daughters and three sons. Hildebrand establishes himself at Fermo. During a carouse with his mistress and children, the castle is set on fire, and countless treasures are consumed. The monks copy these examples, live in villas, and come to Farfa on Sundays to laugh and gossip. Then Alberich, Prince and Senator of the Romans, marches against Farfa with a military force, drives out Campo, and sets up the rule of Cluny in 947 ; but in five years the new Abbot is murdered, and the old wickedness is resumed. If these stories were written down two or more centuries after the date of the alleged events, what is their worth ? If there is anything of reminiscence in such details, it would seem to point to the fact that the precursors of popes and abbots were petty princes, united in some mere military league against the Saracens.

Turning to Cluny, the offspring of Monte Cassino, the new rule is said to date from 910. But Cluny. the archives of Cluny from that century, recently edited by M. Bruel,[1] are full of mistakes, which cast deep doubt upon the genuineness of the whole. They have been compiled, as in other cases,

[1] Paris, 1880.

F

on a system of fraud. Cluny could not have been
founded in the tenth century.

By whatever road we follow the tracks of the Benedictines, wherever we dip into their annals, the same
method of making history is always to be detected.
Thus the monastery near Squillace places Cassiodorus,
an ex-prefect and monk, in the sixth century. The
writings ascribed to him show the impossibility of this
date. They would connect the Roman Empire with the
Old Testament. In like manner Columba and Columbanus, the hero-monks of Scotia, are figures of mythic
retrospection to the monks of the cloisters of Burgundy,
Switzerland, and Lombardy, under the Irish rule in
the thirteenth century. The Life of Columba is said to
have been written by Adamnan, Abbot of Iona, in the
seventh century. But the oldest manuscript comes from
the Benedictine convent of Reichenau on the Lake of
Constance. The Life of Columbanus is ascribed to
Jonas, a monk of Bobbio in Lombardy. The whole
history of Western monachism, it cannot be too empha-
tically insisted on, begins with the Benedictine Order.
And if the evidence forbids us to assume the rise of
the Order earlier than the twelfth century, the fables
referred to fall for want of support.

Through all the cloud of fable, then, we win to a
point of some clearness when we see that the head-
quarters of the Basilians were once at Grotta Ferrata,
those of the Benedictines at Monte Cassino, and that
a literary confederacy existed between them which re-
sulted in the production of the most important works of
dogmatic and polemical Church literature. Mohammedans were all around them. Jews were also numerous. They had opportunities of acquainting themselves
with their traditions. Mosques had long been stand-

ing, synagogues were being built. The theory which explains the origin of the world from Adam, common to the two Oriental sects, had been firmly established in the seats of old philosophic culture, though the traditions of philosophy were not utterly extinct.

Under such conditions the Catholic Church arose, and prepared to struggle for the possession of Rome. But perhaps her true Holy Land is Apulia, Calabria, and Sicily. Surely no student can thoughtfully traverse those regions, observing the remains of the old Greek and Roman, of Byzantine, of Arab, of Norman culture, without feeling that he is on ground far more interesting to our Western humanity than Cappadocia, Syria, or Egypt. We are there in the centre of our world. We begin to understand how the Greeks, stretching out their hands to the East, when the warriors of the Cross had led the way, and the Latins grasping the West, succeeded in founding that great institution of which every Christian sect that has arisen down to our own times is a branch or a scion.

One of the most interesting clues in reference to this subject is furnished by the cult of the Holy Archangel Michael, guardian spirit of so many mountains. Let us take up our station for a moment at Monte St. Angelo, near Manfredonia and Monte Gargano. Here is a chapel in a grotto, an object of pilgrimage at some epoch in the Crusading time. The great festival is celebrated on the 8th of May, and commemorates the ecclesiastical dream of the apparition of the Archangel to St. Lawrence, Archbishop of old Sipontum, hard by, in the year 491. In the Service Book, the Introit is taken from the 102nd Psalm; the Lesson is Apoc. i. 1–5, which speaks of the "seven spirits which are before the throne;" the Gospel is

Matt. xviii. 1–10, on the doctrine of guardian angels. Other parts of the service recognise the intercession of angels, and of the blessed Archangel in particular; but piobably the oldest part of the service is the invocation :—

Alleluia, alleluia. Sancte Michaele Archangele, defende nos in proelio: ut non pereamus in tremendo judicio. Alleluia.

The same mass is sung on Michaelmas Day, September 29, or the Feast of the Dedication of the Church of St. Michael.

When did that prayer of warriors to the archangelic warrior first resound on the slopes of Monte Gargano?

Jews were numerous all along that coast to Bari, there can be little doubt, from the latter half of the twelfth century. But had they during that age already listened to the mysterious oracles of the Book of Daniel, where Michael appears as the guardian angel of the people in a time of great trouble? Rabbindom, whether in Spain or Italy, was in its inception until the epoch of Maimonides, and the synagogue services were as yet incomplete. The great time of trouble for Judaism was the time of the first Crusade. According to these indications, it would be later than that time that the church was dedicated; but Michael, mentioned along with Gabriel in the Koran, earlier belonged to the Mohammedans.

A Rabbin speaks of the Word of the Lord going forth from Bari and Otranto.

Another point of great interest is the cult of St. Nicholas, the successor of Neptune and protector of Bari. The church legend dates the reception of his bones from Lycia in the year 1087; but it is not likely that the tale of merchants from Bari going to fetch these relics could have found acceptance until the Crusading excitement had long set in. The

St. Nicholas of Bari.

Saracenic crypt is said to have been consecrated in 1089, and the church to have been finished in 1139. It should be remembered that the Saracens had been there until 1002.

There can be no doubt that Bari is one of the oldest seats of Christianity in the world, and one of the earliest centres of propagation to the East. The great annual festival, to which multitudes of mariners and of peasants from the east slope of the Apennines throng, is also one of the most important links of the past. It has been said that it is the only occasion in Italy in which the religion of Jesus Christ is seen in the hands of the people as distinct from the priesthood. And if so, the mode of devotion of the pilgrims—their movement round the aisles with the forehead pressed to the pavement—seems to carry us back to Moslem influence, and strikingly to bear witness to the true origin of the church in these regions. And since St. Mark is greatly honoured at Bari, memory takes flight to the Duomo at Venice, with its mosque-like cupola. Since what time has it borne the name of St. Mark, and what was the first worship celebrated there? If this Duomo was finished so early as 1071, it could hardly have been Christian and Catholic.

It is probable that all along the coast the Mohammedans were strong, and the religionists connected with them, the Manichees, throughout the twelfth century. At Lucera, near Monte Gargano, there was a colony of them from Sicily, under Frederic II., in 1223, enjoying religious freedom, which was not put down till 1300.

To revert to the western coast. At Salerno the Cathedral of St. Matthew is dated 1084, and ascribed to Robert Guiscard. The relics of Salerno: St. Matthew. the saint are said to have been brought from the East in

930. Hildebrand, Pope Gregory VII., is said to have died here in 1085. Could his genuine tomb be shown, it would be a great historic landmark; but the actual tomb dates from the sixteenth century. The idea of a Pope in banishment only a quarter of a century after occupying a proud position, said to have been won by Leo IX., arouses reflection, and suggests inquiry into the whole narrative concerning St. Gregory VII. The great medical school of Salerno dates from about the middle of the twelfth century, the flourishing time of the Jewish physicians or of the Jewish Rabbins.

At Amalfi the Cathedral of St. Andrew is said to date from the eleventh century; yet the translation of the relics from Constantinople is referred to the thirteenth century. In the vicinity the tokens of the influence of the Mohammedans are strong. The Saracenic Palazzo Rufalo, at Ruvello, is ascribed to the twelfth century.

At Messina no spot could be more suitable on which
Messina. to deliver a lecture on the history of the Church than the old Norman Church of St. Annunziata dei Catalani, built, it is said, on the site of a temple, then of a mosque. There are perhaps of the faithful who still believe that the epistle sent by the Virgin through the hands of St. Paul to the inhabitants is a genuine document. It was a forgery of Lascaris' in the fifteenth century. Nowhere is it more apparent than in the light of the monuments of Sicily that Maria, Mother of God, is the deified Mariam of the Arabians, even as Isa, son of Mariam, is deified in Jesus.

We may close this excursion by a visit to the beauti-
Monreale. ful cloisters of the Benedictines at Monreale. One of the columns bears the date 1228. This splendid monument of the transition from the Saracen

to the Norman dominion carries our thought to the still greater splendours of the Alhambra, and to the spiritual conquests of the Benedictines in Spain. The like history is repeated yonder to that we have traced in Italy. At Monreale we are not far from the Benedictine cloister San Martino, the founding of which is falsely ascribed to Gregory the Great. There we may meditate, if we please, on the forgeries of the Abbate Vella, and recover from many a long illusion in respect to the documents for the antiquity of the Benedictine Order.

And now let me invite the reader to take a brief review of the legends of the Popes during the important period at which we have been glancing. Let our standpoint be in time the session of Innocent III. (1195–1214), and in place the old Tusculum, now Frascati. Down to 1191 old Tusculum existed, a strong place for a residence of the visible heads of the Church. According to Church tradition, no less than five, and perhaps more, Counts of Tusculum had become Popes.[1] The particulars given in the Book of the Popes, often fabulous in form, reveal the substantial fact that at some time after the first Crusade the monk was beginning to replace the soldier in the direction of the great league of the Cross.

Innocent III. himself is said to have been a Campanian of the lowest rank, to have studied at Paris, and to have been a very learned man. To him is ascribed a work on the Office of the Mass, and a book on ancient Decretals, which he commanded to be observed. In all probability the notorious false Decretals were composed after his time. He is also said to have built, at his own expense, the Hospital of the Holy

Retrospect of Papal History from Innocent III.

[1] See Gregorovius, *Gesch. d. Stadt Rom*, iv. 70.

Spirit in the Leonine City, and to have given silver to all the churches in the city for the making of chalices. He also took the Order of St. Augustine under his protection. He is said to have died at Perugia, whither he had gone to put an end to the strife between the Genoese and the Pisans.

His predecessor, Celestine III. (1188-95), is said to have crowned the Emperor Henry, and to have given him a nun, Constantia, in marriage. He made every effort to recover Jerusalem. Though pressed by many war expenses, he built splendid houses at St. Peter and St. John Lateran. An excellent Pontiff, he was greatly lamented.

Before him Clement III. (1186-88) had declared war against the Saracens. He built the cloister of St. Laurence outside the walls, and "restored" the crumbling Lateran Palace. He waged war with Tancred, tyrant of Apulia.

Gregory VIII. (1186), in his ardour against the barbarians, went, on his accession, to Pisa, reconciled the Genoese with the Pisans, and directed the two peoples to raise the largest fleet they could, and to hasten to Asia for the protection of the Christian religion.

Similarly, Urban III. (1185) had gone to Venice to raise a fleet for the defence of Jerusalem. When he heard of its fall, he died of grief on the way at Ferrara.

Of Lucius III. (1181) the significant fact is related that he strove to abolish the name of Consuls from the Roman Republic, and was cast out of the city. The eyes of his followers were put out. He went to Verona, condemned the license of the Romans at a great council, and exhorted the Christian princes to succour their friends in Asia and Syria. At this late date, then, the Romans still clung to the old form of the Empire, and resisted with success the attempt to impose the rule of the Vicar of Christ upon them.

At the election of his predecessor, Alexander III. (1161–81), a great sedition arose in the city. There was a rival pope, Victor, the nominee of three profane Cardinals, favoured by the Emperor Frederic. Twice Alexander fled, first to Claremont, then to Venice, to the monastery of Carita. He is discovered after three months, and led amidst crosses and solemn ceremonies to St. Mark's. Sitting before the altar, he blesses the Prince, the Senate, and all the people. In the end, he makes peace with Frederic, who comes to Venice, and agrees to restore Rome to the Pontiff. Then there is presented to our view one of those brilliant symbolic scenes in which the pencil of Church artists delight.

Pope Alexander stands before the doors of St. Mark's in the presence of all the people. He bids the Emperor prostrate himself and beg for pardon. The Pope puts his foot on the neck of the Emperor, saying, " It is written, On the serpent and adder thou shalt walk, and tread down the lion and dragon." Frederic replies, " Not thee, but Peter, whose successor thou art, do I obey." " Both me and Peter," the Pontiff answers.

He subsequently bestows the privileges of the white *funale* and the leaden seal on the Doge and Senate, also the ornament of the umbrella on the Doge, and a seat in the theatre. Before this there had been only two seats in the Papal theatre, the right for the Pontiff, the left for the Cæsar. Also on the Feast of the Ascension he grants plenary and perpetual indulgence in St. Mark's. He dies in Rome.

And yet this proud Pope is one of *five* who contend in this period for the Chair of St. Peter, and who nearly succeeded in overthrowing the Roman Church. The tale is a violent affront to common sense in many details.

The Englishman, Adrian IV. (1157–61), is the converter of Norway to the faith. He too is said to have struggled with the Romans, endeavouring to abolish the Consuls. The people beat a Cardinal; the Pope pursues them with curses and interdiction, which weapons he also turns against William of Naples and Sicily. This Pope is a man of war, and fortifies many castles near Volsinum, on the lake of St. Christina. He is the first Pope who dwells in that city. He is unable to remain in Rome, owing to the evil conversation of the Consuls, and dies at Agriganum.

The session of Anastasius IV. (1155) is illustrated by his large charities to the poor during the great famine and pest which raged in the world.

Eugenius III. (1147) is said to have contended with the Romans, who honoured their five Senators. He fled by night to Farfa, and was there consecrated. Returning to the city, he has shortly to take flight, pursued by arrows down the Tiber.[1] He goes to Pisa, then to France, signs Lewis with the cross, and stirs up many against the Turks and Saracens. He returns to Rome, but finally dies at Tibur.

Lucius II. (1146) is Cardinal-priest of the Basilica of the Holy Cross at Jerusalem, which he "restored" or built at his own expense. He busied himself about the expedition to Jerusalem.

Of Celestine II. (1145) nothing is recorded. There was no sedition, owing to the prevalence of the plague.

Innocent II. (1131) makes war on Roger, Duke of

---

[1] The story seems reflected from that of Eugenius IV.

Apulia.   He is taken captive with many Cardinals, but Roger sends him back with great reverence to Rome. There an anti-pope, Peter, has been elected, and all is full of sedition.   Innocent repairs to Pisa, then to Genoa, and to Claremont, where he is magnificently received by St. Bernard.   Peter is there condemned. The Emperor Lothair accompanies him to Rome with a great army.   The anti-pope has disappeared, but the Romans persist in being governed by Senators in the ancient fashion, and Innocent lays down constitutions for the defence of the clergy.

Passing Honorius II. (1126), we come to Calixtus II. (1120), a brother of the Count of Burgundy and a relation of the kings of France, England, and Germany. His name had been Guido.   On his election, he repaired to Beneventum, assembled the Duke of Apulia, the Count of Campania, and other princes, and bound them by oath to obedience to the Roman Pontiff.   He subsequently takes care of the duchy of Apulia and Calabria in the absence of Duke William at Constantinople.   At Rome he holds a council of 900 fathers, and a reinforcement of troops is decreed for Asia; for Baldwin has been taken.   He raises a great fleet of Genoese, Venetians, and Pisans against the enemy.

Gelasius II. (1118) was educated in Monte Cassino under Abbot Odorosius.   His was a stormy career. Cyntius, of the powerful house of Frangipani, seized the Pontiff on his election, cast him to the ground, kicked and pummelled him with his fists, then threw him into chains.   After his liberation, he is persecuted by the Emperor Henry, and flees to Gaul.   He takes refuge in Cluny, and there dies.

Paschalis II. (1100), being a monk, is of course un-

willingly made Pontiff. He has to struggle with an
anti-pope, Gibert. He takes Castellana and Beneventum
by force of arms. He stirs up the Christian princes
to the Asiatic war. He is cast into prison by the
Emperor for refusing to confirm certain heretic bishops.
He comes out after he has confirmed them, but on
Henry's departure, revokes all his promises to him.

Urban II. (1086) had been known as Odo, Abbot of
Cluny. To him are ascribed a number of letters,
succo plenæ, addressed to the Countess Matilda, whose
name has been associated with many church foundations. At Claremont, where he persuaded a Council
to undertake an expedition against the Saracens, he
is said to have signed 300,000 men with the cross.
From this Council is also dated the decree for the
daily observance of the Hours of the Blessed Virgin,
and the celebration of her Office on the Sabbath-day.
On his return to Rome he is troubled by great
seditions under John Paganus, and remains two years
in the house of Peter Leoni, a very powerful citizen
and a Jew, whose descendant later became himself
Pope.

We come to Desiderius, Abbot of Monte Cassino,
or Victor III. (1085). The date is uncertain. He is
said to have been poisoned at the instigation of the
Emperor, because he had been of Hildebrand's party
against the anti-pope Gibert.

Hildebrand, or St. Gregory VII. (1073), has been
made a chief object of idealising Church art. His personality is smothered by panegyric; and all that can
be inferred from the traditions about him is that he
was symbolic of the beginning of an innovation in
Rome. We see him in Church representations celebrating mass on the birthnight of the Lord. He is

seized by Cyntius, son of the Præfect, and shut up in a strong tower. The Romans liberate him next day, destroy the house of Cyntius and put the family to death. Cyntius flees to the Emperor in Germany. Gregory puts the mark of anathema on the Emperor and his party, including Gibert, Archbishop of Ravenna. Then the Countess Matilda intervenes, and at Canosa the Emperor is reconciled to the Church. But peace is again broken, and Henry with Gibert, now made Pope Clement, comes to Rome and besieges Gregory in the Mole of Adrian. Finally, Gregory is freed by Robert, Duke of Apulia, and goes with him to Salerno, where he dies.

Gregory is represented as a great foe of simony, and as the institutor of clerical celibacy and of Sabbath fasts. But when we look to the fraudulent and late Gratianic collection of canons, which is the source of these representations, they are found to be untrustworthy. The ambitions of Monte Cassino and Cluny colour other parts of the representation; and when the monkish colour is expunged, all that can be discerned in this tedious tale of popes and anti-popes is the struggle of factions, of nobles, now with one another, now with the common Oriental enemy. The monks had their reminiscences, but their theory forces them to confuse their reminiscences by importing figures of their own Order into scenes unsuitable to them. The bare fact that the monks of Monte Cassino and of Cluny were beginning to fight for world dominion after the time of the first Crusade is all that we can find that is genuine.

When we ascend to the year 1004, we find the statement that all the princes of Italy formed a league to expel the Saracens from Sicily. When it is added

that William, son of Tancred, with the help of the
princes of Campania and Salerno, in a short space of
time (1004–1006) drove them all out of the island,
the statement is false ; and when it is said that this
was done at the Council of Pope Sergius IV., the
statement is pure fiction.   We must correct these
statements by throwing ourselves into the positions
and feelings of the warriors who led the Crusade.
They were in league to expel the Orientals from the
Mediterranean and to attack them in the East.   At
first they no doubt welcomed as allies the members of
the new spiritual confederacy, which sprung up as
a rival to the confederacies of the Mosque and the
Synagogue, and whose objects were the same with
their own.   But when it was seen that the Abbots of
Monte Cassino and of Cluny, daily growing in wealth
and influence and command of force, were aiming to
set up a new Caliphate in the West, and to overthrow
the old Republic in favour of a new tyranny, no
wonder that the utmost jealousy was inflamed against
them, and that the persons of the Pope were exposed
to constant danger.   But resistance to the pretensions came too late.   The martial manhood of
Europe was drawn off to the East.   It was the great
opportunity for men of business.   When the Crusaders
came straggling back, they found the Jews and the
monks in possession—the Jews absorbing gold and
making slaves, the monks grasping at land and building palaces ; womanhood and the family life deeply
depressed, the intellectual class employed in reducing
reason itself to slavery.

We have not yet recovered from the wounds inflicted
on humanity during that terrible age, the blame of
which falls not so much on the rank and file of the

great monkish militia, as on the ambitious and un-scrupulous prelates who directed their movements from the cloisters.

The history of Catholic Christianity from its rise is, in general, the history of Monte Cassino; and it will appear, on consideration of other branches of the evidence, that it was impossible for the monks to have sat down in the scriptorium of that monastery and to have begun the system of Church fable until some time in the thirteenth century.

Gazing at this notable Church centre, we may gradually recover from that vertigo and giddiness which the inexperienced perusal of the lives of the Popes is apt to produce in the reader. We begin to understand why, although Pope has followed Pope in unbroken series for 800 years, nothing has really progressed, and the like scenes of violence are imagined in the middle of the twelfth century that were imagined in the middle of the fourth. At the earlier epoch, a Vicar of Christ is portrayed leading a band of Roman gladiators and other ruffians to attack a basilica, and to stain its floor with the blood of some 130 persons. For five hundred years a Vicar of Christ is declared to be undisputed sovereign of the city; yet three hundred years later still the Vicars of Christ are struggling with the Senate and the people, are suffering constant defeat, but have not yet usurped the old authority of the præfects. It must be repeated, that the lives of the Popes are a phantasmagoria and an evil dream. It is enough to read in the works set down to the Papal contemporary of Rabbi Moses of Cairo the treatise on the Mass and the Epistles to assure ourselves that in his time the whole hierarchic and mystic system of the Papacy is in its infancy.

CHAPTER IV.

MORAL AND RELIGIOUS TEACHING AMONG THE ROMANS.

THERE is another kind of evidence in respect to institutions of the old Roman Empire, perhaps of even more importance than those to which we have just adverted. It is contained in the records of the Roman philosophic schools, from which we collect what was the best that men thought concerning the problems of existence and the conduct of life. The general feeling upon these matters presents a sharp contrast to that instilled by the monks. Nothing can, on the whole, be more antipathetic than the system of the old philosophers to that of the new; for the Mediævalists delight in the pallium and in the designation of philosophers.

It is unnecessary to enter here into any disquisition L. Annæus on the relation of the Greek masters to their Seneca. Roman disciples. The genius of the Romans made practical and popular the teaching of the Greek schoolmen. They instinctively selected what was helpful towards building up the Roman spirit and the Roman art of conduct. They had little relish for the mere speculative or contemplative life, which carried men out of active fellowship with the body of their fellow-citizens. What is to be admired above all in the Romans is not so much their external works, their roads, their aqueducts, their public buildings, their legions, their system of civil right, as that character which is to be traced everywhere as the base and foundation of all their works. The character of the Roman was the noblest of his traditions, and this tradition the Roman teachers laboured to cherish and hand down intact.

The teaching of the Roman Stoics is the noblest that has ever been given to the world, and the best text-book of their wisdom is the Epistles to Lucilius ascribed to L. Annæus Seneca of Cordova. We say "ascribed to Seneca," because, in the uncertainty that attends upon the authorship of much ancient literature, it is well not to think so much of the name of the writer as of the intrinsic merit of his writings. One is tempted to say that if Seneca, the minister of Nero, was not a good man, then Seneca did not write these Epistles; and if Seneca did write these Epistles, they are the monument of one of the loftiest and purest spirits that has ever risen up to guide and instruct mankind.

In the phrase which Tacitus applies to the teaching of the Stoics, *Sola bona quæ honesta,* we have the summary of this popular teaching. Honesty. We find it expressed in the Epistles in the negative form, *Nihil esse bonum, nisi honestum*[1]—There is no good apart from honesty. Whatsoever is honourable is good, and naught else can be good. The Churchmen have in one place echoed the principle in the ethical lessons of the service-books, although they have lamentably failed to act upon it. Through ages of darkness and dishonesty, the principle, being founded on the nature of man, has never been wholly

---

[1] Ep. lxxi.

G

forgotten ; it reappeared in the manly line of one of
our own poets, "An honest man's the noblest work
of God."

Honesty is the only form of right conduct. The
circle is the circle, no matter what the space enclosed ;
and the good is the good, no matter what space the
man fills in the eye of the world. It is implied that
you are a reasonable being, and that you should employ
your reason to conform yourself to the will of great
Nature, and control those hopes and those fears which
conflict with her laws. The wise and the virtuous life is
ever on one tenor ; it is exempt from change. It flows
from one source, Nature, and her alone. It is implied
that there is a natural source of honesty and of good
in every heart.[1] If this be denied, such teaching is
wanting in all leverage, and can effect nothing. But
it does not occur to the Stoic that there can be
infidels to that Nature who inspires us all, that virtue
which is a heritage from Nature.

Surely Virtue sends beforehand her light into all
minds.[2] Is it not planted in the hearts of
vicious men to approve of better things?
None are shut out from virtue ; all are invited, whether they be freeborn, freedmen, or slaves, whether
they be kings or exiles. You cannot woo Virtue with
gold, you cannot deter her from the door of the poor.[3]
She will accept no sordid lover. If we take her to
our soul, we become stronger, loftier, ampler.[4] And
there is nothing really great, nothing worth our wonder
but the great soul. It dwarfs all else.[5]

Virtue.

[1] Epp. lxxvi., cxviii.
[2] Epp. xvii., cviii.
[3] *De Benef.*, iii. 18, iv. 1, 24.
[4] Ep. lxxvi.
[5] Epp. viii., xviii.

The soul is the true seat of all that is sacred. It clings to its origin beyond time, and, though shut up in this dark and sad domicile, seeks, The Soul. as often as it may, the open air.[1] It is a part of the mind of God; into this mortal breast it has flowed from above. We feel this when we meditate our mortality, when we see that this body is nothing but a hospice, that we must quit when we become troublesome to the host. Must it not be that we come from a loftier seat? Otherwise how should we judge these our surroundings to be so low and narrow, and have no fear of going forth? The soul remembers whence she has come and whither she is going.[2]

Sanity lies in self-content and self-trust. The blessed life is that which needs no addition to it from without. To be wishful, to be dependent on Sanity. benefits, is to be unfinished.[3] You have only to will to be good; the soul will then feed itself, and grow of itself, and exercise itself. We should will to be free, —to snatch ourselves from this universal bondage to fear which is the oppression of mankind. You must free yourself from the fear of death and then of poverty.[4]

Health consists above all in the exercise of the soul in wisdom. *Philosophari est valere.* Mere strength of body is the strength of a madman. Let your first and chief care be the health of the soul, and let the body have the second place.[5] Keep it in bounds as far as you can, and let the soul have laxity and room. The sectary of wisdom cleaves indeed to his body, but the best part of him is away, stretching thought into the sublime. He is like a soldier enlisted; life is a

---

[1] Ep. xli.　　[2] Ep. cxx.　　[3] Ep. lxxx.
[4] Ep. lxxii.　　[5] Epp. viii., xv.

campaign; he is formed neither to love nor to hate
his life, but to endure his mortal lot with the knowledge of better things in store.[1]

True liberty is our goal, and to win it we must be

Liberty. wisdom's servants. That is the paradox:
liberty is service—to no human lord, but to
great ideas, which deliver from lusts and fears.[2] How
great a reward awaits us if we will only break with
the clinging evils of our imagination, and cease to
believe ill of the gods.[3] The hurtful being is as weak
as the being that can be hurt. Absolute liberty is
when we fear neither men nor gods; when we have
no base and no excessive desires; when we have the
greatest authority over ourselves; when we have become
our own man. We must feel ourselves too great and
born for greater things than to be bondmen to our
bodies.[4]

The view of social life and duty is very simple.

Sociality. Nature is our great common mother; we are
begotten of one cause, and for one end. She
implanted in us mutual love and made us sociable
beings. She laid down for us the principles of equity
and justice. By her law it is worse to hurt another
than to be injured ourselves. At her imperial behest
helping hands are ready for mutual succour. Let the
verse be ever, then, in our heart and on our lips:

"Homo sum, humani nihil a me alienum puto."[5]

Briefly, we need but one formula of human duty. All
divinity and all humanity are included in the sentiment,
We are members of one great body.[6]

[1] Ep. lxv.   [2] Ep. viii.
[3] Ep. lxxv.   [4] Ep. lxv.
[5] Ep. xcv.   [6] Cf. Ep. xcii.

It is in accordance with such principles that theology should be as broad as possible. We should understand that all the names whereby men *God.* have defined the unseen causes that operate or seem to operate upon our life mean substantially one thing.

What do we mean by Nature? What do we mean by God?[1] What but a divine reason inserted into the whole world and into its parts? It is Nature who begat us sound and free; it is not she who has reconciled us to vices. It is she who raised our countenances to heaven.[2] God, then, or the gods, or Nature, are expressions that we use for the intelligence that pervades the world. Another term is Providence. The gods did not beget us in a careless moment, and Nature thought us out before she produced us. A man is not a tumultuary and thoughtless piece of work: he is Nature's greatest boast.

The gods are under no external compulsion. Their eternal will is their law, and they change not from their purpose. They cannot seem to *The Gods.* purpose aught against their will. Whatever they cannot leave off, they have willed to continue. They never repent of their first endeavour; they may not descend into the contrary.[3] The immortal gods alone have for their portion virtue and the blessed life. We have some shadow and likeness of that good. It is true that we and they have reason in common, but in them it is consummate—in us on the way to consummation. The bad man does not strive to ascend to the source whence he came. But why should we not suppose that he has somewhat divine in him, seeing that he is a part of God? This element that contains us is one, is God, whose fellows and whose members we are.

---

[1] *De Benef.*, iv. 7. [2] Ep. xciv. [3] *De Benef.*, vi. 23.

The bad man is defective for good, but the presence of virtue and soul in a human body brings the man to a level with the gods ; he tends towards them, mindful of his origin.[1]

In poverty and contempt of riches we may make ourselves worthy of God.[2] The mind of the wise only is worthy of God. We must live in His sight, nothing being closed from His view. He is present to our minds, He intervenes in the midst of our thoughts, yet as one who may at some time depart. A rect and good and great soul, what is this but God sojourning in the body of man? Such a soul may fall to the Roman knight, to the freedman, or to the slave. Knight, freedman, slave! Mere names, the offspring of ambition or of wrong. You may stealthily find heaven from any corner by a leap and bound. Do but arise and make yourself worthy of God.[3]

You need not raise your hands to heaven ; you need not ask the chapel-keeper to let you pour your prayer into the ears of the image, that you may be heard the better. God is near at hand, is with you, within you. I tell you, Lucilius, a sacred spirit sits within us, observer and guardian of our good and evil. He treats us as we treat Him. There is no good man without God.[4]

Remarkable is the protest against verbal quibbles, *One Essence in many Forms.* and the insistance on nominal differences where there is no essential distinction. The effort is always to guide our thinking as well as our conduct *secundum naturam*, according to the realities that we find in our minds. It is idle, for example, to say that we are under debt to Nature and not to God, because these thoughts are inseparable. If you had

[1] Ep. xcii.
[2] Ep. xviii., xcii.
[3] Ep. xxxi.
[4] Ep. xli.

received a good offer from Seneca, you would say you were in debt to Annæus or to Lucius; the creditor would be the same, though the name were changed. Seneca is the same man, whether you pronounce his name, his forename, or his surname. Just so Nature, Fate, Fortune: all are names of one and the same God, who makes a various use of His power. And so in morals. Justice, probity, prudence, fortitude, frugality are the goods of one soul. If you are pleased with any of them, you are pleased with the soul.[1]

These philosophers never perplexed themselves with the idle question whether life was worth living. They recognise that the love of life *The Future.* is so natural, that they direct all the force of their exhortation to fortify the mind against the fear of death. But they felt that life was not to be bought at any price. The main thing is to live well and to die well: the question of sooner or later is an impertinence. We should live as in a tent, expecting to migrate. To die well is to escape the risk of living ill.[1]

The Stoic will not be so inept as to repeat the Epicurean cant, and tell his friend that idle are the fears of hell, and the tales of Ixion's *Hell* wheel, and Sisyphus' stone, and Prometheus' liver. There is none so childish as to fear Cerberus and the shades and ghostly skeletons. Either death consumes us or it sends us forth. In the former case, nothing remains of us. In the latter, better things await us, for we have had a burden removed.

We die daily, for we daily lose some part of life; and when we increase, life decreases. This very day we divide with death. It is not the last drop which drains the water-clock, but all that has flowed down

---

[1] *De Benef.*, iv. 8.   [2] *Ep.* lxx.

before; and the last hour of our existence does not bring death, but only consummates it. We die many times; our last death is that which snatches us away.

A brave and wise man ought not to flee, but to march forth from life. And above all, we should avoid the lust of dying, which seizes upon many.[1] The prayer of Mæcenas was extremely base, on the other hand, when he longed for life, though in the absence of all that makes life a good.[2]

When that day shall come which shall separate this *The Better Life Beyond.* mixture of the divine and human, I shall leave this body where I found it; I shall restore myself to the gods; not that I am now apart from them, but an element of the grave and terrene detains me. Through these delays of mortal time there is a prelude to yonder better and longer life. This space from infancy to old age is like a preparation for a second birth of nature. Another origin expects us, another state of things. 'Tis only after an interval that we can bear heaven. I look intrepidly forward to yonder decretory hour. 'Tis the last hour for the body, not for the soul. Look upon all that lies around you as the furniture of an inn. You may not take out more than you brought in. . . . That day that you dread as your last is your eternal birthday. Lay down the burden![3]

It is sometimes said that Seneca is profuse in words. Is it not to be admired that on topics so trite as life's elementary interests and duties there should be so great an abundance of expression? The stream of eloquence is always sweet and pure, and of clearness undisturbed. He accosts us never as a superior, always as a brother or a friend. A gentle and strong hand

---

[1] Ep. xxiv. [2] Ep. ci. [3] Ep. cii.

is held out to us; we are allured and enticed, never scourged to better things.

After our daily visit to his school we carry away something good, and hope that we return home in saner, or at least more sensible mood. We are, as he says, like one who has visited the shop of the perfumer, and who bears away the fragrance of the place.[1]

A few starry words, a few great guiding conceptions, sum up the whole doctrine. We know not how long after the downfall of the Empire it continued to form the better minds, and to mix with the Puritan feeling of the Arabians. But the Epistles of Seneca, which are a more precious gift to the human race than all the Mediæval books of the Church, were never proclaimed as something sent down from heaven. They have been cast into the shade and the dust as if obsolete, whereas their vital spirit and truth is ever fresh and acceptable to man as man. The great object of the philosopher was to bring us to true *libertas;* the object of all the book-religionists must be to render us intellectual slaves.

The Greek and Roman preacher never sends us to turn Sibylline leaves; he sends us to communion and consultation with the oracle of the heart, for purification and amendment to the energy of the will. Every confidence is placed in reason; none in revelations to a special and privileged class. It is the teaching of souls strengthened and refined by the fire of suffering. Always in the background we see the horse-rack, the prison, the dismal island of exile, the loss of goods; always the deep sense that there are spiritual possessions on which no tyrant may lay his hand.

[1] Ep. cviii.

Claudian three centuries later continues to preach like lofty lessons in high places. They are lessons of gentleness which make conduct and sentiment the essence of piety. Clemency is the guardian of the great world; she dwells in the zone of Jove, gives the middle temperature to the sky, is eldest of the celestial dwellers; she first dissolved Chaos, dispersed the darkness, and poured light upon the ages. She needs no temples, nor altars glowing with incense; she enjoys a seat in the good man's breast, and inspires her lessons of pacific wisdom. The ruler should be slow to wrath and ready to pardon, after the example of the Father in heaven, who casts His bolts on rocks and monsters of the sea, but spares our lives.

The sister of Clemency is Good Faith, and she should share the heart and enter every act. She, the white-robed spirit, forbids you to use a moral dye, to speak the false, to delay the promise, to hide the virus of hatred deep in the bosom, to draw a bright mask over fraud. She confirms friendships by time, and binds them as with adamant that will last. She conquers enemies with arms, and friends with merits. Justice and Patience, Temperance, and Prudence, and Constancy, in like manner religiously personified, join their choirs, and gird themselves in the heart for diverse uses. Vices are importune spirits sent forth from Tartarus' caves— Avarice, with jaws that gape for gold, and her trusty nurse, Ambition, who crouches in the vestibules and doors of the powerful and makes a market of honours. Stilicho, true to the old Roman spirit, will pick out men for advancement from all quarters; he will inquire for merit, not for ancestry—the quality of the man, and not his extraction. The road will be open to genius; the Muses will lift their heads.

Then how glowing is the picture of Rome from the pen of the same poet, as parent of arms, of _{Mother} laws, source of empire, cradle of law. The _{Rome.} same feeling lives in Claudian that inspired the famous lines of Virgil, "*Excudent alii*," &c.

Rome alone takes the conquered to her bosom, and fosters the human race under a common name, after the manner of a mother, not of a domina. Her pacific customs have rendered the Empire the fatherland of all, so that one may change one's abode and still find oneself at home, from farthest Thule to river Orontes. We Romans are all one people, nor shall there ever be a bound to the Roman rule.

When we come to the third and the fourth century of our era, we find a new influence beginning The New to make itself felt in the schools. In theo- Pythagoreans and New logy the philosophers are aiming to establish Platonists. the Unitarian principle, though they continue to speak of "the gods." And in the conduct of life they establish a strict ascesis, which is regarded as a means of arriving at a closer communion with the Divine. Seed was sown in the cities of the East, in Rome, and in South Italy, of which the monks of St. Basil were to reap the fruits after the decline of Islam.

Most instructive in this respect are the lives of Pythagoras, written by members of the Pythagorean sect, Iamblichus, Porphyry, and Numenius. These lives are not in the modern sense biographies. They are poetic constructions of a typical life, which they believed had been once lived among men, about eight hundred years agone, and which they felt to be an exemplar to all members of the Pythagorean communion. The materials of the life have been derived from the actual institutes and customs of that communion. Hence, just as in later ages the life of a Basil, a Gregory, or a Benedict mirrors the sentiments and ideals of the great Orders, so in the great days of the old Empire the life of Pythagoras reflects the sentiments and the ideals of the old Cœnobite philosophers.

They look back upon their founder as one who, Life of while still a youth, attracted to himself honour Pythagoras. and reverence by reason of his gravity and virtue wherever he was seen or heard. Many affirmed, and with reason, that he was a son of God. So religious, calm, and sweet was his whole demeanour, it seemed that some good spirit had come to sojourn in the isle of Samos.[1] In later times, his teaching made so deep an impression upon his disciples, that they refused to call him by his proper name, and designated him "The Divine One," or simply "That Man."

There was in his system a perfect blending of morality with religion. In early life he visited Sidon, Byblus, and Tyre, and from love of *theoria* or contemplation, not from superstition, was initiated in the religious rites of Syria. He visited Carmel, and passed much time in the temple there alone.[2]

He passed into Egypt and imbibed divine wisdom at the fountain-head in intercourse with priests and prophets for the space of twenty-two years.

Finally, he came to Croton, and founded there his Cœnobite school or order, so called because of their community of life and goods. Their number is said to have been six hundred. They met with their wives and children in a *Homacoion*, or common auditorium. So Magna Græcia was founded. His laws and mandates were

[1] The like is said by Eunapius of Apollonius of Tyana.

[2] Which of course gives occasion to the Carmelite Order, founded in the twelfth or thirteenth century, to claim him as one of their fraternity. See P. Tessiere the Carmelite, 1612, in his *Hist. Carmelitanæ*, &c.

received as sent from heaven, from which they would not depart a nail's breadth. Their concord and happiness were universally praised. They looked up to their beloved chief as an Apollo or other spiritual being, who, that he might reform human life, had appeared in human form. He came to impart the saving beams of happiness and philosophy to the race of mankind. A greater blessing hath never, will never, come than this divine gift in the person of Pythagoras. He came to remove blindness from our eyes, that we might see the true principle and causes of the whole universe; that he might establish the best form of policy, concord among the people, community of goods among friends, the cult of the gods, holy rites to the departed, sound legislation, learning, continence of the tongue, abstinence from animal food, temperance and self-control, and all that is worthy of love among true disciples.

He filled the enslaved cities of Italy and Sicily with the spirit of freedom, and redeemed them from the power of tyrants. He removed sedition and discord. Short sayings, delivered now to a small and now to a larger audience, gave the sum and epitome of his wisdom. To expel disease from the body and ignorance from the mind, and put down lavish expense in luxuries, to drive away dissension from the home, and faction from the city, and excess from all lives, these were his aims. Like a loving father, he addressed to each his admonitions. At Delos he had won admiration because he prayed only at the altar of Apollo Genetor, which alone was bloodless.

Winning are the pictures of his activity as a preacher. He would enter the gymnasium at Croton, and the young men would gather about him. He would impress upon them the principle of seniority

in nature, and apply it to teach them reverence
to parents. So unhesitatingly is the good of life
assumed, he said that they should be as grateful to
them who gave them life as a dead man would be
to one who brought him up again to the light. He
even thought, this Confucius of the West, that the
gods would pardon those who gave equal honour to
parents, seeing that our parents taught us divinity.
Fraternal love was to be cultivated, and they were so
to behave that friends should never be converted into
enemies; enemies should be as quickly as possible
converted into friends. And then he would speak of
temperance, and how that it was the only virtue that
befitted alike the youth and the maiden, and women and
the elders. He would remind them that the terrible
calamities of the Trojan War had been brought on by
Heaven in punishment for the incontinence of one man.

He urged them to cultivate the mind. The mere
care of the body was like a hollow friendship, soon
at an end; but education, like an honest and good
friend, would last them to the end, and perhaps confer
an undying glory on their memory. Strength and
beauty, health and courage, could not be transferred.
Riches and public honours could not be recalled, once
they had slipped from your hands; but the man who
imparts learning to another is none the worse himself. The habit of calling in the beauty of old poetic
ideas to enforce moral lessons constantly appears. As
Themis sits by Jove, and by Pluto Dis, so law must
rule in cities, and the man who acts unjustly should
be made to appear a transgressor against all the world.
Senators should not abuse the name of the gods in
oaths, but should so act and speak as to be believed
without an oath at all.

He was strong on the duties of domestic life, the love of children and of wife. Other contracts might be written on parchments or on columns, but that of husband and wife was confirmed by the children. He laid down—a caustic anticipatory critique upon the system of the monks—that it was the greatest of wrongs to tear children and parents asunder.

He said that those who aimed at honours would do well to imitate those who were crowned in the games. These did not injure their adversaries, but only strove to gain the victory themselves. He who arrived at true glory should be indeed what he desired to appear to be in other's eyes. For praise was a more sacred thing than counsel; it concerned the gods to adjudge it. The gods loved to be approached by suppliants who from earliest youth had been imbued with goodness. In a drought, he advised that a band of such boys should be sent to pray for rain. Preaching to the women who assembled in the Temple of Juno, he taught them to think highly of gentleness and goodness of soul (ἐπιεικεια), that they might be the more acceptable to the gods. They should offer to the gods the preparation of their own hands, without the help of slaves,—cakes and honeycombs, and incense,—but they were never to worship the divinity with slaughter and with blood.

Language showed that the Sex had close relations with piety. Each period of woman's life had given a name to divinity. The unwedded girl was called Koré (Proserpine), the wedded woman Nymph, she who bore children Mother, the grandmother in the Doric dialect Maia. It was a Woman who gave forth the oracle at Dodona and at Delphi. Thus were divine virginity and motherhood the reflection of the

human institutes, as they always had been. Nor is it
difficult to understand how, after such preparation, the
Virgin Mother of the Arabs and then of the Catholics
should have laid so strong a hold upon the feeling and
fancy of the peoples of the Mediterranean. It is said
that Pythagoras' preaching was followed by a reformation in the manners of women. They hung up
their costly garments in the Temple of Juno; and the
faithfulness of Crotonian husbands became matter of
fame, after the example of Ulysses, who refused the
immortality offered by Calypso on condition that he
should desert Penelope.

The new Pythagoreans believed that it was the
noblest thing in the world to be a member of the
society of philosophers, and that wisdom was the contemplation of first principles of the fair, the divine, the
incorruptible. One of the most refined features of the
system was the stress it laid on music, to the calming
sounds of which the Cœnobites lay down to rest.
Pythagoras taught them the most comprehensive idea
of friendship ever known : it related them to God and
to all men. Whether sleeping or waking, they were
to be in intercourse with heaven.

Another characteristic of the system was the institute of silence. It was held that the founders of
the mysteries had signified that the most difficult
of virtues was the continence of the tongue. They
who had stood the proof of five years' silence were
thought worthy to know the esoteric doctrines, and
beheld and listened to Pythagoras behind the veil.
They were forbidden to divulge certain doctrines to
the crowd; and a symbolic envelope shrouded them
from all but the initiate. In this, as in other features of the system, a compliance of ancient religious

usage is indicated rather than any jealous reserve of knowledge. He gave out short oracular sayings, as "Take off your shoes when you sacrifice and adore. Turn aside from the broad road, and tread the narrow path. Do not speak of Pythagorean matters without a light."

But we need not pursue these illustrations. One of the greatest services the philosophers rendered to mankind was in their unanimous upholding of the true, the beautiful, and good alike in conduct and in theological contemplation. In popular lore, the gods and dæmons, being above Nature and man, might be, and were, savage, cruel, and immoral. The philosophers, though they dreaded the reproach of superstition, kept up the sacrifices, but rejected bloodshedding, and imparted to the gods that pure and lofty character by which they became the exemplars to humanity. The practices they could not arrest they strove to transform into a better significance. And one of the best illustrations of their influence is to be found in the record of Julian's last campaign, when his friends the philosophers sought to counteract by appeals to reason and experience, the gloomy vaticinations of the Etruscan soothsayers.

The death-bed of that great Emperor is one of the most affecting scenes that ancient literature offers. Whether the words ascribed to him actually fell from his lips or were only considered appropriate to the occasion, we know not. There seems no particular ground for doubting their authenticity. In any case, they reveal the best thought of the time concerning the way in which good men should live and might be expected to die. It is a document of immense weight in reference to our present investigations. We find it hard to forgive those Basilian monks and false pretenders to philosophy, who sat down in their cells some thousand years after that scene, to draw a foolish caricature of the Emperor, to deface him almost beyond recognition, and at the same time to misrepresent those institutes of antiquity from which they were actually borrowing their own. We have not lost the feeling of the Pythagoreans,—that respect for the spirits of the great dead is a chief article of true religion, and shall rejoice if this good comes out of our studies, that gallant and great spirits, like the imperial philosopher, shall resume the place in our reverence of which they have been so long deprived.

Julian exults in restoring life, as a debtor of good faith, to Nature, who claims it again. He is not cast down and sad, for he has been thoroughly taught, in the general opinion of philosophers, that the soul is much more blessed than the body, and he thinks that there is cause for joy rather than for grief when the better condition is separated from the worse. The celestial gods have made death the highest reward of some of the most pious of men. Equally is he a coward who longs to die when he ought not, and who refuses death when death is opportune. Julian rebuked the weeping friends who stood around his couch with all his authority, saying it was unworthy to mourn a prince who had been reconciled to Heaven and the stars. His last moments were spent in conversing with Maximus and Priscus on the sublimity of souls.[1]

If the student compares with such memories the writings of the monks who, under the names Gregory of Nazianzus and Jerome, pretend they were contemporaries of Julian and other " mad dogs against

[1] Ammian, R. G., xxv. 3, 15.

Christ," he will discover the vast interval both in point of time and of sentiment that exists between the old philosophers and the sophists and forgers of the cloisters.

The principles of the philosophers forbade them to submit to any tyranny, human or divine; and it is probable that they looked with a jealous eye upon the Imperial system of government, especially when it began to assume the form of a despotism. Many of their number cruelly suffered on suspicion of conspiracy and treason during the latter part of the fourth century. At the stated time of Mohammed's birth they are altogether blotted out from our view. Nor can they—if we understand them aright—have been reconciled to the men of the Koran or the Mishna. But they prepared the way by their customs and institutes for a class of men who, under the name of Philosophy, had a despotic Christology to introduce.

From the death of Socrates to the end of the old Empire stretches a period of about a thousand years, the most important in the whole history of our culture. Vast is our debt to the philosophers and their schools. It would, of course, be absurd to maintain that the men themselves were always worthy of their noble profession and calling; but the profession itself tended to gather the best spirits together, and to raise and preserve the tone of society. Their interests were the interests of political and spiritual liberty; they were men whose ideas outstripped rather than lagged behind the time. We will sacrifice to candour, and admit any criticism that can be fairly urged against the philosophers and their schools when they are brought into comparison with the Moslems, the Rabbins, or the monks of East and West. Yet, after all, the spiritual

monuments of antiquity give massive testimony, direct
and indirect, in their favour.   The literature that we
have loved so long and well—the literature of Greece,
and Rome, and England—is inspired by the love that
animated their hearts, and all vigour in art is traceable
to virtue and wisdom.   Whether we be Orientals or
Westerns, we own them as our common masters and
friends.   They will not have us for their obsequious
slaves.   *Sit anima nostra cum philosophis!*

In some respects the later philosophers show a
declension of spirit from that of the Stoics.
Miracles. Seneca does not find myth and miracle necessary to recommend his doctrines.   But in Philos-
tratus' Life of Apollonius and in Iamblichus' Life of
Pythagoras both are resorted to; though with nothing
like the luxury and gross extravagance of fiction of
which the monks were to be guilty.   Yet this miraculous element serves to mark the midway point
between the older philosophy or religion and that of
the Middle Ages.

The miracles of Pythagoras are finely conceived as
illustrative of his character and the dignity of his
doctrine.   Egyptian sailors came to take him from
Mount Carmel, thinking that they should sell him for
a great price; but they were awestruck as they saw
him descending the dangerous steep, undelayed by
precipice or stone.   When he came to the skiff, he
simply said, "Is the course for Egypt?" and embarked.   During the voyage he sat silent, fasting for
two nights and two days; nor was he observed to
sleep.   The vessel enjoyed a smooth and unbroken
course, and the sailors concluded that they bore a
divine being into Egypt.   They abstained from evil
words, and were more serious in their discourse than

usual. They landed in perfect calm, and proceeded to raise on the sand, extempore, an altar before him, which they loaded with fruits and with the firstlings of their merchandise. They then made for their port, and he partook of the fruit, and repaired, with his usual tranquil and modest mien, to some neighbouring dwellings.

At Croton he came upon fishers by the shore, who dragged a net loaded with fishes, and he prophesied the exact number that had been taken. They promised to do whatever he bade them if the event should turn out according to his prediction, and the result was that not a fish was lost. The whole were returned to their native element, while the divine one paid the price to the fishermen, who noised his fame abroad, and brought together a multitude, who came to gaze with astonishment on his face, and to believe that he was such a one as in truth he was.[1]

It was a favourite belief that he had power over animals. He tamed the Daunian bear, bound her by an oath to hurt the living no longer, and sent her to the mountains, whence she appeared no more. He whispered bovine language into the ear of an ox at Tarentum, and persuaded him to abstain from beans. The animal was long kept by Juno's temple, and was fed on human diet. The tale is of religious edification in reference to that kind of abstinence.[2] At Olympia he brought down an eagle from the height, stroked it, and let it go. He was another Orpheus. He was also held to have known a previous state of existence, and to have made it his principle to teach men by reminding

[1] Porphyr., *Num.*, 25; Iambl., c. 8. Cf. Plut., *Symp.*, viii. 8; Apul., *Apol.*, 294.

[2] Cf. Plut., *Numa*, 65; Ælian, V. H., iv. 17.

them of the life they had formerly enjoyed. There is nothing gross in these appeals to the feeling for wonder.

Our object is to point out that there was to the latest days of the Empire an intellectual aristocracy of men, whose discipline may be compared, and still more contrasted, with the monachism of six centuries later. The monks have tried hard to force themselves into the society of Porphyry, Celsus, and Julian; but their co-existence in the Empire with the philosophers is a simple impossibility. If by no other fact, by this an impassable gulf is created between the last philosopher and the first monk, that the former have no inkling whatever of a lawgiver, Moses, or of a law and gospel of Arabian or Hebrew origin, whence the precepts of living are infallibly to be derived.

CHAPTER V.

THE ETHICS OF THE MONASTERIES.

As Englishmen, we cannot but look back with wistful regret to the time when the inhabitants of these islands were Romans, and when such sentences as those of Seneca, such verses as those of Claudian, were listened to in Roman houses in London or York during the fifth century of our era. When we pass from the atmosphere of such sentiments to that of Mediæval or Holy Romanism, we find a contrast so violent that nothing but the direst revolution and the lapse of many ages can account for.

The ethics of the Christian Empire are the ethics of the monasteries. The Christian writers can think of no higher mode of life for any of us than the life of monk or nun—no higher destiny than that of the cloister. They who parade so many romantic instances of kings who renounced the palace and the purple for the cell, can certainly offer no higher honour to the mass of mankind. The monks and nuns have always been the pick and flower of Christians, as their modern defender, Count de Montalembert, in effect observes. It is from their lips that we must receive the laws and customs of the Christian life. The New Testament is monastic; nor can we fully comprehend its ethics until we carry them into the light of the monkish commentators.

There is an author esteemed by both the great Orders
Joannes   of St. Basil and St. Benedict, whose writings
Cassianus.   are in this respect valuable, although he
did not write in the age which the catalogues assign
to him.   He passes under the name Cassian, and was
connected with a monastery at Marseilles.   We can
but give a brief indication of the effect produced on
feeling and imagination when we turn from long
occupation with the pages of Seneca to this great
director of the Christian conscience.

Seneca exalts us, inspires us with a sense of the
greatness and the yet unascertained capabilities of
human nature.   Nor can any serious fault be found with
the Stoics' teaching, except that they make too high
demands on human nature—a fault which they admit,
and which wins our love.   But Cassian depresses and
dejects our spirit by incessantly reminding us of the
vices which beset us, of our impotence for good, and of
the immeasurable distance between ourselves and the
divine perfection.

The dress of the monk is shown to be symbolic of
The Habit of Christian virtues in all its parts, and the
the Monk.   proof is drawn from the example of John the
Baptist, who is indeed the prince of monks, and from
that of Peter and of Paul.   Old Testament examples
are also cited.   The hood denotes that they have the
innocence and simplicity of little children of Christ
(Matt. xviii. 1–6).   The colobium, leaving the arms bare,
denotes the mortification of their members upon earth,
their crucifixion to the world; and the rebrachiatories,
that they are apostolic men, studying to minister to
their necessities with their own hands.   The goat-skin
shows them imitators of those who, in the Old Testament dispensation, wandered about in such attire, of

whom the world was not worthy. The staff reminds
of Elisha, and enables the monk to ward off his foes
with the sign of the cross. The monk wears no shoes
because the Gospel forbids them. Sandals are permitted, and reflect Old Testament and New Testament
meanings. The girdle has its sacrament: it signifies
mortification, the denial of the reign of sin, and of the
flesh, which strives against the Spirit, according to the
Apostle. He has much to say on prayer without ceasing, and on the singing of psalms. It appears that the
apostolic delivery of one to Satan means "suspension
from prayer;" and if any ventures to join in prayer
with one so suspended, he makes himself "partaker of
his condemnation."

The example of Peter at Pentecost is called in to
sanction the solemnity of the "third hour," and that
of our Lord dying as immaculate victim and descending to Hades sanctions the "sixth hour" and the
"ninth hour." · There are also the examples of Cor-
nelius, of Peter, and of John. The elevation of
hands at the evening sacrifice is supposed to be typified by the extension of the Lord's hands upon the
cross.

Cassian has a tract on the Institute of Renunciation. And when we study the picture of the
newly-received monk, as he in the midst of ^{Renunciation.}
the brethren is stripped of the garments which are
symbolic of worldly pride, we understand why the
head of the Church has been represented as absolutely
poor. The monk is now to be sustained, not on wealth
gained by the secular arts, or kept back from his
former infidelity, but on the holy and pious largesses
of the monastery. As a soldier of God, he will thus
receive the pay of his service. He will be no longer

anxious for the morrow, according to the saying of the Gospel. He will glory in being numbered with Christ and the poor brethren.

We are dealing with ethical contrasts. It is terrible to observe how the free-souled aspirations which the philosophers had kindled are now replaced by abject submission to the will of their superiors on the part of these soldiers of God. The bright example of the Abbot John is cited, who, in obedience to his senior, fetched a stone for building which it was impossible for many to move, believing that the senior could command nothing vain or unreasonable. Abbot Mark, in his great humility and obedience, cast his little son into a river, at a like command. Abbot Pynaphius, in like passionate love of subjection, quitted the coenobium over which he presided and repaired to a distant monastery. He "was a city on a hill that could not be hid."

Subjection.

This complete renunciation on the part of the Christian soldiers is their mortification and crucifixion in the fear of the Lord. They are dead to anxiety, pride, contention, rivalry. Defunct to all the elements, they send the gaze of their hearts whither they expect to pass, and the eyes of their soul are cast down towards the tomb. This renunciation will avail naught if they turn back from the evangelical plough, or put on again the coat of which they have been despoiled, or come down from the roof of perfection, or take away anything that they have already abdicated. Let them beware of remembering their parents and their old affections, or of building again the things they have destroyed. Only they who persevere to the end shall be saved.

Mortification.

The devil is always lying in wait to the end of our life, to tempt us from humility and poverty, and his "heads," that is, the beginnings of tempt- Humility. ing thoughts, must be revealed to our superior, that they may be crushed. Through many tribulations and by a strait gate and narrow way we must enter the kingdom of God and come to life. We must aspire to be of the few who will inherit that kingdom; for many are called, but few chosen. The way to perfection is an ascent from the fear of God to charity. Examples of this perfection are to be found in one or in a few.

The system expressly aims at the debilitation of the mind. The monk must be as deaf and mute and blind to all but his ideal, immobile under abuse and reproaches. He must be a fool in this world that he may be wise. He must exercise no discernment nor judgment on the orders given to him. He must judge that only to be sanct, useful, wise, which either the law of God or the examen of his senior has pointed out to him. Under this discipline he may endure for ever in the cœnobium. In short, the ladder by which he may easily climb to perfection consists of these steps: the fear of the Lord, which gives birth to salutary compunction, from which proceeds abrenunciation of all things. This bareness procreates humility. Humility generates mortification of desires, by which all vices are extirpated and wither. Virtues then fructify; in their pullulation purity of heart is acquired, and by purity of heart the perfection of apostolic charity is possessed.

A moral discipline thus founded in fear and self-distrust, and employing an artificial psychology, could only produce results the very opposite to those arrived at in a system that makes the *secundum naturam* its principle.

There are eight principal vices with which the monk has to struggle, and they assume the shapes of malignant "spirits" to his enslaved imagination. They are Gluttony, Fornication, Love of Money, Wrath, Sadness, Anxiety, Vainglory, and Pride. The struggle with these is that *Agon*, or Olympian contest, which is rewarded by the crown. The monk is the true athlete of Christ, and all the apostolic passages which use this figure are applied to him. It is he who runs, and boxes, and wrestles, and there is no cessation to his fight with principalities and powers. Much is said of fasting which explains dark passages in the Gospels.

It is made clear that the New Testament ethics and legends of apostolic times are the reflections of monastic teachings, no less than the opinions ascribed to St. Basil. Judas, Ananias, and Sapphira furnish the prototypical warnings against love of money, along with the Basilian saying to a senator who kept back a part of his goods, "You have ruined a senator and not made a monk." Another warning is to be found in the rich fool of the parable. Amidst these depressing deterrents, we come upon one remedial piece of advice ; that of manual labour, especially gardening, as recommended by the example of Abbot Paul. Many a vice-haunted monk must have gone mad but for this resource.

In connection with the vice of vainglory, it should be remembered that the discipline which aimed at the eradication of this propensity could never permit a monk to earn literary renown for himself. It is too often forgotten that the fame

The Eight Vices.

Love of Money.

Vainglory.

of literary Fathers of the Church was never enjoyed by those who had really earned it by their pens. The literature, like the architecture, is the work of men compelled to renounce the "last infirmity of noble minds." Nay, the fine distinction of vainglory and pride must yield another vice to be trampled on. It may be remarked in passing that it is this monkish vice of *kenodoxia* which has been reflected upon the philosopher Peregrinus in a tract falsely ascribed to Lucian.

As we proceed in the study of Cassian, it becomes apparent at every step that the New Testament is the production of minds kindred to his own, which are saturated with the same ideas. They alone know what "the Apostle" means, whose sentences appear to have been thought out in the Latin tongue.

Thus the destiny, the scope, or end of the monk is expressed in the works: "Having your fruit The Destiny in sanctification, but the end eternal life." of the Monk. His scope is purity of heart, justly named sanctification, without which the aforesaid end cannot be apprehended. The definition of this end is otherwise given by the Apostle when he says, "Forgetting the things that are behind, extending myself to those which are before, I pursue towards the destined prize of the supernal vocation of the Lord." In the exposition of this passage we are led again into the way of renunciation. Some attempt it without charity, and become infructuous and sterile, as the Apostle foresaw when he said, "If I distribute all my goods to the poor and give my body to be burned, but have not charity, it profits me nothing." He describes the members of this charity, which consists in purity of heart alone.

Cassian proceeds to dwell on tranquillity of mind, and on that effort towards the contemplation of divine things which is illustrated in the Gospel by the allegory of Martha and Mary. The Lord said, "Martha, Martha, thou art anxious and troubled about many things : few things are needful, or even one. Mary has chosen the good part, which shall not be taken away from her." The chief good has been placed by the Lord in theory alone, that is, in divine contemplation. All other virtues are secondary to this. The Lord promises the reward of the kingdom of heaven to those who have practised the labour of fasting, the instancy of reading, the works of mercy, justice, piety, and humanity.

Contempla-tion.

There never was a state of the world in which it can have been so difficult to practise the virtue of theoria, or the fixed contemplation of Christ, as that in which we now live. The creed on which we act is that the world in its variety is to be wisely yet as largely as possible enjoyed. We approve those who extract the most pleasure and profit out of existence, and at the same time profess to follow a rule which condemns the rich man to the intolerable ardour of eternal fire, and denounces her that lives in delight as dead while she lives. We must be dead in body, says the monk, with Abraham, Isaac, and Jacob, and should desire, with the Apostle, to depart from this flesh that we may be joined to the Lord, to become strange and foreign to the body that we may be present with Him. This most lively state of souls detached from the body is represented by the Apostle when he speaks of Mount Sion, and the Civitas Dei, and the celestial Jerusalem, and the throng of many thousand angels, and the Church of the primitive enrolled in heaven, and the spirits of the perfected just.

Surely if there be a philosophy of the mind at all, it teaches, and ever must teach, that the source of thought is one. What but perplexity and self-torture can result from the teaching *Three Sources of Thought.* which recognises three sources of thought—God, the devil, and ourselves? Yet this principle, says Cassian, explains not only the language of the ancient prophets, but that of the Son of God when He refers to the Spirit of the Father speaking in the disciples, and that of the Vessel of Election when he says that Christ speaks in him. It explains how the devil entered the heart of Judas the Iscariot, or of Ananias, or of the Pharisees. Hence the precept of the Lord that we should be as "approved money-changers," whose skill is in the discernment of the pure gold from the spurious coin. We must distinguish the mint of the Spirit from Jewish superstition or swelling secular philosophy.

We wish we could think that the monks claimed Seneca as a doctor of the Church because they admired and coveted his noble wisdom. *Hatred of Liberal Culture.* Alas! they tell us that they would never have enrolled him in the list of their illustrious had he not exchanged letters with the Apostle Paul; these letters being their own forgery. They detest the bright light of philosophy. They find in their own consciousness that its spirit is not of God; that is, it is not congenial with their system. There are unhappy men, who, after they have embraced the profession of the monk, have been deceived by the gold-like glitter of philosophic teaching, which is false bronze coin. They have been deceived and rendered naked and miserable, going back to the noise of the world or the heretic errors and presumptions. A most alarmed sense of the perils which beset the quiet of the cloister is here revealed. The director of consciences is aware how much of human goodness is outside, exerting its baneful attraction upon the inmates. Yet these inducements are but "imitations of the coin of the true King, because they seem for the present full of piety, but they are not from the legitimate *monetarii, i.e.,* not stamped by approved and Catholic Fathers."

There is a danger in excess of fasting, watching, and prayer, and the desire of spiritual gain. Sometimes a precept, however useful, must be cut off and cast aside, and the monk must enter weak into the kingdom of heaven, rather than run the risk of falling into some scandal, or losing the whole body of his works in Gehenna. The devil produces illusions by assuming the guise of sanctity. Abbot John, after an exhausting fast of two days, went to refection. The devil came in the form of a black Ethiopian, and falling at his knees, said, "Indulge me, Abbot, because I laid this labour on thee." The Abbot understood that he had been circumvented by the craft of the devil; had kept an unnecessarily weakening fast; had, in short, been deceived by false coin.

Discretion.

Discretion is therefore eminently to be desired. This is that "light of the body" of which the Gospel speaks. It is "the sun" which should not set upon our earth; it is the solid food of the perfect. Terrible was the fate of the old man Heron, who, with want of discretion, went to excess in fasting, mistook the angel of Satan for an angel of light, and flung himself into a deep well. He was taken out and died on the third day, obstinately refusing to believe that he had been made the sport of devilish craft. So deep was his disgrace, he was hardly accorded the usual rites of

burial, although his spiritual status had before been of
the loftiest. Truly a tearful story. When these soldiers
of God have carried their enthusiastic subjection to the
point of madness, and suicide results, their memory is
disgraced, because their end has so tragically censured
the system.

It was found that the recruits to the spiritual army
had been over-goaded to fasts and watches. But discretion in those practices was only to be gained by
following the example of the elders. Private judgment
cannot of course be permitted. It must be remembered
that Paul, after his visitation, consulted Ananias, and
later the apostles at Jerusalem. Yet what discretion
of any kind, original or borrowed, was to be expected of
men who were brought to church to hear that they
must hate father and mother, children, wife, and lands,
and that, if they would be perfect, they must sell all
they had and give to the poor; of men who were
horrified by the pestiferous end of Judas the traitor and
parricide, as they were captivated by the example of
the inimitable Paul? If all experience teaches that
wealth, or at least competency, is to be deemed a
condition for the cultivation of virtue, what is the confounding of rich men with the wicked and the doomed
but the confounding of the moral perceptions?

Another mode of intellectual torture is provided in
discussions on the flesh and the spirit: an- The Flesh and
other example of artificial or false psychology. the Spirit.
Our being is not thus sundered; and he who follows
what the monks term the concupiscence of the spirit
arrives at a state of more dangerous self-elation than
he who frankly admits that all desires are of mixed
quality. The deep distrust of self, the contempt of the
only source whence manly acts and sentiments can

spring, darkens over the whole system.   Nature is everywhere pitchforked out of it; and terrible, perhaps sometimes beautiful, must have been the effect when she came running back to redeem the cloister from absolute inhumanity or incurable frenzy.   We find in Cassian a treatise on friendship, but he seems to have no idea of mutual esteem and admiration.   He thinks only of a transcendental charity, another name in his system for the idea of the transcendent God.

The fine vocabulary of the old Roman is gone, or is strained to some inhuman meaning.   As for the old motto, *Sola bona quæ honesta*, it is never heard; it must have been unintelligible.   The monk, trained to fix his mind on the impossible and unattainable, falls into inconceivable pettiness and worse than childishness in his actual conduct.   As we lend our ear to Cassian, and imagine ourselves for the time to be on the way to monachic perfection, we find ourselves falling into attitudes and affectations and hypocrisies.   We are sacrificing ourselves to an idea.   We are assisting at the parade of an ancient Salvation Army, whose collective force is secured by the effacement of the individual.   With Seneca we had felt ourselves to be freemen; we are now intellectual slaves.   Weary of the long tension, we cast off our cowl, resume our old habit, pass to the station of spectator and critic, listen by anticipation to the mockery of Rabelais, or to the drolleries of the abbeys of Touraine.

The ethics that obtained in the schools of the Roman Empire attempt to reflect the meaning and purport of Nature; the Mediæval ethics strive to subvert Nature.   The former aim at the making of individuals; the latter at the annihilation of them.

The former see only personal worth; the latter the worth only of a system. The former rest on common feelings and disclaim all theological theory; the latter are nothing but a theory, destitute of all support in the facts of our human experience. Had we no other evidence than these violent contrasts, we should decide that many ages were requisite to bring about such a revolution in the world once ruled by the old Roman spirit; and we should also decide that the New Testament is the chief of monastic books, and that it cannot be detached from the atmosphere of the monasteries and made to fit our modern life without glaring contempt of the fitness of times and things.

CHAPTER VI.

THE TRADITIONS OF THE MOSQUE.

LET us now suppose, for the sake of steadying our thoughts, that we, children of Esau, as the Mollahs and the Rabbins call us in their traditions, are visiting Spain and the Mediterranean at any time during the age 800–900, when the great empire of Islam is the all-impressive fact, and when the habit of pilgrimage to Mecca, to the holy places in Syria, and to Cordova has set in, when one great dogma and legend resounds through all the dominions of the Arabs. Suppose that we are acquainted with the literature of the Greeks, and with their sacred legends of Genesis and the deluge in the time of Deucalion, as they stand in the compilation of Apollodorus.

Now for the first time we are to listen to the dogma of creation by the will of Allah, of the first man Adam, and of the long line of prophets and apostles, stretching from him to the second Adam, the son of Mary, and from him to the renowned and latest apostle. It is some two hundred years before the Rabbins in this same city of Cordova prescribe the Saturday Sabbath in place of the Moslem Friday, and some four hundred years before the Benedictines have brought hither the Koran, misrendered into Latin. Listening to the preaching of the Moslem clergy, we are listening to the earliest form in which the substance both of the Old and New Testament were known to our world.

The Moslems are, in fact, by virtue of their traditions, the unanswered, and, as we hold, the un- Critics of the answerable critics of the legends both of the Church The Synagogue and of the Church. If, in a broad Moslems. illustrative sense, there are three branches of Christendom, Islam, Judaism, and Catholicism, then Islam is the eldest. Arabia is the common mother of the great Mediæval tradition. The order of the three days of worship, Friday, Saturday, Sunday, represents the chronological relation of the three systems.

The Moslem sources are above all the Koran and the first chronicle of Al Tabari, which is the The Koran foundation of all the Mediæval chronicles. and the We may suppose, in our ignorance of the Chronicle exact time of the first redaction of the Koran, that in the ninth century, when mosque-building was going forward in East and West, and when the higher Arabian culture was in its inception, the book which is to the Moslem the Word of God had assumed nearly its present form. There may have been later interpolations ; but if so, they are not of such a kind or extent as to affect our argument. The chronicle is said to have been composed about 900–920, and it covers the period from the creation of the world to the epoch of the author. About 963 it is said to have been translated into Persian. Of the original, fragments only remain. The oldest Persian MS., used by M. Zotenberg for his French translation (1867–74), is believed by him to date from the thirteenth century. Yet only a vague and confused notion of the Catholic dogma of the Trinity is in one place hinted. The careful study of these two sources teaches us that the great Arabian tradition is prior to, and therefore independent of, the traditions of the Synagogue and of the Church.

The truth has been long concealed from us on this matter, owing to the fact that the Benedictines first mistranslated the Koran in the interests of Church dogma, and that the prejudice so created has never since been removed. The Latin translation is ascribed to the impulse of Peter, Abbot of Cluny (1143). It is said to have been executed by Robertus Retenensis, deacon of Pampeluna, and Hermannus Dalmata.[1]

The gross and wilful mistake has been made by the translators,—that they who had resolved to denounce Mohammed as an impostor and false prophet have introduced the name of Jesus Christ into their translation. Now, neither Jesus nor Christ, nor the dogma of the person of Christ as held in the Church, is to be found in any part of the Moslem Word of God. To this day every true follower of Islam denies, and must deny, with the vehemence of faith and of intelligent conviction, that there is aught in common between Isa, son of the virgin Mariam, sister of Harun, the glorious prophet, last in the succession before Mohammed, and the crucified one of Catholic tradition.

A further wilful blunder consisted in the rendering of the phrase "People of the Book" in the Koran by "Jews and Christians." The only people who can furnish us with an account of the origin of the term *Jehudim* are the doctors of the Synagogue; and certainly they have nothing to tell us concerning *Yahood* at Medina in the time of the rise of Islam.

[1] Fabricius, *Bibl. Med. et Inf. Lat.*, x. 660. The date is proleptic, probably by at least two centuries.

The only class of men who can historically explain the term *Christiani* is the great Basilian and Benedictine confederacy. The word is their own coinage. The Koran knows nothing of Christiani. A fresh and exact rendering of the book is sorely needed in the interests of literary science.

When we come to the Koran with minds disabused of the Mediæval dishonesty, we find that the book is nothing less than the original Bible, *i.e.*, the source of those legends of Origins which have been retold by the Rabbins in Bible and Talmud. It is also the source of the Catholic legend of Mary, mother of Jesus, or, in their altered version, Mary, mother of God. As this subject is so utterly misunderstood, we subjoin a brief outline of the oracles of the Koran and the connected Chronicle.

First, Allah created the world, the earth as a carpet, and the heaven as a roof, and caused to descend from heaven water, with which He produced the fruits (Sur. ii. 20). He estab- *Legends of Genesis in the Koran.* lished the sun to give light, and disposed the moon in stations, that the number of years and the reckoning of time might be known (Sur. x. 5). He created the heavens and the earth and all that is between them in six days (Sur. l. 37). But one day is for the Lord as a thousand years (Sur. xxii. 46); the work of creation therefore occupied six thousand years (Chron. i. 3).

The earth was created in two days (Sur. xli. 8–11). The creation of trees and water followed, then that of the seven heavens, and stars, and the angels. Lastly, Adam was created and placed in Paradise. The angels were bidden to worship him. Allah felt no fatigue after the work of creation (Sur. l. 37).

The Djâns or genii were created of flaming fire, and
Adam. the world was given to them (Sur. lv. 14);
but to them Allah declared that he would
establish on earth his vicar (Sur. ii. 28). Adam was
created out of the dust (Sur. xxii. 5), through the
ministry of Gabriel, Michael, and Izrail. Allah
caused him to know the names of all things. And
the angels adored[1] Adam, with the exception of Eblis
(Sur. ii. 32, xv. 30).

And Allah said, "Why didst thou not adore
Adam?" He answered, "Because Thou didst create
him of earth and me of fire: I am better than he"
(Sur. vii. 11).

And Allah said, "My curse shall be upon thee
till the day of judgment" (Sur. xxxviii. 79). His
form was changed to that of a devil because of his
pride.

And Allah said to Adam, "Dwell in Paradise, thou
and thy wife. Eat abundantly of the things that it
produces where ye will; but draw not near to this tree,
that ye may not be of the number of the unrighteous"
(Sur. ii. 33). It was on Friday that Adam entered
Paradise, and he dwelt there five hundred years of this
world (Chron. i. 26).

And Eblis tempted Adam and Eve, saying, "Your
The Tempta- Lord hath not forbidden you this tree, but
tion. lest ye should become angels or immortal"
(Sur. vii.).

He caused them to fall through deceit; and when
they had tasted of the tree, their nakedness appeared
to them, and they gathered leaves of Paradise to cover
them. They were ashamed of one another. A voice

---

[1] *i.e.*, honoured, as distinguished from worshipped in the highest sense
(Chron. i. 26).

was heard; trees and angels spoke on all sides, and the guilty pair were stupefied.

The chronicle tells that the serpent, the most beautiful creature next to Adam, had introduced Eblis in its mouth to Paradise. Four branches of the trees of Paradise were lowered; each attached itself to a body of Adam, Eve, Eblis, and the serpent, and so they were chased from Paradise. It seems that Paradise was conceived as the seventh heaven; thence they are cast down upon earth.

The Serpent.

It is the legend of the origin of sin and shame; and the proper standpoint for its intelligence is the mosque at Mecca. Adam was cast down on Mount Serandib in Hindostan, Eve at Djidda by the sea, seven parasangs from Mecca, the serpent at Ispahan, Eblis at Simnan. Allah was wroth with the serpent and took away his four feet, so that he crawled on his belly. He became the enemy of the children of Adam, and was condemned to eat dust.

The naïve effort to trace the origin of human antipathies to primeval guilt is also seen in the legend of the peacock, who led Eve to the forbidden fruit, so sinned against Allah and lost his voice. Certain plants are traced up to Adam's tears of sorrow or of joy. For after four hundred years Gabriel was sent to Adam to assure him of the mercy of Allah.

"He learned words from his Lord, and the Lord returned to him, for it is He who returns, the Compassionate" (Sur. ii. 35).

Adam reconciled to Allah.

He was then taught agriculture and other arts of life. His stature was reduced; for he had touched the first heaven and could hear the voice of angels; his physical structure was adapted to his life in this world. Then there was brought down from heaven by order of Allah "the visited house," and placed at Mecca on the site where now stands the temple. The black stone was then white and brilliant (Chron. i. 27).

Adam and Eve, reunited, went to Mecca, and made procession round "the visited house." They then repaired to Mount Serandib, tilled the earth and built houses. They were alone in the world.

Then Eblis demanded and obtained of Allah the boon of life until the last day, when Israfil should sound his trumpet and the dead should come forth. (At that epoch the living will never die. Death itself, in the form of a sheep, will be brought and slain.) Then Eblis a second time sought to deceive Adam. The children of Adam and Eve died. When Eve was about to give birth for the fourth time to a child, Eblis foretold a long life for it, and gained from Adam the promise that it should be his. Adam consented, and named the child Abdal-Hareth, because Hareth had been the name of Eblis before he rebelled against Allah. But the child died at the end of two years.[1]

Then Eve bore two sons, Kâbil and Hâbil. Adam Kábil and would have given to Hâbil the twin-sister Hâbil. of Kâbil to wife, but Kâbil was not satisfied. Therefore Adam said to them, "Go and offer a sacrifice ; and to him whose sacrifice Allah shall accept, I will give this young girl." The sacrifice of Hâbil the shepherd was accepted, and that of Kâbil the husbandman was rejected. Adam gave the young girl to Hâbil. Then said Kâbil to Hâbil, "I will slay him," and after that sought occasion to slay him.

---

[1] This act was imputed as a sin to Adam. The dedication of children to evil beings is a strong theme in popular tales.

One day when Hâbil was asleep on a mountain, Kâbil went thither, took a great stone, cast it at the head of Hâbil and slew him. In fear of Adam, he took the corpse on his back and went through the world. He knew not what to do with the body. Then Allah inspired two ravens to go before Kâbil and fight with one another. One slew the other, then digged a hole with his beak and hid the dead bird in the earth. Kâbil said, " I have not so much sense as this raven! I will place my brother under the earth." Then he buried Hâbil. Kâbil was the first murderer, Hâbil the first to be buried. Adam, hearing of the death of his son, went to seek Kâbil, but found him not, and recited an elegy bewailing his unjust death (Sur. v.; cf. Chron. i. 30).[1]

Origin of Murder and Burial.

Young Adam made a pilgrimage from Serandib to Djidda, near Mecca. On one occasion he slept in a valley, and Gabriel was sent to him to cause all his posterity that should be born until the day of judgment to come forth from his loins and to be shown to him. There were 120 male children. Half were placed on his right hand, half on his left. He said to them on the right, " These shall surely be in Paradise," and to them on the left, " They shall certainly go into hell " (Sur. vii. 171 ; cf. Chron. i. 31).

The Posterity of Adam.

Pre-existence of Souls.

In the same connection another legend impresses a precept of the law on the memory. When Gabriel came to the Prophet David among Adam's posterity, Adam gave him forty years of his own life. At the end of his life Adam repented, and said to Allah, " Give me back these forty years," and denied the surrender of them. And Allah said, " When you

The Two Witnesses.

[1] It is the Rabbins who *borrow* this story in part. Pirké, c. 20.

give aught to any one, take witnesses." "Call in witness
two men from among you" (Sur. ii. 282; cf. Chron. i. 31).

Seth was born to Adam at the age of 120 years.
The name is said to signify "Gift of God."

Seth.

He succeeded Adam as lord of the earth, was
a prophet, and had the most numerous posterity. Allah
sent from heaven 114 books: of these, fifty were sent
to Adam and Seth, thirty to the prophet Noah, twenty
to Abraham, and ten to other prophets. The last were
the Law, the Psalter, the Gospel, and the Koran,
sent to Mohammed (Chron. i. 32).

When Adam died, Gabriel was sent to Seth to bear
him the gift of prophecy and to order him to
wash the body of Adam, and wrap it in a
cloth and bury it. The custom has obtained to this
day among the children of Adam, and will obtain till
the Resurrection. Seth recited over Adam the *tecbirs*
or legal prayers. Many say that Adam's tomb is near
Mecca. Eve died a year later, and was buried with
him. It is said that at the deluge Noah placed their
bones in the ark, and afterwards buried them at the
Holy Place (Ib. i. 33).

Burial
Customs.

Seth had a son and successor, Enos, and Enos had a
very wise son, Cainan. These two were kings,
but not prophets. Cainan begat Malaleel,
and Malaleel, Jared. Jared was not a prophet, but his
son Edris received the gift of prophecy.[1]

Enos.
Cainan.

Edris was of Hindostan, but dwelt in Yemen. In
his time men were fire-worshippers. Edris
read to them the books of Ibrahim, and
called them to Allah. He was the first
writer with the reed, also the first tailor. So devout

Edris (cf.
Enoch in the
Bible).

---

[1] The name Enoch is Syriac. I have generally followed Zotenberg's
rendering of the names.

was he, that during about ten years he never lay down at night, but prayed and read the books of _{Invention of} Ibrahim. _{Writing.}

The angel of death then came to him, and bade him ask some boon at his hands. Edris replied, "I ask that thou wilt take my soul." The angel replied that the time of Edris was not come. Then Edris prayed the angel to take away his soul for a few moments. Finally, Izrail took away the soul of Edris, and at the same moment Allah restored it, and the remainder of his days was granted to him (Sur. xix., Sale's *note*).

Years later, Edris asked of Izrail that he might see hell. The Compassionate granted the prayer, and Edris was shown the seven stages of hell, and the various punishments of sinners. In like manner, he was admitted to Paradise, and there remained to this day.

Edris was succeeded by Mathusalem, who called men to true religion, and converted them from fire-worship. He had a son Lamech, and Lamech had Noah, who was a prophet. Between Edris and Noah there were 1700 years, during which time there was no prophet (Chron. i. 35; cf. Sur. xix.).

The Chronicle here interposes an account of a series of terrestrial kings, who serve to explain the origin of inventions. The last of these was _{Beyourasp.} Beyourasp. To him the Prophet Noah was sent. Beyourasp was an idolater, as the Koran _{The Prophet} shows (Sur. lxxi. 20, xxix. 13). The life _{Noah.} of Noah was of a thousand years. He was treated with scorn and contempt, but behaved with _{His Unbeliev-} patience. His wife was unbelieving (Sur. _{ing Wife a} lxvi. 10). Her children were Sem, Cham, _{Prototype.} Japhet, and Canaan. The first three were believers; the last, with his mother, infidel.

Noah prayed that Allah would destroy the unrighteous and show mercy to the faithful (Sur. lxxi. 27–29).
Allah heard the prayer, and bade Noah plant a *teck*,
which takes forty years to grow. At the end of the
time the punishment of the infidels was due.

Noah dwelt at Kufa, and had in his house an oven,
which was said to have belonged to Adam. It was a
sign set by Allah, as we read in the Koran: "When
"an order shall be come, and the oven shall be in
ebullition " (Sur. xxiii. 27 ; cf. Hyde and Lord on the
Persian traditions, p. 9 ; Sale on Sur. xi.).

Allah bade Noah uproot the *teck* and make planks,
and sent Gabriel with an order for the building of the
ark (Sur. xi. 39–42). It was finished in forty days.
Canaan, deaf to the appeal of his father, declared that
he would retire to a mountain. The water rose and
drowned him. The Lord declared that he was no son
of the family.

Eblis entered the ark, holding by the tail of the
ass.

The ark was entered at Kufa ; it went to Mecca,
and turned about the Kaaba. Sometimes turning to
the east, sometimes to the west, it went also to Syria.

Commemora-
tion of the
Flood.
After six months it rested on Mount Djoudi,
in Armenia (Sur. xi. 46). Noah had entered
the ark on a day kept as a fast, tenth Redjeh ;
he came forth on the day *Aschoura*, the tenth of
Moharrem.

An entertaining account is given of the creation of
the pig and the cat in the ark. They existed not
before the Flood.

Noah remained forty days on Mount Djoudi, and
sent forth a raven, which came not back. Then he sent
the dove, which burned its talons in the bitter waters

and lost its feathers.   The species is seen to this day, and they are dear to the heart of men.

The town which Noah built at the foot of Djoudi, called *Souk-al-themanim*, "Market of the eighty," reminds of the eighty believers who were with him when he landed.

The history of the eighty and their posterity is written in all the books sent from heaven, from Adam to the time of Yezdegherd, son of Schariar, king of Persia in the time of Omar.   They are, among others, the Book of Ibrahim, the Law of Moses, the Gospel of Isa, and the Koran of Mohammed.

The deluge was universal, as the Koran teaches (Sur. liv. 12).

After Noah, all peoples descend from his three sons. From Sem descend the Arabs, Persians, men of white complexion, lawyers, sages, and the best people.   For Sem, having seen his father asleep in an indecent posture, had turned his eyes away and covered his father; Japhet and Cham had laughed.   When Noah awoke, he cursed these two; and thenceforth the men and the fruits of the land of Cham became black.   The Turks, the Sclaves, and Gog and Magog (Hungarians ?), with other peoples descend from Japhet (Chron. i. 41). *Sem, Cham, Japhet.*

Semites: the People of Culture.

There follows in the Chronicle the story of the King Dhohak of the race of Cham, who reigned a thousand years after the deluge.   He was idolatrous and cruel, and a revolt was raised against him in Ispahan by a smith, who became governor of the city, and whose leathern apron became a victorious standard in war under the next king, Afridoun.   When his line became extinct, Kousch of the children of Cham succeeded.   After him came *King Dhohak.*

Afridoun. Kousch.

Canaan. They were both idolaters. Nemrod followed

Canaan. Nemrod. Canaan; he had a vizier Azar, son of Nahor, son of Sarug. Now Azar was father of Ibrahim, the friend of God.[1]

From the deluge to Ibrahim there were three thousand years. There was no prophet, and the people of Ad revolted against Allah. He sent to them the Prophet Houd (Chron. i. 43.)

The Chronicle next relates the legend of Mecca
Prophetic Legends of the Foretime. concerning the mission of the Prophet Houd to the old Arabian tribe of Ad, who were of the posterity of Sem. "We have sent to Ad their brother Houd" (Sur. vii. 63).

The Adites dwelt in the desert of Hedjaz, and were
The Prophet Houd. of superhuman stature and strength, and Cyclopian builders (Sur. lxxxix. 5–7, lxix. 6).

Refusing in their pride to listen to the voice of the prophet, a great and terrible word was sent against them (Sur. xli. 14). During fifty years he preached to them in vain (Sur. xi. 57). Then they were destroyed. The wind lifted them into the air and dashed them in pieces on the earth (Sur. lxix. 7, liv. 19). The prophet with the few faithful was saved.

In like manner to the Themoudites of the same
The Prophet Salih. desert, in the valley of Hidjr, their brother Salih was sent (Sur. xi. 64). He had grown up among them, but had not shared their idolatry. When he called them to the service of the one Creator, they defied him and demanded a miracle in proof of his mission (Sur. xxvi. 153). And he replied. in the words of the Koran: "O my people, this she-

---

[1] He becomes *Terah* in the Bible (Gen. xi. 24) or *Thara* (Luc. iii. 34), in the Talmud *Zarah*, and in Eusebius *Athar*.

camel, which shall come from God, shall be for you a miracle" (Sur. xi. 67).

The miracle consisted in his calling forth by means of prayer a she-camel with red hair, with a little one, from the groaning rock. They cried out that he was a magician; whereupon the camel drank up their spring of water. It was predicted that a boy with red hair and blue eyes should destroy the camel, and that calamity would ensue. At last, after nine boys had been slain through fear in their infancy, "the slayer of the she-camel," a son of one of the chief men, was preserved. The deed was done; and after three days the divine vengeance fell on the Themoudites (Sur. xi. 69). Salih and the faithful were saved. Abou Ghalib, one of the people, was at Mecca at the time, and fixed his abode there till his death.

The interest of these legends consists in the feeling excited by the view of memorials of a vanished past,—the broken column, the rock-hewn dwelling, and in the ætiologic action of fancy which suggests dramas of past sin and retribution. The scenery and the ideas are thoroughly Arabian. The writers have their eyes fixed on Mecca and the desert.

Between Salih and Ibrahim there was no prophet. Nemrod, son of Canaan, succeeded him as king. He lived in the land of Babylon, on the site of Bagdad, and was the most wicked and idolatrous of all kings. His vizier Azar was a sculptor of idols. His name in the *pehlvi* is Tharé. He was descended from Noah through Sem, Arphaxad, Canaan, Salé, Heber, Phalez, Reu, Sarug, Nachor.

The Story of Ibrahim.

Azar.

Then follows the legend of the birth of Ibrahim,

preceded by prophecies of the astrologers concerning the great Iconoclast. Nemrod caused every pregnant woman to be watched, and the male children to be slain.

The Birth of the Iconoclast.

When the mother of Ibrahim bare him, she hid him and declared that he was dead. She carried him to a cave in a mountain, and rolled to a stone. After a few days she found him living with his finger in his mouth, miraculously drawing nourishment therefrom. The boy grew marvellously. One night his mother took him forth, and gazing at a star, he said, "Is this my Lord?" When the star set, he exclaimed, "I love not them that set." In like manner he refused to own moon or sun for his god (Sur. vi. 76–78).

When Azar heard of those things, he loved the boy greatly; and Ibrahim in his father's absence overthrew his idols and spurned them. The scene which ensued between father and son is reported in the Koran (Sur. xix. 42).

On a great feast-day, Ibrahim excused himself, perhaps by a subterfuge, from attendance at the feast, on the plea that the stars had warned him of an illness (Sur. xxxvii. 86).

It is said by many that he never lied but on this occasion and on the occasion when the king of Egypt took Sara, and Ibrahim said, "She is my sister."

In the absence of the priests, he entered the temple with an axe, and saw meats of all kinds placed before the idols. He said, "Do ye not eat? Why do ye not speak?" (Sur. xxxvii. 89). Then he smote them with his axe and cast them to the ground. On the largest idol he hung his axe and departed. The priests returning, warned Nemrod of what had befallen. He went to the temple and said,

Iconoclasm.

"Who has treated our gods in this fashion?" (Sur. xxi. 60).

They gave him Ibrahim's name. Brought before Nemrod, Ibrahim declared that the great idol had wrought the destruction. Nemrod ordered him to be burned, but delayed the execution. In the discussion which followed the infidel remained confounded (Sur. ii. 260).

It is deeply impressed on the conscience of Islam that Ibrahim had interceded for his father because the latter had conditionally promised to believe.

On the death of Azar, Nemrod ordered Ibrahim to be cast into a fiery furnace (Sur. xxxvii. 95). Fiery Trial of Ibrahim. During the space of a year, wood was brought by mules, camels, and asses. But the camels ever cast their burden to the earth, and refused to carry it: wherefore they were blessed by Ibrahim. The mules and the asses contrariwise were accursed. An immense pyre was finally constructed by the servants of Nemrod. Fire was set to it, and the sparks rose to heaven. Ibrahim was brought in chains; but none could approach the pyre. Then Eblis clothed himself in a splendid robe and came before Nemrod, who knew him not. He pretended to be an old man who had served Nemrod for two hundred years, and who was willing to show him how to cast "the magician" into the flames.

Eblis then made a *balista;* Ibrahim was placed in it and hurled into the air. But Gabriel was Device of Eblis. sent to support him and to inquire what was his need. Ibrahim resigned himself to Allah: let Him do with him as he would! Then Allah called him his friend, and said to the fire, as we read in the Koran, "Fire, become cold and healing for Ibrahim!" (Sur. xxi. 69).

When he fell into the fire, it separated on this hand and on that, and gave passage to Ibrahim. A spring burst forth from the fire, and about the spring was a garden. His chains fell from him by the power of Allah; and Nemrod, from the height of a tower of wood which he had built above his palace to view the fire, saw Ibrahim in the midst, seated on the verdure by the running spring of water. Some say that an angel was by his side; but this was not so; for Ibrahim had not sought the help of Gabriel, but had placed all his confidence in Allah.

Nemrod was amazed, and cried out with a loud voice, "Ibrahim!" And Ibrahim replied, "What wilt thou, O enemy of Allah?" And Nemrod replied, "Who has refreshed the fire for thee?" And Ibrahim said, "He who created fire!" Nemrod said, "Ask of thy God that thou mayest come out of this fire, O Ibrahim, that I may behold thee!" And Ibrahim arose and passed through the burning fire. Wherever he placed his foot, the fire became cold and pleasant beneath the foot of the Friend of God. And Nemrod said, "Thou hast a powerful God; I would show him hospitality." Ibrahim replied, "My God needs not thy hospitality."

The legend goes on to relate how Nemrod made a vast animal sacrifice in presence of Ibrahim; but Allah accepted it not. Nemrod then resolved to make war on the God of Ibrahim, and rose into the air in a vulture-borne chest. He shot three arrows into heaven, which Allah sent back, soiled with blood, by the hand of Gabriel. Then Nemrod said, "I have destroyed the God of Ibrahim," and returned to the earth.

Nemrod wars against Heaven.

The Koran tells how all such artifices of the infidel shall be vain (Sur. xvi. 28).

Nemrod could do naught against Ibrahim, nor against Allah. Finally, he besought Ibrahim to depart from Babylon (Chron. i. 46).

Ibrahim had a brother, Haran, who had left a son, Loth. Loth followed the faith of Ibrahim, as it is written in the Koran (Sur. xxiv. 25), "Ibrahim said: I will go to my Lord, and He will direct me" (Sur. xxxvii. 97). *Flight of Ibrahim, the Friend of God.*

So Ibrahim and Loth quitted the land of Babylon. Ibrahim wedded Sara, daughter of Haran, his paternal uncle. She was of surpassing beauty. There were believing friends of Ibrahim who, refusing to listen to the remonstrance of their wives, set out with Ibrahim. The example was used to instruct those who left their wives to follow the Prophet from Mecca to Medina (Sur. lx. 4). What nobler calling could there be for the true Moslem than to act as the friends of Ibrahim had acted in the foretime?

Ibrahim came to Haran, in Syria, and there remained some time. The king of Haran was Noubil, an idolater, brother of Azar, and uncle of Ibrahim.

Ibrahim departed for Egypt; but the dwellers in certain towns of Syria, *Al Moutafikât,* "the convinced of lies," begged him to remain with them. Loth and other followers of Ibrahim did remain. When Ibrahim came into Egypt, the people were astonished at the beauty of Sara; and when the prophet came *Sara.* before the king of Egypt, he said that Sara was his sister. This was true; because, as the Koran saith," Believers are brothers" (Sur. xlix. 10). Though Ibrahim thrice lied in the course of his life, his lies had truth in them.[1]

The king of Egypt demanded the hand of Sara; but she, who had consented to the subterfuge, said,

[1] Presumably his example justifies subterfuge in certain cases.

" Let the hand that hath been stretched out to a woman who belongs to a prophet be withered ! " His hand was withered, but at the prayer of Sara was restored. A second time, as he stretched it forth to her, it was withered, and again restored. The fourth time he abstained from touching Sara, and accused her of magic ; but she replied that she was wife of a prophet of Allah.

Ibrahim meantime was praying in his distress, and Gabriel was sent to remove the veil between him and the king of Egypt, so that Ibrahim saw Sara, and heard her voice and that of the king. When brought before the king, Sara was sent for and loaded with presents, and the like were offered to Ibrahim, but he refused them. The king had four hundred young daughters. The name of one was Agar, and her rank _Agar._ was superior to that of the others. When she and Sara met, they conceived an affection for one another. The king gave Agar to Sara, and dismissed Ibrahim with honour, who departed to Syria, and established himself at Saba, a desert place, _Saba (Beer-sheba)._ with Sara and Agar. He dug a pit, and there flowed forth sweet water.

The settlement were reduced to hunger, and Ibrahim going forth with a sack to find supplies, and returning empty, a miracle was wrought in his favour. Some sand which he had placed in the sack was changed into flour while he slept. There were grains of corn among the flour; he sowed it, and all his riches came from that handful of sand turned to flour by the power of Allah. Ibrahim brought sheep to his settlement, which gradually became a great town. As the number of men increased, they became _Chat (Heth)._ a burden to the prophet, who established himself in another place, Chat, of the same land.

Then the people of Saba began to decrease, and repenting, they sought the prophet to bring him back. He refused to return, but Ibrahim gave them seven goats, that they might be a blessing for the increase of the spring at Saba. And Allah blessed the prophet at Chat with great wealth of cattle and slaves. He showed great hospitality to strangers (Chron. i. 47).

Nemrod continued with his insolent defiances of Heaven, in spite of the warnings of an angel *Death of* sent to him by Allah. He challenged the *Nemrod.* King of Heaven to battle, and gathered 100,000 men. But the angel prophesied that he should be destroyed by the feeblest of creatures. Then Allah gave orders to the gnat, least of animals in the divine host, and an army of them fell on the hands and faces of the accursed infidels. The wounds inflicted were incurable; the horses reared and threw their riders, and the host of Nemrod was put to flight. A gnat entered by the nostrils into the brain of Nemrod and devoured his brain. He could obtain relief only from blows struck upon his head. After a life of 1400 years, he died, and his kingdom passed to Qantari, who reigned a hundred years. Then the kingdom passed to the Arameans, and was with them for three hundred years. Then it passed to the Persians.

Sara being childless, gave Agar to Ibrahim, and she had a son named Ismail. The rite of cir- *Ismail.* cumcision of women is then traced ætio-logically to the jealousy of Sara against Agar. The rite was also imposed on all the family of Ibrahim. It seems that circumcision is regarded in the *Circumcision.* conscience of the faithful as a punishment for the sin of Sara (Chron. i. 50). At last Ibrahim took Ismail and Agar and went forth, not knowing whither.

And Gabriel appeared to him, and bade him take them into the sanctuary of God, where was the "visited house." The place was desert, without water or grass. But the prophet put his trust in Allah, and placing a bottle of water and the food that he had before the mother and child, committed them to Allah. He then returned to Sara.

The place where Agar and Ismail were is the site of the Kaaba and the well of Zemzem. The child wept and smote the earth with his heel, and there appeared a spring, the spring which feeds the well of Zemzem. Agar banked it up, otherwise it would have formed a great river, because of the blessing on Ismail. The birds of the air gathered about the spring: it is by the song of birds that the travellers in the desert know the places of water springs. Men of the tribe of Jorham, in the territory of Mecca, finding their well dry, wandered in search of water and found the spring. They proposed to Agar to share it with her, and to relieve her of solitude, and she consented.

The Kaaba and Spring of Zemzem

The Tribe of Jorham.

When three years had elapsed, and Ismail was five years old, Ibrahim learned through Gabriel of the good estate of the boy, and went to visit him, riding on the Borak of the prophet.

Ibrahim Annually Visits Ismail.

When Ismail was grown, Agar died. The men of Jorham, knowing that the well belonged to Ismail, and that if he departed, it would be dried, sought to detain him by giving him in marriage a maiden of their tribe. This first wife Ismail repudiated, because of the displeasure of Ibrahim, who yearly visited Ismail. He took another wife of the tribe of Jorham. Upon her, who hospitably received the prophet, he bestowed his blessing; and the consequence is seen in the abundance of meat, of milk, and of dates that obtains at Mecca. The wife of Ismail did not offer him bread, otherwise there would be of that also abundance.

In the place near the Kaaba called the "Station of Ibrahim" is still to be seen the print of his footstep. *The Station of Ibrahim.*

Isâk occupies a subordinate place to Ismail in the Arabian oracles and legends. The Koran says, "We have announced to Sara Isâk, and after Isak, Yakoub"[1] (Sur. xi. 74). *Isâk*

This was at the time when Ismail at Mecca was five years old, and when Gabriel and Michael were sent to destroy the people of Loth. The cities of Loth, called *Al Moutafikât,* were Cana, Maschhouh, Gomorrha, Adama, and Sodom. In each there were more than one hundred thousand men. The Koran says these places were on the "straight road" (Sur. xv. 76), that is, from the Hedjaz to Syria. *The Cities of Loth.*

The wife of Loth was infidel, and his children idolaters. They were the first to be guilty of unnatural sin, as the Koran declares (Sur. vii. 78, xxix. 28). Loth prophetically warned them, and was mocked at and despised (Sur. xxvi. 160 *seq.*). *Origin of Unnatural Sin.*

He prayed and asked help of God. Then came Gabriel, Michael, and Israfil in the guise of beautiful young men to Ibrahim, who said, "We have received guests who are like to angels." He brought them a roasted calf (Sur. xi. 72). But being angels, they needed not to eat. *Visit of Angels to Ibrahim.*

A sacred custom is explained from this occasion, that of saying *Bismillah,* "In the name of God!" at the beginning, and "Praise to God!" at the end of a repast. Thus the price of the food which *Meal Customs.*

---

[1] Cf. Sale's note on the laughter (?) of Sara.

belongs to Him is paid.   Gabriel said, "Rightly is Ibrahim called the Friend of God!"

Ibrahim feared, because his guests refused to partake, but Sara "laughed," as the Koran says.   Then the angels made themselves known as the apostles of Allah, sent to destroy the people of Loth, and to announce the birth of Isâk, who should have a son, Yakoub, the father of a great posterity.   Sara, being aged, was astonished at this word, as the Koran relates (Sur. xi. 75, li. 29).

But the angels bade them not to despair of the mercy of the Lord (Sur. xv. 56).

Then Ibrahim was troubled concerning Loth, and the angels promised his deliverance and that of his house, save the unbelieving wife (Sur. xxix. 31, li. 35).

The legend proceeds to relate how the angels came to Sodom, and how the wicked were punished. Gabriel, standing at the edge of *Al Moutafikât*, passed his wing over the soil, detached the towns by the divine power, and raising them into the air, turned them upside down.   A black water came forth from the site (Sur. xi. 84).

Destruction of the Cities by Gabriel.

The wife of Loth looked back, and one of the stones of the ruined cities fell on her head and slew her. Loth went and settled in the land of Ibrahim.

Ibrahim had promised in the days when they desired a child, that if it were a male, he would sacrifice it to the Lord.   He had forgotten his vow; and Allah, to honour him, reminded him of it in a dream.

The Sacrifice of Ismail.

There are arguments in the Koran in favour of the sacrifice of Isâk; others in favour of that of Ismail;[1] but the latter are decisive (Chron. i. 53).

[1] The dispute seems to represent rival traditions of Mecca and Hebron.

When Ibrahim came to the mountain, the scene of this new trial, the angels wept, and the mountain groaned and trembled. Eblis also was afflicted, and sought to tempt Agar, and also Ismail, from their submission to the command of Allah; but he was faithfully resisted.

Weeping, the father prepared to immolate his son, but the blade of the knife was miraculously turned. Ismail besought him to make a fresh attempt, but at that moment Gabriel was sent from heaven with a ram, white, with black eyes and long horns. A voice was heard, " O Ibrahim, now thou hast accomplished thy vision " (Sur. xxxvii. 105).

Ibrahim trembled, let fall the knife, and cried out, " Allah is great! " Gabriel repeated the words. And when they saw the angel they cried again, " There is no God but Allah ! Praise to Allah ! "

Thus the origin of the *Tekbir*, or prayers recited on the feast of sacrifices, is traced to the authorship of Gabriel, the Spirit of God, of Ibrahim, the Friend of God, and of Ismail, the Victim of God. And Allah granted to Ismail that for his sake the sins of the faithful who should appear before him might be forgiven. Origin of Sacrificial Prayers.

The place of the immolation is Mount Mina, where the stones are cast and the victims are sacrificed. For the ram escaped from Ibrahim, who cast seven stones at it. Finally it was sacrificed. In the Koran Allah saith, " Thus will we reward them who do well" (Sur. xxxvii. 110). The example of the Friend of God is that of a greatness the tradition of which shall be preserved till the day of judgment. Mount Mina.

Some say that the ram was the same with that
sacrificed by El Khâlil; that Allah had kept
it in Paradise to feed there till the hour of
Ismail's immolation.[1]

El Khâlil.

In the time of Noah and the deluge, the "visited
house," the object of Adam's yearly pilgrimage, had been raised to heaven. The site
was vacant when Allah said to Ibrahim, "Arise, go
to Mecca, and build a house on the place where was
the visited house" (Sur. xxii. 27; Chron. i. 54).

The Kaaba.

Ibrahim went to find Ismail, and they prepared to
obey the divine command. But since they were
ignorant of building, Allah sent a cloud of the size
of the Kaaba, that the building might fill the space
described by its shadow. The Koran says, "When
Ibrahim and Ismail raised the foundation of the house,
they said, Lord, receive from us this house, for Thou
art He that heareth and knoweth" (Sur. ii. 121).

Then they prayed that the holy ceremonies of pilgrimage might be made known to them.
And in the time of Mohammed, he is said to
have declared himself the object of another
prayer of Ibrahim, "Send a prophet from among my
descendants, that he may recite Thy verses to his
brethren, that he may cause them to know Thy book
and Thy wisdom; and purge them, O Lord, from their
sins" (cf. Sur. iii. 158; Chron. xii. 54).

Moslem Ceremonies Revealed

And Gabriel was sent to Ibrahim to teach him the
rites of pilgrimage and the visitation of Mount Mina
and Mount Arafat, the processions around the Kaaba,
the casting of stones, the assumption of the pilgrim
habit, the offering of sacrifice, the shaving of the head,
and all that concerns the pilgrimage.

---

[1] *Vide* Sale's notes on Sur. xxxvii. 105 *seq.*

Then Ibrahim confided the temple of Mecca to Ismail and to his children, that it might be theirs until the day of judgment. Standing on Mount Thabir, he turned his gaze now on Syria the fertile, now on Mecca the desert. In answer to his prayers, Mecca, though desert, became abundantly supplied from Egypt, Yemen, and Maghreb.

Ismail in Charge of Mecca

The voice of the prophet was heard by all creation, calling men to make pilgrimage to the house which God had built for them. And they who were pre-destined to bliss replied, "We are ready to obey, O Allah! There is none but Thee! We are ready to obey!" And faithful pilgrims now and until the day of judgment are of them who obey the voice of Ibrahim.

After these things Ibrahim returned into Syria to Sara. Yearly he continued to make the pilgrimage to Mecca.

When Isâk was grown up, Sara had another son, named Yakoub, as the Koran saith (Sur. vi. 84). Isâk also had two sons, Esau and Yakoub. They were twins. At the moment that Esau was born, Yakoub seized him by the heel. Hence his name.[1]

Birth of Yakoub.

Esau and Yakoub.

Yakoub and his posterity were prophets; but no son of Esau was a prophet, except Job (Ayyoub).

Isâk became blind during the lifetime of Sara. Sara died at the age of 130 years, and was buried in the land of Canaan.

Ibrahim then wedded Keturah, daughter of Joktan. She was also of the land of Canaan. They had six sons — Zamram, Jeksan, Madan, Madian, Jesbok, Sué.[2]

Keturah and her Children.

---

[1] *Al-aqib*=the heel.

[2] Cf. Gen. xxv. 11.

The Koran saith, "Recall when Ibrahim said: Lord, cause me to see how Thou wilt raise the dead " (Sur. ii. 262).

It was the last year of his life, when he was 199 years old, and was returning from Mecca. And Allah said, "Take four different birds, slay them, cut them in pieces, mingle them, and place on the mountains a piece of each bird. Then call, and they shall come swiftly to thee." Ibrahim took four birds—a heron, an eagle, a hawk, and a vulture. The pieces of the slain birds were placed on four mountains. There arose a wind which carried the pieces from one mountain to the other, so that all that belonged to one bird were reunited. Then he called the birds, and all four swiftly flew to Ibrahim. Then Allah said, "So will I do at the day of judgment" (Chron. i. 58).

The legends tell how the beard of Ibrahim becoming white, it was revealed to him that it was a sign of intelligence and gentleness. The Angel of Death was sent to take his soul by his own consent, and appeared to him in the form of a very debile old man of 202 years. And Ibrahim learning that his debility would be like that of his visitor should he live to his age, resigned his life, and the angel bore away his soul. Isâk washed him and placed him by Sara in Syria.

After the death of Ibrahim, Isâk buried him, then visited Ismail at Mecca. Ismail paid a yearly visit to the tomb of his father. Ismail was an apostle and prophet, and preached to the idolaters of Hadramaut and Egypt. His daughter Basemath he gave in marriage to Esau. He died at Mecca, appointing Isâk his executor, and he was buried by the side of Agar. His posterity were dispersed, but his two sons Nabit and Kedar dwelt at Mecca. Nabit and Kedar.

The dwellers in the Hedjaz, in the desert, and the Arabs are all children of Ibrahim and of Ismail.

These legends form a network connecting the sacred places of the Mohammedans in Arabia with those in Syria. From the standpoint of the old mosque at Hebron, which takes its name from the "Friend of Allah," and from that of the mosque at Mecca, the genesis of the sacred poetry can without difficulty be understood. To call in the Bible at this point is but to confuse the narrative.

This legend is designed to explain the enmity that was felt to be a standing one between the peoples of whom the twins are symbolic. Legend of Esau and Yakoub. Blind Isâk prays that the gift of prophecy may fall on Yakoub, who has set before him by a ruse a dish of roast-lamb. Yakoub feared the vengeance of his brother, yet prayed for him, and his posterity became numerous.

The Chronicle explains that by the race of Esau is meant "the Greeks," and that Roum was a son of Esau, whose children gained posses- Romans and Arabians. sion of the land of the Greeks. In other words, the Arabians mean, by the sons of Esau, the inhabitants of the Roman Empire. The Jewish chronicles designate the same by Edom.

Yakoub is made to flee by night from Esau to his uncle Laban in Syria. His name, Israel, re- Yakoub= Israel. ceives an Arabic etymology—*asra ila Allah*, "he went by night to God." In Syria he served Laban, and received Lia and Rachel as his wives. At that time, and until the law of Musa, it was lawful for a man to wed two sisters, but in the Koran this is forbidden (Sur. iv. 27).

He had by Lia Ruben, Simeon, Judah, Levi, Zabulon, and Issachar. By Zelpha, handmaid of Rachel, he had Dan and Nephtali. By Bala, handmaid of Lia, he had Gad and Esau. By Rachel he had Joseph.

Then he desired greatly to return to the land of Canaan, and Esau desired to see him. When the two brothers met, Esau wept for joy and exclaimed, "Yakoub is not the servant of Esau, but his beloved brother." For Yakoub had said in Syria, "I am the servant of Esau."

Return of Yakoub.

After a year Benjamin was born. Then Yakoub as a prophet calls men in the land of Canaan to Allah. Esau resigns the land to him and bids him an amicable farewell.

Benjamin.

It is again said that Esau took with him his son Roum and went to the land called Roum, and that all the Greeks derive from him.

The Land of Roum.

The method of the Arabian historic mythology is essentially the same with that of the old Greek tribal mythology. Twins who quarrel are symbolic of rival tribes or peoples. The rivalry of the Roman and the Arabian empire is expressed. The religious empire of the prophetic Yakoub is destined to supplant that of the unprophetic Esau. The domination of the Romans in the land of Canaan is represented symbolically by the wedding of Esau to a daughter of the prophet of Mecca. The flight of Yakoub in poverty and fear, his return in wealth, is analogous to the double wanderings in Greek legends. The tendency is to show that Yakoub, as representative of the orthodox belief, "came back to his own," and was admitted to be in his rights there by the "elder brothers." So often in myths of conquest a certain conscience makes itself felt, and a pretext of justice is cast over deeds of violence.

The chronicler says that there is no story more marvellous or more instructive than that of Yussuf; none concerning which the Koran has a greater number of verses. *The Story of Yussuf (Joseph).*

The legend is in substance that of the Bible, yet with ampler details. The eleven brothers plot against the favourite son of Yakoub. Yahud interposes to save him. The chronicler speaks of the pit into which Yussuf was cast as existing to his day. The extraction of the prophet from the pit by the leaders of a caravan on its way from Arabia to Egypt is dramatically told. He was sold for twenty dirhems of nominal value.

There was at the time an Amalekite king of Egypt, a Semite called Rayyan. His treasurer was the grandee of Egypt, Putiphar, son of Amir. He was impotent, and his wife was the greatest beauty in Egypt. *Yussuf in Egypt.* She tempted Yussuf, but he saw a sign from Allah. He had a vision of Yakoub entering from the wall of the room, biting his finger and saying, " O Yussuf, alas! alas!" And he fled from her.

Further details of his trials and of his imprisonment follow. He interprets the dreams of the king of Egypt, is made intendant of the granaries, and on the death of the grandee, weds his widow, Zulaikha, who excuses her past conduct, and who is proved to be no adulteress, and by whom he has the sons Ephraim and *Ephraim and Manasseh.* Manasseh. He becomes vizier.

Then follows the story of the reconciliation of Yussuf with his family, and the arrival of Yakoub in his house in Egypt. Yussuf as prophet calls the king of Egypt to Allah, and he believes. The brethren wed wives in

L

Egypt, and the number of the family increases from seventy to 1,700,000 souls at the date of the Exodus.

Yussuf chooses Yehud for his executor, who places his body in a marble coffin and casts it into the Nile. When Moses went out from Egypt, he carried the coffin to the burial-place of Ibrahim, Isâk, and Yakoub in Syria.

The children of Yakoub (or Israel) have been placed in Paradise by Allah. Their comprehensive designation of the chosen people is "Ibrahim, Ismail, Isâk, Yakoub, and the tribes" (Chron. i. 65).

Then follows the story of Job the patient. He is Job (Ayoub) the Patient. grandson of Esau, and the only prophet of Esau's stock. He is located in Basan, a tract between Damascus and Ramla. His village is called Qarya-Ayyoub, and the spring near it Ain-Ayyoub. The trials of Job and his wife Rahma, due to the enmity of Eblis, are similar to those related in the Old Testament, but there are great variations.

One of Job's sons was Bischr, called Dsoul Kefl. Allah speaks of him in the Koran : "Ismail, and Edris, and Dsoul Kefl, they were all patient" (Sur. xxi. 85).

Schoaib descended from Ibrahim by Madian, eponymus The Prophet Schoaib. of Madian in Syria. He called the unbelieving people to Allah, and their disobedience was punished by a great heat and fire sent down from a cloud, while Gabriel sent forth a terrifying cry.

The Chronicle, in its attempt at a retrospection of the King Minotschehr. dim past, reverts to the kings of Persia, who dwelt in the land of Babylon, in the province of Irâk. The Arabs and the dwellers in Maghreb were never entirely subject to those kings, with the exception of Minotschehr. He was a just king, and reigned for 120 years. In his time Moses appeared.

Walid, the most unjust of all the kings of Egypt, was on the throne when Musa was born. He *Predicted* represented himself as God, and called upon *Birth of Musa* men to adore him (Sur. lxxix. 23, xxviii. *(Moses).* 38); but Asija, his wife, followed the religion of Yussuf and of Israel.

The Pharaoun saw in vision a fire coming from Syria to Egypt to destroy the Copts and their houses. The astrologers warned him that an Israelite child would be born to destroy the Egyptians. Precautions were taken to slay the male children (Sur. xiv. 6). Then there was the respite of a year.

Imram was of the family of Levi, son of Yakoub. His father was Isaar, and his grandfather *The Family* Kaath. During the year of respite his wife *of Imram.* gave birth to Harun, and in the next year to Musa. Allah inspired her to cast him into the river, *Harun and* as we read in the Koran: "If thou fearest *Musa.* aught for him, cast him into the river, without fear and without affliction, for we will restore him, and appoint him one of our apostles" (Sur. xxviii. 6).

Properly speaking, this was an inspiration rather than a revelation, for she was no prophetess (*cf.* Sur. xvi. 70).

The coffer which she made for the child was an inspiration from God (Sur. xx. 38).

The maker was one Harbil, the only believer among all the Copts. He is praised in the Koran (Sur. xl. 29). Musa had a sister. The mother bade her follow the child (Sur. xxviii. 10).

The coffer was carried to the palace of the Pharaoun at Memphis, and left among the trees. The slaves drew it forth, but dared not open it. They carried it to Asija, who also dared not open it. Finally, it was opened in the presence of Pharaoun, who proposed to slay the child; but it was spared at the intercession of Asija (Sur. xxviii. 7).

The child was called *Musa*, signifying *water* and *tree*, because he had been found amidst the water and the trees.

The sister introduces the mother as nurse, and the child is taken home. Each week it is carried to Asija. One day Asija placed the child, who was then five years old, on the knee of Pharaoun, and said, "It is thy child." The king replied, "It is thine." But when the child plucked at his beard, Pharaoun took his hand and said, "This is the child of the Israelites that I seek, and I will slay him." But Asija said, "I will prove the child and see whether he acts with discretion." She placed him between two basins, the one filled with fire, the other with rubies. The child turned to the basin of rubies, but Allah ordered Gabriel to carry the hand of Musa to the fire. The child took up a glowing coal, placed it in his mouth, and burned his tongue. So was his ignorance proved and his life saved.

A knot was found at the end of his tongue, so that he could not pronounce the letter *Siu*. When he became man and prophet, he prayed to Allah, "Loosen the knot of my tongue, that my words may be heard" (Sur. xx. 28–29).

At the age of ten he rode to and fro in Memphis between his mother's house and the palace, attended by a great train of servants. He was called *Son of Pharaoun*, and was beloved by the king, who had him at his side when he rode forth. Musa was endowed with great wisdom. At thirty years of age he received a wife from Pharaoun, and there was rejoicing in Memphis as at the wedding of a king. He had two sons, Gersam and Eliezer.

The chronicler, at home in Memphis and the adjacent towns, each of which has its mosque, proceeds Flight of Musa and Madian and Schoaib. to tell how the time came when Musa should deliver his oppressed brethren. He came to Heliopolis seeking Pharaoun, who had gone thither. At noon he saw an Israelite and an Egyptian in combat, and when the Israelite cried to him for help, Musa slew the Egyptian. Then he felt remorse, though the man was an infidel; for he had not yet found the gift of prophecy, and had not yet been commanded to slay the infidel. But He who pardons, the Merciful, forgave him (Sur. xxviii. 14).

And Musa vowed that he would no more bring help to the infidel; for the Israelite he had succoured was an infidel.

Next day Musa met the same Israelite, who was assailed by another Egyptian. Musa upbraided the Israelite, who gave information to Pharaoun against him. Finally, Moses fled to Madian, the city nearest to Memphis in the direction of Syria. Allah sent an angel to show him the road. Barefooted he walked eight days and eight nights, till the skin of his soles fell from them.

Schoaib, prophet of the faithful surviving Midianites, was a great shepherd. He had two daughters, Sephora and Abra, the former fair, the latter dark, and both beautiful. These young shepherdesses sought a hireling shepherd.

It is said in the Koran, " When Musa came to the well of Madian, he found about the well a multitude who were giving their flocks to drink. And he found two women who kept their sheep far from the water " (Sur. xxviii. 22).

Now this well was closed by a stone which only forty

men could lift. And the daughters of the old and blind prophet of God could not approach the well until the men had withdrawn. Then Musa himself advanced, removed the stone and the seal, and gave the sheep of the daughters of Schoaib to drink. Then he seated himself in the shadow of a tree, and hungered. And when the daughters of Schoaib told their father, he bade them call the man. When Musa came and related the story of his flight, the heart of the prophet was fastened on him, and he offered him one of his two daughters, on condition that he would serve as hireling for the space of eight years or for ten years.

At the end of ten years Musa came before Schoaib, and Sephora was given to him. After a time Musa desired to visit his family in Egypt, but he remained another year until the sheep should have lambed. Then each sheep had twice he-lambs. They were given to Musa. He remained another year at the request of Schoaib, and in like manner each sheep had twice she-lambs. They were given to Musa, who thus had flocks greater than those of Schoaib.

Now an angel had left with Schoaib a shepherd's staff which was forked. Schoaib knew not that it was an angel, for he had the form of a man. This staff proved to be the rod by which Allah desired to work miracles to prove the prophetic mission of Musa. So when Schoaib bade him choose a staff to support him on the way, Musa found again and again this staff coming to his hand. Finally, Schoaib gave him the staff. Afterwards he repented, and ran after Musa, and demanded it back. Musa refused, and while they parleyed, there came by an angel in the form of a man ; to him they referred their difference. The angel said,

"Cast the rod to the ground, and it shall be his who can lift it from the ground." Musa alone was able to lift it.

The Koran saith, "When Musa had reached the term agreed on, and was gone forth with his house, he saw fire on the side of Mount Sinai" (Sur. xxviii. 29). *Prophetic Mission of Musa.*

And again : "Hath the story of Musa come to thee ? When he saw fire, and said to his family, Wait here, for I have seen fire ? " (Sur. xx. 8).

This was when he had travelled five days from the land of Schoaib, and was near Mount Sinai, and a great darkness had fallen over the land. He took his rod and went on. Presently he saw fire at the top of a tree. It was the thorny tree called *aousadje*, the first tree that came forth from the earth.

Musa was seized with fear and would have returned ; but, as Allah saith in the Koran, "A voice cried to him from the right side of the valley in the blessed place, above the tree: Musa, surely I am Allah, Lord of creatures " (Sur. xxviii. 30).

Musa prostrated himself; and Allah graciously said to him, "Surely I am thy Lord ; take off thy shoes, for thou art in the holy valley of Towa" (Sur. xx. 12). *The Holy Valley.*

In this place the Lord taught Musa all parts of the system of the Unity of God, and caused him to know the law. Allah spake three words to Musa by which His Unity is explained :— *The Divine Unity.*

"Surely I am Allah ; there is no other god but me " (Sur. xx. 14).

"Surely I am thy Lord" (Sur. xx. 12).

"Surely I am Allah, Lord of creatures" (Sur. xxviii. 30).

To Musa also He said, "Serve me and make prayer in commemoration of me" (Sur. xx. 14). The precept of prayer is placed before all other precepts of the law and of worship.

The Precept of Prayer.

And again, with reference to the Resurrection Allah said, "Surely the hour of judgment shall come; I will surely manifest the same, that to each soul may be rendered according to its deeds" (Sur. xx. 15).

The Resurrection.

Then Allah conferred on Musa the gift of prophecy and sent him to Pharaoun (Sur. xxvi. 9).

He caused him to see the miracle which confirmed his mission, saying, "What is that thou dost hold in thy right hand, Musa?" (Sur. xx. 18).

The Sign of the Rod.

The change of the rod into the serpent was effected before Musa went to Pharaoun, that he might not fear, but might be accustomed to the sight, and be perfect in all things.

And then the Lord said, "Put thy hand in thy bosom; it shall come forth white without any harm" (Sur. xxviii. 32).

Then Musa prayed for the loosing of his tongue, and that Harun, his brother, might be given him as counsellor (Sur. xx. 26 *seq.*).

His prayer was heard; and how great is the word which Allah addressed to His servant, "I have chosen thee for myself" (Sur. xx. 43).

So Musa came from the place where he held converse with Allah, loaded with favours, endued with the gift of prophecy, with the knowledge of the law; and Allah called the place the Blessed Valley (Sur. xxviii. 30).

So Musa returned to his wife, not with fire, but with the light, the most brilliant that is.

A writer in the Chronicle expatiates on the number of moralities there are to be found in this interview of Musa with Allah. He well observes that in the Koran the story is even as the tree, and the morality is the fruit When you sit beneath the shade of a tree, you should also enjoy its fruit.

Passing over many interesting details in the Chronicle, Musa appeared before Pharaoun, and declared *Musa before* himself the apostle of the Lord, the Creator of *Pharaoun.* heaven and earth. Pharaoun mocked, and said to his courtiers, " God has sent you an apostle who is mad ! "

Musa cast his rod to the ground, which became a great serpent. It opened its mouth, placed its lower jaw on the throne of Pharaoun, and would place its upper jaw on the roof of the palace, so as to carry it bodily away. The monarch cried out with fear. Musa seized the serpent by the neck, which again became a rod. The second sign of the whitened hand then appeared (Sur. xxvi. 32).

The noise of these things spread through Egypt, and all the Israelites believed in Musa. The magicians, on the other hand, were sent for, and gathered together, it is said, to the number of 15,000. The most skilled, seventy in number, were selected. Of these, the four chief were Schâboun, Gâboun, Hâtit, and Mosfa. On a great feast-day the trial of skill took place. The magicians had an apparatus of sticks and cords, by which they contrived to represent serpents raising themselves as if to attack the company, and the eyes of the spectators were fascinated, and they were afraid (Sur. vii. 113).

But when Musa cast his rod, it became a serpent greater than the others, struck the earth with its tail, rolled the end of its tail about the dais of Pharaoun,

and then swallowed up all the other serpents. The
The Magi-   magicians saw that the miracle was from
cians become Allah, and they believed in him. Pharaoun,
Believers and
Martyrs.   believing them to be in complicity with Musa,
ordered their hands and feet to be cut off, and then their
crucifixion. They died as willing martyrs for the true
faith. Movingly the chronicler says: "In the morning they were magicians, enemies of Allah; in the
evening they were martyrs and in Paradise." Pharaoun
departed, wretched and despised, as we read in the
Koran (Sur. vii. 116).

Musa remained twenty years with the Egyptians,
calling them to Allah and working miracles, but
Pharaoun hardened himself in his belief. At last he
declared, "I will ascend myself to heaven, and see the
God of Musa." Then he bade Haman make a great
tower of chalk and bricks. It required two years for
its construction. It is said that Pharaoun was the
first to make bricks. Having ascended the tower, and
neither seen nor heard anything, Pharaoun came down
and said, "Musa, surely I hold that he is of the number of liars" (Sur. xxviii. 38).

Allah saith in the Koran, "Surely we have given to
The Nine   Musa nine evident signs" (Sur. xvii. 103).
Signs.   He wrought a miracle each year, and Pharaoun
besought him, "If thou wilt take away this chastisement, we will believe." But when the chastisement
was removed, they broke their word.

The nine signs formed a climax, each being greater
than the preceding (Sur. xliii. 47). They were:—

1. The rod changed into a serpent.
2. The hand of Moses become white and brilliant.
3. The famine (Sur. vii. 127).
4. The deluge.

5. The locusts.
6. The Qourmals (lice).
7. The frogs.
8. The water changed into blood.
9. The putrifaction of all that belonged to the Egyptians.

The contest between Musa and Pharaoun lasted for two years. Now Pharaoun, though he had destroyed the idols and ascribed divinity to himself alone, nevertheless revered the bull. He prostrated himself and adored the sacred animal, and abstained from its flesh. Finally, the time that Allah had fixed for his destruction arrived, and the word came to Musa, "March with my servants during the night, for ye will be pursued" (Sur. xliv. 22, xxvi. 52).

When all things were ready for the exodus, the elders of the children of Israel reminded Musa of the testament of Yussuf (Joseph), *The Exodus.* bidding them open his tomb and carry his remains with them to Syria, to repose by Ibrahim, Isâk, and Yakoub. But the tomb of Yussuf was un- *The Tomb* known. After inquiry, an old Egyptian *of Yussuf.* woman, a believer, named Mariam, daughter of Nâmousi, was found, who promised to show the tomb of Yussuf on condition that she should be taken with the Israelites, and that Musa would ask of Allah Paradise on her behalf. Then she said, "The tomb of Yussuf is in the midst of the river Nile, which passes in the midst of the city of Memphis, in such and such a spot." At the prayer of Musa, the water retired, and the coffin of Yussuf was found. It was of marble and without joints.

There follows an account of the borrowing of the ornaments of the Egyptians, in accordance with the command of Musa. The Israelites were bidden to gather together at a spot outside the city. Each was

The Sacrifice at the Exodus. to sacrifice with his house a sheep, a lamb, or a fowl. When they went forth, they were to dip their hands in the blood, and to smear the doors of the houses, that their friends might know they were gone forth.

At midnight the host assembled, to the number of 620,000 horsemen, besides footmen, women, children, and old men. Harun was placed with the advance guards, and was ordered to march to the sea, where Gabriel had promised to join Musa and the army. Troop by troop and tribe by tribe the host followed, Musa being with the rear-guard. It was the ninth night of the month Moharrem, the night of Sunday. In the morning the Egyptians found that the Israelites had departed, but in each house a lamp burned; and there was not an Egyptian house in which there was not a corpse of young or of old.

The next day was the day called Aschoura, the tenth

The Day Aschoura. of Moharrem. Pharaoun gathered his army, and placed with the van-guard Haman with 2,000,000 foot-soldiers; himself occupied the centre with 5,000,000 horsemen. At daybreak they set out (Sur. xxvi. 60).

When the Israelites were overtaken, Allah inspired Musa to strike the sea with his rod, and the waters divided and stood as mountains. The Israelite tribes which descended from the sons of Yakoub entered the sea by twelve different routes (Sur. xxvi. 63). The black mud at the bottom of the sea became at the prayer of Musa dry like sand.

As Musa stood at the brink of the sea, Gabriel, Michael, and the angels arrived and said, "O Musa, pass the sea! for Allah hath ordered us to tarry here till Pharaoun shall have entered the sea with all his host." And Musa urged his horse into the sea, crying, "In the name of Allah, the merciful and compassionate!" and all the children of Israel followed him. Between each of the twelve roads there were walls of water, so that the several tribes could not see each other. At the prayer of Musa these watery walls opened in the form of an arcade, so that the Israelites could see from one end to the other, till the passage had been made.

Pharaoun, beholding these things, was terrified, but Haman persuaded him that as Musa had passed by means of magic, so he could pass by means of his divinity. And when he with all his host were in the midst of the sea, Musa from the other bank would have smitten the sea with his rod, but was detained by a word from Allah (Sur. xliv. 23).

When Pharaoun came to the opposite bank, he urged his horse ashore, but Gabriel stretched forth his hand, struck Pharaoun on the face, and cast him into the sea. And Allah ordered the sea to sink upon the host, and drown them. Pharaoun cried from the midst of the waters, "I believe in the same God with the children of Israel; there is no God but He; I am of the resigned. I believe in the word of Musa" (Sur. x. 90). And Gabriel answered, "Now thou dost believe, but before thou wert a rebel, and thou hast been of the number of the wicked." And fearing lest Allah in His mercy should pardon Pharaoun, he passed his wing over the bottom of the sea, raised some of the earth and cast it into the mouth of Pharaoun, who was drowned.

It is said that Gabriel recognised two great enemies on

the earth : Eblis, who refused to adore Adam, the vicar of Allah, and Pharaoun, who declared, "I am God."

The day of Aschoura was kept as a fast. The next day the brother of Pharaoun and his host were carried to be cast up from the sea for a sign (Sur. x. 92).

The sea remained agitated for ten days ; nor will it be appeased on that spot until the day of the Resurrection. The place is called Bab-al-Tâgath, "Gate of the cupola."

But the Israelites yearned after a god that they might see and adore, like the Amalekites and the Copts, who had idols with the form of a bull's head (Sur. vii. 134).

Now there was among them a man called Sâmeri, whose true name was Musa, son of Dzafar.

Sâmeri.

He was of the people of Akhberi, a village of the land of Irâk, who were idolaters. According to another and better accepted version, Sâmeri was an Israelite and a descendant of Levi, son of Yakoub, who had been exposed at the time of the slaughter of the male children, and had been preserved through Gabriel's ministry (Chron. i. 74).

It had been promised to Musa that Allah would speak to him on Mount Sinai and give him the Law. He sent Gabriel to him and called him to the revelation in Sinai. The Law was sent entire and at once, not like the Koran, in pieces, each day a Surah and each moment a letter.

The Revelation on Mount Sinai.

On Sinai Musa was to fast for thirty days that his stomach and his mouth might become pure for the reception of the words of Allah. And Musa said to Harun his brother, "Replace me with my people ; do justice, and follow not the path of the wicked" (Sur. vii. 138).

The children of Israel desired that the chiefs and the elders of them should go with Musa, to witness that the words were indeed the words of Allah. Musa consented, and they chose out seventy (Sur. vii. 154). The day of revelation was the 10th of the month Dsoul'hidje; and the time between the death of Pharaoun and the revelation was eleven months. During the month Dsoul-qu'ade, Musa fasted with the seventy, and then came Gabriel with an order for the prolongation of the fast for ten days of Dsoul-'hidje: altogether forty days.

At the end of the thirty days the children of Israel gathered to Harun and murmured against Musa. Then Sâmeri saw that the moment to destroy them had come. He hinted to Harun that perchance Musa was wroth with them because they had taken the gold and the silver of Pharaoun and the Copts, which was forbidden. Then Harun told these things to the children of Israel, and bade them gather the booty that it might be covered with dust till Musa should return.

But Sâmeri said, "This shall serve you naught; Musa will not return until ye have burned all this." Now Sâmeri had recognised Gabriel at the time he came to call Musa to the revelation. And where Gabriel placed his foot, Sâmeri raised of the earth trodden by him. He now made a calf of the gold and placed some of the earth in its body. The The Golden Calf. calf began to low; they say it had become flesh and bone, that it walked and ate of grass. Then the children of Israel said, "This is our God and the God of Musa; but Musa hath abandoned him" (Sur. xx. 90).

Then they worshipped the calf. It is said in the Commentaries that but 12,000 abstained. On the fortieth day, when Musa ascended the summit of the

mountain to be in the presence of Allah, the Lord said
to him, " I have proved thy people after thy departure,
and Sâmeri hath led them astray " (Sur. xx. 85–87).

At the moment of revelation, as Allah conversed with
The Revela- Musa, a white cloud rested on the head of
tion. the prophet, so that he was invisible to the
seventy. Musa was in the presence of Allah, who conversed with him, though by means of no bodily organ.
He gave him the Law written on tables, as He saith in
the Koran, " We have written for him on the tables
concerning everything " (Sur. vii. 142).

When the revelation was ended, Musa prayed that
he might behold the Lord. But Allah replied, " Thou
canst not see me. Look at this mountain; if it remains
in its place, thou shalt see me." The mountain was
reduced to dust, and Musa fell fainting. On recovering he said, " Glory to Thee ; I bring Thee my repentance ; I will be the first of believers." He made the
request that we might know that no eye can penetrate
to Allah.

Later a cloud enveloped the elders along with Musa,
and they heard Allah conversing with Musa. Then
they said that they would not believe in that which
they had heard until they had seen the God who spoke.
Then the fire of divine wrath came down from heaven ;
a terrible noise was heard, and they fell to the ground.
The world was darkened, and they gave up the ghost.
But Musa interceded, and Allah hearkened, and raised
them up (Sur. ii. 52–53). The seventy then offered
their repentance to Him.

Musa went down with the seventy, bearing the
Tables of the Law. Some say that the tables were of
gold ; others, that they were of rubies and emeralds,
and covered with images.

Coming down to the people, they found them in sin, worshipping the calf. Musa, in wrath, cast the tables from his hands. He reproached Harun and the people and Sâmeri (Sur. vii. 149, xx. 94 *seq.*). Sâmeri was condemned to be set apart from mankind so long as he should live, and not to be approached. He should render an inevitable account in the world to come. Musa burned the calf and reduced it to powder.

The Israelites repented, and Musa announced to them from Allah, "Return to your Creator or yield to death; this shall profit you with Him. He will pardon you, for He loves to pardon. He is merciful" (Sur. ii. 51).

The Repentance and Expiation.

It was better for them to die with the pleasure of Allah than to live in His wrath. So on the morrow each rested in his place, his hands placed on his feet, his face turned to heaven, doing penance and imploring pardon of Allah. Then the 12,000 who had not sinned smote the remainder with their swords and beheaded them. The father slew the son, or the son the father. And Musa threw himself before Allah in prayer, weeping and crying. And Allah sent a black cloud to stand in the midst, that they who slew might not see their victims. The massacre lasted from daybreak to midday. The children and the weak sat about Musa and cried. Then at noon Allah hearkened to the prayer of Musa. He showed mercy, and accepted the repentance both of the dead and the living, and Musa rendered thanks to Him (Sura. ii. 49–50). Seventy thousand men had perished.

Then Allah commanded the reading of the *Taurath* or Law to the children of Israel. And they found the verses ordaining prayer, fasting, alms, &c., too hard. Then Musa called the seventy

Reading of the Taurath.

M

elders to bear witness of the words of Allah. But they added to his words, saying that He had declared, "If ye cannot fulfil them, do not so" (Sur. ii. 70).

Then Musa appealed to the help of Allah, and Allah ordered a mountain in Syria to quit its place and to remain suspended over their heads (Sur. vii. 170).

In the end Musa prayed, and the Law was made easier (Sur. ii. 61). Then Musa led them back to *Return to Egypt.* Egypt, and Allah gave them the palaces and the dwellings of the Copts and of Pharaoun for their heritage, as it is written in the Koran (Sur. vii. 133).

The children of Israel possessed all this land as far as Maghreb and Mazenderan and Spain, and they remained there many years, and Musa remained with them, and gave them counsels each day, reminding them of the benefits of Allah (Sur. ii. 38, vii. 137).

There is some dispute among the Moslem doctors as *Musa and Khidr.* to the personality of Khidr, some identifying him as Elias, others as Jeremy and Elisha. He is said to be guardian of the seas; and whoever falls into the sea is by him washed, and Khidr pronounces over him the legal prayer. Elias is guardian of the deserts and friend of wanderers. Those guardian spirits are invisible except at their own will. Khidr is connected with the legend of the Quest of the Water of Life, which gives immortality till the day of the Resurrection.

It was revealed to Musa that Allah had a servant wiser than himself, namely, Khidr. Musa went with Joshua, son of Nun, to seek him at "the confluence of the seas;" an account of their adventures is to be found in the 18th Surah of the Koran.

Qâroun, son of Yeshar, a descendant of Levi, was cousin of Musa. He was a goldsmith, and by means of some alchemy acquired great riches. He became filled with pride, and when alms were demanded from him, he refused to give. He then suborned a woman to charge Musa with fornication, but Allah changed the word in her mouth, and she betrayed the intrigue of Qâroun (*cf.* Sur. xxxiii. 69). The earth opened and seized Qâroun as far as the ankles; at the repeated command of Musa it seized him as far as the knees, and so gradually he entirely disappeared. With him were swallowed up the seventy who had apostatised with him. At the day of resurrection they will be sent to hell. And all the treasures of Qâroun were swallowed up also (Sur. xxviii. 81 *seq.*).

Story of Qâroun (Korah).

On his return to Egypt, Musa was bidden by Allah to lead the children of Israel into Syria. There were in that land three great cities— Balqâ, Arihâ (Jericho), and Ilyâ. The people were giants, the remains of the people of Ad. The greatest among them was Oudj (Og), who, when standing on the sea-shore, would take a fish from the water and hold it in the sun till it was roasted.

Fight of Musa with the Giants.

Musa issued the word, "O my people! enter the Holy Land that Allah hath destined for you (Sur. v. 24).

The twelve chiefs of the twelve tribes perceived Oudj advancing to meet them. He regarded them as so many ants, placed them in his boot, and showed them to the people in his house. He would have slain them, but at the intercession of his wife they were spared, and went back and described the giants to the affrighted hosts of Israel. They re-

Oudj (Og).

fused to advance. Musa and Harun went forward alone.

But though the Israelites sought to return to Egypt, they returned, in spite of themselves, to the same spot. Musa, after slaying Oudj, returned to them. Then Allah sent a vision by Gabriel, saying, "They shall be condemned to wander in the desert for forty years; afflict not thyself because of this perverse people" (Sur. v. 29).

When they prayed for food in the desert, where there The Manna was naught but thorns, Musa prayed, and and the Allah caused manna to drop from the ends of Quails the thorns. Then the quails were sent for meat (Sur. ii. 54).

Then Musa struck the rock with his rod, and each The Rock of the tribes drank of a separate spring (Sur. and the ii. 57). In their want of faith, the people Twelve Springs. took a great quantity of quails against the morrow, and Allah sent no more, until Musa prayed, and He relented.

A cloud was sent to remain above them each day until the evening and to give them shade (Sur. ii. 54). Their clothes wore not out; each child as it came into the world was dressed, and its garments grew with its growth.

The rock that gave the water was carried by Musa on an ass, and the water burst forth from it.

At the end of thirty years, Harun died in the desert; three years after, Musa and all the chiefs. Musa instituted Joshua his successor, who received the gift of prophecy; and after the death of Joshua, Caleb, son of Jephone, was prophet. On the day that the children of Israel came out of the desert, Joshua and Caleb alone survived of those who had entered it.

When Allah would call Harun to himself, Musa took
him to the distance of a parasang from the
people.   Harun saw a beautiful tree, beneath
which was a bed covered with a carpet.
Harun lay down and slept, and Musa remained seated
at his side.   The angel of death took the soul of Harun,
and Musa found him dead.   Presently the couch and the
tree and Harun disappeared, and Musa knew not whether
he had gone upto heaven or had descended into the earth.

When, on his return, the Israelites accused him of
having slain his brother, Allah caused the bed to descend
with the body of Harun, that they might see he was
dead (*cf.* Sur. xxxiii. 69).

Three years later, at a warning from Allah, Musa
called Joshua and went forth from the midst of the
people.   A wind arose from the east; terror laid hold
on the heart of Joshua, for he knew not what it meant.
Musa pressed him to his bosom.   The moon was
obscured, and Musa disappeared, leaving his garment
behind him.   On his return, the people accused Joshua
of having slain Musa, and imprisoned him under a
guard of ten men.   But in the night they saw an
angel clearly from heaven, saying, "Deliver Joshua, for
Allah hath called Musa to him."   Then he was released.

Another account is that Musa went forth with Joshua
and saw angels digging a tomb.   Musa asked, "For
whom is this tomb?"   They replied, "For a servant of
the number of the servants of Allah.   See how the
tomb is made!"   Musa went down, and the angel of
death, who was among them, took his soul.

Joshua, son of Nun, was of the tribe of Yussuf.   His
mother was Mariam, sister of Harun.   Seven
years after Musa's death he led the Israelites
against Ariha and slew its giants.   Then he attacked

Balqa, the capital and royal residence. Among its idolatrous inhabitants was a true believer and servant of Allah, named Bilaam, son of Beor. When the inhabitants besought his aid in prayer, he said, "It is the army of my God; I will not pray for evil upon them." The king, Bilac, sent for him, but Bilaam refused to pray. Then the king bribed the wife of Bilaam with great presents of silver and jewels, and Bilaam yielded to her request and consented to pray (*cf.* Sur. vii. 174).

On the day of attack, he went forth as a pious man upon an ass. But the ass halted and refused to advance, and Allah gave it a voice, so that it cried, "Bilaam, whither goest thou? Thou wouldst fight against God and curse the prophet of Allah." Bilaam turned back. And Eblis came as an old man and tempted him, saying that an ass had never spoken. So Bilaam a second time sought the mountain for the purpose of cursing Israel. And Israel began to flee.

Then Joshua in turn betook himself to prayer, beseeching the Lord that the true faith might depart from among the infidels. And Allah hearkened, and true faith came forth from the mouth of Bilaam in the form of a dove and rose to heaven. Then Bilaam, thus foiled, counselled the king to send forth beautiful women to seduce the Israelites. The device succeeded, but Allah sent a plague upon the guilty ones.

Phinees, son of Eleazar, a descendant of Harun, took
Phinees. a lance, went to one of the guilty couples, and transpierced them. Then he carried them forth and cried in a loud voice, "Behold and take warning!" In this day 70,000 died of the pest.

The next day the city was taken, and Bilac and Bilaam were slain. A man named Adjezán had, contrary to the law, taken a part of the booty; he was cast into the fire with the booty, and the spot is called Adjezán to this day.

Other kings of the land, Kouma, Djioun (Sihon), and Baraq, are named. Baraq believed, but afterwards denied the law of Musa. Joshua died at the age of 128, having led the children of Israel during twenty-eight years. He was succeeded by Caleb and Khazqil (Ezekiel), who was of the tribe of Jehud. They attacked the apostate Baraq and his people, and cut off the thumbs of Baraq, who had treated in this way seventy kings. After seven years' war the army of Israelites went back to Egypt. Many had been slain, many remained in the land, where their descendants dwell to this day.

The chronicler fixes all these events in the time of King Minotschehr. He was succeeded by his _Kings of_ grandson Zew or Zab, who founded Bagdad. _Persia._ After Zew came Kaiqobád, who resided at Balkh. The events that happened in Israel after Musa's death occurred in this reign.

It is said that Khazqil is the Dsoul-Kefl of the Koran. He is also called Ibn-al-Adjouz, as son of an aged pair who had no children. Khazqil _The Prophet Khazqil (Ezekiel)._ was one of the three prophets who raised men from the dead; Musa and Isa were the other two. A great multitude had lain dead for several years, after a pest sent upon them for disobedience in refusing to make war on the infidels. At the prayer of Khazqil, Allah raised them up, and they lived again till their term was come. It is said that their descendants exhale an odour of death (see Sur. ii. 244).

Unlike the Bible, the Chronicle gives the genealogy of Elias as a descendant of Harun. He was _Elias._ sent to turn the people from their idolatrous worship of Baal. At his prayer rain ceased and famine

ensued, which lasted three years.   None had bread
except Elias, so that when in any place bread was
smelt, men said, "Elias passed by here yesterday."

He brought bread to the house of an aged woman
and her son, Eliseus, whom he cured of paralysis.

At the end of the three years Elias and Eliseus went
to the king and bade him pray to the idol. As the
prayers were unheard, Elias prayed, and it began to
rain, and the corn and the grass grew.

But the people again became infidel, and Elias
prayed for their salvation. But when they had anew
renounced the worship of God, he turned his heart from
them, and going forth from the town with Eliseus, cried,
"Lord, take me from amongst them!" So Allah took
him, and granted him to live until the day when Israfil
shall sound the trumpet of judgment, and gave him
Paradise for a dwelling. He appointed Eliseus his
successor, and God made him a prophet.

While he lived, Eliseus called the children of Israel,
who had forsaken the law of Musa, to Allah.
Eliseus After his death there was no longer a prophet,
but there were sages, blessed of Allah, who exhorted
them.

They had an ark with them called *Sakiné:* the head
The Ark. of it was as the head of a cat. He who had
any wish, went to the ark, addressed his
prayer to God, and obtained what he asked. In war,
the ark was carried before the army; a noise like the
cry of a cat went forth from it, and Allah filled the
hearts of their foes with fear, so that they fled. The
trust of the Israelites was in this ark, as it is said
in the Koran, "The ark, on which shall be security on
the part of your Lord, also the relics of Musa and of
Harun, and angels shall bear it" (Sur. ii. 254).

The relic of Musa was the rod, that of Harun his mitre. There was also a small quantity of the manna which they had brought back from the desert; also fragments of the Tables that Musa had broken. The ark passed from the hands of Musa to the other prophets, till it came to Eliseus. After his death, the people gave themselves up to wickedness, and only a few adhered to the law of Musa. Then Allah gave the people into the hands of an oppressor. Their king, Ilâq, was attacked by the Amalekites, who obtained possession of the ark and sent it into the Maghreb. The Israelites remained without a prophet until Allah sent to them a prophet, Samuel, and gave to Tâlout the kingdom. Then the ark returned into their possession.

In the space of 460 years twenty kings reigned over the children of Israel. They were Ilâq, Kings of Israel Chusan, Noufil, brother of Caleb, Khafawend, Nasir. Then appeared a prophetess, Diwan; she slew the king and made Barak king in his place. Then there was a king from the Hedjaz, of the race of Loth, named Sarir, then Abmak, Taris. A troop of Philistines invaded the land, and called to them the Beni-Ammon. Then, after eighteen years, there was another Israelite king, Jephel, followed by Akroun. Then there was an interregnum of twenty years. Then there was a man named Ali, who was priest, and exercised the royal power. He was weak, and the ark fell into the hands of wicked men. At the end of thirty years Allah granted the prophetic functions to Samuel, son of Rayyan, son of Alqama. The Israelites, exhausted by their oppressive kings, were then governed by Djâlout, of the Amalekite race. Samuel appointed Tâlout their king.

The kingdom of Djâlout was in Syria. The Israelites, oppressed by the descendants of the
ancient giants, with the Adites and the
Themoudites, asked of Allah a prophet who should
renew the law and religion of Musa. Rayyan, the
descendant of Harun, left a wife with child, who was
confided to the care of the sage Il. She gave birth to
a child called Samuel, who was instructed by Il in the
law and religion of Musa up to the age of seven years.
At forty years he received the gift of prophecy from
Allah.

One night while Samuel slept, Gabriel came and
made a noise, so that Samuel awoke. He saw no one,
and said, " Master, didst call me ?" and Il said, " No."
This was repeated the next night and the third. And
Il said, " My son, if in the night some one call thee,
answer : Here am I, what dost thou command? I
am in thy hands ! " Samuel did so. Then Gabriel
appeared to him, and communicated to him the will
of Allah.

Il had two grown sons, whom he had taught the
duty of sacrifice after the law of Musa, and nothing
more. And Samuel said, " Allah hath said : Why hast
thou neglected to perform the sacrifice, so that thy
sons add to it or take from it? Why hast thou not
directed them ? Because of this sin I will deliver thee
into the hands of an enemy, who shall slay thy sons,
take away the ark, and cause thee to perish." Then
Djâlout came, made war on the children of Israel, and
slew the sons of Il ; and Il died of grief. The ark
was lost.

Then the Israelites said to Samuel, " Pray that
Allah may give us a king, that we may make war to
take the ark again." And the prophet said to them,

" Allah hath appointed Tâlout your king" (Sur. ii. 247–248).

Tâlout was of the race of the children of Israel. He was poor, a water-porter like his ancestors, who had asses for this use. Now the father *Tâlout.* of Tâlout had lost an ass, which had fled into the desert. Tâlout had gone to seek the ass, and Samuel sought Tâlout to make him king. Seeing him afar off, Samuel called him and said, "Thou shalt be king of the children of Israel." Tâlout replied, " O prophet of Allah! thou knowest that my tribe is the least of all tribes, and that I am the poorest and the weakest of all the children of Israel." Samuel said, " It is the order of Allah." Then he poured on his head the sacred oil, which was said to *Royal* have been inherited from Yussuf, son of *Unction.* Yakoub, and was in the hands of the prophets. In appointing a king, they poured it upon his head and face, that his skin might become brilliant and pure.

The tribe of which came the prophets was the tribe of Levi ; that of which came the kings was *Levi and* the tribe of Yehud, which in the eyes of the *Jehud.* people was despised. The Israelites said, "Why should he reign over us? We are worthier of the royalty than he " (Sur. ii. 248).

Tâlout was the wisest man of all the tribes, and had the loftiest stature ; therefore he was called Tâlout. Samuel said, " Allah gives the power to whom He wills." The people said, " Show us a sign!" Samuel said, " The sign of his kingship shall be that the ark shall return " (Sur. ii. 249).

Now none knew where the ark was. Some said that the enemy had cast it on the dung-heap, and that Allah had sent angels with the order to raise the ark into the air. Others said that the idolaters had placed it in their temple. And when they went to the temple, they saw the ark placed above the idols, and the idols stretched on the ground. The infidels said, "It is the talisman of the children of Israel : put it out of this house." Then they took it and attached it to the tails of two cows, each of which had a calf. Allah caused the cows to be guided by angels, that they might place the ark in the midst of the Israelites. Then the cows returned and their calves. The people having received the ark, recognised Tâlout as king and submitted to his orders.

The Chronicle proceeds to relate how Tâlout made war against Djâlout under the direction of Samuel, as we read in the second chapter of the Koran, of which narrative there is a variant in the Biblical first Book of Samuel, where Gideon, in the incident of the lapping of the water, takes the place of Tâlout. In the end, there remained with Tâlout only 313 men—the same number that the prophet Mohammed had with him on the day of Bedr.

The battle was delayed by direction of Allah, for David, son of Isai—a little man with grey eyes, thin hair, timid of heart, and delicate of body—was destined to slay Djâlout. "Thou shalt recognise him," said the divine voice, "by this : when thou shalt place the horn upon his head, the oil shall come forth." Samuel went to Isai, but neither of his eleven sons was chosen. At last Samuel found David in a valley, withdrawing his sheep two by two from a torrent. He doubted not that this was the chosen one, and placing the horn upon his head, the oil came forth.

Djâlout proudly challenged Tâlout to single combat, and Talout took a coat of mail given him by Samuel,

Daoud (David).

and clothed successively each of his band therewith, but it fitted none. Finally Isai, father of David, spoke of this remaining son, and it was found that the coat of mail fitted him. David was willing to encounter Djâlout, and went forth to meet him in his shepherd's attire, armed only with a sling and three magic stones which had spoken to him from the road, saying, "Take me!" One of these stones was that cast by Musa on the enemies of Allah, another had been cast by Harun. The third was to carry doom to Djâlout. Tâlout promised him the half of his kingdom and his daughter should he vanquish Djâlout. David replied, "I will slay him by the power of Allah!" And as a good Mussulman, advancing before the line of battle, he paused and pronounced the sacred formula, *Bismillah!*

Djâlout, at the head of 100,000 men, clad in cuirasses and casques and fully armed, despised David and taunted him. Then David put his hand in his bag, took one of his stones, placed it in the sling and hurled it, crying out, "*Bismillah!*" Allah ordered the wind to lift the helmet of Djâlout from his head, that the stone might strike him. The stone crushed his head, and his brains came forth. He fell from his horse and died. The stone fell to the earth and broke into a multitude of fragments, which struck all the horsemen on their heads. A great number were killed by this single stone; as it is said in the Koran, "They put them to flight by the permission of Allah, and David slew Djâlout."

Then Tâlout put the rest to flight, returned, and told Samuel the story of David. Samuel said to Tâlout, "Accomplish thy promise!" And Tâlout gave David his daughter in marriage, confided all affairs to him, and gave him his ring, and all the people were subject to his orders.

Tâlout in course of time became jealous of David, but dared not show this to Samuel. Then Samuel died, and Tâlout plotted to slay David. He proposed to go in the middle of the night and cut him in twain. But David's wife gave him information. Then David filled a bottle with wine, placed it in his bed, covered it with a garment, and went his way. Tâlout came in the middle of the night with a sword dipped in poison, and cut the bottle in two, and as the wine escaped, Tâlout said, "He drank much wine yesterday!" Then he discerned that it was a ruse of his daughter, and would have slain her, but she fled. The next night, when Tâlout was asleep, David came and placed about his head four arrows, on which was written his own name. When Tâlout awoke, he said, "David is more generous than I; for if I had had him in my power, I would not have done him grace; but he has done me no harm."

One day, pursued by Tâlout, David hid in a cavern of a mountain, and Allah inspired a spider to close the entrance to the cavern with his web, so that Tâlout found him not.

The sages of Israel united against Tâlout, who slew them all. There remained only a wise woman, whom he had delivered to his chamberlain, a man of good heart. Presently, Tâlout, smitten through a dream with remorse, inquired of the chamberlain if there was no sage of whom he could demand expiation. Then the chamberlain spoke of this sage woman who had been delivered to him to be slain. She was brought before Tâlout, and he said, "What is my expiation?" She

[margin note:] Tâlout Plots to Slay David.

answered, "Lead me to the tomb of a prophet, that I may pray ; perhaps Allah will cause him to speak." They went to the tomb of Samuel. She prayed, and Samuel said, "His expiation shall be that he go with his sons to the Valley of Giants and fight them till he die." Now Tâlout had twelve sons. He called them all and asked them, "What say ye?" They answered, "We obey!" So they went to the city of the giants, made war, and were all slain.

On the death of Tâlout David prospered, and Allah granted to him the gift of prophecy. His genealogy is traced up to Azer, father of Ibrahim. His unassailable power, which is referred to in the Koran (Sur. xxxviii. 16, 19), was seen in the guard of four thousand horsemen at the gate of his palace.

The Prophet David.

None was at the same time king and prophet, except David and Suleiman, for Yussuf was but the treasurer of a king. David had not asked the kingship of Allah ; Suleiman did so (Sur. xxxviii. 25, 34).

The function of David as judge and deputy of Allah himself is dwelt upon. The Psalms were sent to him : they contained neither law nor prescriptions, but were entirely consecrated to the establishment of the unity of God. His voice was incomparable, and when he began to sing the praises of Allah, the birds of heaven came and placed themselves about his head and listened. The mountains also joined with him in song, as it is said in the Koran (Sur. xxxiv. 10, 17, 18, 21, 79).[1]

David was an obedient servant of God and just among men. He had ninety-nine wives beside concubines. He divided his time into three parts, occupy-

[1] Cf. Ps. cxlviii., and the Talmudists (Sale).

ing one day with the affairs of this world, and with the administration of justice, consecrating the second day to the service of God and to the affairs of the other world, and the third day recreating himself with his wives in permitted pleasures.

When David prayed that he might attain to the The Trial of degree of distinction of the ancient prophets, David. Allah reminded him of the trials in which Ibrahim, Yakoub, Yussuf, Musa, and Ayoub had proved their perseverance. David prayed that he too might be tried, and Allah granted his request.

Years passed, when one night, as he was in the attitude of adoration before Allah, Eblis under the form of a dove came and fell before him, simulating death. David would have seized the dove, but it fled by the window of the chamber. The eye of David, in following it, rested on a woman seated opposite him, naked, and who was washing her head. He was smitten with love, and demanded of his confidant who this woman was. The reply was that she was wife of Uriah, of royal race, and that Uriah had gone forth with David's army to make war with the infidels. David sent a letter to the commander bidding him place Uriah before the ark; for those who were in this position would not return; they must conquer or die. Uriah marched at the head of the army three times, but the fourth time he was slain. His death was announced to his wife, Bethsabe, who put on mourning for him according to the law. Then David proposed to make her his wife, and she consented, on condition that if she should have a son, the son should be appointed his successor. The son was Solomon.

David was one day celebrating the praises of Allah

in a lonely place, according to his custom. When he
had finished his adoration, two angels appeared on the
side of the Mihrab and seated themselves before him,
and David was afraid (Sur. xxxviii. 20).

They said, " Fear not; we are two adversaries; the
one of us has acted unjustly towards the other. Judge
between us with equity; direct us in the even way.
This my brother had ninety-and-nine sheep, and I
had but one. He said, ' Give her to me to keep,' and
he disputed her with me." David said, "He hath
acted unjustly towards thee in asking thy sheep to
add to his. Many of those who are associated together
act unjustly towards one another, except those who
believe and do what is right; but their number is
small." And when David perceived that Allah tried
him, he implored pardon of his Lord, prostrated
himself and repented (Sur. xxxviii. 20–23). He wept
so much, that he could plunge a cup in the water of
his tears. He drank therefrom, and there sprang up
before him a tree. So he remained forty days and forty
nights. Then Allah sent to him Gabriel, who said
to him, "O David! the Lord commends to thee His
salvation." He understood that it was a reproach, and
wept still more. It is said that during these forty
days he shed more tears than Adam and his descendants had shed or shall shed until the day of resurrection for their sins.

Allah received his repentance; the good news was
brought by Gabriel. And David said, "O Gabriel!
how on the day of resurrection shall Uriah act toward
me?" Gabriel answered, "Allah hath not told me."
David began again to weep, to adore, and to pray, until
Allah sent word to him, "O David, on the day of resurrection, when Uriah shall accuse thee, I will give

N

him so great a part of Paradise that he shall be satisfied with thee." Then David understood that Allah had shown him mercy, and his grief left him. But the remembrance of his sins was ever with him, and he wrote them on his hand, that, looking, he might recall them to himself.

Afterwards David asked of Allah that he might gain his living by the exercise of an industry; and Allah gave him power over iron, which became between his hands as paste and as wax. He ordered Gabriel to teach him the art of making coats of mail, as it is recorded in the Koran (Sur. xxxiv. 10, xxi. 80).

These coats of mail, the rings of which are without joints or sutures, are called Davidian to this day.

After David had reigned twelve years, a famine and The Temple at Ailia. an epidemic afflicted the children of Israel, and a great number died. They assembled at the place now called Ailia, and prayed that the cures might be removed. When their prayer was heard, they said, "We must build here a temple, for it is a blessed place." They did so; and thence is the privilege of this temple. When David was ready to die, the temple was not finished, and he charged Suleiman with its completion. The foundations of it are of hard stone, because Suleiman, after the death of his father, forced the Divs to raise the foundations in stone. When you come to the spot at the present day, you see that the columns and the gates are alike of stone, as in the mosque of Damascus. Only the columns of the temple of Ailia are from twenty to thirty cubits in height and of a single piece, so that there is no binding with cement; a proof that such a thing cannot have been made by men. It is said in the Koran that "all the dæmons, architects, and divers were subject" to Suleiman (Sur. xxxviii. 30).

The cause of the famine is said to have been that David desired to know the number of the children of Israel. Allah approved not of this, and said, " O David ! didst thou not know that I promised to Ibrahim and to Yakoub to bless their descendants by making them so numerous that none can know their number?" Then Allah said, "Choose one of these three things : three years of famine, three years of the enemy, or three days of death." David said within himself, "1 could not endure three years of famine, and three years of the enemy is a great calamity." He therefore chose three days of death. Then the plague broke out among the children of Israel, and there died so many the first day that their number could not be counted ; and David feared that after three days there would be no more Israelites. He prayed and said, "O Lord! it is I who have drunk sour wine, and the children of Israel have pain in the bowels ;" that is, I have committed a sin, and they are punished for it. "If thou wouldst punish, punish me, and remove death from them." And Allah heard his prayer.

It is recorded in the Koran, "We have given to Loqman wisdom" (Sur. xxxi. 11). He lived Loqman the in the time of David, and was with him for Sage thirty years. The saying is ascribed to him, "Silence is wisdom, but few practise it."[1]

To Suleiman Allah granted the gift of prophecy, along with the royalty, as heritage of David. Suleiman, He was David's assessor during his lifetime son of David.

---

[1] There are numerous stories of Loqman ; but Tabari has not reported them, because his object in the Chronicle was simply to fix the epoch of each personage (cf. Sale's notes to Sur. xxix.).

(Sur. xxi. 78, xxvii. 16). A story is told different from
that in the Bible illustrative of the sagacity and dignity
of Suleiman.

Passages in the Koran which allude to the great
power of Suleiman are then adduced. He was a great
builder, employing for this purpose the services of the
Divs. His throne of rubies is especially named, above
which were represented two vultures sheltering Suleiman
with their shadow. Diving also began in Suleiman's
time for pearls, and the Divs were employed in it.

He had also a carpet, five hundred parasangs long,
on which were placed three hundred thrones of gold
and silver; and Suleiman ordered the birds to join
their wings for shelter to him and his suite. He had
also a thousand crystal houses, abodes of his thousand
wives, of whom three hundred were legitimate. He
would then bid the wind to raise the carpet, with all
that was upon it, to the distance of a mile or so. And
thus he would travel from place to place. In the morning he would be at Damascus, and in the evening
at Ailia, as it is reported in the Koran (Sur. xxi. 81,
xxxiv. 11, xxxviii. 35).

With the same wild and audacious fancy, the Chro-
Suleiman and nicle tells of the expedition of Suleiman to
Balkis.   the desert of Arabia; but the compilers, as
usual, had a clear topography in their mind's eye.

He learned that in the land of Yemen there were
idolaters. He caused the carpet to be prepared, drew
up thereon his army, and bade the wind carry the carpet
from Syria to Yemen. His route was by the Hedjaz.
Arrived at Mecca, he bade the wind let down the carpet,
and made the procession about the temple, saying,
"From this place there shall go forth a prophet from
among the Arabs; his dwelling shall be at Medina,

and his tomb shall be also at Medina; and on the earth there shall be no man nobler than he before Allah." Then he left Mecca and went out of the land of Hedjaz. The road crossed a burning desert, and his people suffered from thirst. Suleiman desired to ascertain if there was water; the *houd-houd* (lapwing) alone knew the places of water. His seeking for this bird and finding it not is alluded to in the Koran (Sur. xxvii. 20).

Now the *houd-houd* had gone to the place where Balkis was, in the territory of Saba, of which she was queen. Her beauty was surpassing, for her mother had been a Peri and her father a prince. The *houd-houd* of Suleiman found another *houd-houd* at the palace, and recited the power of his master. The other replied, "The queen adores the sun."

The *houd-houd* returned with the news to Suleiman, and he gave her a letter, which she carried to the Queen of Saba, calling upon her and her people to become true believers. The Chronicle proceeds, expounding and explaining the 27th Surah of the Koran, to relate the circumstances which led to the wedding of Suleiman with Balkis, and the conversion of all her army. He had a son by Balkis. A fourth chapter narrates the story of the miraculous birth of Balkis.

In Surah xxxviii. 33 it is written, "We have proved Suleiman, by placing on his throne a body." The Ring of The explanation of this allusion is as follows. Solomon. There was a king of an island kingdom. He had great power, and was an idolater. Suleiman resolved to attack him; so preparing the carpet, he was transported upon it, two months' journey, to the island. He attacked the king, slew him, and converted all the people to the true religion. He then brought back with him the king's daughter, who was most beautiful. But she was greatly grieved, and in his perplexity Suleiman took counsel of the Divs, who made a figure of marble resembling the father of the girl. On seeing it, she was glad, and caused a royal throne to be made for it, and day and night adored it. This was known to none but to Asaf, son of Berakhya, who knew the great name of God, and was steward in the house of Suleiman. He informed Suleiman that in his house was an idol, wherefore Suleiman ordered the statue to be broken and the young girl to be punished. Then he put on a pure robe and said, " O Lord, Thou knowest that it is not worthy of the sons of David that they should adore in their houses another than Thee, after all the benefits wherewith Thou hast loaded them. But as for me, I knew it not. Come to my aid ! " And he lamented, asked pardon, and wept.

Suleiman had a ring on which was engraved the great name of Allah, by means of which he was the master of the universe. His wife and mother of his children was called Djerade. Suleiman had more trust in her than in his other wives, and occasionally the ring was left in her custody. One day, by the will of Allah, when the ring was in the hand of Djerade, one of the great Divs took the form of Suleiman. He received the ring and seated himself on the throne of Suleiman ; and all submitted to his orders because of the ring. When Suleiman returned and demanded the ring, Djerade said, "I have restored it to thee." Suleiman denied this, and they disputed together. Then Djerade said, "Thou art not Suleiman ; he who is seated on the throne is Suleiman ; thou art a Div who hast taken the form of Suleiman." He was astonished and went out of the house, saying that he was Suleiman to all whom he met. But they beat him and answered, "Thou art a Div!" In the end, some fishermen made him work for the wage of two fishes a day. But at the end of forty days, Allah pardoned him and restored his power. The ring was found by him in a fish; men, dæmons, and birds unite about him; the usurping Div is by the aid of the Peris brought from the depth of the sea, and is thence cast back tied to stone and iron, where he remains till the day of the resurrection.

His reign was of forty years. Towards the end of his life he would often repair to the temple at Ailia, and remain there a month or two Death of Suleiman. without coming forth, wrapped in prayer and adoration. None dared approach him as he stood in this devout attitude, neither man nor dæmon. Now in his *mihrab* there grew every day a tree to him unknown. Suleiman asked, "What is thy name and thy use?" The tree replied, "Such is my name and such is my use." Then Suleiman had it transplanted to another place; and if it was of medicinal use, he caused its nature to be inscribed in a book. One day Suleiman saw a new tree in his *mihrab*, and asked, "What is thy name and thy use?" The tree replied, "For the destruction of this temple: make of me a staff and lean on me." Suleiman said, "None can destroy this temple so long as I live;" and he understood that the tree had warned him of his death. He pulled up the tree and made a staff, leaning on it when he prayed. Knowing that the temple was far from finished, and that when he should be dead the Divs would not execute it, he said, "O Lord! cause the event of my death to remain unknown to the Divs and the Peris, that they may finish this temple." Allah heard his prayer for the completion of the temple and that the Peris might be belied.

When his life came to its term, Suleiman stood up, praying, leaning upon the staff. When Allah had commanded the Angel of Death to take his soul, Suleiman remained thus an entire year; and all who approached saw him in this attitude, and were afraid to come near. Meanwhile the Divs were toiling day and night in the temple till it should be finished. When the soul had quitted the body of Suleiman, Allah the same day bade the white fly which eats wood to come from beneath the earth and gnaw the staff. Each day it gnawed a little; and had only finished at the end of a year. The Divs had then finished the construction of the temple; the staff was broken, and Suleiman fell, as it is recorded in the Koran (Sur. xxxiv. 13).

It says that when Suleiman fell, the lies of the Divs and of the Peris became manifest to men; for they had pretended before that they knew hidden things. Had they known hidden things, they would have known that Suleiman had been dead a year.

The wise men and the learned gathered together, and shut up the ant for a day and a night, that it might gnaw wood. Then they compared the space gnawed with the extent of the staff, and so found how long Suleiman had been dead. And now, whenever the white fly gnaws wood, the void is filled with clay and water by the Divs and the Peris. It will be so till the day of resurrection, because of their gratitude to her who delivered them from Suleiman. If not from them, whence could water and clay come in the midst of the wood?[1]

---

[1] There seems to be a reflection of the story of the building of the temple by Genii in 1 Kings vi. 7, and the Rabbins *ad loc.* (Sale).

The Chronicle proceeds to narrate the story of the ant, alluded to in the 27th Surah of the Koran; also the adventure with the horses, alluded to in the 38th Surah as sacrificed in expiation for his neglect of one of the daily prayers prescribed to the faithful.

Suleiman is thoroughly a Mussulman king, and his territories are Syria, Hedjaz, Saba, Yemen, Maghreb, and Arabia.

The Chronicle next interposes an account of the kings of Persia contemporary with Suleiman.

Suleiman is succeeded by his son Radjaim, who was king without being prophet, and who reigned only over a part of Syria and of the children Kings of Israel. of Israel, who had many kings. The son of Radjaim was Abim, who became king of the two tribes of Yehud and Benjamin, and who was succeeded by his son Asa. There was war between him and the king of Hindostan, named Zarh, who was conquered and slain.

Abim abandoned the religion of Musa, of David, and Suleiman, and introduced idolatry among the children of Israel, which spread in Syria and the sacred city of Ailia. Asa recalled the people to religion. He put to death his mother, who was an idolatress. Then many of the people who were idolaters migrated to Hindostan, where the king adored the sun and moon. He invaded Syria, and Asa in his distress offered a prayer which is cited as a model to good Mussulmans, beginning, " O Allah! Lord of the seven heavens, Lord of the great throne! God of Ibrahim, of Israel, of Isaac, of Yakoub, and of the twelve tribes! Thou remainest hidden from Thy creatures when Thou wilt. Man cannot attain Thy dwelling, nor seize the substance of Thy greatness. Thou art the watcher who sleepeth not, the Great One, upon whom neither days nor nights

have effect." The prayer goes on to call to mind divine
deliverances in the sacred history of Islam.

"Thou raisest the dead, and Thou dost preserve the
world eternally. Thy strength perishes not; Thou art
great and dost not diminish. My God! have pity on
me and hear my prayer."

In a dream he is assured of the friendship of Allah
and of His aid. He was made a prophet, and finally
the army of Zarh was defeated by an army of angels.[1]

Asa was succeeded by Josaphat, and he by Athalia,
who slew the descendants of the kings and reigned
seven years. Then Joas, son of King Ochozias, came
from his retreat and put her to death. He was succeeded by Amasias, and he by Azarias, Joatham, Achaz,
Ezechias.

Ezechias was a great king, a believer and a just man.
Ezechias and A prophet, Isaiah, was sent to him, who was
Isaiah. well received by Ezechias, and who converted
the people from idolatry. And Allah preserved the
kingdom for the sake of the prophet.

Now Ezechias was lame and paralytic, and had a
wound on his leg which hindered him from riding on
horseback. Hearing of this, Sennacherib, who reigned
in Moussoul, invaded Syria. His general, Nabuchodonosor, warned him that already in a previous expedition an army had been annihilated in answer to the
prayer of Isaiah, which raised a great wind. But
Sennacherib heeded not his counsel and marched to
the holy city.

At the prayer of Isaiah, Allah sent a vision and
declared, "I will protect this temple of Ailia, and I
will remove from thee this enemy. But say to the
king that his life is arrived at its term, that he must

[1] The story has found some reflections in the Biblical Chronicle.

make his will and intrust the kingdom to another, whom I will protect."

But in answer to the king's prayer, a vision came to Isaiah again: "Tell the king, I have added to thy life fifteen years, and I will deliver thee from the enemy." Then Isaiah was ordered to take water from a certain well and wash the feet of Ezechias ; thus the wound was cured. The army of Sennacherib was destroyed, and he was taken captive and sent back to Moussoul.

Ezechias was succeeded by Manaseh, and he by Ammon. They followed the true religion. Then came Joakim. The people did ill and sought to slay Isaiah, who fled from the city and hid in a tree which Allah caused to open. But Eblis seized his cloak, and when the tree closed, a part of the cloak remained outside. When the Israelites saw it, they brought a saw, and sawed the tree which held the prophet.

After some years, Nabuchodonosor came with a great army from Moussoul, made the king prisoner, put out his eyes, and slew his sons before him. He destroyed the temple and all the towns, and carried away the children of Israel into Persia, whose king at that time was Gouschtasp. He gave all the kingdom of Syria and of Ailia to Nabuchodonosor.

Some say that Jeremy is another name of the prophet called Aziz, who is referred to in the Koran (Sur. ii. 261). After the conquests _{Jeremy the Prophet.} by Nabuchodonosor, he returned to Iraq with many prisoners, among whom was the prophet Daniel.

Set at liberty by Nabuchodonosor, Jeremy, obedient to the divine voice, mounted an ass and came into Syria and Palestine. When he saw the holy city in ruins, and found none to give him bread, he plucked some grapes and figs, and sat down and ate of them in a field. Having no water, he pressed the grapes into a cup and drunk. He exclaimed, "How shall God cause this dead city to live again?" Not that he doubted of the resurrection at the day of judgment. Towards noon he tied his ass to a tree and slept in the shade. Then Allah took from him his ass, and he remained dead one hundred years, as it is recorded in the Koran. Allah raised him up again when Gouschtasp succeeded to the throne of Persia, and Nabuchodonosor had returned to Babylon, and the great men of Israel had returned to Palestine and had rebuilt the cities (Sur. ii. 261).[1]

On this resuscitation of Aziz, Allah said, "We have made of thee a sign for men." He gave him prophecy, taught him the *Taurath* or Law, and sent him into the holy city. For in the destruction of the city the Law had been burned, with all other books of knowledge of the children of Israel. On coming back and rebuilding the temple, they knew nothing of the Law; they had no knowledge of religion ; and they were afflicted.

When Aziz appeared they demanded a sign of him, and he said, "I am that Jeremy whom Allah sent as prophet to the children of Israel and who were cast into prison." He told them how he had been dead for one hundred years, and they said, "Allah is almighty." But still they demanded a sign, and he said, "I will recite the whole Taurath." Never before had this been done, neither by Musa nor Harun. He then recited the Law, and they committed it to writing, recognising that he was a true prophet, and rendering thanks to Allah.

In the time of neglect, when Isaiah was prophet, he had made a copy of the Law in fair writing, and had placed it under one of the columns of the temple, one

[1] Cf. Sale's note on the Biblical parallel.

of the great monoliths made by the Divs in the
time of Suleiman. Aziz directed them to dig under
such and such a column, and they found the Law in a
coffer of wood bound with iron. They compared it
with the Law dictated by Aziz, and there was not a
letter too much or too little. They were seized with
astonishment and said, "It is not the deed of a man!"
For this cause they became infidels, as it is said in the
Koran, "The Yahud say that Aziz is the Son of God."
Then Allah refuted their saying, "They take their
doctors and their monks for their lords, to the exclu-
sion of Allah" (Sur. ix. 30–31).[1]

The Persian king Gouschtasp was a great protector
of the cult of fire. The prophet of the $_{\text{Zerdusht}}$
Mages, Zerdusht, who is the author of their $_{\substack{\text{and the} \\ \text{Mages.}}}$
religion, who brought the Zendavesta to the
people, lived under his reign. Formerly he had been a
disciple of Aziz, but had become his opponent. Then
Aziz prayed to Allah, who disfigured him, and the
children of Israel cast him out of Ailia. He went to
Iraq, thence to Balkh, and presented himself before
Gouschtasp, claiming to be a prophet and enjoining the
cult of fire. Gouschtasp believed in him and prescribed
his religion in all Persia. The Persians say that
Zerdusht descended from Minotschehr.[2]

In the reign of Bahman, king of Persia, Nabucho-
donosor, invested with the government of $_{\text{Second De-}}$
Babylon, and of Iraq as far as Syria and $_{\substack{\text{struction of} \\ \text{the Holy}}}$
Maghreb, was sent a second time to destroy $_{\text{Place.}}$
Ailia. He took with him three wise men whom he

---

[1] It seems an entire misunderstanding to refer to the *Jews* and *Christians*
in this passage

[2] The Moslems thus claim the magians as dissenters from themselves,
as the monks pretended that the followers of Manes were in some sort
Christians.

made his viziers, Daryousch (Darius), Kirousch (Cyrus), and Ahasuerus, his son.

After destroying the holy place, he brought with him captive the king Zedechias, son of Joiacim, who was put to death by Bahman.

In his government of Babylon he had 100,000 youths, descendants of the prophets, in his service.

Daniel
Among them was the prophet Daniel, who was endowed with wisdom. Evilmerodach, son of Nabuchodonosor, succeeded him ; then Balthasar reigned. Revolting against Bahman, he was put to death by Daryousch.

Ahasuerus was sent against the king of Hindostan, who had revolted against Bahman ; he slew him in battle, and obtained the kingdom, as well as that of Babylon and Iraq, on the death of Daryousch.

Ahasuerus treated the captive children of Israel with
Ahasuerus and Esther.
kindness and delivered them from slavery. He had a wife of high birth ; she committed a fault, and Ahasuerus caused her to be slain. He took a wife of the children of Israel named Esther, and had by her a son named Kirousch. Esther distinguished the children of Israel, saying, "They are my relations ; they are descendants of prophets and sages ; they must be honoured." For fear of Bahman, she dared not send them back to the Holy Land, but treated them with kindness.

Kirousch, succeeding Ahasuerus, also treated them
Kirousch (Cyrus).
with kindness, because they were of the race of his mother. Daniel, grown up, had received from God the gift of prophecy. He called Kirousch to God and to the true religion, and he abandoned the cult of fire, although in secret, for fear of Bahman ; on the death of the latter he publicly pro-

fessed the religion of Daniel, and placed him at the head of his kingdom. Daniel demanded permission to return with the people to the Holy Land, to restore the city and the temple. Kirousch refused, saying, " Were there a thousand prophets like thee, they should all remain with me." But the Israelites were permitted to return. Seventy years had elapsed since their deportation by Nabuchodonosor. On the death of Kirousch Daniel returned to the holy place and worshipped Allah.

CHAPTER VII.

THE TRADITIONS OF THE MOSQUE—*Continued.*

THE Chronicle now takes up the succession of the
kings of Yemen, from the death of Queen
Balkis to the epoch of Bahman. All the
kings of Yemen were Himyarites. One of them,
Tobba, made a victorious expedition to China.

The Himya-rite Kings.

To return to Persia and King Bahman. The surname of Ardeschir—Longhand—was given
to him. He adored fire and held the Magian
religion in esteem. His mother was called Astoniya;
she descended from Tâlout, king of the children of
Israel. Bahman had a posthumous son, Dara,
who had been exposed in infancy, and who
came to the throne as Dara the elder.

Persia.

Dara the Elder.

In the land of Roum and of the Maghreb was a great
empire, that of the Ionians (or Greeks). King
Philip was a descendant of Esau, son of Isâk.
In his kingdom there was a town, Macedon, residence
of the kings of Greece. In this land were the Greek
sages, and all the wisdom of the world came from them;
they were such as Aristotle, Hippocrates, Plato, Socrates,
Hermes, Apollonius and Agathodæmon. Their books
on philosophy, medicine, and the other sciences are
numerous and well known. To-day there remains
naught of them, and their cities are ruined. Their
books only are in the hands of men. Philip rendered

Philip of Macedon.

the land the most flourishing between Roum, Yemen, and all the countries of the West.

Philip paid tribute to Dara, like the other kings. But when Dara the younger succeeded, he was attacked and slain by Alexander, reputed son *Alexander.* of Philip, who is called Dsoul Qarnaim, because he obtained the empire of all the earth. Alexander was in reality son of the Persian king Bahram, and of a daughter of the king of the Greeks When Philip died, he took the crown, and his mother informed him of the circumstances of his birth. His conquest of Persia and the death of Dara is described; and it is said that Alexander collected the Persian books of wisdom, had them copied and translated into Greek, and sent to Aristotle, the greatest of the sages. He is said to have invaded Hindostan, Tibet, and China, and the Maghreb, and to have arrived at the obscure region. Thence he returned to Iraq, and died at Zour.

Alexander, as Dsoul Qarnaim, is mentioned in the Koran (Sur. xviii. 82–84, 92). He was so *Dsoul* called because he went from one end of the *Qarnaim.* earth to the other. In his expedition to the East by Tibet, he constructed the wall of Yadjoudj and Madjoudj (Gog and Magog.)

He appears to be claimed as a prophet by some, by others as an inspired man on the ground of *Gog and* the allusions in the Koran. The race of Gog *Magog.* and Magog are said to descend from two brothers, sons of Japheth, who, after the deluge, fixed their seat behind the mountains of the East. A fabulous account is given of these unbelievers, who were walled out by Dsoul Qarnaim. In another passage of the Koran it is foretold that they will come forth and spread over the earth (Sur. xxi. 96).

The Chronicle gives an account of the successors of
Alexander. Ptolemy Lagos, it is said, placed at Ailia
a chief from among the children of Israel that he
might practise the religion of the Law. Ptolemy
Decianus succeeded; and the commentaries say that
he ruled the "people of the cavern." At the end of
240 years the empire of the Greeks passed to the
Romans, to a man who descended from Esau, namely,
Augustus. He reigned fifty-six years; and

Augustus. in the forty-second year [1] of his reign Isa, son
of Mariam, was born. Between Isa and Alexander
there was a space of 319 years.

The Chronicle resumes the story of the kings of
Persia and of the princes after Alexander.

When the empire passed from the Greeks to the
Romans, a king came from Rome, crossed the Tigris,
and made conquests. His name was Antio-

Antiochus. chus. Aschk, son of Dara the elder, opposed
and slew him in battle. Several years after, Constantine, a king of Rome, came to avenge

Constantine. the death of Antiochus. One of the "kings
of the provinces" gave him battle, defeated him, and
pursued him to Rome, destroying that city. Then
Constantine fled and founded Constantinople.

Aschk was followed by another Aschk, and he again
by Schapour, who reigned sixty years.

The Asch-
kanian During this reign the children of Israel
kings. slew the prophet Yahia, son of Zachariah;
and they fell into the hands of Schapour, who slew
or reduced them to slavery.

In the fortieth year of Schapour, appeared Isa, son
of Mariam, the prophet.

The Chronicle continues the succession of the

---

[1] Other MSS. in the fifty-second year.

Aschkanian kings down to Ardeschir Bâbegân the Sassanide, who put an end to the "kings of the provinces," and recovered Syria and the Maghreb from the Romans. From the epoch of Alexander to him there elapsed 520 years.

Meantime there had passed among the children of Israel many events. Allah had granted to Zachariah the gift of prophecy and the authority over the holy place of Ailia, the temple and the worship. Mariam, daughter of Imram, had come into the world; she had been consecrated and brought into the temple as a child. Finally, the birth of Yahia, son of Zachariah, and the birth of Isa, son of Mariam, took place in the time of the Aschkanians. *Origin of the Christian Legend.*

During the time of the Ptolemies, the people were happy and the temple cult was flourishing. It is said that there were four thousand to five thousand servants who fasted by day and prayed by night, and who went not out of the temple. But there was no prophet among the children of Israel. Then Allah gave the gift of prophecy to Zachariah, and the people accepted him. He was son of Yahia, and descended from Radjaim, son of Suleiman. He was consecrated, like the four thousand servants in the temple. Now there was a custom among the Israelites that when a man offered a sacrifice to Allah during the pregnancy of his wife, he said, "O Lord, if there should be born to me a son, I will consecrate him to Thee," and the mother said the same thing. If the child was a girl, the vow was not obligatory. *The Prophet Zachariah.*

It is said that the origin of the custom of the consecration of children was the prescript of Allah to Musa in the Law, "I love for servants youths without sin." They were to be pure before Allah, and occupied all their life in His service. The sense of the word *mou'harrer* or *consecrated* is to be free from the occupations and cares of this world. When one had two sons, necessarily one of them must be consecrated.

The four thousand servants received Zachariah as their spiritual superior in the temple. He had a cousin, Imram, son of Mâtan, also a descendant of Suleiman, who was with him in the service of the temple, and beloved by him. There also was another man of the family of Zachariah, named Qâpour. He had two daughters, one of whom he gave in marriage to Imram, the other to Zachariah. The latter was called Isâ; she became mother of Yahia. The wife of Imram was called Hanna. Zachariah had no children; Imram had many; and when his wife became anew pregnant, the husband and wife both consecrated the child. This was Mariam; as it is said in the Koran, "The wife of Imram said: Lord, I have consecrated to thee the child in my womb" (Sur. iii. 31).

Allah here mentions the mother first, because the child has a more direct affinity with the mother. And there is in the word of the wife of Imram much precious instruction relative to the service of Allah. If one performs an act of submission, if the act be diminished and rendered improper, and the servant knows and confesses it, Allah pardons him, and accepts none the less his imperfect act. This was the case with the mother of Mariam. Believing that she should give birth to a child fit to be offered to God, she consecrated it beforehand. When she was delivered and saw that it was a girl, she was afflicted and ashamed because of the hindrance of her vow, and lamented. She craved pardon of Allah, pronouncing sadly these words, "I have given birth to a daughter." Allah accepted from her this girl as a boy, even as it is said in the Koran, "Her Lord accepted her with grace" (Sur. iii. 32).

Allah said in a vision to Zachariah, "Tell the mother of Mariam, I accept from thee this girl as a boy; take her to the temple and consecrate her." The Conse-cration of Mariam. Never before had a girl been consecrated in the temple, and none had been consecrated to remain there always, because woman is impure, and when subject to impurity may not remain in the temple, nor touch a book, nor recite prayers, even as a man who is subject to any defilement.

When the mother of Mariam brought her child to the temple, the servants and the devout were very astonished, and gathered about Zachariah the prophet and said to him, "What new custom has the wife of Imram introduced in consecrating her daughter?" And Zachariah said, "It is the order of Allah." Then they were appeased, and each desired to take and rear the child. But Zachariah said, "I have greater rights over her, for my wife is her aunt." They answered, "If any has greater rights over her than another, it is her mother." As they disputed thus with respect to Mariam, Zachariah said, "Let us cast lots, The Casting and he who shall be by lot indicated shall of Lots. take Mariam." They consented, and brought the reeds with which they wrote the Law, and each put his name on his reed; then they gathered them together and covered them with a turban. Then they said to one, "Put in thy hand and take out a reed; he whose name shall be written therein, shall bring up Mariam." It is said in the Koran, "Thou wert not among them when they cast their reeds" (Sur. iii. 39).

So they consulted the lot thrice, and thrice the name of Zachariah came forth. Then they knew that he had greater rights over her, and he took her; as it is said in the Koran, "Zachariah had care of her" (Sur. v. 32).

He constructed in the temple a cell for Mariam, and brought her up in it. He fixed upon it a lock, of which he kept the key always with him. When Mariam was five years old, he made a sanctuary for her in her cell, and there taught her the worship of Allah.

Zachariah was seventy years of age and had no children. He asked a child of Allah, but his wife was past the time of bearing. He had finally lost all hope of a child, and had ceased to pray for one. All his fatherly affection was given to Mariam, whom he brought up till she was twelve years old. None other than Zachariah had access to her. He opened the door once by day and once by night, gave her to eat and drink, and instructed her in worship.

One day Zachariah opened the door and found with Mary, though it was winter, fruits and other produce of summer. It is said in the Koran, "Each time that Zachariah entered, he found food with her" (Sur. iii. 32).

Allah sent to her in winter fruits of summer, that Zachariah might have no suspicion with respect to Mariam. For if it had been fruits of the season, terrestrial fruits, Zachariah might have thought that some one had had access to her by stratagem and brought her these fruits. But seeing fruits that existed not in the earth in this season, he suspected no one, and understood that they came from Allah. He said to Mariam, "Whence comes this?" She answered, "It comes from Allah, for Allah nourishes whom He wills without measure" (Sur. iii. 32). Zachariah understood that Allah alone could give these fruits at this epoch. He observed this appearance for one or two days, and he was struck with this thought, " If Allah can produce in the winter season the fruits of summer, He can cause me to beget a child, though I be hopeless thereof." He began to pray with a free heart, and asked of Allah that He would give him a child, as it is recorded in the Koran (Sur. v. 33).

It is said in the Koran, " Recite the mercy of thy Lord toward his servant Zachariah when he Birth of invoked his Lord with a secret invocation " Yahya, the son of (Sur. xix. 1–2). Zachariah.

He prayed in secret, because he and his wife were old, and they were ashamed to ask Allah publicly for children and to tell their friends. He prayed in secret, saying, " My bones are weakened, and my head shines with whiteness ; I have never been deceived in the prayers I have addressed to Thee. I fear my nephews who shall come after me " (Sur. iii. 5).

He signified by his nephews the children of Israel. He had no property that he should fear they would take away his heritage ; but when a prophet dies without leaving a successor, his people alter his religion and abandon the Book of Allah. Therefore he said, " Give me an heir coming from Thee, who may inherit from me and from the family of Yakoub ; and O Lord, cause him to be pleasing to Thee" (Sur. v. 6).

Allah sent Gabriel to announce to him the good news. Zachariah prayed in the sanctuary. Gabriel spoke to him with a loud voice, as it is said in the Koran, " The angels called him while he prayed in the sanctuary : Allah announces Yahya to thee " (Sur. iii. 33–34).

Again it is said, " O Zachariah ! we announce to thee a son, whose name shall be Yahya. We have given him this name that none have yet borne " (Sur. xix. 7–8).

Allah gave him the name Yahya because his parents were aged people, as if he had received life from two that were dead. Then Allah described to him Yahya, saying, "He shall confirm the Word of Allah; he shall be a lord, chaste, and a prophet of the number of the just" (Sur. iii. 34).

Allah gave the name of lord to no prophet but to Yahya. In the commentaries it is said that the meaning of the word is *clement*. Allah saith, "I have made him gentle that he may remove from my creatures their ills and their pains, that he may show gentleness and become great; for none become great except by gentleness; and greatness rests on gentleness and patience." Allah saith, "I have made him chaste, so that Yahya shall have no commerce with any women, because he shall know that men are destroyed by women. He shall be removed from women that he may not contract this habit, and he shall have no carnal need; however strong the desire in him, he shall surmount it."

Hearing these words, Zachariah was astonished, and said to Gabriel, "Whence shall I have a child? Old age hath reached me and my wife is barren" (Sur iii. 35). Gabriel answered: "Thus Allah doeth as He wills." Then Zachariah demanded a sign. And he said, "The sign that thou askest shall be that thou shalt not speak to men for three days except by sign" (v. 36).

Allah did not approve this demand of Zachariah. He said to him, "With this announcement of my messenger and of my angel thou dost still demand a sign?" Allah took away his speech from him, but hindered him not from pronouncing the name of Allah and praying, as it is said in the Koran, "Pronounce the name of God and His praises without ceasing, morning and evening."

And again: "Thou shalt not speak to men during three nights, though thou hast no infirmity" (Sur. xix. 11).

Zachariah was Imaum in the sanctuary of Ailia. When the time of prayer arrived and they were all assembled, he came out of the sanctuary and signed to them to go and pray, as it is recorded in the Koran, "And Zachariah went out of the sanctuary and made signs to them" (v. 12).

When Yahya was born, Allah granted him the quality of prophet, even during the lifetime of his father, and before the prophetic mission of Isa, who only obtained it after Yahya. It is said that Yahya was among the number of prophets to whom Allah granted a book. For it is said in the Koran, "O Yahya! take this book with firmness." Others say that the book meant is the Law (v. 13).

From his infancy Allah distinguished Yahya: "We have given him wisdom from his infancy," that he might know Allah and the prophets of Allah, and that he might confirm the mission of Isa while yet in his infancy.

"We have given him clemency and purity. He was neither violent nor disobedient" (v. 13, 14).

Then Allah blessed him and gave him salutation, saying, "Peace be on him, the day of his birth, and the day of his death, and the day that he shall rise" (v. 15).

The chronicler concludes this recital with the observation that it would not have been suitable to omit the story of a servant so great, praised by Allah in the Koran in terms so distinguished from his birth to the day when he shall appear before Him. Yahya is purely a Mussulman prophet.

There is not agreement as to the epoch of the birth of Isa. Some say that it was six months after that of Yahya; others say that it was three years later. The conception of Mariam and the birth of Isa are in the Koran mentioned in these terms: "Remember in the Book, Mariam, when she retired from her family to a place exposed to the sun.[1] She hid herself behind a veil. We sent to her our spirit, who appeared to her as a perfect man" (Sur. xix. 16–17).

In the Commentaries it is said that Mariam was not of mature age until she was in her thirteenth year. Gabriel was sent that he might breathe in her sleeve, so that she might conceive.

Imram was dead, they say, at the time of the conse-
Yussuf the cration of Mariam. Imram had a brother
Carpenter. Yakoub, son of Matan, who had a son in like manner consecrated. He was called Yussuf, and after the death of his father, had been brought up, like Mariam, in the temple. Zachariah confided the service of the temple to this cousin of Mariam, who having attained the age of thirteen years, learned the trade of carpenter. He served in the temple, and there did all the necessary carpenter's work.

Yussuf alone was suffered by Zachariah to enter the
The Annun- cell of Mariam; he carried water thither that
ciation. she might wash her head immediately before the visit of Gabriel. She had finished washing, she was purified, and covered with her garment when Gabriel appeared in the form of Yussuf the carpenter. She had seen no man except Zachariah and Yussuf. Thinking that this was the latter, she said, "I implore

[1] Hence, says Al Beidâwi, the custom of Orientation.

the protection of Allah against thee, if thou fearest him" (v. 18).

Gabriel, seeing that she feared, said to her, "I am the envoy of thy Lord, to give thee a holy son" (v. 19). "That is, a son pure from all taint. Allah hath created him in thy womb."

When she understood that it was not a man who spake with her, she became calm, and answered, saying, "How should I have a son, seeing that no man hath ever touched me, and that I am not a sinner?"

He answered, "Thus shall it be; thy Lord hath said, It is easy for me" (v. 20, 21).

Gabriel said, "Allah hath said: I will create this child without father, and I will make of him a prophet. It is the decree of the Lord that causes thee to give birth to a child without intercourse with a man. Allah hath called him Isa and Masich. When he shall be born, give him this name." It is said that Gabriel spoke to her further, as it is said in the Koran, "Allah announces to thee His word; he shall be called the Masich, Isa, son of Mariam" (Sur. iii. 40).

He was created, for Allah said, "Be," and he was, apart from human generation. The name Masich is a symbol; he shall so be called because whenever he shall place his hand on a sick person, there shall be instant cure, and the blind man shall recover his sight.

Then Gabriel added, "He shall be illustrious in this world and the next. He shall be of the familiars of God, and he shall speak to man in his cradle and in his full age, and he shall be of the number of the just. Allah shall teach him the Book of Wisdom, the Law, and the Gospel; and he shall be His apostle to the children of Israel" (Sur. iii. 41, 43).

When Mariam heard, she believed in the word of

Allah and in the revelation that Allah had sent by the mouth of Gabriel. She was convinced of its truth, and kept no doubt in her heart. Allah hath praised her in another place in the Koran, along with the believing wife of Pharaoun, who became a martyr for the faith, and was taken up living into Paradise: "And Mariam, the daughter of Imram, who preserved her chastity, and into whose womb we breathed of our spirit, and believed in the words of her Lord and his book, and was of the devout and obedient" (Sur. lxvi. 12).[1]

When Gabriel had comforted the heart of Mariam, he breathed upon her by order of Allah, and Mariam conceived of this pure breath, as it is said in the Koran, "Isa remained in the womb of his mother, and when she prayed, he offered his praises to Allah."

There are sectaries who pretend that Isa was the illegitimate son of Yussuf and Mariam; but they are condemned by the above passage in the Koran.

<small>Heresies concerning Mariam and Isa</small>

Isa was upon the earth an instrument of proof. He proved men, and by him a great number of the unbelievers were cast into hell, both among those heretics who have transgressed the bounds of belief, and among those who believe not at all.

The former have not understood the manner of the conception of Mariam nor the true rank of Allah. There are three sects among them. Some say that Allah is the third of three, the other two being Mariam and Isa. Others pretend that Allah is Isa, son of Mariam. He came down from heaven into the womb of Mariam,

---

[1] The commentators ascribe to the Prophet the saying that there had been many perfect among men, but only four among women : Asia, wife of Pharaoun ; Mariam, daughter of Imram ; Khadijah, the Prophet's first wife, and Fatima, his daughter.

went forth, and was shown to men under the human form. Then he returned to heaven. This their opinion has sprung from ignorance of the true power of God.

The belief of Islam is this : that Isa was in this world by the power of God and by His order. For The Creed of Allah had ordained that he should exist in Islam. the womb of his mother without the aid of a father; and He was! Even so with every other creation of which he said, "Be," and it was. Even so He created the heaven and the earth, men and angels. For all that God hath created or will create, He has no need of basis nor of model. Thus He created Adam from dust, without father or mother, as it is written in the Koran, "Isa is before Allah, even as Adam. He formed him from the dust, then He said, 'Be!' and he was" (Sur. iii. 52).

When the pregnancy of Mariam was far advanced, she was ashamed to show herself to Zachariah, The Birth and told Yussuf, her cousin, of the message of Isa. she had received. And Yussuf, knowing that no man had approached her, believed her word. As her hour drew near, she went out alone from the holy place and the city. She directed her steps to a withered palm-tree, whose leaves had fallen and whose branches were broken. She sat down beneath it, as it is written in the Koran, "The pains of birth came upon her under the trunk of a palm-tree" (Sur. xix. 23).

When she had brought forth Isa, pain and shame caused her to utter these words, "Would to God that I had died before this, and that I had been utterly forgotten!" And a voice beneath cried, "Be not grieved, for Allah hath provided a stream beneath thee; and shake the trunk of the palm-tree, and ripe dates shall fall for thee" (vers. 24–25).

Allah caused a spring of water to burst forth on the spot, that Mariam might wash herself and the babe. Then she shook the tree, and immediately dates sprung forth, ripened, and fell. She ate, and recovered strength. It is from Allah that the custom of giving dates to the newly accouchées has been learned.

And Gabriel said, "If thou see any man, say, 'Verily, I have vowed a fast unto the Merciful One : wherefore I will by no means speak to a man this day.'" So she brought the child to her people. They said, "O Mariam! now thou hast done a strange thing. O sister of Harun! thy father was not a bad man, neither was thy mother a harlot" (Sur. xix. 28–29).

She is here called sister of Harun, by way of explanation and reproach, because her brother Harun was a pious man. It is also said that there is an allusion to Harun, brother of Musa, because the father of Mariam descended from Suleiman, son of David, who descended from Harun. Even as when one is designated by the name of his tribe, "brother of Temim, or of Aad," Mariam is thus designated as member of the tribe of Harun. According to another account, Harun was a perverse man in the midst of the children of Israel, and they reproached her with likeness to him.

Mariam answered not, but pointed to Isa, as it is written in the Koran. And they said, "How shall we speak to an infant in the cradle?" And he spoke, saying, "I am the servant of Allah; He hath given me the Book, and hath made me a prophet, and hath made me blessed wheresoever I may be, and hath commanded me prayer and alms so long as I shall live; and made me dutiful to my mother, and hath not made me proud or unhappy. And peace on

Isa Speaks in the Cradle.

me the day wherein I was born, and the day wherein I shall die, and the day wherein I shall be raised to life" (Sur. xix. 30 *seq.*).

It was thus that Allah caused the child to speak, to show his prophetic character; and Isa thus purged Mariam, Zachariah, and Yussuf the carpenter from the accusation which weighed upon them. He established first his quality of SERVANT OF ALLAH, and so gave the lie to those heretics concerning the three things which they say of him, and which are not suitable to Allah. Then he said that Allah had given him the BOOK, that is, had taught him the GOSPEL. When his mother prayed, he, in the womb of his mother, recited the Gospel and addressed praises to Allah. Finally, he said, "Allah hath made me PROPHET, though I be still a child." None had before been prophet in his infancy. Then he added, "I am blessed, &c., that men may learn of me knowledge and wisdom; He has given me the Way of Religion, that they may find the right path." It is written, "Such was Isa, son of Mariam, according to the Word of Truth, of which they doubt. It is not for Allah to have any son; Allah forbid! When He decrees a thing, He only saith unto it, Be, and it is!" (Sur. xix. 36).

The holiness of Allah comports not with wife, nor with children, nor partners.

It is related that at the moment of the birth of Isa, all the idols in the earth were overthrown The Fall of and fell to the earth. And all the dæmons the Idols. of the earth gathered about Eblis and said to him, "There has passed an event upon the earth, we know not what it is." Eblis undertook to travel on the earth, and marched three days and three nights, till he came near Isa, who was just born. He understood that this was the event, and would exert his power on Isa. But the angels repulsed him; for the mother of Mariam had placed Mariam and her son under the keeping of Allah against the Divs, saying on the day of the birth of Mariam, "I put her under Thy protection, her and her posterity, against Satan, driven away with stones" (Sur. iii. 31).[1]

"Our prophet," the Chronicle adds, "hath said, No child sees the day without being subject to Eblis, except Isa, son of Mariam."

Then Eblis said to the dæmons, "The event is that a child is born to a woman without concourse of a father. He shall be prophet of Allah and illustrious. If to-day all the idols of the earth are fallen, know that later this child shall procure us joy." They said, "How?" And Eblis said, "Many men shall be infidel because of him, and shall go to hell."

Like other prophets distinguished by Allah,—Ibrahim, Musa, and Mohammed, who had to undergo flight and exile,—Isa was destined to flee. His mother Mariam took him and transported him from his birthplace to a place situated a month's journey from the holy place, in Egypt, and caused him to dwell there thirty years. Then he returned to Syria, Palestine, and made his message known to men, and taught them the Gospel, and the precepts of the Gospel.

Flight of Mariam with Isa.

The cause of the flight was this: Isa was born after Alexander, in the time of the "kings of the provinces." All the lands situated beyond the Tigris, as far as Egypt, Yemen, and the Maghreb, were under the dominion of the Greeks, as the Chronicle has told. At the epoch

---

[1] The legend is here explicative or ætiologic of the custom of the pilgrimage of Mecca, of throwing stones at the devil in the valley of Mina.

of Isa there was a Greek king named Augustus. Some
say that he was a Roman and emperor of Rome. He
reigned fifty-six years, and in the forty-second year of
his reign Isa was born.

There was in Palestine, Syria, a king appointed by
Augustus named Herod. He treated with kindness
the children of Israel, the temple and the servants of
the temple, and favoured Zachariah. When Herod
heard of the birth of Isa, son of a virgin, he was astonished. Ten days later there came men from Syria to
the holy place to see Isa. They were learned astrologers, who had found in their books that on such a day
a child, of maiden born, would see the light. They
came, bringing gold, myrrh, and incense; and Herod
sent and inquired of them the reason of their coming.
According to another account, they had been sent by
a king of one of the towns of Syria, who had read in
the stars; or it was a king of Persia, read in the books
of Daniel, who had sent them. Herod inquired the
significance of their presents, and they said, "Gold is
the most precious of all the jewels of the world, even
as this child is above all creatures of the world. Myrrh
is a cure for all kinds of wounds, and this child shall
cure wounds, maladies, and infirmities by his efficacious
prayer with Allah. Incense is an aroma the odour and
smoke of which rise in the air to heaven, a property that
belongs to no other perfume. When this child shall
be great, Allah shall raise him to heaven. These three
objects then are his symbols."

Then Herod was jealous of Isa, and resolved, when
these men were gone, to slay him. Mariam was warned
of the design, some say by a divine inspiration, others
by a revelation, an angel having brought her the order
to remove Isa from the holy place. She mounted an

P

ass, took Isa before her, and caused Yussuf the carpenter, her cousin, to accompany her. She quitted Palestine, passed the frontier of Syria, and repaired to Egypt. She took up her abode in one of the villages of that land, and brought up Isa with great care. It is said that she and Yussuf gleaned ears of corn. Mariam intrusted Isa to no one, and sometimes gleaned having him attached to her back.

The village where they lived, seated on a lofty hill, had many springs and was full of delights. Some say that it was in Syria, in the *Ghawtah* of Damascus, in the midst of the sand,—one of four places celebrated in the book *Masâlek* for delights. The Koran says, "We appointed the son of Mariam and his mother for a sign; and we prepared for them an abode in an elevated place of the earth, sure and provided with springs" (Sur. xxiii. 52).[1]

The Chronicle comments: "Allah said: As Mariam and her son had no safety at the holy place, because of the fear which the king inspired them with, I have given them surety in a delightful village, full of springs and abundance."

Mariam educated Isa till he was twelve years old. There was in the village a farmer who was kind to the poor. Each evening the poor ate in his house, and often many passed the night there. His house was never empty of poor. Mariam and Isa were often there, and the farmer showed them kindness, saying, "It is a strange woman and a young orphan." And Mariam was freed from care with respect to him.

The Rearing of Isa.

---

[1] The commentators cannot fix the topography; whether the hill be at Ailia, Damascus, Ramleh, in Palestine, or Egypt. It is the religious ideal which absorbs thought.

The first miracle that Isa wrought when he had attained the age of twelve was this. One day the treasure of the farmer had been robbed, and knowing not to whom to impute the theft, he was greatly grieved, as was also Mariam. Seeing his mother in sadness, Isa inquired the reason. She said, "This farmer, who treats us with so much kindness, is afflicted by the loss of his goods." Isa went and found him and said, "Bring all the poor who have passed the night in thy house." The farmer did so. Among them there was a blind man, who, apart from this infirmity, was in good health, and a lame man, who also was in good health. Isa bade the lame man seat himself on the neck of the blind man. He did so, and the blind man was bidden to rise. The blind man said, "I am too weak to rise." Isa said, "How couldst thou rise yester evening?" Then he made him rise, and said, "Yester evening thou didst thus: This lame man tied a cord between his shoulders, and put the end of the coil between the hands of the blind man, who dragged the other to the place of the treasure, where he took the money; then he carried it in the same way out of the house, and himself went in again." Both confessed the deed, and restored the money to the farmer, who was filled with joy, and offered a part of it to Mariam. As she would not accept, he said to her, "Give it to thy son." But he would not accept it. Then the farmer said, "Remain, thou and thy son, in my house, and go not elsewhere." Mariam consented, and remained with Isa in the house of the farmer, who made Isa his treasurer.

A second miracle which the farmer saw Isa work was the following. He had made a great feast to celebrate the wedding of his son, and had invited a large

The First Miracle of Isa.

number of guests.   At this epoch the drinking of wine
was permitted, only later Allah had forbidden it in the
Koran.   After the wedding the farmer received one
day some guests, and the wine failed.   He was vexed,
and Isa seeing this, went into the house where there
were twelve pitchers, passed his hand over each and
went his way.   And all the pitchers over which Isa
had passed his hand were filled with wine.   Thus each
day he wrought a new miracle till he had attained the
age of thirty years.

Then King Herod died, and his son Archelaus succeeded him.   He was succeeded by his son Herod,
who is called Herod the younger, while his grandfather
is called Herod the elder.   When Isa had completed
thirty years, Allah taught him the Gospel entirely, and
instructed him in knowledge and wisdom, and he laid
down the precepts of the Gospel and of religion.   Isa
wrought many miracles in Syria in the midst of man.
Allah said to him in the revelation, "Return to the
holy place and call men to Allah, that they may believe
in thy quality of prophet.   Preach to them the Law,
the Gospel, and my religion, that they may receive it."
So Isa and Mariam returned to the holy place at Ailia.
At the time they had quitted Ailia, Zachariah had
been slain.

When Herod had heard of the story of the birth of
Isa, and that Mariam had fled into Syria, the
children of Israel said to Zachariah, "Thou
hast been prophet, but thou art become infidel,
for thou hast been guilty of fornication with
Mariam ; and for fear that she should tell us, thou
hast sent her into Syria and Egypt."   Then they would
slay him, and told Herod, saying, "This man must be
slain, because he has committed fornication with

The Murder of Zachariah and the Pro-phetic Func-tion of Yahya.

Mariam." Now the king sought Isa to slay him, and when they told him that Zachariah had removed Isa and Mariam, he ordered that Zachariah should be pursued and put to death. Zachariah fled in the direction of Syria to rejoin Mariam. The children of Israel pursued him. At the gate of Ailia there was a hollow tree; Zachariah hid himself therein, and when his pursuers came, they did not perceive that he had gone in. Then Eblis appeared to them and said, "Zachariah is in this tree; cut it with a saw; you shall see if he is therein, and you shall cut him with the tree; if he is not therein, you shall have no great damage." They found his reasoning just, and brought a saw, and sawed the tree and Zachariah in two. His blood flowed. None knew of this event. Some say that Allah had given the tree the command to open, that Zachariah might go in, and then to close again. When the tree closed, Eblis seized a part of the cloak of Zachariah, so that it remained outside the cleft. When the others came, they recognised by this sign that Zachariah was in the tree. But this account is not exact. For the same God who could dispose the tree that he might enter, could have taken from Eblis the part of the cloak.

After the death of Zachariah, Yahya remained hidden till the death of Herod. Allah gave him the quality of prophet, and he fulfilled his mission among the people. When he had fulfilled thirty years, the children of Israel recognised him as a prophet. He taught the Law and called men to Isa, preaching to them the coming of Isa, who should work miracles and bring from heaven a Book and a Law. When Isa came, the first who believed in him and his mission was Yahya, as it is said in the Koran, "Verily Allah promiseth

thee Yahya, who shall confirm the Word from God"
(Sur. iii. 34).

When Allah had caused Isa to enter again the holy
city among the children of Israel, he conferred upon him the quality of prophet and
gave him the Gospel. Isa went into the
temple and called the people to Allah and recited to
them the Gospel. The first who believed on him was
Yahya. Isa said to them as it is recorded in the Koran,
"I come to you with a sign from Allah." They
answered, "What is this sign?" He said, "I will
make from clay the figure of a bird; I will breathe
thereon, and by the permission of Allah it shall become
a true bird" (Sur. iii. 43). They said, "Do it!"
Then Isa made them a bat, which is visible every morning and night, and which up to that time had not
existed in the world. They formed this figure of clay,
and Isa breathed thereon, and the bird flew into the
air. It is the strangest of all birds. While others fly
by means of their wings, this has none upon its whole
body. It is composed only of flesh and bone, yet it
flies. The people said to Isa, "Hast thou no other
sign?" He said, "I cure the blind from birth, and
the lepers." Had Isa cured only ordinary blindness,
he would have done the work of a simple physician;
it would not have been the work of a prophet. But
Isa cured the blind from birth, which the physicians,
by their confession, cannot cure, and thus he showed
his quality of prophet; and so with the leprosy, which
the physicians are impotent to cure.

Then the people said, "Hast thou another sign?"
Isa said, "I raise the dead by the order of
Allah: whom would ye that I should raise?"
They inquired who was he that had been

The Pro-
phetic Office
of Isa.

Raising of
Sem from
the Dead.

longest dead; for they saw not who could have died
before Noe and his sons. In the midst of the mountains of Palestine there is a valley in which was buried,
as they had found in the Law, Sem, son of Noe, the ancestor of the children of Israel. The children of Israel
said to Isa, "The tomb of Sem, son of Noe, is in this
valley; he is our ancestor; raise him." Isa stood at the
end of the valley surrounded by the people. He cried
with a loud voice, "Sem, son of Noe, arise, by the
command of Allah!" Then the earth opened where he
was buried; Sem raised his head and shook the earth
from his hands and his face. His beard was all white;
none had had the beard white before Ibrahim. The
children of Israel said, "O Isa! it is not Sem, son of
Noe, for his beard is white." Isa spake thus to him,
"Who art thou?" He answered, "I am Sem, son of
Noe." Then Isa said, "Who am I?" The other said,
"Thou art Isa, son of Mariam, prophet of Allah." Isa
continued, "Wherefore is thy beard white, since in
thy time none was white, and that all died having their
hair black?" Sem answered, "I also died having
black hair; but when I heard thy voice, I thought that
it was that of Israfil, and that it was the day of the
last judgment, and then my hair became white."

Isa said, "Wilt thou, O Sem, that I ask of God that
He will grant thee to live with me?" Sem said, "O
prophet of Allah! though I should live yet a long time,
I must die at last. I remember still the bitterness of
death; I would not know it a second time. Ask of
Allah that He will cause me to return to the earth in
my former state." Isa prayed, and Sem disappeared in
the tomb, and the earth covered him as before. Not
being able to deny the event, there were those who
said that Sem was raised, but that he remained only one

hour seated in his tomb, without speaking; that he fell back afterwards, and that the earth covered him as before.

Another miracle wrought by Isa was this.   He said, "I will tell you what you have eaten and what you have kept in your houses." He said to each one, "Thou hast eaten yester evening such a thing, and there has remained so much."   He added, "These things are signs for ever if ye are believers.   I come to confirm the Law, and I make lawful for you certain things which are forbidden" (Sur. iii. 43–44).

Among the things forbidden in the Law and that Isa permitted was mutton-fat.

It is said in the Koran, "We have forbidden them all animals having a hoof, and of bullocks and sheep we forbade them the fat of both," &c. (Sur. vi. 147). But this was permitted by the Law of the Gospel; and when our Prophet appeared, he also permitted what was permitted by the Law of the Gospel. Another interdiction of the Law which was abolished by the Gospel was that of fishing on the Sabbath-day.   It was forbidden to work on the Sabbath-day, but Isa, according to the Law of the Gospel, permitted it, and after him our Prophet also.[1]

When Isa had wrought all these miracles before the people, who saw and heard them, they remained infidel and would not believe.   They said, "All this is of magic."   It is said in the Koran, "Isa, son of Mariam, said: O children of Israel! I am the apostle of God, sent to you to confirm the Law that was before me, and to announce an apostle who shall come after me, and whose name shall be Ahmed.   And when he pro-

---

[1] See Surah lxii. 6 seq. The allusion appears to be simply to the Friday, the Moslem "day of assembly."

duced evident signs, they said, It is evident magic "
(Sur. lxi. 6).[1]

Abd-allah-ibn-Abbas says, "No prophet has come to
the perfect fulfilment of his mission without having
announced the coming of Mohammed and promised it."
In the Commentaries it is recorded that Isa remained
thus two years among the people, and that he accomplished his divine mission, working miracles and deeds
of wisdom. He was wont to travel, and never remained
two nights in the same place; none knew of his house,
his hut, his horse, or his ass.

After he had made known his mission to the people
of Palestine, and none believed on him, Isa, because
of their unbelief, abandoned them, and went from
town to town in Syria, Egypt, Yemen, as far as the
Maghreb, and, leaving no town on one side, called men
to Allah.

At first, on quitting the holy place at Ailia, none
was with him except his twelve disciples. The Twelve
They were fullers, called in Arabic *qaṣṣar*. Disciples.
They are also called *hawâri*, "because they whiten
garments." The day that Isa perceived that the
people of Ailia, in spite of the miracles they had
seen, remained infidel, like King Herod, he left the
city and turned to Allah, seeking some one who might
recognise and believe in him, and he said, "Who will
be my helpers unto God?" (Sur. iii. 45). The disciples
said, "We will be the helpers of God" (Sur. iii. 46).

Then these men left their trade of fulling, and went

[1] There can be no doubt that the Moslem doctors are sincere when they
insist that the passage in the Fourth Gospel of the Church (John xvi. 7)
concerning the coming of the Paraclete—the Periclyte, as they insist the
word should be—refers to their Prophet Mohammed; and it is one among
many incidental proofs of the priority of the Koran over the New Testament.

with Isa. In every town there were persons who believed, and others who were infidel. The believers followed Isa, but the disciples occupied the first rank. It is said of them in the Koran, "O ye who believe, be the helpers of God," *i.e.*, be subject to Mohammed and protect the religion of Allah, "even as Isa, son of Mariam, said to the apostles: Who will be my helpers unto Allah? And the apostles answered: We will be the helpers of Allah" (Sur. lxi. 14).

"Do as they did, who were less than you," says the chronicler. "A part of the children of Israel believed, and a part believed not; but we strengthened those who believed above their enemy; wherefore they became victorious."

The Chronicle states that Tabari has recorded none of the stories relative to Isa. He has simply said, in reference to his prophetic action, that Isa came to the children of Israel in the quality of a prophet; that he remained three years among them; that none believed on him; that he was seized to be put to death, and that Allah raised him to heaven.

But the narratives of Isa, his miraculous and prophetic acts, are too remarkable to be thus curtailed. There are many in the Koran, and the others which have been recounted have been taken from the Commentaries. The following history is well known; it is found in the Koran, and is too admired by men to be omitted after that Allah has related it in the Koran.

It is recorded in the Koran :—"The apostles said: O Isa, son of Mariam! is thy Lord able *History of the Table from Heaven.* to cause a table to descend unto us from heaven?" (Sur. v. 112).

Wherever Isa went upon the earth, he was accompanied by a multitude of believers, and also by a multitude of unbelievers, who followed him to see his miracles. One day, going to the west, he came into a country of Egypt called Andalos. The men had no provisions and were hungry. They found the apostles, and said to them, "Speak to Isa, that he ask of Allah to send food from heaven, that we may satisfy ourselves, and at the same time there may be a miracle." The apostles spoke to Isa. He answered, "Fear Allah, if ye are believers." They said, "We desire to eat and that our hearts may be revived; we shall know that thou hast spoke the truth, and we shall bear witness thereof" (Sur. v. 113).

Then Isa prayed, saying, "O Lord, cause a furnished table to descend unto us from heaven" (Sur. v. 114). The word *maïdé* in the text of the Koran designates a table or cloth on which bread and other food is placed. Isa added, "Let it be a feast-day for the first and the last among us, and a sign from Thee. Feed us, for Thou art the best provider."

The commentators explain the words "first" and "last" by "our time and our people and our co-religionaries who shall be after us." Allah said, "I will cause it to descend to you; but whosoever among you shall disbelieve hereafter, I will punish him with a chastisement the like of which no creature hath felt" (Sur. v. 115).

Isa announced this to the disciples, and caused men to know this condition. Next day all the people were gathered together, and Isa prayed. Men lifted their eyes to heaven. Then a table appeared in the air, and came down before Isa and his disciples. It was covered with a cloth. Isa stretched forth his hand and seized the cloth. Twelve white loaves were placed upon it, according to the number of the disciples, a great fish fried, salt, and vegetables. According to Abd-allah-ibn-Abbas, there were all the kinds of vegetables in the world, except the porrum, garlic, and onion. The men sat and ate, and were satisfied. When one ate a morsel of bread or of fish or of vegetable, an equal quantity always replaced that which had been taken. In the evening, after all had eaten, the table returned to heaven. This day was a Sunday. The morrow, at the moment of breakfast, the table came down again; all ate, and with the evening it returned to heaven. And so on the third day; then it returned not. Among these men there were unbelievers who had shared in the meals, and who said, "This is of magic, which lasts three days and not more." Then they slept the night, and on the morrow, when they rose, they were changed into swine and entirely disfigured.

According to another story, no table came down from heaven, but the miracle passed thus. One day Isa said to the apostles, "Have you nothing to eat?" One of them, named Simeon, offered him two fried fish and five cakes. Isa divided them into small pieces, and Allah sent his benediction, so that all the people ate thereof and were satisfied, and each had food during three days. In spite of that, the fish and the cakes were not diminished. Then some remained unbelieving, and Allah changed them into swine. So they lived for three days, then they died; for this metamorphosis is a chastisement of Allah. He who is smitten by it cannot live, and has no posterity.

Some theologians deny this event, and say the table did not come down from heaven. When the apostles had demanded it of Isa, and Isa had prayed, and caused them to know the condition of the severe chastisement if they remained unbelieving, they answered, " We have no need of the table, for we are believers, and faithful to our belief."

The Chronicle here digresses in order to narrate the story of another metamorphosis in the olden time, near to that of David and Sulei- man—of certain villagers who had sinned against the law of the Sabbath, and were changed into apes (Sur. xvii 163). Sin against the Law of the Sabbath.

Not only had the fish enjoyment of sabbatic repose, but stags and other beasts of chase, when they enter the sacred territory of Mecca, are safe and friendly with man. Here is an instruction from Allah. The animals are inspired by him.

The transgression of the Sabbath took place when there was no prophet in Syria, but there were wise men who exhorted the sinners; and occasion is here taken to dwell upon the duty of mutual exhortation among believers to the doing of good and the avoiding of evil (Sur. ix. 72).

To return to the narrative of Tabari.

He says that Isa remained three years among the people. But in the books which treat of the narratives of the prophets it is said that he remained only two years. Towards the end of his life he returned to the holy place of Ailia, after the event of the table coming down from heaven. The people resolved to slay him, and gained the friendship of the king of Ailia, Herod the younger, who followed the religion of the Greeks. They said to him, " Isa is a magician who deceives the people." Herod gave them orders to slay him. Then they sought to seize Isa, but he hid himself; they could not find him in any house.

One night he was with his disciples in a house, and said to them, " Pray this night for me." But they fell into a heavy sleep. Isa said, "Ye have delivered me to my enemies. It shall come to pass also that ye shall deny me and betray me."

The next day, one of his disciples, Simeon, went The Betrayal of Isa. out. The people seized him, saying, "It is a companion of Isa. Show us where Isa is." Simeon said, "I have forsaken Isa, and am not of his friends." He denied and became infidel. Then they seized another disciple who had gone out, and said to him, "Show us where is Isa, or we will put thee to death." The disciple said, "If ye give me a reward, I will tell you where he is." They consented, and this disciple sold Isa for thirty dirhems, and took them to the house where Isa was. The people seized him, and tied him head and feet, and the disciples fled. The people said to Isa, "Thou hast practised magic before men, and thou hast said that thou raisest the dead; wherefore now dost thou not deliver us from the hands of men?" They dragged him to a place where they had made ready a cross to crucify him, and a great number of the people gathered around him. They had a chief named Isoua, who was also among them. When they would bind Isa to the cross, Allah removed him from their sight, and gave the form and aspect of Isa to Isoua, their chief.

When Isa disappeared, they were astonished, and Crucifixion of Isoua in Isa's Stead. said, "He employs magic and has escaped from our eyes. Wait a little and the effect will soon be past, and he will reappear; for the magic has no duration." When they looked, they saw Isoua entirely like to Isa, and they seized him; and he said, "I am Isoua." They answered, "Thou liest; thou art Isa, and thou didst escape our eyes by magic; now the magic is past, and thou hast become visible." He protested in vain that he was Isoua; they slew him and bound him to the cross. As for Isa, Allah raised him to heaven, as it is said in the Koran, "They have not slain and have not crucified him, but some one who resembled him" (Sur. iv. 156).

Isoua remained on the cross for seven days. Each night Mariam, the mother of Isa, came and wept at the foot of the cross till morning. The eighth day Allah caused Isa to come down from heaven to Mariam. This night Mariam saw him, and knew that he was not dead, and her heart was consoled. Isa was that night in the house of Mariam, and caused Yahya, son of Zachariah, to be called. The apostles had been at first of the number twelve. One of them, Simeon, had denied Isa, and another had sold him for thirty dirhems and had delivered him to " the Jews;" there remained only ten. Isa this night caused them to be sought for, but found only seven. He inquired of them, "Where is he from among you who sold me for thirty dirhems and delivered me to the Jews?" They answered, "He repented, and knowing that he has committed a crime, has slain himself." Isa said, "If Allah accepted his repentance, he ought not to have slain himself; for there is no sin which may not be repaired by the pardon of Allah."

Then Isa commanded Yahya and the seven disciples to keep his faith and call men to Allah. He sent them each into a part of the world to call men to Allah, to the belief of his mission, of his religion and of the Gospel. He sent two disciples to Rome and into Greece, one called Peter, the other Paul, and confided all the West to them. He sent another named Thomas to Babylon

The Seven Apostles.

Peter and Paul.

Thomas.

and into Iraq, and confided to him all the East;
Philip.   another, Philip, to Kairouan; another, John,
John.   to Ephesus, whence were the "people of the
cavern." He ordered another to remain at Ailia with
James.   Yahya, son of Zachariah; his name was James.
He sent another into the Hedjaz towards Maghreb;
Bartholo-   his name was Bartholomew. When Isa had
mew.   appointed these seven disciples [1] and Yahya
his successors, and had given them his commands, he
Ascension of blessed Mariam, and towards dawn prayed
Isa   Allah to raise him to heaven. The heretics
to-day celebrate as a feast the night when Isa descended and went up again to heaven. They burn
perfume and incense in great quantities in their houses
and in the churches.

The next day the apostles presented themselves in
the midst of the people and said, "This night Isa descended from heaven and commanded us to call men
to the belief of his prophetic mission." The people
seized them, struck them, and detained them, making
them undergo violence that they might be forced to
deny Isa; but the apostles refused. While Herod the
Tiberius and younger reigned at Ailia, the king of Rome
Herod be- was informed that among the children of
come Be-
lievers. Israel a man had appeared named Isa, who
had wrought miracles before men, and who had
come fatherless into the world; that the Jews had
killed and crucified him, and that now they tormented
his companions to make them deny him. The king
of Rome came with a numerous army to Ailia, and
slew a great number of the people. He delivered the
apostles from their hands, believed in the religion of

---

[1] In the work of Kessæus, cited by Sike, p. 691, the names of twelve
disciples are given.

Isa, and took with him those of them whom Isa had appointed his representatives at Rome.   He commanded the others to traverse the world and call men to the religion of Isa, as he had ordained.   Herod, king of Ailia, also accepted the religion of Isa, and followed the words of the two apostles whom Isa had appointed at Ailia, and many men believed in Isa and his faith, which spread in Syria.

The king of Rome took the wood on which they said Isa was crucified and made of it a Qiblah. *The Cross becomes a Qiblah.* Christians when they pray place it before them, pretending that it is the wood on which Isa was crucified, and that from thence Allah raised him to heaven. For this reason they show reverence for this wood.

But their pretension is not based on fact.   For it was not Isa who was crucified on the wood, but some one who resembled him ; and Allah raised Isa to heaven before he was upon the cross, as it is related in the Koran (Sur. iv. 156).

When the religion of Isa was greatly spread abroad, Eblis made his appearance, and on a feast-day, when a great number of men, followers of Isa, were gathered in the temple at Ailia, *Heresies concerning Isa.* he presented himself there, accompanied by two Divs. They had taken the form of three old men, sat in the midst of the people and entered into conversation, saying, "We have all three come from the west. Having heard speak of your religion, we have found it good, and have believed ; but we have desired to hear what you say concerning Isa."   The men answered, "Isa is the prophet, the spirit of Allah, and the son of Mariam ; he was not begotten of a father."   Eblis said, "This is not possible.   I think that Allah is the father of Isa."   One of the Divs said, "This word is a folly,

Q

for Allah hath no children and hath no commerce with a woman; but Isa is Allah himself, who came down from heaven and entered the womb of Mariam. He went forth to show himself to men under the form of a man, then he returned to heaven; for Allah hath power to be where He wills, and to show to men what He wills." The other Div said, "Your words are insensate. For me, I hold that Allah loved Mariam, and caused Isa to be born from her without father; and He has established him among men as a sign of His omnipotence; then He associated with Himself Isa and Mariam, that they might be honoured equally with Allah."

That day Eblis showed himself to men and then disappeared. These words fell into the hearts of men, who said, "Necessarily Isa must be in one of these three conditions." Then when Eblis and his companions had disappeared, he led men astray, who pretended that it was three angels whom Allah had ordered to instruct us on the true origin of Isa. Then the heretics were divided into three sects, each of which accepted one of these three doctrines, which since then have remained among them.

All Gentiles have become infidel in respect to Allah on the subject of Isa; they know neither Allah nor Isa.

Some say that the event of the three Divs and their discourse took place in the lifetime of Isa; but this is not so. It was after Isa that the occurrence took place in the midst of the people.

When Isa had ascended to heaven the apostles spread his religion among men, and each betook himself to the land that Isa had assigned to him, and called men to Allah. Yahya, son of Zachariah, and the Apostle James remained King Herod treated them kindly and accepted

Death of Mariam and Murder of Yahya, Son of Zachariah.

at Ailia.

the religion of Isa.   Mariam died six months after Isa.

Now the king had a niece named Herodias; according to another story, she was the daughter of his wife. The king loved this young girl and desired to espouse her; on this he consulted Yahya. But he said, "It is not lawful for thee to espouse her, for according to the Law and the Gospel it is forbidden to a man to wed the daughter of his brother or the daughter of his wife." So Yahya dissuaded him. Then the young girl and her mother were angered against Yahya, and the former received the following instructions from the mother: "When the king shall tell thee to demand a grace (each day she had liberty to demand a grace), say, I desire that thou cause Yahya, son of Zachariah, to be slain." When she made this request, the king said, "Ask something else, for Yahya is a prophet of Allah, who must not be slain." Next day the young girl repeated her demand, but the king granted it not. Then the mother and the daughter waited till one day the king made a banquet. Then the mother adorned the young girl with fine raiment, and brought her before the king, that she might serve him to drink. When he was drunk, and had returned to his room, he called the young girl and would approach her; but she said, "I will not give myself to thee unless thou place here before me the head of Yahya." The king in his drunkenness ordered that Yahya should be put to death. He was beheaded, and his head was carried in a dish and presented to the woman. Then the head began to speak, and said to the king, "It is not lawful for thee to take this woman." The king was filled with terror and remorse. The blood of Yahya, in the place where it had been poured, ceased not to boil. When the king was informed of it, he ordered the earth to be covered; but the blood ceased not to boil, however great the quantity of earth cast upon it.

There was a king of Persia, on the hither side of Tigris, one of the kings of the provinces, of the Aschkanian race, named Kherdous. He was warned that the children of Israel had just killed their prophet Yahya, and that they had crucified another prophet named Isa. He was wroth with them, gathered an army and marched against Ailia. He halted at the gates of the city and ordered his general to enter, saying, "I have vowed that I will slay of these people so many that the blood shall flow as a river." The name of this general was Pirouzadan. When he came into the city, and saw the blood of Yahya boiling, he asked what was this blood. The people answered, "It is the blood of the sacrifices that we have offered to Allah, which he has not accepted." The general, knowing that they spake not the truth, brought them by pressing questions to confess, saying, "It is the blood of a prophet who has been slain among us; you are come to punish us for this." The general asked what was necessary that rest might be given to the blood; they said, "Unless thou bringest the murderer and slayest him by pouring his blood on this, the blood of Yahya will not cease to boil." But none knew where the murderer was, and King Herod was hidden. Then the king of Persia caused a massacre of the children of Israel, men and women, pouring their blood on the boiling blood of Yahya; but it ceased not to boil until 70,000 persons had been slain.[1]

King Kherdous. (margin note)

---

[1] There are other accounts, showing how impressive was the idea of the boiling blood which cried out for vengeance.

Then the general caused inquiry to be made of the king, who was outside the city, what he should do. The king said, " Continue the massacre until the blood flows into my camp." Pirouzadan pitied the children of Israel, and bade them gather all their beasts together for slaughter, that the blood might flow to the camp of the king. And they did so   Then the king ordered the general to profane the temple by casting into it impure objects, and finally that he should destroy the temple. He put an impost on the people, and promised to remit it from those who should cast filth into the temple. All did so; and the temple and city were entirely destroyed, more so than in the time of Nabuchodonosor. All descendants of the prophets were taken into captivity.

It is told that Pirouzadan afterwards embraced the " Jewish " religion and separated from the king, who left the children of Israel captive in his kingdom until his death. Then they returned to the holy place and rebuilt the city.

Some traditionists say that this Persian king was Nabuchodonosor; an anachronism which the chronicler corrects: King Kherdous was contemporary with the successors of Alexander.

Some also here connect the prophet Daniel and five other descendants of the prophets with this king, assumed to be Nabuchodonosor. It was reported to him that Daniel and his com- *The Prophet Daniel in the Lions' Den.* panions followed another religion than his, and that they ate not the flesh of sacrifices. When interrogated, they avowed that they worshipped Allah. Then the king ordered a great pit to be dug, and them to be cast in along with a famished lion. They were left there a whole day. In the evening, the king, looking in the trench, saw the lion couched far from the men, who were in all safety, and with them a seventh person. He made them come forth, and asked them who was this other person. Now it was an angel, who struck the king on the face, and changed him into a wild beast. He went forth from his kingdom, and lived with the beasts of the desert seven years; then he died.

Tabari, however, says that this legend is false; that this king was not Nabuchodonosor, but Kherdous; also that every king who did evil was called by the children of Israel Nabuchodonosor;[1] and so in this sense Kherdous may be called by that name.

The chronicler, continuing, says that under the Romans Syria and Rome formed one empire, and that kings of Rome succeeded one another from Tiberius, under whom the death of Isa took place, and who became a follower of his religion, down to Heraclius, in whose time Mohammed appeared. He has not a solitary word of those fables of the Synagogue which tell of wars of the Romans against the Jews during this period. The Aschkanian kings reigned on the other side the Tigris as far as Reï, and when they ceased to reign the Arabs occupied their place. For they had been ill at ease in the desert, in the Hedjaz, and in Yemen. They came and dwelt in Bahram and in the Yemana; and when the Aschkanian kings quitted Iraq, the Arabs came forth from the territory of Koufa and Hora and occupied Iraq. A portion of the territory remained in the power of the "kings of the provinces," who were not subject to the Arabs. The Arabs occupied all the land of Iraq to the frontiers of Syria. Syria with Rome formed the empire of the Romans.

[1] An important fact in reference to the Biblical legends of Nebuchadnezzar.

Ardeschin subdued the "kings of the provinces," and made himself master of the lands inhabited by the Arabs, and confined them to the desert on Hedjaz and Bahram.[1] He endeavoured to wrest Syria from the Romans, but could not succeed. Nor could any of the Persian kings obtain possession of Syria; it remained united to the Roman empire from the epoch of the ascension of Isa to the time of Mohammed, or from Tiberius to Heraclius, a period of 585 years.[2]

Ardeschin, Son of Babek.

An imperfect list of Roman emperors follows. The writer says that under Nero the two apostles sent by Isa to Rome, who called him to the religion of Isa, were crucified head downwards. Vespasian was a believer in Isa. He sent his son Titus to Ailia to destroy the city and the temple and slaughter the children of Israel, to avenge upon them the death of Isa. But no war under Hadrian is recorded. A bare list follows, down to Heraclius, to whom "our Prophet" addressed a letter and sent a messenger.

From Nabuchodonosor to the Hegira there elapsed 1000 years; from Alexander to the time of Mohammed, 926 years;[3] from Alexander to the birth of Isa, 303 years;[4] from the birth of Isa to his ascension, thirty-three years; and from the ascension to the time of Mohammed, 585 years.

Passing over some annals of the Arabs in Iraq, Mesopotamia, and Yemen, we come to the legend of the "People of the Cavern." These were of an idolatrous city in Syria, Ephesus, in the time of the great King Decianus, after Alex-

The Young Men of the Cavern.

[1] Cf. Part II. c. 11. It was 400 or 523 or 266 years after Alexander.
[2] The following passage is only in MSS. A and B, used by Zotenberg.
[3] Or 920, according to Part II. c. 65.
[4] Or 369, ib.

ander. They were of the number six, the sole believers in all the city knowing Allah. The king summoned them to him, and said, "Who do ye worship, and what is your God?" They confessed their religion before the king, and Allah strengthened their hearts, so that they had no fear, and they said, "Our God is the God of heaven and of earth, and we own no other than Him. If we spoke otherwise, we should lie." So Allah hath spoken of them in the Koran (Sur. xviii. 12).

At this time there was no prophet on the earth; by their own intelligence they came to the knowledge of Allah. It was before the appearance of Isa, Yahya, and Zachariah; there was no prophet in Syria.

These men were all of high birth, and the king could not lightly put them to death. The king had a Cadi whose son also professed the true faith, but dared not avow it in public because of the king. The king said to the Cadi, "What thinkest thou? how must we act with them?" The Cadi answered, "They are all of good family; they must not lightly be slain. Give them the space of this night, that they may reflect, and return, it may be, to reason." The king granted them this space, and they retired. In the Koran they are honoured by the name "young men." They had enjoyed the immediate direction of Allah in the right way.[1]

Their names were Maximilianos, Malchos, Iamblichos, Martinianos, Dionysios, and John. By night they left the city and repaired to the mountain Yahlos. There they met a shepherd named Antoninos. They said to him, "Is there in this mountain a place in which we

[1] The doctors and commentators say that the expression "young men" is only employed twice in the Koran in reference to believers. Once it is applied to Ibrahim (Sur. xxi. 61). To infidels it is twice applied (xii. 36, 62).

may hide for some days?" The shepherd said to them, "Who are you?" They answered, "We profess another religion than the king and the dwellers in the city; we worship a God different from their idols. We have fled from the king, fearing for our life; we seek a hiding-place." And when they had explained to him their belief, he too accepted it, and said, "I will go with you."

He had a dog which followed them, and which refused to quit them, though the shepherd struck it and would have driven it away, for fear that its bark might betray them. At last Allah gave a voice to the dog, which said distinctly, "Why do ye strike me? I also believe in the same God in whom ye believe!" This was for them a sign and a miracle on the part of Allah. Then they set forth and came to a great cavern known to the shepherd. The Koran says: "Thou mightest have seen the sun, when it had risen, to decline from their cave towards the right hand; and when it went down, to leave them on the left hand. And they were in the spacious part. This was of the signs of God. Whomsoever God shall direct, he is directed; and whomsoever He shall cause to err, thou shalt not find any to defend or direct. And thou wouldst have judged them to be awake while they were sleeping, and we have caused them to turn themselves to the right hand and to the left. And their dog stretched forth his forelegs in the mouth of the cave. If thou hadst come suddenly upon them, verily thou wouldst have turned thy back and fled from them, and thou wouldst have been filled with fear at them" (Sur. xviii. 16 *seq.*).

Allah sent them sleep, and during sleep He took away their souls, and that of the dog. In vain the king sought for them during a month. They remained in the cavern 309 years. Each week Allah sent them an angel to turn them from one side to the other, to hinder their flesh from corrupting by contact with the earth, and their bodies from being decomposed. The mountain was situated towards the south, at the left of the west; and the entrance of the cavern was turned to the side of the north, so that the sun in rising was on the right of the cavern, and on its left when it set. The north wind blew in it, and hindered any cadaveric odour from being perceived.

Under the first of the Roman kings of Syria Isa had appeared, and informed the children of Israel of the event of the young men of the cavern, announcing that they would arise, would be seen of men, and would die anew, that men might be convinced of the resurrection of the dead.

At the end, therefore, of the 309 years, saith Allah in the Book, "We awaked them from sleep, that they might ask questions of one another. One of them spake, and said, 'How long have ye tarried?' They answered, 'We have tarried a day, or part of a day.' They said, 'Your Lord best knoweth the time of your tarrying. Now send one of you with this your money into the city, and let him see which hath the best and cheapest food, and let him buy your provision from him, and let him behave circumspectly, and not discover you to any one. Verily, if they come up against you they will stone you, or force you to return to their religion; and then shall ye not prosper for ever.' And so we made men acquainted with them, that they might know that the promise of Allah is true, and that there is no doubt of the hour, when they disputed anything of this matter" (Sur. xviii. 18–20).

So all the people of Syria and of Roum (Asia Minor) believed in Isa and read the Gospel, and they knew this event. But it was not said in the Gospel in what country of Syria the cavern was situated, as the Koran indicates it. So they waited to see from what land they would come.

It was Iamblichos who was sent into the city. He recognised the houses and the bazaars, but not the men. He saw men in prayer worshipping God, and in astonishment said, " A day ago we started, and the people has become believing !" Then he went to a baker's to buy bread ; but the baker saw that his money was not current coin, for it was the coin of Decianus, of whom he knew nothing. The present king, he said, followed the religion of Isa and worshipped Allah. Iamblichos was brought before the king, who listened to his adventure, looked at the coin, and recognised that it was one of the Companions of the Cavern whose story he had read in the Gospel. He then caused Iamblichos to recite his story in presence of the citizens, the doctors, and the readers of the Gospel. And all agreed that the adventure of the cavern was that foretold in the Gospel. And Iamblichos entered the cavern in the sight of the king and the people, to tell his companions that they had slept the sleep of 309 years.

The Koran relates, " They said : Erect a building over them ; their Lord best knoweth." They who prevailed in their affair answered, " We will surely build a chapel over them."

For when Iamblichos had spoken to his companions, he fell and died, and the others also died. The king and people waited, but as none appeared, and as they dared not enter the cavern, they proposed to build a chapel at the door of the cavern, that men might pray and their prayer might be heard. So they built the chapel, and inscribed on the stone of the cavern wall the history of the men of the cavern, as it has been here told after the commentators.

Tabari says further, "Some of the doctors say that these Young Men entered the cavern before Isa, and came out after Isa; and that both events were in the time of the 'kings of the provinces,' after the epoch of Alexander and before that of Ardeschin son of Babek." Another account is that they entered the cavern after the appearance of Isa, having believed on him in the city of idolaters; and that one of the apostolic missionaries of Isa having come into this city, had called the inhabitants to Allah; that they had not accepted his preaching, and that the Companions of the Cavern had accepted it.

Another story is that the king, being an idolater, had placed at the gate of the city an idol; all that entered the city worshipped it. Now one of the apostles of Isa came to the city, and refusing to worship the idol, entered not the city. Near the gate was a bath, to which he repaired; he hired himself to the proprietor for wages. He fasted during the day, and spent the night in prayer. The keeper of the bath was blessed in his industry, and he said, "This blessing comes to me because of this servant." So he treated the apostle with respect and made a friend of him. After a certain time the apostle expounded to his master the religion of Isa, and the keeper of the bath accepted it. Also to the young people of the city who visited the bath-keeper the apostle preached the faith of Isa, and they accepted it. They were the Companions of the Cavern.

One day the king's son came to the house with a woman of evil life. The apostle said to him, "Art thou not ashamed to come to the bath with this abandoned woman?" The king's son struck him, reviled him, and entered the bath. He and the woman were suffocated and died. When the king was told that his son had been slain in the bath, he came thither, called for the keeper and his servant, and said, "Who are they that frequent the keeper of the bath?" Then the young men, on search being made, went out of the city and fled. At a certain place they met a peasant, who had a dog, and who also professed their religion. They said, "The king seeks us." The man was afraid, and he went with them, followed by his dog. The keeper of the bath, the peasant, the apostle, and the young men of the city all went together and entered the cavern. The king arrived at the door, and as none dared enter, he caused them to be walled in, that they might die of hunger and thirst. The Companions of the Cavern slept there 309 years. Then, when Allah willed their reappearance, a shepherd came by; he was cold and turned to the mountain. He found an opening, entered with his sheep and passed the night, then went his way. Allah awoke the Companions of the Cavern and restored their life. Then they sent one of them with the money which they had. The author says that at this time each dirhem had the value of ten, was seven times the weight of the later coin, and was as large as the sole of a young camel.

There are further discussions as to the exact number of the Men of the Cavern, the strong opinion being, according to the Koran, that they were seven, and the dog the eighth.[1]

[1] From the Moslems the legend of the Seven Sleepers found its way among Jacobites, Nestorians, monks of St. Basil, and monks of St. Benedict. See Simeon Metaphrastes and Gregory of Tours.

In the Koran we read, "Jonas (Yunus) was of those

'who were sent,' when he fled into the loaded ship, and they cast lots among themselves, and he was condemned; and the fish swallowed him, for he was worthy of blame. And if he had not been of those who praised Allah, verily he had remained in the belly thereof until the day of resurrection. And we cast him on the naked shore, and he was sick; and we caused a plant of a gourd to grow up over him; and we sent him to a hundred thousand persons, or they were a greater number, and they believed; wherefore we granted them to enjoy for a season" (Sur. xxxvii. 139).

Jonas is said to live in the time of the "kings of the provinces." He was of the children of Israel, a prophet, and an envoy of Allah. He was sent to a city of the territory of Moussoul, including seven towns, all given to idolatry. As the people refused to believe, Allah threatened to send upon them a chastisement should they not repent. On the day appointed, Jonas went forth from the midst of them. During the night and at daybreak, Allah sent a red cloud filled with fire, which hovered above the city. The king and the people gathered together, and knew that the chastisement was near at hand. And the king said, "Seek Jonas, that we may believe in Allah; for what he has told us is the truth." When Jonas knew that they sought him, he said with anger, "Why did they not believe before this day?" He fled from them, and showed not himself; as again it is said in the Koran, "Remember Dhuhun,[1] when he departed in wrath, and thought that we should not exercise our power over him. And he cried out in the darkness, 'There is no

A surname of Yunus.

God besides thee : praise be unto thee ! Verily I have been one of the unjust.' Wherefore we heard him and delivered him from affliction ; for so do we deliver the true believers " (Sur. xxi. 87).

The king on the departure of Jonas caused all the people to go forth out of the city, with all their quadrupeds and birds. They covered themselves with dust, and the king said, " O Lord, though Jonas thy prophet be gone, we lose not confidence in thee. We believe on thee, Allah, and in thy prophet." Then the king caused all the idols to be destroyed ; and all the children to be separated from their mothers, and the young from their dams. Cries and tears, and prayers and sobs from the great multitude rose to heaven ; heaven was afflicted with earth ; and the angels wept and pardoned the city. Three days and three nights supplication continued ; on the fourth day Allah had pity on them, and remanded the chastisement. Never before had Allah pardoned a people who had not believed at the appointed time, as it is said in the Koran (Sur. xc. 8).

They adopted the faith and believed in Allah ; but Jonas was not there to teach the religion and worship ; and they waited till Allah should send Jonas or another prophet.

Jonas meanwhile in his wrath knew not that he committed a sin that Allah would punish. Crossing to the shore, he went on board a passing vessel, and when it came to the middle of the sea Allah caused to come from the depth of the sea the fish, into the belly of which Jonas was to be cast, and the fish stopped the vessel. The crew prayed and wept, and prepared for death. Then Jonas knew that he had committed a sin, and he said to them on board, " It

is I whom the fish desires, cast me to it!" When he
declared his name and quality, they refused to cast
into the sea a prophet of Allah. Then they cast lots,
and the lot fell upon Jonas, as it is said in the Koran,
"They took pieces of clay, and wrote upon each the
name of one of those on board, and prayed that the
name of the appointed one might swim and the others
fall. The name of Jonas came to the surface. Then
he cast himself into the sea and was swallowed by the
fish. But Allah charged the fish to do him no hurt.
This species of fish has by His will a raised back like
the roof of a house; and to this day is held sacred
from pursuit."

After forty days Allah would deliver Jonas, and
Jonas was inspired with the thought of prayer. Allah
sent an angel to lead the fish to the shore at the place
where Jonas had embarked. When cast ashore, he was
weak as a new-born child. But Allah inspired a doe,
which came and gave him of her milk; and she returned
again in the evening. The sun scorched the body of
Jonas, and Allah caused a gourd to spring from the
ground, which wound about a dry trunk and put forth
large leaves to give him shade. Forty days, night and
morning, the doe came to give him milk, till he could
rise and pray. At last the gourd withered, and Jonas
was aggrieved. Then Allah exhorted him because he
was not grieved for the many thousands of His servants
whom he had deserted; and Jonas was sent anew to
the people.

When he came to the territory of the city, he met a
shepherd with his sheep, who told him of the condition
of the city, and how they were seeking Jonas. Jonas
declared himself, and bade the shepherd go and tell
the people. The shepherd said, "O prophet of Allah!

where shalt thou be?" Jonas answered, "In this mountain." The other said, "Who will show me the road to thee?" Jonas answered, "This she-goat." The shepherd said, "Who will bear witness to the people that I have seen thee?" Jonas said, "Thy dog." Then Jonas entered the mountain, and the shepherd went and told the king, who with the people came out of the city. The shepherd said to the dog, "Bear witness for me, as the prophet commanded." The dog began to speak, and said distinctly, "Jonas, son of Mataï, prophet of Allah, was here." Then the shepherd said to the she-goat, "Be our guide." She led them to Jonas, who was found deep in prayer. He rose and went with them to the city; they believed, and he remained with them till his death.

In another place in the Koran it is written: "Wait patiently the judgment of thy Lord; and be not like him who was swallowed by the fish, when he cried, being inwardly vexed. Had not grace from his Lord reached him, he had surely been cast forth on the naked shore, covered with shame; but the Lord chose him, and made him of the just" (Sur. lxviii. 50).

That is, Jonas was elect when he came from the belly of the fish. The story was revealed to our prophet by Allah, saying, "Be patient, whatever the afflictions that thy people cause thee, and quit them not like Jonas, son of Mataï."

"This history, from beginning to end," says the chronicler, "is as the doctors and commentators have given it in their books, in the same order." [1]

---

[1] The tomb of the prophet Jonas (Yunus) is shown near Moussoul.

R

In the times also of the "kings of the provinces"
occurred the event mentioned by Allah in the
Koran :—"Propound unto them for an example the inhabitants of the city when the
apostles came thereto, when we sent unto them two,
but they charged them with imposture; wherefore we
strengthened them with a third" (Sur. xxxvi. 12).

The Two Apostles Succoured by a Third.

This was the city of Antioch, which formed part of
the country of Moussoul and of Syria, as the commentators explain. These apostles were in number
three, Sadoug, Sadig, and Saloum. There reigned in
the city a Roman king, Antiochus, an idolater, like all
the people. Allah sent two apostles, who were treated
by them as liars, then a third, and all were prophets.
Tabari says there are differences in the traditions.
Some say that they were disciples of Isa, and that their
mission was by Isa's command. But the commentators
rely on the above passage of the Koran.

In the commentaries also we read that the names of
these apostles were Thomas, Paul, and Simeon. For a
year they called men to Allah, but none believed. But
there was a carpenter, Habib, who had believed; he
was a stranger, and dwelt outside the city. Each day
he divided his gains—gave one part to the poor, the
other to the needs of his family. After a year, rain
failed, and the people threatened to stone the prophets.
But Habib cried, "O my people! follow the apostles of
Allah! Follow Him who demandeth not any reward of
you; for these are directed." And when they answered,
"Thou hast followed them," he replied, "Why should
I not adore Him who hath created me? For unto Him
shall ye return" (Sur. xxxvi. 21).

The people surrounded him and said, "Thou art a
stranger, and takest thy bread and water from our city,

but thou hast alliance with our enemies." They trampled him under foot, and smote him so that he died. Allah sent him to Paradise, as it is said in the Koran, "And when Habib saw the splendours of Paradise he said, 'Ah! if my people knew what Allah hath granted me because I have followed His prophets, surely they too would follow.'" You may still see the tomb of Habib the carpenter at Antioch. Then Allah commanded Gabriel to sound, and they all died, as it is said in the Koran, "There was but one cry, and behold, they were utterly extinct." [1]

Samson is also referred to the time of the "kings of the provinces." He was not a prophet, but a believer, dwelling in one of the cities of Roum and worshipping Allah. His mother had made a vow and had consecrated him to Allah, who had given him so much strength that none could master him. When bound with cords or fetters, he broke them, and nought could hold him. The inhabitants of the city were idolaters. Samson's house was a parasang from the city; thence he came and called them to Allah, but they believed not. He made war upon them alone, armed with the chin-bone of a camel, from an opening in which Allah caused a spring to issue for his drink. In all battles he slew a great number, made many prisoners, and took much spoil. Whatever ruse was employed against him, they could not seize him. Then they said, "He must be caught by means of a woman." They offered great wealth to his wife, who belonged to them, that she might bind him and tell them afterwards, and they gave her a strong and stout cord. When Samson slept, she tied his hands to his neck; but on awaking he tore the cord, and his wife said that

The Story of Samson.

[1] See Sale's note _ad loc_

she had done this to prove whether it was by his
strength that he resisted, or through the weakness of
his foes. Another night the men brought her a chain
of brass, but Samson shook his hands and broke the
chain when he awoke. Then she said, "I have proved
thee to see how strong thou art; now I know that no
man in the world is stronger than thou art." Samson
said, "There is but one thing by which I may be bound
and in which I cannot move;" and after much entreaty he
said that it was only by his own hair that he could be
bound. His hair was so long that it reached his feet.
So when he slept his wife bound him with his hair,
and when the men of the city came they cut off the
ears and nose of Samson, put out his eyes, and took
him into the city to the court of the king, where they
placed him. The king was on the terrace, and looked
at him. Samson implored Allah to give him back his
strength and all that had been cut from his body.
Then he wrenched the columns from the terrace and
caused them to fall. All the people perished.

George was a believer in the religion of Isa in the
time of the "kings of the provinces." He
was of Palestine, a travelling merchant, who
distributed all his income to the poor year
by year, reserving to himself only the capital. There
was at Moussoul a king of Syria, a giant and an
idolater, Dadyane (said to signify Diocletian). He
had an idol named Apollo. George and other believers
in Isa kept their religion a secret, and George with his
friend went to Moussoul to gain the protection of the
king, taking with him great riches. He found that a
proclamation had been made against all who refused to
worship idols, and that the king had called an assembly outside the city, had brought the idol Apollo, and

Story of
George
(Dschirschis)
the Martyr.

caused a great fire to be kindled before him. Those
who refused to adore were to be cast into the fire.

George resolved to call the king to Allah ; either the
king would believe, or he would punish George with
death, and Allah would reward his faithfulness. So
George gave away all his goods to his friend and came
poor before the king. He preached to him the doctrine
of the Creator and denounced the helpless idol. He
described himself as lowliest of the servants of Allah.
The king derided his poverty, pointed to the wealth
of his own idolatrous servants, and said, "Thy God
must be a slave like thyself, destitute and bare."
George replied, "The graces of my God are of another
world, not of this. If thy idol has servants like
Theophilos, my God has servants like Elias and Idris,
who were prophets, and raised to heaven to be with the
angels. If thou hast servants like Machlitos, my God
has servants like Isa the Masich, son of Mariam, whom
God has set apart from all men." He spoke long of
the merits of Isa, and further said, "If thy idol has
slaves like Inbil, a wealthy woman of high family, my
God has handmaids like Mariam the mother of Isa ; "
and he recounted her merits.

The king refused to believe on these ideal beings, and
ordered that George should be stretched naked on a
plank, and be furrowed with iron combs ; yet he died
not. Vinegar and mustard were placed on his wounds ;
yet he died not. An iron nail was brought, heated red
hot, and thrust into his head ; yet he died not. He
was then plunged into a boiling cauldron ; yet he died
not. Then the king was amazed, and calling him,
cried, "George, who art thou?" He answered, "I am
a man." The king said, "Hast thou felt no pain from
these punishments ? " George replied, "This God to

whom I call thee turns from me the pains of thy
punishments, that this may be an argument from Him
with thee." Then the king cast him into prison. His
friends said, "He must be tormented in prison, that he
may be busied with himself and not debauch the jailers
by calling them to his religion." The king ordered
him to be stretched on his face in the prison, and his
hands and feet to be nailed to his body with forty iron
nails. There was a column of marble which twenty
men could hardly lift; it was placed on George's back,
and he remained in this state all day. In the night
Allah sent an angel and gave him a vision. Before
this he had not received a message from heaven. The
angel took away the stone and the nails, and gave him
to eat and drink. Then he said, "In the name of
Allah, O George! bear with my enemy and suffer his
torments; he shall kill thee four times, and I will give
thee life thrice, and the fourth time I will deliver thee
from martyrdom."

In the morning George came before the king, and
told him that he had been brought from prison by One
whose power was greater than his. The king caused
him to be placed between two planks of wood and
to be sawn in two, and each half was cut into seven
morsels. The morsels were cast into two lion's cages,
but the lions smelt and refused to touch them. In
the night Allah collected the pieces, restored the body
and the soul of George, who went before the king,
saying, "It is my Lord who can accomplish such
things." The king said, "Who is this man, and what
shall we do with him?" They said, "He is a magician; he charms the eyes. Cause the magicians to come,
that they may triumph over him." The chief magician demanded an ox. He breathed into the two ears

of the beast and transformed it into two. He demanded corn, sowed it, and it sprang up, came to ear, and ripened. He cut and crushed it, had it baked and eaten. The king was delighted, and said, "I see thou canst confound George. Canst thou transform him into a dog?" He answered, "I can." Then he had a cup of water brought, breathed upon it, and gave George to drink. He took it, saying "Bismillah!" and felt no harm. The magician was confounded, and said, "O king! were there magic in these things, I should have conquered, but these are the acts of the God of heaven."

Then one of the familiars of the king told him how there was in the city a poor woman who had a cow which gave milk on which she lived. The cow died, and the woman cast forth the body, and the dogs and birds devoured it. After a long space of time, she went and found George. He pitied her, and gave her a rod, saying, "Take this and strike the cow, and the cow shall return to life." And when she told him the cow had been devoured, he said, "Bring a bone, no matter which." So she brought a bone which remained, and George touched it with the rod, and the cow came to life. The king said, " Has this miracle happened?" The courtier replied, "Surely, and I have accepted the religion of George, and have believed in him." Then the king ordered that his tongue should be torn out.

The story became known, and that day four thousand men believed in the God of George. The king caused them to be put to death with torments. And when he asked George why he had not prayed for their restoration to life, he replied, "The delights they have found are to be preferred to the life in this world."

A further miracle was wrought by George. He

caused fourteen seats, on which guests sat at table with the king, made of fourteen kinds of wood, to put forth leaves and fruits, that they might eat, at the request of one of the guests. The king said, "None can surpass him." Then the same courtier asked permission to subject him to a torture against which magic would not prevail. A hollow bull of bronze was filled with naphtha, sandarac, sulphur, and lead. George was placed therein, and a fire was kindled and kept burning three days. Then came a violent storm and the world was black as night. Men trembled and remained in amazement for three days. Then Allah sent the Angel Michael to overthrow and break the statue. He made a noise that was heard in all Syria; all that heard fell and fainted, no less than the king and his guests.

George came forth, and appeared again before the king, and spake to him, and the king and his guests recovered their senses. And one said, "O George! I know not if it is thou who workest these prodigies or thy God. If it is thy God, bid Him raise the dead from this cemetery, that we may speak with them, and they may give testimony." Then George went to an old cemetery in their sight, and said, "Allah accomplishes this to prove the truth." He prayed, and seventeen persons came living from their tombs to them; nine men, five women, and three children. Among them was an old man. The king said, "What is thy name?" He replied, "Toubil." "When didst die? "At such an epoch." They reckoned the time: he had been dead four hundred years. And the familiars of the king said, "There is no torture save hunger that he has not undergone." So then he was detained in the house of a poor old decrepit woman, where there was naught to eat and drink. To her George expounded the faith, and she believed. Then he prayed, and a pillar that upheld the house became green, furnished leaves, and gave all manner of fruits for food. Its summit became a lofty tree. When the king was informed of this, he ordered the tree to be uprooted and the house to be destroyed. Then the tree withered and became as it was before. They left the house, and caused George to come forth. The woman had a son, deaf and dumb, blind and paralysed. She said, "Pray that my son may be cured." George breathed into the ear of the son and upon his eyes, and he recovered hearing and sight. She said, "Pray also for his tongue, his hands, and his feet." George said, "Another time." He was again brought before the king.

The king caused to be fixed to his chariot, driven by forty oxen, swords, knives, daggers, and spikes, and drove over George, who was cut to pieces. The fragments of his body were burned and reduced to ashes, then cast into the sea. Allah ordered the wind to carry these ashes to the sea-shore in the sight of man, and restored George to life. And George again appeared before the astonished king, who declared that he would believe in him, were it not that men would say he was vanquished. "Do for me," he said, "a thing that shall save us both. Go into the temple of my idols ; there are many idols, of which the greatest is Apollo. Offer him adoration and sacrifice, and I will believe in thy God and adopt thy religion. So men will not say thou hast vanquished me." George consented, and the king kissed his head and face. When the news spread, a great number of the people who had adopted his religion were greatly distressed.

George passed that night in prayer and singing of psalms with a loud voice. His voice was very sweet. The queen heard, and came and stood behind him praying. And George, seeing her, expounded to her the faith, and she believed, saying, "Keep this secret."

The next day all the people went to the temple-gate to see what George would do. The old woman with whom he had lodged had been told that the king had seduced George with gold and power, and had tempted him to abandon his faith. In great grief she took up her paralytic son and went to the temple-gate. As the king entered with George, the paralytic recovered the use of hands, feet, and tongue, and went into the temple, placing himself before George, who recognised him and said, "Call me those idols." There were seventy-one of them, each placed on a throne of gold. At the word of the young man they all fell to the earth at the feet of George. He struck the earth with his foot, and they all disappeared under the earth.

Now Eblis was in the temple; it was he who spoke from the interior of the idols to those who came to worship George seized him in sight of all the people, and said, "Cursed one! why dost destroy and lead astray all these men? What pleasure hast thou in this?" Eblis said, "O George! if Allah said to me, 'Choose the kingdom of heaven and of earth, and all that is included in it, or the power to lead a single man astray,' I would choose to lead astray one of the sons of Adam, because before Adam the kingdom of the earth belonged to me. Allah ordered me to adore Adam; all the angels adored him, as Gabriel, Michael, and Israfil, but I did not, and I have lost my power, without having taken care of it." George let him go, and he disappeared under the earth. The king said

"George! thou hast deceived me, and hast destroyed my gods." George said, "I have done so intentionally, that thou mayest know they are not gods; and as they cannot protect themselves, they cannot protect you."

The queen made known her faith, and said to the king, "There is no prodigy that George hath not wrought before thine eyes, save that he has not prayed that thou shouldst disappear under earth, even as these idols. Why dost not believe in him?" It was seven years that George had dwelt among them, and 34,000 men had believed on him. The king ordered that the queen should be attached to the same wood to which they had bound George on the first day, and that her flesh should be furrowed with the same iron combs. She said to George, "Pray that Allah may soften my torments!" He bade her look toward heaven. She did so and smiled, and when the king asked wherefore, she said, "I see above my head two angels with vestments of Paradise, ornaments, and crowns; they come to take my soul, to carry me to Allah." Then she gave up her soul amidst torments. When she was dead, George lifted up his hands and said, "O Lord! thou hast protected me in all these torments, and hast made me support them; thou hast granted the recompense of martyrs in the death that I have undergone. This is my last day; thou hast promised that thou wouldst raise me to thyself, and that thou wouldst deliver me from these ills. O Lord! before thou dost take me to thyself, bring to nought these men before me who have not believed in me, and have made me undergo torments. O Lord! whosoever after me shall be in woe or affliction, and who shall call on thee, give him joy by thy pity and by my intercession, and save him as thou hast saved me."

When George had finished this prayer, a cloud covered the heaven, and a rain of fire fell on those who had not believed in him, and the 34,000 men and women who had believed in him were present. As the fire fell on the king and his followers, they seized their swords, fell upon George and his disciples, and slew them all. The unbelieving were all devoured by the fire.

It was at this epoch the reign of the "kings of the provinces" came to an end, under Ardeschir, son of Babek.

The chronicler describes his reign and that of Scha-

Mani. pour, in whose time he says Mani the heresiarch appeared. There followed Hormuzd and Bahram. It is said that during the reign of the latter the doctrine of Mani was recognised to be false, and he was put to death. Bahram caused him to be flayed, his skin to be filled with straw. He was hanged at the gate of the city of Tcheudi-Schapour, and all his followers were put to death.

After three short reigns, we come to that of Schapour Dsoul Aktaf. There was, it is said, in Roum a king named Elianus (Julian), of the family of Constantine, who believed in the religion of Isa, but who afterwards returned to the religion of the Romans that was before Isa. He caused all the "churches" of Roum to be destroyed and broke all the "crosses." It is said that 70,000 Arabs joined him, and they formed his vanguard under Jovianus. They are said to have given Schapour battle and to have crushed him, so that he fled to Ctesiphon, and escaped to Iraq. Some further particulars of the campaign and the death of Elianus, which depart from the account in Ammianus, are given. Jovianus surrendered Nisibis to Schapour, and is said to have reigned five years.

The references to religious affairs now become scant till the time of Mohammed ; and it is clear that where the chronicle is supposed to refer to " Jews " or " Christains," neither members of the Synagogue nor of the Church are signified.

Thus Noman, an Arab vassal king of Hora, has charge of Bahram, son of one of the Persian kings, for whom he builds a *khawarnaq* or palace. Noman was an idolater, but had a Syrian vizier who followed the religion of Isa, son of Mariam. One spring day he sat with the vizier on the terrace of the palace, and looking on the beauty of the landscape, the river Euphrates, Sawad and Iraq, he said, " Is there in the world a place whose aspect is more pleasant than this ? " The vizier replied, " It is very beautiful, but it has one fault : it lasts not." " What is there that is lasting ? " asked the king. The other said, " The religion of Allah and His worship and the other world." Noman came down, adopted the religion of Isa, put on a frock, and retired from the world after a reign of twenty-two years. None ever saw him again or knew what became of him.

At the time of the birth of Mohammed, all Arabia, the Hedjaz, Mecca, and Medina, were given up to idolatry, except that there were some " Jews," Yemen. whose ancestors had fled from Nabuchodonosor, in the Hedjaz, and who followed the religion of Musa. At this epoch " Judaism " had fallen, and the religion of Isa prevailed, but only in the land of Roum and towards the Orient. All other lands were plunged in idolatry.

Then we read that " Jewish doctors " prophesied the uprise of Mohammed in the territory of Mecca and of his flight to Medina ; that they had found this in the Law, the Book of Allah sent down to Musa ; that they expounded the religion of Musa to the Himyaritic king, and that he accepted it, renouncing idols. That these doctors were invited by him to go and convert Yemen, and that they did not call the city of Medina to Allah, because, as they said, "These men will believe by Mohammed." Clearly these were not Rabbins.

At Mecca, the same doctors declare the temple to be a temple of Allah, and bid the king shave his head and make processions about the temple. To this king is ascribed the act of first removing the idols from the temple and covering it with cloth. In Yemen the inhabitants are said to renounce idolatry under the direction of these doctors and to embrace "Judaism." The doctors speak as Mussulmen about Divs, and clearly are Mussulmen, that is, in so far as they prepare for the coming of the Prophet.

It is said that Zora otherwise Dsou Nowas, the most The People respected of all the kings of Yemen, made an of Nadjran. expedition against Nadjran, all whose inhabitants followed the religion of Isa. He called them to "Judaism," but they refused; whereupon he plunged them into a fiery fosse. Here we have a reference to the Koran, which makes it clear that the people of Nadjran were not "Christians," but faithful Moslems, followers of Isa, and that their persecutors were certainly not "Jews."

" Cursed were the contrivers of the pit of fire supplied with fuel, when they sat round the same, and were witnesses of what they did against the true believers. They afflicted them for no other reason than because they believed in the mighty, the glorious Allah, whose is the kingdom of heaven and earth. Allah is witness of all things. Verily for those who persecute the true believers of either sex, and afterwards repent not, the

torment of hell, and for them the pain of burning"
(Sur. lxxxv.).

These people of Nadjran were all Arabs of the Beni
Thalab. Formerly they had been idolaters;
but there came to them one Fimiouu, a Syrian, Fimioun.
and descendant of the disciples of Isa. He went from
town to town earning his living; fled to the territory
of Moussoul, Mesopotamia or Iraq; was made captive and
sold back to Nadjran. His master found his chamber
illuminated at night though he had no torch; he was
praying and reciting. Next day, on being questioned,
he said that he preferred the religion of Isa, son of
Mariam, and was reciting the Gospel, the book of God.
He gave a proof of the superiority of his religion by
praying at the foot of a tree where the people held
their idolatrous rites, when Allah, in the eyes of all the
people, gave order to the wind, and the tree was entirely
uprooted. The people broke their idols and embraced
the religion of Isa, alone among the Arabs. It is impossible that such a legend, in the belief of the
chronicler, should refer to any missionary monk of the
Order of St. Basil, whose christology was to the Arabs
an abomination.

In the short Surah cv. of the Koran it is written,
"Hast thou not seen how thy Lord dealt with
the masters of the elephant? Did He not The Men of
make their treacherous design an occasion of phant.
drawing them into error, and send against them flocks
of birds, which cast down upon them stones of baked
clay, and render them like the leaves of corn eaten?"

This is said to refer to the conquest of Yemen by
the Abyssinian kings. Yousouf Dsou-Nowas, the "man
of the fosse," already referred to, returned from Nadjran
to Yemen. One of the "Christians" of Nadjran, named

Dous, had fled upon his horse Thalab. He now returned to Nadjran, called forth the living refugees from their retreats, and said, "Build again your churches and set up the Christian cult; I shall not rest till I have had vengeance." He rode to find the Cæsar, who was "Christian," taking a half-bound Gospel with him. At this epoch Nouschirwan, a fire-worshipper, was king of Persia. He cared naught for the burning of the "Christians." So Dous came to the emperor and showed his half-bound Gospel. The Cæsar was afflicted and wept, but excused himself from making an expedition to so distant a land. He would, however, write to the Gentile king of Abyssinia. And Dous went with the letter to Nadjaschi, king of Abyssinia, and showed him the half-bound book. The king wept with his people, and resolved to attack Dsou-Nowas with a numerous army, and to act with the "Jews" in a ruder manner than they had acted with the Gentiles.

Dsou-Nowas, adopting a ruse, contrived to break up the Abyssinian army and slaughter them. Then Abraha was sent with another army of 100,000 men and conquered the land. At the city of Cana he assumed the crown, proclaimed "Christianism" and built "churches," compelling the people to renounce "Judaism." The king of Abyssinia became jealous of Abraha, and sent Aryat to summon him. Aryat was treacherously slain.

Then the king of Abyssinia swore by Allah, by Ïsa, by the Gospel and the cross that he would not rest till he had shed the blood of Abraha. But the latter made a timely submission, was pardoned, and left in possession of Yemen. He established "Christianism" in Yemen, and led an army with elephants to Mecca to destroy the temple of the Kaaba. Allah caused him to perish, as it is written in the above text of the Koran.

Abraha had built a magnificent "church" at Cana called Qalis, which was visited by "Christians" from Roum, Syria, and other lands. It far surpassed the beauty of the temple at Mecca. It contained paintings and other splendid works of art. An Arab of the desert visited and defiled it; in vengeance for which act Abraha resolved to attack Mecca.

When Abraha came to the sacred enclosure, his elephant Mahmoud refused to advance a step. Then Allah sent birds, swallow-like, which flew to the sea and took up grains of sand in their beaks; then they returned to Mecca and hovered over the Abyssinians. A vapour came from hell and changed the sand into stones, which fell on the heads of the soldiers; the fire entered their bodies, the flesh left their bones, and their bodies became a mass of wounds. They returned to Yemen and died.

After this event the inhabitants of Mecca were held in high respect by all the Arabs, as guardians of the holy city and sanctuary. When a caravan of a hundred or a thousand camels went from Mecca, they attached to each camel's neck a branch with a cord of wool, and it was thus protected from robbers and marauders.

The Prophet himself was born in the era of the Elephant, in the reign of Nouschirwan. Epoch of the Elephant.

According to another legend, the king of Abyssinia desired to build at Antioch a "church" bearing his name. He shipped a great quantity of wood to Syria, but the vessel was wrecked near Djeddah. Much of the wood was collected. At the time the temple at Mecca was about to be rebuilt. So the elders of Mecca went to Djeddah and asked that the wood might be sold to them, and that they might hire the Abyssinian carpenters. A letter was sent to know the pleasure

s

of the Abyssinian king, who wrote in return, "I give all this wood to the temple of the Kaaba. Go to Mecca with the carpenters, build that temple, and use the money thou hast with thee for the expenses." And the inspector did so. The temple remains as it was then built, with the exception of a corner, destroyed by an engine of war. Mohammed was then thirty-five years old.

There are in the Chronicle some further references to the cross marked on the dress of the Roman emperor, the symbol of a different religion. But the cross was an old Roman sign of victory, and has nothing to do with the crucifix.

Whatever, then, be the date and the meaning of such legends, they cannot refer to Christianism in any sense understood by the Christians, that is, by the monks themselves.

Again, Khadidja, the wife of Mohammed, is said, at the time when Gabriel appeared to him and saluted him as the Apostle of God, to have repaired to a learned Gentile, Waraga, son of Naufal, who lived at Mecca in the religion of Isa and practised the worship of Allah. He had read many books, knew the Gospel, and that the time had come for the appearance of the Prophet. Khadidja said to him, "Hast thou not found anywhere in the ancient books the name of Gabriel, and knowest thou who Gabriel is?" Then she related what had occurred to Mohammed, and how Gabriel had recited to him the Surah called *Iqra*. And Waraga replied, "Gabriel is the great Namous, the angel who mediates between Allah and the prophets, who brings to them the messages of Allah. He came to find Musa and Isa. If what thou sayest be true, Mohammed, thy husband, is the prophet who is to be raised up at

Mecca in the midst of the Arabs, and who is mentioned in the Scriptures." And he added, "If he had ordered that men should be called to Allah, the first who would have answered and believed in him would have been myself. I have waited for him for long years!" This was not the language of a Christian.

Nothing can be more impressive then the simple message which Gabriel brings to Mohammed the second time, as he lies sleeping in his cloak, chilled with fear. "Rise, thou that art covered with a cloak! Rise and preach, and magnify thy Lord. Cleanse thy garments and flee abomination; and be not liberal, in hopes to receive more in return; and patiently wait for thy Lord" (Sur. lxxiv. 1–7).

Here Allah (says the Chronicle) has resumed for the Prophet prayer, religion, purity, faith, liberality, good nature, and perseverance; all parts of religion and the qualities of the prophetic office.

Beautiful is the legend which tells how Khadidja in joy answered her husband, when he in despondency exclaimed, "Whom shall I call, and who will believe on me?" "Thou canst at least call me before all other men, for I believe in thee!" Then Gabriel called for water and taught him the manner of ablutions and of prayer; the Prophet repeating after him, and Khadidja after the Prophet. How beautiful, again, the incident of the boy Ali coming in and witnessing the scene, and departing to consult his father whether he should abide in idolatry. Turning back from the door, he says, "O Mohammed, Allah hath created me without consulting my father. What need have I to consult Abou-Talib to follow the religion of Allah and the worship? Teach me the religion that hath been ordained thee!"

This simple spiritual creed had nothing in common with the Catholic christology as we know it from the earliest documents of the Church. It is simply the turning from the idol to the Eternal, from the creature to the Creator.

When the situation of the few believers among the persecuting infidels became intolerable, the Prophet bade them go to Abyssinia, "whose people are Christians, possessors of a sacred book, and nearer to the Mussulmen than the idolaters. The king never commits an injustice." They were seventy who took part in this first Flight; they found security with the king, who refused to extradite them at the demand of the Qoraischites. He is said to have held "many discussions with the Mussulmen on the subject of Islam and Christianism;" but these are not in Tabari. The king is said to have believed in his heart, and to have declared in public, "I think that Mohammed is the person spoken of in the Gospel." But the inhabitants refused to forsake "the Christian religion." The king therefore practised his religion in secret. On his death, when the Prophet had been five years at Medina, Gabriel enabled him to see from Medina to Abyssinia, and ordered him to pray for the king. Mohammed saw his body stretched upon the bed.

There is nothing in the records of Catholic Christianity to confirm the notion that it had entered Abyssinia before the time of Mohammed. Nothing is left us to infer but either that these legends are of very late date, or that they refer to some form of religion to us unknown. Another incident records how Mohammed, persecuted and weary, was resting near Taif and praying for the people, "O Lord, punish them not, for they know not that I am thy prophet!" It was near a vineyard owned by some cousins of Mohammed, Otha and Schaiba, and they had with them a˙ slave of Schaiba's, a Gentile from the city of Nineve. Nineve is towards Syria, the land of Jonas. This slave had read the Gospel and the Law, and practised the orthodox cult at Mecca. It was the time of vintage, and the Prophet, not knowing whose was the vine, sat by a cistern to rest and to wash his feet and hands and face. His cousins saw and recognised him, but were unwilling to show themselves. Schaiba said to the slave, "Thou seest this man; he is a magician and possessed; wherever he goes, he is struck and hunted by men. But he is our relation and is hungry; we pity him; carry him a plate of grapes, and return without speaking, for he may seduce thee and cause thee to lose thy Christian faith." The slave took the dish, and remained at a distance looking on. Mohammed took a grape, and having detached a stone from it, put it in his mouth, saying, "*Bismillah !*" The slave said, "Young man, what word hast thou pronounced? Since I left my country, I have not heard it." And when the slave said he came from Nineve, the Prophet said, "It is the town of my brother Jonas, son of Matai." And when the slave asked him who he was, he replied, "I am a prophet, and Jonas was a prophet; all prophets are brethren." Finally, he gave his name, "Mohammed and Ahmed." "Art thou," the slave asked, "that Ahmed who is named in the Gospel? It is there said that Allah would send thee to the inhabitants of Mecca, who should make thee go forth from the city, and that Allah should bring thee back, to subject them by force, and that thy religion should reign in the world." "Assuredly," said the Prophet. "Tell me the faith," said the slave, "for I have been long seeking thee." The Prophet presented to him the formula of Islam, and the slave made profession of it; then he fell at the feet of the Prophet and kissed them.

Mohammed ate the grapes and departed.

Here again "Christianism" is obviously not Catholic dogma. On the contrary, it is a Christianism which is conceived as a foreshadow of and preparation for Islam and the Prophet. And the story is perfectly consistent with what the Moslems ever maintain, that the Gospel, in their sense of the word, foretells Mohammed, the Periclyte. It would appear that the "Judaism" of the Chronicle is the religion of Musa, and the "Christianism" the religion of Isa—both, as it might be said, earlier and imperfect forms of Islam. But the words are mistranslations.

The Koran says: "Remember when we caused Conversion certain of the *Djinns* (or genii) to turn aside of the Peris. unto thee, that they might hear the Koran. And when they were present at the same they said, 'Give ear;' and when they had heard, they went back to the people, preaching. They said, 'Our people, verily we have heard a book which hath been revealed since Musa, confirming that which was before it, directing unto the truth and the right way. Our people, obey God's preacher, and believe in him'" (Sur. xlvii. 28 *seq*.).

The names of these Peris are given. Later, they came to the Prophet at Medina and said, "Our companions have become believers; they desire to see and hear thee." Then they gathered in the Valley of the Djinns, at two parasangs from Medina, towards the desert, where none dares pass at night. The Prophet promised that one night he would go to them. Here again the commentators think that the Peris must have previously been of the Jewish religion, *i.e.*, the religion of Musa, but by no means that of the Synagogue.

Again, it is said that at the time of the great Flight the villages of the Medina territory were inhabited by "Jews," or Arab descendants of the Beni-Israel, who had come from Syria and Ailia, fleeing from Nabuchodonosor, and that they had strong and solid castles. They knew from the Law the description of the Prophet, and had believed in him. But they thought *The Beni-Israel and the Arabs.* he would be of the Beni-Israel, of the descendants of Musa; they did not know that he would come of the Arabs. The Law had contained the very description of Mohammed, but the ancient Jews had suppressed it, so that these descendants did not know he would be an Arab. Each time they were attacked by the Arabs, they took the Law, seeking for the passage concerning the Prophet, putting their hands on it and saying, "Lord, aid us against these enemies because of the prophet," and they obtained help. Now when the Prophet appeared, and they saw that he was Arab and not Israelite, as they had thought, they would not believe in him, and said, "This is not the prophet that we expected;" as it is said in the Koran, "When a book came to them from Allah, confirming what was with them, though they had before prayed for assistance against the unbelievers, when that came to them which they knew, they had not believed therein; therefore the curse of Allah shall be on the infidels" (Sur. ii. 83).

The Rabbins knew nothing of all this; and it is once more clear that the "Judaism" of the Chronicle and the commentators is the system of the Law, adhered to especially by the Syrians and their descendants.

The sacred customs of the Arabs bear no trace of being founded on those of the Synagogue or the Church.

In the middle of the month Schaban, Allah commanded the Prophet to turn no more in prayer
The Qiblah to the holy place of Ailia, but to the Kaaba,
as the Arabs did. The "People of the Book" turned to Ailia, where was Solomon's temple, an illustrious place, towards which Musa and Isa both turned. When the Prophet came to Medina, where the cult of the "People of the Book" prevailed, who turned to the holy place at Ailia, Allah ordered him to turn also thither, that he might not vex them. Yet he longed to turn to the Kaaba, the Qiblah of Ibrahim and Ismail. Finally his prayer was heard in the second year of the Hegira, as it is recorded in the Koran, "We will that thou turn to a Qiblah that shall please thee. Turn to the holy temple" (Sur. ii. 139).

Here again, "Jews and Christians" is a misrendering. What distinctly appears is, that the followers of the prophets Musa and Isa in the Hedjaz and Syria turned to the holy place of the north, while the old idolaters of Mecca and the Moslems turned to the Kaaba. It is no affair of the Synagogue or of the Church.

In the month of Moharrem next year, it is said that
The Fast of Mohammed observed that "the Jews celebrated
Ramadan. on the tenth of the month a feast called
Aschoura," in commemoration of the deliverance of Musa from the sea. Then the Prophet ordained a fast to the Mussulmen on that day, saying, "I am worthier to follow the example of my brother Musa, son of Imram." Then the Prophet, seeing that "Christians" fasted during fifty days, desired to have a like fast in his religion. The Koran says, "O true believers! a

fast is ordained for you, as it was ordained unto those before you, that ye may fear" (Sur. ii. 179).

Who were those before the true believers? The Chronicle says, "Isa had ordained a fast of only thirty days; the 'Christians' have made the number fifty. Musa also had to observe the fast only of thirty days of the month Dsoul-qada, the time of his converse with Allah, but he added thereto eleven days." The Koran ordains the month Ramadan for the fast, the month in which the Koran was sent down. At the expiration of the fast the Prophet established the obligation of alms at the feast of the fast-breaking. Next year he left Mussulmen free to fast or not on the day of Aschoura.

It is needless to argue these points at length, because the Chronicles of the Rabbins supply no confirmation of the existence of Hebrews, or Hebrew teachers, or Hebrew literature in Arabia either at or before the time of Mohammed.

The Chronicle indeed frequently speaks of a people called *Yahoud* who had fortified places in the vicinity of Medina, and who were either expelled to Khaubon or put to death by Mohammed. They appear, however, to be clans of Arabs, who, though holding the Law in the Moslem sense, refused to submit to Islam and to the Prophet. There is nothing to connect them with the *Yehudim* of the Bible, except the fact of their common resistance to Islam. It appears probable that the term *Yehudim* was, like a number of other terms, such as *Taurath*, *Nebi*, &c., borrowed by the Rabbins from the Arabian tradition.

It is necessary, therefore, that the question of Geiger's prize-essay, "What did Mohammed borrow from the Jews?" should be reconsidered. Let us state the question in a more general form, "What did the

doctors of the Mosque borrow from the doctors of the
Synagogue?" Then the answer must be, according to
the evidence—absolutely nothing. Or if, again, the
question be stated thus, "What is the debt of Arabian
religious literature to Hebrew religious literature?"
The answer again must be, that the debt lies on the
other side, and that without exception. The Arabs
know of no Hebrew books containing revelations of
the will of Allah bequeathed from the dim foretime.
The Hebrews, on the other hand, who directly admit
that the Arabians were their masters in philosophy,
indirectly admit that they were also their masters in
religious lore, as we shall see when we come to examine
the traditions of the Synagogue.

And now, disengaging ourselves from the spell of the
great tradition stretching down from the first Adam
to the second, and again to Mohammed himself, and
reverting to the world of fact in place of that of inspired fancy, let us glance around us during the period
700-900 of our era.

The Koran, and the mass of religious legends on
which the Koran reposes, must during this period have
become fixed, and must have been known at Damascus,
Ailia, Bagdad, as well as at Mecca and Medina, and
equally in Africa and Spain, at the time when the
Rabbins and the Monks were not yet heard of in the
world. The Moslems had come to conceive of themselves as the people elect out of all the nations of the
earth to witness for the sole Deity of Allah, elect also
as Protestants and Iconoclasts in reference to the system
of worship that had so long prevailed in East and
West. They believed that a great Prophet had arisen
among them to teach them these things, and to close a
long prophetic and apostolic succession that could be

traced up through 6000 years to the first Adam.　They
believed that before Mohammed, had appeared Isa,
son of Mariam, about the beginning of the Roman
Empire, and it seems that the Roman emperors from
Tiberius had been mostly Masichists or followers of
the Masich.　The Chronicle even states that when
Mohammed made his first summons in the name of the
new religion to the princes of the earth, the Emperor
Heraclius had at once submitted, and had proclaimed
Islam in his dominions.　They believed that before Isa
had been Musa, and before Musa, Ibrahim the friend
of Allah, and his sons Ismail and Ishak.　They had
brought their chief sacred places into connection with
this great system of retrospection.

Such was the great effort of national and ecclesiastical
will, acting upon the imagination of one of the most
powerfully imaginative peoples in the world, the success
of which has had effects so momentous upon our
lives.　It may safely be said that this great Chronicle of
the Moslems is the foundation of all the mediæval
chronicles, not only of those compiled in the synagogues, but of those more numerously compiled in the
cloisters of the Orders of St. Basil and of St. Benedict.
We here touch the foundations of our Christianity;
we here arrive at last at the root of those conceptions
of the world and its origin, which, however beautiful
and impressive they may be in the light of sentiment,
have too long troubled our intelligence and impeded
the march of more useful knowledge.

It is needless to pursue this great Chronicle to the
end, and to dwell upon the particulars of the conquests
of Islam or of the life and death of Mohammed.　It
is apparent beyond question that down to the time
given as that of the death of Tabari, or about the year

920, that the Moslems ignore both Jews and Christians in our sense of these words. The like answer must be given to the question, What did Mohammed learn from the Christians? that we have already given to the corresponding question in reference to the Jews. The doctors of the Mosque know of followers of the Masich, of the Word of Allah, the created human son of Mariam; but they know nought of those Catholic Christians whose primitive spokesmen are solely the Basilians and the Benedictines. They condemn, apparently beforehand, and as if prophetically, the dogma that he was Son of God as infidelity. It is not the Rabbins nor the people of the Synagogue whom they accuse of conspiring against him, but unbelieving predecessors of their own; nor is the denial of his crucifixion directed against the monks. The whole is their revelation, and every page of Catholic polemic against the Docetic belief bears witness that it is they who are bent upon forcing their dogma of a crucified God-man upon an unwilling world.

It will be necessary now to show how the literature of the Rabbins followed upon that of the Moslem doctors, and that of the monks upon Rabbindom.

CHAPTER VIII.

THE RISE OF HEBREW LITERATURE.

THE rise of Hebrew literature in Spain, from the latter decades of the tenth century or from the beginning of the eleventh, is a fact of the utmost importance with reference to the rise of Christendom itself.

What is the date of our oldest Hebrew text of the Scriptures? Our English Revisers say, in their Preface of 1884, that "the earliest MS. of which the age is certainly known bears date A.D. 916." It would be more accurate to say that we have no certain knowledge of the age of any MS., and that the date given is probably too early by more than two centuries.

Date of Hebrew MSS. of the Old Testament.

Recently Dr. Wickes of Oxford[1] has discussed the antiquity of the Codex in the Synagogue at Aleppo, of which he has given a facsimile page in his work on the accents. This Codex has an epigraph assigning it to Aaron Ben Asher, at the beginning of the tenth century, which epigraph Dr. Wickes has no hesitation in treating as a fabrication. And he proceeds to remark: "How many other epigraphs of Jewish texts would, when carefully tested, have to be rejected, notably that of the Cambridge Codex 12, which makes a Spanish MS.,

---

[1] A Treatise on the Accentuation of the Twenty-one so-called Prose Books of the Old Testament. By William Wickes, D.D. Oxford: Clarendon Press, 1887.

unquestionably younger than the one we have been considering, written in the year 856." [1]   He adds that he has no doubt, from personal inspection, that a Codex in the Imperial Library of St. Petersburg, dated 1009, is also much younger than that date.

It is admitted, then, by experts that we have as yet no satisfactory criterion for determining the date of MSS., and that few, if any, can be assigned to an earlier date than the twelfth century of our era; a most important admission.

The question is part of a wider one, namely, at what epoch were the synagogues founded, with that system of worship and of instruction of which the Hebrew Scriptures formed a part? The whole subject stands in a clear light so soon as we draw a horizon line, as sharply as may be, between the imaginary retrospect of the Rabbins, which in great part is the same with the retrospect of the doctors of Islam, and the actual beginning of their literary activity.

In the first place, Hebrew writing, by their admission, was in its infancy as a sacred art during the tenth

Hebrew Writing and Grammar.

century. Hebrew grammar is not heard of till then, and its founders are said to be the Gaonim of Spain, who were pupils of the Arabians. The very name Gaonim is said to be of Arabic derivation; and the whole impetus to study and culture received by the early Rabbins came from Arabian culture and civilisation.

Orientalists have not yet arrived at an understanding

The Semitic Mother-tongue.

as to the mother-tongue of the various Semitic dialects; but were it not for the long pre-possessions in reference to the history of the Jews, it is tolerably clear that the Arabic would be

---

[1] The MS. is probably of the thirteenth century.

recognised as the parent of all the rest.   The late Dr.
W. Wright, in his Grammar of the Arabic language,
remarked : "The Hebrew of the Pentateuch and the
Assyrian, as it appears in even the oldest inscriptions,
seem to me to have already attained nearly the same
stage of grammatical development (or decay) as the
post-classical Arabic, the spoken language of mediæval
and modern times."

As an example of the prepossession to which we
have referred, the following may be cited from M.
Renan : "It was natural that the Gaonim should desire
to apply to their sacred tongue, so closely related to the
Arabic in point of grammar, the culture that the Arabs
used in respect to their idiom.   We should believe,
nevertheless, that before the labours founded on those
of the Arabs, of which the Gaon Saadia is regarded as
the 'beginner, the Jews were in possession of the
elements of a grammatical instruction." [1]

But the learned critic produces no argument in
support of such a belief, which should be abandoned
if it rests on no producible evidence.

It is equally clear that not only the forms, but the
substance of early Hebrew literature was *Hebrew Tra-*
derived from the traditions of the Arabians *dition de-*
—in other words, that the Biblical legends *pends on the Arabians.*
are based on those in the Koran and the Chronicle of
Tabari.   The resemblances and the variations presented
in the Moslem traditions, in the Chronicle of Josippon,
who is supposed to have been an Italian Jew, most
probably of the eleventh century, and in the *Antiquities*
of the pretended Jew Flavius Josephus, whose works
were produced by the Basilian monks, probably in some
monastery of Southern Italy, and lastly with the Hebrew

[1] *Hist. des Langues Sémitiques,* 172.

Bible, cannot be here considered in detail. It will be
sufficient to point out that if these writings are posterior
to those of the Arabians, it will be impossible to deny
the indebtedness of the traditions of the Synagogue
to those of the Mosque.

The Rabbins call their people *Ibrim*, Hebrews,
Ibrim and Eber. for whom they find an eponymous ancestor.
Eber, a name probably of Arabic origin.
They also have the name *Yehud*, corresponding to the
Arabic name already noticed, in the books of Daniel
and Ezra. *Yehudim*, Jews, is synonymous with *Ibrim*
in one prophetic passage, and they have another
eponymous, Yehudah, the *fourth* son of Yakoub. They
are also Yisrael, or Beni Yisrael, whose eponymous
is Yakoub-Yisrael; and they have a distinction of
"kings of Yehudah" and "kings of Yisrael," said
to date from the death of Solomon. Again, the ten
tribes of Yisrael are designated Ephraim, and their
eponymous is the younger son of Joseph.

Now the name Heber is recognised in the Chronicle
of Tabari in Mohammed's genealogy, who is traced up
to Kaidar, son of Ismail, and the line then ascends
though Ibrahim, Tharé, Nahor, Sarug, Ragon, Phaleg,
Heber, Salé, Arphaxad, to Sem, and from Sem to
Adam.[1]

Yehudah is recognised as *third* son of Yakoub in
the same Chronicle, and Yisrael is another name of
Yakoub. The Chronicle, as we have seen, also recognises Israelites as the designation of the people on whose
sacred history it rests down to the time of the rise of
Islam; although it ignores Rabbins and synagogues.
The Chronicle also gives Yussuf two sons, Ephraim
and Manasseh. The former has two prophetic sons.

---

[1] Chronicle ii. 356, Zotenberg. Cf. Gen. xi.

The Bible agrees with the Chronicle in tracing all mankind up to the three ancestors Sem, Ham, and Japhet; and the Bible, in making Sem father of all the Beni-Heber, whose younger son, Joktan, is the eponymous of the Joktanite Arabs, Almodad, and the rest, shows that the term Ibrim can hardly exclude the Arabs.[1]

Again, the Bible gives as Ishmaelites the people of Nebaioth, Kedar, and ten others, who dwell "from Havilah unto Shur, before Egypt, as thou goest towards Assyria." The Chronicle fixes Nabaioth and Kedar, the two sons of Ishmael, at Mecca, and says that all the people of the Hedjaz were descendants of Ibrahim and Ismael. And the Biblical legend also allows Ismael to be the elder son of the father of the faithful; an important admission, almost equivalent to the admission that the people who trace themselves to Isaac are younger in the religious tradition.

But leaving the dreamy indications of genealogies and geographies,—where the Rabbins show their antipathy to the Arabian tradition is in degrading the mother of Ishmael into an Egyptian bondwoman from an Egyptian princess, as she is in the Arabian tradition, in denying joint-heirship to her son with the son of Sara, and in transferring the honours of Ishmael to Isaac. There is no resort to such antipathy among the Arabians: they admit Isaac without depreciating him, reserving the preference to Ishmael. Their word is "the God of Ibrahim, Ismail, Isaac, and Yakoub."

More distinct are the constant indications in the poetical Old Testament books that the Bible lessons were written for a people who habitually considered

---

[1] Gen. x. See, on the tribe of Kahtan in Spain, *Mohamm. Dynasties,* by Gayangos, vol. ii. 24.

themselves captives, exiles, servants of other lords, and who were taught to look back upon imaginary splendours of a reign of David by way of consolation in their weakness, and stimulus to those hopes of dominion which beat high in the Jewish heart from the time of the Normans.

The tradition about David and the holy place at The Davidic Ailia evidently comes from the Muslim, as Tradition. also probably the name *Salem, Jerusalem.* It has never been shown that these names, and those of *Zion, Ariel,* have in general other than a poetical signification in the literature of the Rabbins ; for there is absolutely no evidence from architecture, from coins, or any other documents of antiquity, that this people ever enjoyed dominion in the city founded by the Romans as Aelia Capitolina, and conquered by the Arabs. But wherever in the Middle Ages there was a synagogue and a burial-ground, there was a "Zion" and a "Jerusalem" or "Ariel." [1]

One of the most remarkable things in the Old Testament writings is the hints it gives, not The Plot against the only in the Book of Esther, which was deJewish People. signed to explain and illustrate the festivity of Purim—a feast, we must believe, of purely mediæval origin—but elsewhere of plots against the whole people of the Synagogue to destroy them. And in the violent and allegorical language which the Rabbins habitually employ there are symbolic words which sufficiently reveal their meaning. "They have said, Come and let us cut them off from being a nation, that

[1] On a bronze ewer in the Bodleian Library, found in Suffolk in the seventeenth century, there is an inscription : "The gift of the martyr Rabbi Yechiel, who answered and directed the congregation as he desired, in order to see the face of Ariel, as it is written in the law of Yekuthiel, Righteousness delivereth from death."

the name of Israel may be no more in remembrance. For they have consulted together with one consent; they are confederate against thee; the tabernacles of Edom and the Ishmaelites."[1]

Now the mediæval chroniclers say expressly that Edom means the Roman Empire,[2] or the European powers. It is well known that the mediæval Rabbins take delight in employing a great number of synonyms, drawn from the Biblical chronicles and genealogies, to express the same idea. Just as with the Arabians "Nebuchadnezzar, king of Babylon," is a symbolic expression for a power inimical to the Semites, so with Assyrians, Chaldees, Ammonites, Moabites, Philistines, and the like. In the same way the Moors in Spain called tribes alien to them Philistines and Amalekites. There is little, however, in the Biblical writings which points clearly to the sons of Ishmael as enemies of the Jews, distinguished from the Romans. We have but occasional reference to Hagarenes, Ishmaelites, sons of Kedar. Ephraim appears to denote a large branch of half-Israelites, " a cake half-turned," regarded by the Jews as inferior to themselves, who honour Jehuda; while the Mohammedans, who so highly honour Joseph, say that Jehuda was the smallest and most despised of the tribes. Amidst the dense obscurities of the Biblical books one point at least is luminous. The Jews with the Mohammedans are children of Jacob or Israel. The Jews are not children of Ishmael; they honour the younger son of Abraham. But both branches of the stock regard Esau-Edom, *i.e.*, the Greeks and Romans, as elder brethren of the

[1] Ps. lxxxiii.
[2] One of the earliest is Benjamin of Tudela, c. 1160, who calls Rome the Edomite capital, and the Pope the head of the Edomitish religion. The book is of dubious date.

Israelites. The earlier part of the catalogue of nations in Genesis x. is full of Greek and Latin names, according to the explanation of the Jerusalem Targum; and there are more Greek and Latin words in Biblical Hebrew in general than is commonly known.

These are but general observations. But it may be safely said that if the Bible, which, regarded as a chronicle of ancient times, has hitherto defied all the efforts of ordinary criticism, is ever to be understood, it must be in the light of the dialect and the peculiar world of thought in which the mediæval Rabbins lived and moved.

Let us turn now to the question of the origin of the
The Tal-
muds.
Talmuds, in which citations from the Bible lie embedded, even as citations from the New Testament lie embedded in the commentaries of the monks. The Rabbins who constructed the Talmuds alone were in the secret of the date of the composition of the Hebrew Scriptures. The Talmuds, moreover, are their most valued books. They have a saying that while the Scriptures are as water, the Mishna is as wine, and the Gemara as spiced wine.

Now the traditions which still linger in the syna-
Popular
Jewish
Mythology.
gogues with respect to the origin of the Talmuds will hardly bear critical scrutiny. There is evidence in them of that same straining after an imaginary antiquity which is characteristic of all new peoples and departures. In a current Anglo-Jewish almanac, e.g., we read in a chronological table of an edict of the Emperor Augustus in favour of the Jews in England of the year fifteen of our era; though but recently a Jewish scholar, Mr. Joseph Jacobs, has shown that there is no evidence of the arrival of any Jews in England until about the year 1070.

We find the datum of the burning of the temple and

the capture of Jerusalem in the year 70, but it appears from some of the Jewish mediæval chronicles that the year 68 or 69 is given. Nor can the idea of any such event be traced higher than the tenth—more probably the eleventh century

The next incredibility is the capture of Bither, and the slaughter of 600,000 Jews, which may be traced to similar sources. The date given is the year 134.

Then the Mishna is said to have been written by "Rabbi Judah, the Prince," in 141, the Jerusalem Talmud to have been completed in 469, and the Babylonian Talmud in 504.

We read of "the first mention of the Jews in the English chronicles" in the year 740. These chronicles of the monasteries have been shown to be false and antedated, as we have already observed; nor are there genuine notices in monkish chronicles of the Jews in any part of Europe until, at the earliest, the thirteenth century.

But now we come upon a date which may possibly be accepted; it is "Solomon Isaacides or Rashi flourished 1062." And again: "The Crusaders commenced what they termed the holy war by murdering the Jews of Europe, 1096."

It is, in fact, about the middle of the eleventh century that the Ibrim, or Jehudim, or Beni-Israel of the synagogues enter the field of historical observation. Between the years 1000–1200 falls the first period of Judaism and its most important literature.

There is indeed a tradition concerning a Rabbinical succession from a much earlier time; there were Tanaim; there were Amoraim in the time of Antoninus Pius, with whom the Talmud is supposed to have originated; there were Rabanim of

Dogma of the Rabbinical Succession.

Pumbadita in Persia, and finally Gaonim of that and other places.[1] Great was the legendary renown of these Eastern academies, and from them the Rabbinical illumination is said to have passed to Spain in the tenth century. But the tradition demands critical attention. It is a "far cry" from Mesopotamia to Tarshish, and one would expect stronger historic links connecting these extreme points of Rabbinical culture. Moreover, had Rabbinical schools been famous for so many centuries in the East, the westward migratory doctors must have brought with them a whole system of theology and of devotional literature wherewith to furnish the synagogues of Spain. But the facts of Spanish Rabbindom down to Maimonides, distinctly negative this supposition. Everything relating to the Synagogue cult had to begin in Spain. Consequently the whole theory of a succession of Rabbins and of "Princes of the Captivity" in the East, reaching up so high as even the seventh century of our era, breaks down on examination. It seems to be, in fact, a case of reversed or double wandering, similar to those frequent in the old Greek historical mythology, that we have here before us. The splendour of the Jewish status in Spain has reflected itself upon schools of the East in reality later than those of Spain, and on "Princes" who probably did not flourish in the East till the twelfth century.

Actual Rise of the Spanish Schools.

---

[1] See S. Ben Virga, *Hist. Judaica*, c. 42 ; D. Ganz, *Tschemach David ;* Depping, *Die Juden im Mittelalter*, p. 63 ff. Isaac Disraeli, *Genius of Judaism*, 1833, remarks on the entire incompetence of the Rabbins for history, and dates their efforts at historiography from the time of the contest with the Karaites or anti-traditionists. He refers to the *Sepher Juchaism* of Zacuto, 1500, as the most important of Jewish histories, along with the *Seed of David* and the *Sceptre of David* of Ganz and De Virga, p 9 *seq*.

Let us look a little more closely at the tradition Two "Fathers and Teachers of Israel" are supposed to have flourished at Pumbadita in the tenth century, R. Scherira and R. Hai. To the former is ascribed a "secret roll," not extant, also judicial "Responses" and authoritative "Epistles." Further, he is said, about 987, to have produced a chronicle of the Rabbinical succession. But it is admitted that doubts were rife about the antiquities of the Israelites in his time. and that he was not an impartial writer.[1]

And yet upon so frail a link as the personality and authority of these Rabbins we are invited to make our belief in a history of some 400 or 500 preceding years depend.   We are to thank Scherira for "the continuity of the thread from the close of the Talmudic epoch down to his time," though he can produce no more than a bare skeleton of names and years, by which he links the past of Rabbindom with himself.   He is succeeded by his son, Hai, "who sat upon the throne of his father, and his rule was greatly strengthened." His epoch is given as 969–1038.   But this Rabbin is said to have been more an Arabic than a Hebrew scholar ; and the statement is made concerning him, which will hardly surprise the reader who has followed our argument, that he read the Koran and the Moslem traditions in order to understand the Bible.[2]   It is also said that he learned versification from the Spanish Rabbins, which he employed in order to embody moral precepts similar to the proverbs ascribed to Solomon. It is Spanish and African Jews who glorify the memory of this Father in Israel.

[1] Graetz, *Gesch. d. Juden.*, v. 387.
[2] Ibid. vi. 8.

Another earlier name in the lists of Jewish illustrious men is that of R. Saadia, of Faium, in Upper Egypt (892–942), who is said to have been the master of Hai.   How so, if the school of Pumbadita was earlier?

R. Saadia.

But we have no distinct knowledge of Saadia, and it is admitted that there was not much Talmudic knowledge in Egypt till two centuries later, and that, in fact, the ideas about Saadia, who is said to have first translated the Scriptures into Arabic, to have made some attempts at Hebrew grammar and lexicography, and to have framed a Rabbanite or orthodox festal calendar, may be traced to the school of Maimonides.

We have no writings of Saadia, and he himself, in his personality unknown, became probably from the twelfth century an object of retrospective honour to the ad- herents of oral tradition in Egypt.   The origin of the school of Maimonides itself carries us back to Spain, his birthplace.

Advancing down the stream of time, we are informed that North Africa was "deprived of its schools and teachers" about 1015–1055.   We can only understand this as a mediæval expression denoting that they had not yet been founded.   About 1027 is given as the date of the dawn of Rabbinical schools in Spain; a little later the Gaonim are said to be extinct in the East. As we understand the drift of such legends, they lead us to infer that it was the schools of Spain which began to supply Rabbins to Africa, Egypt, Syria, and Persia during the eleventh century; and that the legends about the priority of Pumbadita and Sura owe their genesis to the later prosperity and ambition of these schools.   It was natural, moreover, that Orientals in

Spain should desire to make out an early connection with the East.

Let us attend to the striking and pathetic legend of the rise of the school at Cordova. Rabbi Moses and his son, R. Henoch, are supposed to arrive in rags of sackcloth about the year 980,[1] and entering the school, to take part in a discussion on the day of atonement. The presiding Rabbi, Nathan, rises, impressed with the learning of the stranger in rags, and cedes to him the place of judge of the congregation of Cordova. The tale ran that R. Moses had been captured by a Moslem Emir, who had assailed his beautiful wife. She, inquiring if the sea would give up its dead at the day of judgment, and receiving an affirmative answer from her husband, had cast herself into the waves. The Rabbin himself was sold and redeemed by his countrymen at Cordova, while his companions on the same vessel, R. Shemariah and R. Hoshiel, were sold to Alexandria and to Alkihoran in North Africa, where they became respectively chief Rabbins.

The legend is more luminous than authentic facts could be. It shows that the Rabbins of Spain and of the West generally looked upon the tenth century as a dim and almost unknown past; that their predecessors had been poor wandering slaves under the Moslem rule, and that practically the origin of the schools of Cordova was not within the ken of the historical inquirer. With such data before us, it is impossible to admit that Cordova could have "taken over a great heritage of learning from Judea, Babylonia, and North Africa, in order to increase it manifold for coming generations." No; for in the eleventh century ignorance of Hebrew

_____
[1] The date is uncertainly given.

reigned in the East, while in the West the knowledge of it was beginning. It is only in Spain and during the eleventh century that we move out of the legendary mist into historic daylight, and can pass in review a long line of scholars whose work is crowned by the great Rabbin, the true Moses of the Synagogue, who fixed its creed and its law, Maimonides.

To the famous Samuel the Prince (Nagid) of Granada (1027) is ascribed a number of works, the very titles of which should indicate that the Biblical literature of the Synagogue was beginning. He is said to have written a Psalter, a Book of Proverbs, a Koheleth or Ecclesiastes. He is said to have methodised the Talmud, which we may perhaps take to be a figure of speech for the inception of the Talmud. He too busied himself with the catena of tradition; in other words, with the contrivance of an ecclesiastical retrospective, leading up from his time to the phantom scholars of the "Great Synagogue" through the various dynasties between. He also wrought at Hebrew grammar and at a practical commentary on the Talmud, which became canonical. He corresponded with brethren in Syria and Egypt. His name may clearly stand as denoting that the canonical time of the Synagogue has at least begun.

Samuel the Prince was a beloved ideal among the Spanish Rabbins through all the Middle Ages. Two of them who lived in the fifteenth century say of him that "he showed good to the Jews in Spain, Maghreb, Africa, and Egypt." But after his time those events began which have been written in blood for the unhappy people of the Synagogue. The son of R. Samuel, named Joseph Halevy, say the good Rabbins, who write and who think in the dialect of the Bible, "walked in the ways of his father; he stood behind him in nought, save that he was not so lowly as he, because in his youth he had no need to fear ; so he became proud to his destruction, and the great men of Granada envied him, so that they did not speak friendly with him. They rose against him on the Sabbath, the ninth day of the tenth month (Tebet), and slew him with the whole congregation, and the Jews who had come from far lands that they might know of his learning and his greatness, with the sword in that fatal time. The mourning for them spread through all lands when these horrible tidings were heard. Observe it, O God, and behold and plead Thou their cause!"[1]

At Cordova, Jona Marinus (995–1050) is said to have been the creator of Hebrew syntax, and to have surpassed his rival Samuel of Granada in mastery of the sacred tongue. His great interest was Biblical exegesis, and he is said to have abandoned childish interpretations. These dates must be received with caution.

Then at Malaga we come upon the Jewish Plato —an inflated title—Salomon Ibn Gebirol or Avicebron (1021–1070). But this early Ibn Gebirol. mediæval philosopher passed for an Arabian, and must have been the pupil of the Arabians. His work *Mekor Chaiim*, "Fountains of Life," was translated into Latin in the next age—the first age for translations into that tongue.[2] It may be recalled in this connection that the Arabians produced a line of savants from the ninth century—Al Kindy, Al Farabi, Ibn Sina

---

[1] *Emek Habacha* of R. Joseph Hacohen, by D. M. Wiener, 1858. Cf. *Schebet Jehuda*, § 5, *Chronicles of R. Joseph*. The date is very uncertain, 1064–1084. The fast of Tebet is on the 10th.

[2] So Jourdain, *Recherches*, &c., iii. 8.

(Avicenna), Al Ghazil in the East ; Ibn Badscha (Avempace), Ibn Tofail, Ibn Roschd (Averroes), in Spain and Africa. Ritter observes that the names of Saadia, Gebirol, and Maimonides may represent the beginning, middle, and end of the connection of the Jews with Arabian philosophy. The like remarks may be made of their connection with Arabian religion. It is probable that the earlier Rabbins wore the turban, and it is doubtful whether any public synagogue could have been built before the eleventh century.

It is unnecessary to cite the long roll of names of Hebrew grammarians, Talmudists, commentators, writers of psalms and prayers for sacred use in the synagogues during the period 1000–1200. They all write in a classical Hebrew, little differing from that of the Bible ; nor can we discover any schools where the Bible is so likely to have been commenced as in those of Spain. So far as the scenery and customs are concerned, there is no land which appears better to reflect the Bible than Southern Spain ; as Richard Ford in his charming Handbook frequently notices.

It has been sometimes remarked as strange, if Hebrew literature be of immense antiquity, that Moses Maimonides (c. 1140–1205) should be looked up to by the Rabbins as the great authority for the creed and the customs of the Synagogue. But in the light of the facts just considered, it is evident that no scholar could have been better acquainted with the whole formation of the literature of his people and the kind of authority it possessed. It was only in his time and that of the Emperor Frederic II. that the learned world became distinctly conscious of three rival traditions, the Mohammedan, the Jewish, and the Christian, and of an inter-relation between them. On the part of the

Rabbins themselves there are not wanting confessions to the effect that the pretensions to a high literary antiquity were not founded on fact. Thus Ben Jasus of Toledo is said to have anticipated modern criticism, and to have asserted that the Book of Genesis was written many ages "after Moses." The criticism may have been meant to apply also to the Arabian tradition.

Let us try to form to ourselves a picture of the rise of the Jewish communities in Cordova, Granada, Seville, and Toledo. The Moslems conquered Spain, which they call Andalus, early in the eighth century. Our historian is here Al Makkari, who is believed to have written only in the eleventh century. He makes one or two references to the people called *Yahud,* which can no more be understood of the congregations governed by Rabbins than the similar references in the Koran or the Chronicle of Tabari can be. He knows nothing of Christians and their churches, although he has some quaint allusions to the worship of a Virgin which probably relates to some old Roman goddess. He says that Karnattah (Granada) was handed over to *Yahud* to keep. He has an obscure reference to a Jewish poet, who was thought to be an Islamite at heart. The indications are extremely faint and dubious ; nor is there a word in this writer, amidst all his descriptions of the splendours of Cordova and the other cities, which would lead us to infer that he knew of flourishing synagogues belonging to a rival sect. The evidence is blankly negative, equally with that of the chronicles of the Spanish Rabbins.

We must assume, then, that in the most palmy time of the Western caliphate, a little later than Al Makkari, the people called *Jehud* began to establish themselves as a distinct community, ruled over by men who wielded the imaginary "sceptre of Judah," and who persuaded themselves that they were in the line of descent from the famous King David or Daoud, honoured alike by them and by their Moslem masters. With culture, toleration became the fashion of Islam ; and the Jews, who had always differed in certain customs from the Hagarenes, ventured to acquire a literary art, a holy language, and a sacred architecture in imitation of their neighbours.

Of peculiar interest is the Jewry at Toledo. The *The Jewry at Toledo.* older synagogue shows horse-shoe arches springing from bastard Gothic capitals. The decoration is Moorish. The date of its erection has not been discovered. In 1405 it was converted into a church under the persecuting San Vicente de Ferrer. Its ceiling—an illustrative fact—is said to have been made from beams of Lebanon cedars. The other synagogue, built in the fourteenth century, shows a mixture of Moorish and Gothic with Hebrew. It passed to the Order of Calatrava in 1494. The walls of these synagogues must be conscious of all that was important in the rise and growth of Judaism. Men may have worshipped there at the time when William the Conqueror was landing on these shores, who knew all that was to be known concerning the formation of a community of wandering traders into a nation and a Church. But when they first landed in Spain, they were doubtless like a rope of sand, or like the scattered bundle of sticks in their favourite proverb.

They met in private assemblies, and encouraged one another in the feeling of a common nationality and religion. They formed a system of dissent from Islam, on grounds that are imperfectly known. They learned to look up to the Patriarch Jacob-Israel, and to his son Jehuda, as their progenitors. Their great ideals in the nearer retrospective were Moses and David. The Ideal of David became the founder of their state, the David. builder of "Zion," in a poetic sense. Their hearts beat high with the hope of deliverance from their subject condition under the renewal of the glory of the house of David. Son of David became the name of the hoped-for Prince or Messias; and one may suppose that this projection of the Messiah into the future was connected with a rejection of the Moslem Masich, Isa, who had appeared in the past. In their oracles David became first-born son of God. "God and David" became the watchword of religion and freedom.[1] As the new Pythagoreans had delighted to refer to Pythagoras works of their own composition in a very late age, so the simple-hearted Rabbins delighted to trace up all prophecy to its fountain-head in Moses, and all psalmody to David. They read lessons from the Law which they conceived, in common with the Moslems, to have been given in the Arabian desert. We may listen to the echoes of their prayers and songs in the Psalter, and in the writings of such as Halevy, while their sermons lie embedded in the books ascribed to Isaiah, Jeremiah, Ezekiel, and the other prophets. The mediæval Cohanim and their Levites persuaded themselves that they stood in a glorious sacerdotal succession from the priests and Levites of the Temple of the days of old.

Looking out from their humble meeting-places, they encourage one another to believe that the tyranny of Edom—that is, of the Europeans—is doomed. The

[1] Ps. lxxxix. 27–28; Hosea iii. 5; Jer. xxx. 8, 9; Ez. xxxiv. 22–24; Zech. xii. 8. Zunz, *Die synagogale Poesie des Mittelalters*, 1855, p. 4.

intensity of their sufferings is reflected in the violence
of their imagery, and is followed by the reaction of
extravagant hopes. Every legend about Egypt or
Babylon in the past becomes a prediction of deliverance.
The Eternal stands in indissoluble covenant with His
Spouse, the Beloved of the mystic "Song of Solomon."
He is Father, Friend, King, Redeemer. Prayer, since
the time of the uprise of the Iconoclasts, has replaced
sacrifices; it is a higher duty, and protects from the
pains of hell. A simple ritual, consisting of the
Schemah or confession of the Divine unity, the Tefilla
or prayer proper, and the Keduscha or glorification of
God, was gradually formed and enriched during this
period. The great Day of Atonement reminded of the
religious duties of repentance and amendment as the conditions of forgiveness ; while Purim cemented natural
feeling in recollection of sufferings and a deliverance,
which, under the form of allegory, may be regarded as
strictly historical.

If, in the light of a strict scrutiny of the evidence,
Persecutions the rise of Hebrew literature in Spain cannot
of the Jews be regarded as a renaissance, but must be
regarded as a beginning, the Bible and the Talmud
first become of close and vital interests as the literature of a people who have become known to us since
the time of the Norman conquests. They become the
mirror of actual history, and no longer of our own
capricious fancies. We listen to the cries of the people
against the incessant extortion of Edom, whose word is
ever, "Give ! give !" their plaints of poverty, and of the
endeavours of their foes to rob them of what was left,
their moral reputation, and even of their lives. They
are treated as dogs, as the filth of the streets, as lying
witnesses, sitting in a corner and daring no reply to

slanders. They are taunted with the failure of their Messianic hopes. "Where is their God? Where is this edifice of the Judaism of the future? Why are the sons of kings so cast down?" cry the worshippers of Moloch and of Baal. "Why does not the son of Jesse come? Why do the chariot-wheels of Jehovah delay?" The oppressors shake their heads as they cast a glance upon the poor, mad, dreaming Rabbin. His hope flees like the cloud, they say, and his eyes run down with tears. The famous passage in the fifty-third of Isaiah is the very ideal, painted in the deepest colours of experience, of the Mediæval Rabbin. Was there ever sorrow like his?

One cannot read the chronicles of the Rabbins relating to the Crusades without burning shame and indignation. The rank and file of the warriors of the Cross were mostly composed of what honest Prebendary Thomas Fuller calls the "Devil's Blackguard." One would fain hope that the atrocities they committed in the synagogues have been exaggerated. They appear, however, to be too well authenticated by the voices of too many witnesses from the Synagogue, which has more justly earned the honours of saintdom and martyrdom than any religious community in the world. "Beware of denying the Only One, of forsaking thy faith, of breaking thy truth," the Rabbins incessantly exhort; and in response, to quote from Zunz, "Noble spirits exerted their finest sap, pressed flowers gave forth their perfume, and the fettered became freer than the jailors." It is later that the warnings in the best Jewish moral literature against the "worship of the dead," meaning the rites of old religion, and against idols, belong. The Gentile cultus is Baal's worship; baptism is defilement; a church is a "house of errors."

U

Terrible are the tales of suicide, of the sacrifice of children by their own parents, that the sin of apostasy might be avoided and that the unity of the Eternal might be exalted. Beautiful women, youths and aged men, went to their fiery doom, chanting, "Hear, O Israel, the Lord our God is one God!" It was the last cry of bride and bridegroom, who were united in life, and were not divided in their sacrificial death.

Writing of the English persecutions, honest Thomas Fuller says, "Endless it were to reckon up the indignities offered unto the Jews, on occasion sometimes given, but oftener taken. Apprentices nowadays do not throw sticks at cocks on Shrove Tuesday so commonly as then on that day they used clubs on the Jews, if appearing out of their houses ; a people equally unhappy at feasts and at frays. For whensoever the Christians at any revels made great entertainments, the Jews were made to pay the reckoning. And wheresoever any brawl began in London, it ended always in the Old Jewry, with pillaging of the people therein. What good heart can, without grief, recount the injuries offered to those who once were the only people of God ?"

We dwell upon these matters because no literature can be understood except in relation to the life of the people from which it springs, and because it may be said that the Biblical writers, in the larger sense of the term, extend down to the seventeenth century, and yield us massive evidence of the real historical conditions under which the whole of the Synagogue literature was composed. It is one of the strangest things in the world that in our churches should still be chanted psalms of malediction, which no doubt "never cost a Christian his life," but which must have been directed by the Rabbins against the precursors of the Christians.

At this late epoch in the history of literature, we have still to ask, How it has come to pass that the Old Testament remains an un- intelligible book to the critics? For it can- not be denied that what is called Old Testament criticism is nothing but the record of a series of fumblings and stumblings on the part of learned men, and that little has been gained except the gradual conviction that these writings are of much later origin than tradition has accustomed us to believe.

The Bible in the Light of Mediæval Times.

The cause of this failure has been the baseless assumption as to the origin and date of the Hebrew books ; and secondly, the assumption that they were designed to impart exact geographical and historical information. In so far as the contents of the Bible run parallel to the great Arabian tradition, we have shown that these contents are based upon the Arabian tradition, or upon some tradition common to both the Arabians and the Jews. And with regard to those parts of the Old Testament which are peculiar to the Synagogue, we may in a few words show that they are alone intelligible in the light of Mediæval times.

The' analogy of the Koran and the Old Testament holds good so far, that neither the one book nor the other can be understood apart from the light shed upon them from the class of men with whom they originated ; that is, in the case of the Old Testament, from the authors of the poetry, the sermons, and the expositions composed for the use of the Synagogue, and further from the chronicles of Mediæval Rabbins. It will be necessary to offer only a few illustrations of the sym- bolical use of Bible names, which will indicate the actual world in which the Bible writers were actually living and moving.

Let us revert for a moment to the Table of Nations in Genesis x. It is a Mediæval brain-map, derived from classical and Arabian sources. By the sons of Japhet, the Jerusalem Targum understands Africa, Germany, Media, Macedonia, Athens, Assos (?), Thrace, Asia, Phrygia or Persia, Barbaria, Hellas (or Elis ?), Tarsus, Italy, Dodona, vers. 2–4.

Under the kingdom of Babel, Edessa, Nisibis, and Ctesiphon are named ; under the Assyrian, Nineveh and Artagigarta, vers. 10, 11. Then we find after Mizraim the names Mareotes (Moors?), Pentapolis, Lusitania (or Lycia), Pelusium, Pantascenitæ, Philistæi, and Cappadoces, Hivuæus, Tripolis, Arcæi, Caparossa, Antaraḍos, Emessa, Antioch, vers. 13–18.

R. Joseph sees in the Gomer and Riphath the Franks of the Gironde and the Seine, and the Bretons of the Loire.

The Semitic tribes are all, as children of Eber, Ibrim or Hebrews. Yet the names Joktan, Almodad, Sheleph, Hazarmaveth, Jerah, &c., all point to an Arabian source, as the place Mesha probably denotes Mecca.[1]

There is, then, nothing distinctly Jewish in the Table of the Nations, nothing even that indicates a writer viewing the world from a standpoint in the East. It sketches a map of the world ; and if we are to judge of his position by considering what objects he describes most clearly, we may place him in the West of Europe. There is some advance in geographical description over the Moslem chronicler, who simply sets down the Arabians and Persians and the best

[1] See Al Makkari, of the eleventh century, in Gayangos

people as Semitic, the black people as Hamitic, and
the Turks, Sclaves, and Magyars as Japhetic.

But there is little geographical information in any
other part of the Bible.   The constantly _{Symbolism}
recurring names, which we have been wont ^{of the Bible.}
to understand of cities and lands, are really symbolic
of institutions, societies, powers.   The historical principle of the Biblical writers is very simple.   The
world revolves about Judaism.   The interest of the
present and future is concentrated in the chosen
people of the Synagogue, and is reflected in the forms
of historic retrospection or allegorical contemplation.
The world exists as a theatre for the enactment of a
divine drama in which the Synagogue is always acting
or suffering the leading part.   There is no interest
in the nations except as the conquerors, allies, or possible subjects of the Jews.

Judah and Jerusalem are, in general, poetic terms,
signifying the people of the Dispersion, who are the
Praise of the Lord, and the Heritage of Peace, amidst
whom kings of righteousness have reigned, where is
the altar and hearth of the Most High, and whence His
Word hath ever gone forth.   The people is the Vineyard planted by the right hand of the Eternal in the
midst of an idolatrous multitude, of whom Baal is the
constant symbol; she is the Vine itself, "brought up
out of Egypt," that is tended in the state of captivity
by the Divine hand.   She is the Bride, the Spouse, the
Garden of the Eternal.   When the poets sing of
Lebanon, they seem to be thinking of some superb
roof like that of the synagogue at Toledo.   The grief
of the persecuted worshippers is the mourning of
Lebanon, the desecration of the synagogues its fall.
Bashan, and Carmel, and Gilead have the like symbolic

reference to the sacred place of meeting in a strange land; Jordan is a symbolic river, separating the chosen people from the world; the land of Jordan and the pride or swelling of Jordan are no prosaic allusions to physical phenomena, but to national ideas.

Profuse is the employment of the image of the valley by the poets, still in no topographical sense : the Vale of the judgment of God, the Vale of decision, the Vale of sorrow, the fat Vales, the Vale of acacias, the Vales of blessing and of weeping, the Vale of vision, and so on, signify the homes of Judaism.   The Hebrew words are quite general and vague.

The holy cities, the cities of Judah, their watch-towers, denote the settlements of Jews; and the con-gregation of God, and "all the holy places of God in the land," are plainly the synagogues, viewed by the psalmist in an affecting picture as broken down, their fine wood-work hacked to pieces (Ps. lxxiv.).   Their *Bâmoth*, or high places, sanctuaries or chapels served by their Cohanim or priestly Rabbins, and their rich furniture, are also simply the Mediæval synagogues, contrasted with the high places of Baal, the temples in which images are still preserved—the tents of vanity, or the houses of Baal Peor.   The Mediæval Rabbins delighted in considering that, as sprung of a royal and sacerdotal stock, the name David is symbolic of their pretensions, which are set forth in the Bible under the figure of the Horn of David, the Throne of David, the Tower of David, and the House of David, the Sprout of David, and the like.

There is something almost childish in the vanity with which the Spanish Rabbins delighted in rivalry with the "nobles of the Hagarenes."   Their status was no doubt splendid to ostentation (a weakness of the Jews) until the calamities of the latter part of the eleventh century fell upon them. A chronicler of the fifteenth century describes them as riding out of Toledo each day in 700 chariots; and all will remember the striking invectives ascribed to the Prophet Isaiah against the finery of the Jewish ladies.

Where were these synagogues? There is a poetic passage in the Bible which plainly indicates that they were at the date of its composition to be found in Spain. The consideration of this passage leads us into the heart of Mediæval Judaism. Biblical Reference to Spain and France

"They of the south occupy the Mount of Esau, and they of the plain the Philistines.

"And they of the mountains occupy the fields of Ephraim and the fields of Samaria, and Benjamin, Gilead.

"And the banished ones of this coast[1] of the sons of Israel the cities of the Canaanites unto Zarephath.

"And the banished ones of Jerusalem which are in Sepharad occupy the cities of the south.

"And saviours come unto Mount Sion to judge the Mount of Esau,

"And the kingdom becometh Jehovah's."—OBAD. 19, 20.

Now Sepharad means in the holy language of Judaism Spain and nothing but Spain. Zarephath no less distinctly means France. Nor is it possible to throw a clearer light upon the passage than by citing from the Spanish Rabbin Joseph (c. 1496–1575), who describes himself as "son of Joshua, son of Meir, son of Jehudah, son of Joshua, son of Jehuda, son of David, son of Moses, of the priests who went forth from Huete from the land of Sepharad." His book is "a memorial of the multitude of afflictions which we have experienced in the countries of the Gentiles from the day that Jehudah was led captive Rabbi Joseph of Sepharad.

[1] Or host or fortress.

from his country until this day; and of the wars of the kings of the Gentiles which they have warred in the land of Jehudah and Jerusalem, and the exiles from Zarephath and Sepharad, that the sons of Israel may know it. And I have gathered in Israel after the reapers, as my hand hath found it, here a little and there a little. Therefoie also I shook my lap to write a book of the chronicles of the kings of Zarephath and of Sepharad and of the kings of the house of Othman; and to put these times in a book, and to write how these Egyptians wronged us as well as our fathers, that the remembrance thereof may not pass away from among the Jews, nor the memory come to an end from their seed, until the lame shall leap as a hart and the tongue of the dumb sing. Sing praises unto the Lord, for He hath done glorious things? This is known in every land."

In his chronicles, Esau or Edom constantly stands for the Roman Empire in the mediæval sense; Ashkenaz is Germany; "Egyptians" means the same with "Edomites."

The passage in Obadiah, in the light of this commentary, is simply a description of the Jews living in the midst of the "Idumeans," *i.e.*, the people of the provinces of the old Roman Empire. The Israelites dwell in "Mount Esau," that is, in old Roman territory, chiefly in Spain. Plainly, therefore, "cities of the Canaanites," is simply symbolical for cities of Israel's enemies in that land, and "Canaan" is constantly a symbol of an idolatrous people. Philistines probably stand for the Moors; Ephraim, Samaria, the Mount of Samaria, and Gilead, and Manasseh, and Benjamin appear to be all poetic synonyms. If the "Gate of Benjamin" is in the north of Jewry proper, is identical with the "Gate of Ephraim," the Jews in the north of Europe may be signified.

In order to show that the vivid representations in the Prophets of the prostrate and desolate condition of the Jews after some terrible persecution really refer to the time of the Crusades, it is of course necessary to show that they cannot be related to any earlier event in the history of Judaism. Now the fact is that the Book of Tradition, or the Rabbinical chroniclers down to the sixteenth century, have no distinct knowledge of any occurrence of the kind until they come to the year 1096. Their meagre and inaccurate account of the preceding thousand years has been borrowed chiefly from the Arabians and the monastic chroniclers. The fact that a Spanish Rabbin should begin with Adam, and dispose of the interval between him and the first Crusade in a few rambling pages, seems decisive of the question.[1] In the *Valley of Baca*, by the same author, he admits that he used Christian books. It seems, then, conclusive that the Biblical writer of a late time is a sure index to the date when the memory of the first Biblical writer begins.

Reflections on the Crusades.

Now what is the Rabbinical-Hebrew account of the first Crusade? Let us try to separate his own thoughts from the particulars he has derived from the monks, and ascertain how far he follows in the wake of the old Biblical tradition.

The First Crusade.

R. Joseph says that there arose against the Jews "a nation of fierce countenance, that spared not the persons of the old, nor had compassion on children."

---

[1] So Abraham Zacuto, a Spanish Rabbin, formed a Rabbinical succession from Adam down to 1500 A.D. I. Disraeli, *Genius of Judaism*, 84. I have not been able to see Zacuto's work

He says that the year 1096 was one of sorrow for
Jacob; that they were given over to plunder in the
countries of the uncircumcised in all the places where
they were scattered. He says that "their sorrows and
desolations are written in the Law of Moses." And
indeed in the Book of Deuteronomy, with the corresponding passages in the Prophets, we find his terrible
description almost word for word.[1]

He compares the invading hosts to a multitude of
locusts, precisely as the Prophet Joel does.[2] He iden-
tifies the Germans and the French with the people of
"the fierce countenance." He tells how they resolved
to destroy the Jews from being a nation (in revenge
for their Messias), so that the name of the Jews should
be had no more in remembrance, unless they would
change their glory and be as themselves. He tells
how the Ashkenazim or German Jews had their hearts
melted and became as water; how fear took hold on them
and pain as on a woman in travail; how they bare their
lives in their hands, proclaimed a fast, and cried to the
Lord in their distress,[3] who covered Himself with a
cloud that the prayer should not pass through.[4]

In Trier, on the Sabbath-day, 18th of Iyar, ten men
of the congregation were slain with the edge of the
sword "because they would not be defiled with the
proud water."[5] A pious woman chose death rather
than life; she took a knife and slew herself because
she would not be defiled. She was the first of them
that slew themselves. She said, "The Lord is my portion; I wait on Him."[6] The rest were saved by the

---

[1] Deut. xxviii. 49 seq., Jer. v. 15, vi. 22. The terror always comes
from "the North."

[2] Chap. ii.   [3] Cf. Joel i. 13-15.   [4] Joel ii. 2; Lam. ii. 1, iii. 44.
[5] This detail is probably proleptic.   [6] Lam. iii. 24.

hand of the "bishop," for his eyes had compassion on them, and he delivered them out of the hand of the enemy. Eliezer, son of Nathan the Levite, wrote an elegy for the slain.

At Worms, the 23rd of the same month, was another "day of the Lord's vengeance." The books of the Law were cast to the ground and trodden under foot, and the oppressors uttered their voice in the house of the Lord as in the day of solemn fast.[1] They devoured Israel with open jaws, and left but a small gleaning, whom they turned away from the Lord, the God of Israel, but who, when the storm was overpast, returned to the God of their fathers. They that were slain had sanctified the Holy God of Israel, and chose death rather than life, that they might not be defiled. Many slew themselves, each his brother and his neighbour, his dear wife and his children, even compassionate mothers their children,[2] with all their heart and with all their soul, who cried, "*Hear, O Israel!*"[3] when they breathed forth their spirit on their mothers' bosoms.

Seven days later, on the 1st Sivan, there was another massacre, and again the martyrs slew their neighbours, and the mothers and children were dashed to pieces in the day of the Lord's anger.[4] A small remnant only escaped. The number of those who died during twelve days was eight hundred souls. Simchah Ha-Cohen, a young priest, slew a relative of the "bishop's," a councillor of the city, and was pierced with swords that he died.

The good Rabbin weeps and laments for those martyrs

---

[1] Cf. Lam. ii. 7 and Ps. lxxiv. : "He hath thrown down in His wrath the strongholds of the daughter of Judah."

[2] Lam. iv. 10.　　　　　　　　[3] Deut. vi. 4, 5.

[4] Cf. the vindictive passages, Isa. xiii. 16 ; Ps. cxxxvii 8, 9, with Hos. x. 14, xiii 16 ; Neh. iii. 10.

with a mourning like the jackals or the daughters of the ostrich.[1]

On the 3rd Sivan there ensued a massacre at Mainz, and again the unhappy martyrs put forth their hands to the desire of their eyes and slew their wives and children.[2] The women took part in the slaughter on that accursed day. Some of the old men covered themselves with the praying-veils, and said, "He is the Rock; His works are perfect."[3] "Teach the daughters of Israel to lament for this, and one woman to teach another lamentations; for behold! valiant ones lament in the streets and ambassadors of peace weep bitterly for this holy congregation, against which the hewers have come up with axes as hewers of wood."[4] Thirteen hundred souls were spoiled at this dread time.

It is when we peruse these awful details that we begin to understand in what age the cry was heard of the preacher in the synagogue, "Thy holy cities are a wilderness, Zion a wilderness, Jerusalem a desolation. Our holy and our beautiful house, where our fathers praised Thee, is burned up with fire, and all our pleasant things are laid waste. Wilt Thou refrain Thyself for these things, O Lord? Wilt Thou hold Thy peace and afflict us very sore?"

There is nothing in all tragedy more affecting than the story of Uri and of Isaac, who had two daughters. They were subjected to force, but returned to the God of their fathers. Isaac slew them on the Feast of Weeks in the evening, kindled his house and brought to the Lord a sacrifice; for with his friend Uri he went into the house of God before the ark, and they died before

---

[1] Cf. Mic. i. 8.   [2] Cf. Ezek. xxiv. 16.   [3] Deut. xxxii. 4.
[4] See the laments in Jer. ix. 19; Isa. xxxii. 7; and the image of the hewers with axes in Ps. lxxiv. 5; Jer. xlvi. 22; Ezek. xxvi. 9.

the Lord as the flame went up, and their souls fled to heaven. "My heart," exclaims the Rabbin, "is with the slain, and with them which are burned in the fire; my soul refuses to be comforted. Plead, O Lord, the cause of the souls; judge righteous judgment, and avenge Thou the blood of Thy servants which was spilled; as it is written, I will demand their blood that I have not cleansed, for the Lord dwelleth in Zion."[1]

Similar scenes of horror were enacted at Cologne and other places. At Wevelinghoven old R. Samuel took a knife and slew his young son, pronouncing a blessing on the sacrifice, the youth crying Amen! Who is it that here exclaims, "Behold and see, all ye that pass by the way, if there be any sorrow like unto their sorrow. Was there ever such a thing heard from the day that the Lord created man upon the earth? Woe unto the eyes which beheld it!"[2] The beadle of the synagogue, a young man, strengthened himself, and slew the father on the corpse of the son. After this massacre there were not left save two or three berries on the top of the uttermost bough.[3]

R. Isaac Ha-Levy, who drowned himself in the Rhine, has applied to him the text, "I will bring back from the depths of the sea."[4] At another vineyard of the Lord in the same district three hundred souls consented to martyrdom; and at Santen others in like manner "hallowed the day when the woodcutter came upon" those cedars of the Lord.[5]

A striking incident is recorded in connection with the synagogue at Meurs, where the governor of the city

---

[1] Cf. Joel iii. 21 ; cf. Jer. iv. 19, "evil from the North," xxxi. 15 ; the symbolic Rahel, Lam. i. 16.

[2] Lam. i. 12.   [3] Isa. xvii. 6, xxiv. 13 ; Jer. xlix. 9; Obad. 5.

[4] Ps. lxviii. 23.   [5] Cf. Jer. xxii. 7.

intercedes for the Jews and delivers a political speech to them, which awakens reminiscences of scenes connected with King Hezekiah and the Prophet Isaiah.

At Gilria the people, says the chronicler, were made to drink of the cup of the Lord's fury to the dregs.[1] He gave them to be robbed and plundered, and none escaped nor remained in the day of the Lord's anger. The language of the prophets constantly rises to his lips, "Those that I have swaddled and brought up hath mine enemy consumed."[2] He repeats the elegiac strain of the Lamentations, "his eye flows with water."[3] He calls upon the daughters of Israel to weep over the slain. "Clothe not yourselves in silk garments, put not on crimson; for because of our transgressions is glory despoiled from Judah."[4]

Treves and Metz and Ratisbon and Prague all contributed martyrs during that terrible summer. And here again a curious light is reflected upon an obscure Biblical passage. In Chron. iv. 9, amidst a long catalogue of the descendants of Jehuda, we read of Jabez "the Sorrowful," that he was held in peculiar honour. Of others we read, "These were the potters, and those that dwelt among plants and hedges; there they dwelt with the king for his work" (v. 23).

The chronicler applies these words to the German martyrs, and they are said to mean that they were the workmen and gardeners of the Eternal, furthering by

[1] In Jer. xxv. 9 *seq.* the calamity of the "families of the North" is described. After seventy years the "king of Babylon" and the "Chaldeans" are to be punished. All nations, all the kings of the North, no less than Judah and Jerusalem, are to drink of the wine-cup of fury and become mad because of the sword sent among them. In Isa. li. 17-22 Jerusalem has drunk of this cup, but shall drink no more.

[2] See the terrible context, Lam. ii. 15-22; cf. Hos. ix. 12, 13.

[3] Lam. i. 16, iv. 21. Here too Edom—Rome—shall drink of the cup.

[4] Cf. Jer. ix. 17-20.

their sufferings His designs for the salvation of the world. "They gave up their souls for His sake, whose blood was spilled like water. And He will give back to them according to their doings, and according to the works of their hands; and their souls will be bound up in the bundle of life,[1] in the temple of the King, the Lord of Hosts; and their purity and their righteousness will stand as a defence for us. Amen and Amen."

The Rabbin here declares that he has taken his account of the martyrs of the Crusade from a contemporary writer, R. Eliezer, and that he has compared the German annals. He is, in fact, confirmed by those of Mainz and Hildesheim. He then proceeds to trace the fate of the Crusaders on the march; how the Eternal avenged upon them the blood of His servants; how the uncircumcised fell by the sword, by famine, and by pestilence, so that few were left; how they took and polluted the land of Israel and Judah with their abominations and idols for eighty-eight years, till at last the verse was fulfilled, "Your enemies shall be desolate upon her."

About fifty years later great calamities fell upon Israel. The Rabbi Joseph says that about 1142 the academies ceased, and the study of the Law was at an end. The date is not quite certain, but the evil time is marked in memory by the death of the pious Spanish Rabbin Joseph Halevy and by "years of exile and suffering." Ben Tamari arose in the land of the Arabs, an enemy of the Jews. He issued a decree in all the cities of his kingdom that they should renounce their God, so that they had to quit their abodes, doomed to death, to the sword, to famine, to captivity. He said, "Go to, we will destroy

Cessation of Schools.

Tamurt or Tamurath.

---

[1] 1 Sam. xxv. 29.

them from being a nation, that Israel's name may be remembered no more;" and he left them no name in his whole kingdom and provinces, which he had conquered from the end of the earth unto Al Mahadia.[1]

In those days the hand of Alphonso VIII., son of Raymond of Burgundy, was heavy on the Ishmaelites of the land of Sepharad, and his kingdom was established. He took from the Ishmaelites Gaberkah or Calatrava, which was on the way from the land of Ishmael to his own country; and the rebellious people in the land of Philistia (Saracens of Africa) passed over the sea into Sepharad; and there was no remnant of Israel left from Tangiers to Al Mahadia. The Jews, hearing that the rebellious ones were coming to cast them away from the God of Israel, fled for their lives; and the parents scarce had compassion on the children for the weakness of their hands. Some of them were bound by the hand of Edom, and were sold to them, that they might escape from the land of Ishmael; some fled barefoot, and their children vainly asked for bread. But their cry went up to God, and He put it into the heart of Alphonso to set over Gebarkah as treasurer R. Jehuda the prince, son of R. Joseph ben Ezra, descendant of the great men of Granada, whose power in Jerusalem was hereditary.

This noble offshoot of the stem of Judah was a great benefactor to the remnant of the Captivity. He delivered them from chains, fed and clothed them, and sent the weak on horses and mules to Toledo. His goodness and generosity were equal to his influence; he wrought out the ordinances of the Eternal for Israel.[2]

---

[1] On this occasion the famous R. Joseph Kimchi, or his father, R. Yischak, settled in Narbonne.

[2] Deut. xxxii. 21. Wiener, *Schebet Jehudah,* 3rd part.

The second Crusade (1146) was also a time to the house of Jacob "of sorrow and oppression, The Second of emptiness, desolation, and destruction, of Crusade. smiting of the knees together. Much pain was in all loins and their faces gathered blackness."[1]

A new series of atrocities began in the towns of Germany, and the Jews ran to the rocks and strongholds to save their lives from the confederates of Baal. After a massacre at Wurtzburg (1147), it is said that all who were slain were next day gathered together, and "were carried in waggons, every sound limb, thigh, and shoulder, and the thumbs of the hands," and they were buried in the bishop's garden. It was bought by R. Rachakiah and his wife Judith for a burial-place.[2]

After an account of the martyrdom of Rabbins in France and Spain in 1171, the chronicler ob- The Fast for serves that the fast which followed should be the Events of greater than the fast of Gedaliah, and that 1171. the Jews then began to observe a fast for the occasion.

After the account of the massacre in London (1190), the chronicler relates how at Bruges the Gentile murderer of a Jew was seized, brought out on the day of Purim, and hanged on a tree, although he was servant to the king of Zarephath. This was followed by the burning of eighty Jews. Next year occurred the massacre of York, and the story of bloodshed continues to the end of the century.

Upon this review of the evidence it seems impossible to resist the conclusion that the "great slaughter" of 1096, allegorically spoken of as the coming of "Nebu-

---

[1] Nah. ii. 10.

[2] To what can the fearful parable, Ezek. xxiv. 3 *seq.*, of the boiling pot with the good pieces, the thighs and shoulders, the choice pieces, refer but to some such occurrence ?

chadnezzar" against Judah and Jerusalem, was the event which has left so unparalleled an impression on the literature of the synagogues and on the fasts of the Jews. When we look outside the Bible to the Rabbins of the twelfth century, we find in their commentaries, their songs of Zion, their elegies and prayers, the most decisive evidence of the correctness of this view. The Targum on the Prophets from the thirteenth century is full of mourning over "the temple in ruins." Rome is inveighed against precisely as the prophets inveighed against Edom or Esau. Germany is identified with a name in Ezekiel (xxxviii. 6). Here we have, in the words of E. Deutsch, a "masked history, written under the bloody censorship of Esau—Rome." It points out a large number of Messianic passages in the Bible which began to inspire the people not earlier than the twelfth century. The whole world of Biblical legend is here what Islam has said or sung in all its tongues.[1] The Targum on the Pentateuch, describing the breaking up of the Western Empire, mentions the Turks (Gen. x. 2), and so on. The Targum to Daniel shows a writer who looks back on the first Crusade and the calamities of the Jews; he talks of the Messiah, son of Joseph, of the true Messiah, son of David, of Gog and Magog; in short, he is full of the events that led to the foundation of the Latin kingdom in the East. In the Targum on Zech. xii. 10, Messiah, son of Ephraim, is described as warring against Gog, by whom he is slain.

With regard to the fasts of the Jews, all, with the exception of the Day of Atonement, appear to have been instituted in memory of the attack of the allegorical "king of Babylon" on the

The Fasts.

[1] E. Deutsch in Smith's *Dict. of Bible*, art *Versions Targum*.

synagogues. As to Gedaliah, the account of him closes the Biblical legendary record. He, after the siege by Nebuchadnezzar, becomes ruler of the remnant of Judah. He comforts them and assures them of safety under the "Chaldeans," precisely as the good Spanish Rabbin is said to have done. Then one "Ishmael" is said to smite both the Jews and the Chaldeans, and a migration takes place to "Egypt." Finally, another "King of Babylon" takes the "King of Judah" out of prison and exalts him to honour. The meaning is tolerably transparent, however symbolic the imagery may be. After the terrible events with which the eleventh century closed and the next opened, there was on the whole a recovery of hope, as the uprise of Alrui and other Messiahs showed. In some of the late prophecies ascribed to Zechariah, the preacher seems to tell the people that so much mourning is now idle, and that it were well to turn the fasts to more moral account, and to celebrate them with the gladness of hope.[1]

The like feeling is plainly shown in the Book of Esther, and in the idea of the feast of Purim, when they recalled the days wherein they rested from their enemies, and the month which was turned unto them from sorrow to joy, and from mourning into a good day.

We come to a point of great importance, namely, to ascertain when and where the literature of the Synagogue became known to the monks of St. Basil and of St. Benedict, who are the earliest writers in the interests of the Church. It can hardly be denied that apostates from the Synagogue were in some sort allies of the founders of the Catholic

Connection between the Rabbins and the Abbots.

[1] Chaps. vii., viii.

Church. The activity of informers and apostates was
an additional thorn in the side of the persecuted people.
These men, induced by revenge, vanity, or lucre, are
said to have been the authors of the worst slanders
launched against their people; the charges of slaughter-
ing children, drinking blood, poisoning springs, and
the like. To them also has been traced literary
forgeries, which have had their influence in concealing
from us the knowledge of the past.[1] Informers are
denounced in the Law, and a Rabbin explains the
"sons of my mother who were incensed against me" in
the Song of Songs (i. 6) of treacherous Israelites who
ally with idolaters against their brethren for the sake
of gold. Such complaints are constant in the period
under consideration. It was this class of men who
helped the monks to contrive those clamorous writings
adversus Judæos, which the monks then proleptically
referred to the fourth century and later times, when
the Jews had not yet been heard of in any part of our
world.

The two Josephi, namely, Josephus Hebræus and
Flavius Josephus, are both spurious writers.
The former has long borne the name of the
false Josephus, but the second has no more claim to be
genuine than the former.

The Two Josephi.

The first, or Josippon Gorionides, is said to have
been an Italian Jew of the tenth century. We may
remark, however, that all particulars concerning Jewish
writers in Italy before the eleventh or twelfth century
are equally indistinct with those concerning the Jewish
writers in Spain, and it is more probable that Josippon
wrote in a later age.

His Chronicle is conceived in Biblical language and

[1] Zunz, *u. s.* 13

style, and is held to have been based upon an Arabian Chronicle.[1] The fact is important, for "Flavius Josephus" closely resembles Josippon in the general character of his legends; and since both Flavius Josephus and Philo, together with the Greek chronographers, such as G. Syncellus, are solely traceable to the monks of St. Basil, we appear to have here detected the channel through which the notions about the antiquities of the Jews were received into the cloisters. There are also some notices by the interpolator of the Lexicon of Suidas, who can be none other than a Basilian monk, which appear to have been derived from Josippon.

But neither of these Chronicles of these forgers of history, nor the LXX. itself, follow the Hebrew canonical text. And it is difficult to suppose that if that canonical text had been fixed so early as the end of the eleventh century, it should not have been followed by these chroniclers. The Basilian Order probably did not arise in South Italy or Sicily until the twelfth century. At that time there were probably a large number of Jews in Calabria, who were parties to the hopes and ambitions of the rising synagogues, and who aided in the construction of its literature. The canon of the Hebrew Bible may not have been fixed until the time of Maimonides. We may therefore fairly conclude that the first attempts at Jewish historiography, based upon that of the Arabs, were made during the century 1050–1150.

The most important clue, perhaps, on the side of the monks of St. Basil which connects them with the Jewish scholars is contained in the St. Nilus. Life of St. Nilus, honoured at Rossano, in Calabria, and

---

[1] Zunz, *Gottesd. Vorträge*, pp. 150, 281, n. 2; Graetz, *Gesch. d. Juden.*, 5. 281, 356.

founder of the celebrated Basilian cloister of Grotta
Ferrata, near Frascati, according to the traditional date,
about the year 1002. The date is no doubt proleptic
by more than a century. And the Life of St. Nilus,
which may be read in the Bollandist *Acts*, is in the
usual official style, betraying a distance on the part of
the writer from his subject. But in the Life of St.
Nilus it is said that he invited the Calabrian Jewish
scholar, S. Domnolo of Oria, near Otranto, and
another to visit him in his cell, and to read the Law
and Prophets as long as Moses tarried on Mount
Sinai, but that they refused. This Domnolo is recognised in Jewish mediæval records as the author of a
"Commentary on the Book of Creation;" but as Dr.
Graetz states, his work did not become generally known
until the twelfth century, the age, in all probability,
when the Lives of the great saint of the south, St. Nilus,
and the great saint of the north of Italy, St. Romuald,
were composed.

About 1040–1070 Messina and the east coast of
Sicily, Calabria, and Longobardia were part of the
Eastern Empire. About 1105 Sicily and the south of
Italy had passed into the hands of the Normans, and
the Latin kingdoms had been formed in Syria through
the Crusade. It was a most important epoch, not only
for the general history of the world, but specially both
for Judaism and Monachism. The districts referred to
became a sort of Holy Land of Monachism. Cape
Garganus, with its church dedicated to the archangel
Michael, was a great resort of pilgrims; it is connected
in legend with the names of Otto III., and with
Adalbert of the great house of Monte Cassino. At
Beneventum was the tomb of St. Bartholomew. North-
wards, we trace the course of the Basilians to Gaeta,

where the legend tells that St. Nilus was living with his brethren like nomads in "the tents of Israel." Here Otto III. is supposed to play the part of a penitent David, and lays his crown in the hands of St. Nilus, a scene destined to be embellished by the pencil of Domenichino in Grotta Ferrata. As at Messina, Palermo, Monreale, Saracinesco, we are reminded of the transition from the Saracen to the Norman architecture, so in the early records of the Italian Jews, the Basilians, and the Benedictines of Monte Cassino of the thirteenth century are traced the beginnings of that great Catholic system which followed in the wake of the Saracens and of the Jews.

Slowly the monks appear to have won a seat for themselves in Rome. It is obvious that in Rabbins in no part of the world could they have made Rome way until the Jews, against whom their arguments are ever directed, had appeared. We hear of a Rabbin in Rome about the year 1050 who writes against the symbolical Edom precisely like the prophet Obadiah, and doubtless with the same meaning. But it is not till about a hundred years later that we hear of the rise of the Leoni family, who give an occupant to the chair of St. Peter, or that we hear of a schola or synagogue of the Jews.

Nothing can be more important on the side of the Synagogue than the evidence which it supplies of an unbroken series of Rabbins from the eleventh century onwards, and of the almost complete darkness in which the people are enveloped, both in East and West, before the beginning of that age. Equally dark to our gaze is the state of Rome and the Roman world, as the monkish annals profess to represent it before the twelfth century. If we conceive the Italian league of the

eleventh century to have prepared the way for the
Catholic Church, if the fighting Popes are merely
metaphors for militant heads of such a league, still it is
not to be confounded with the Catholic Church, whose
writers distinctly admit the priority of the literature
and religious beliefs of the Hebrews. In a word, the
generation that witnessed the conquests of the Normans
in Italy and England witnessed the rise of the synagogues, with all that fierce anti-Semitic feeling which
the kinsmen of the Hagarenes aroused; they witnessed
the revenge of the Crusade, and they witnessed the
rise of the Catholic Church.

It would be interesting could we certainly detect
references in the canonical Hebrew literature to the
conquests of the Turks and Normans. The difficulty
is that the Rabbins habitually employ symbolical
language, of a vague description, the key to which
cannot perhaps be wholly recovered, and that they
scruple not to write their oracles under the names of
mythic ideals of the great foretime. Thus Nathan of
Rome, who is probably ante-dated into the tenth century
of our era, makes the prophet Elijah preach and exhort
as if he were yet living. He alludes to Gog and Magog,
whose "judgment has already come upon the people."
The Hungarians or Turks are supposed to be meant,
but this is not certain, any more than the same reference
is certain in the descriptions of the Biblical Ezekiel.
In Spain, according to Ford, the Moors meant by Gog
and Magog the Normans of the ninth century.

The same Nathan, when he speaks of "Babylon," is
said to allude to the city of Rome. We touch on these
points [1] because we desire to insist upon a principle of
criticism, namely, that from dreary and aoristic books

[1] Rapoport, *Biogr. d. Natan Romi*, n. 43 (from Graetz.)

like those of the Rabbins exact dates are not to be extracted. The approximate dates should first be discovered at which the writers flourished; we may then ascertain what is the significance of their symbolic allusions.

It may be hard to dispossess the mind of long-inherited ideas about the city of " Jerusalem." Yet the evidence plainly teaches that no such city ought to appear on any historical map until the twelfth century and the time of the Latin kingdom. It is not till the middle of that century that we hear of Rabbins like Jehuda Halevy, their minds sharing the contagion of the times, pilgriming to Syria, only to meet with disappointment. The city was still the holy place of the Moslems, and the Jewish Theocracy of God and David had still to be discovered in the "heart of the earth." Jewish mediæval records tell how, about 1211, 300 Rabbins from France and England made the pilgrimage to the Holy Land. There may have been a settlement of Jews at Tiberias so early as the first Crusade, but elsewhere they appear to have had no strength. R. Nachmanides much later finds but a mere knot of his people, for whom he is trying to obtain a synagogue in the ruins near the city. The condition of the Jews in the caliphate of Bagdad and at Jerusalem during the twelfth century has been touched by the light ironical pen of Benjamin Disraeli, himself a descendant of the Spanish or African stock. He appears to have perfectly understood the genius of the Rabbins, and how little historic worth there was in the dreams of past Davidic glories and of the existence of their " Tombs of the Kings." [1]

---

[1] "This imaginative people," he calls them. A curious example of their literary habits is their ascription of the book *Sohar*, probably written in the

On the whole, therefore, the evidence appears to force us to the conclusion that the first period of Hebrew literature falls between 1000–1200 of our era, and that its contents began to be communicated by lax or apostate members of the Synagogue to the Basilians and Benedictines of Italy, who were densely ignorant of the Hebrew language themselves, as the writings ascribed to "Philo," "Josephus," and "Origen" bear witness, from the time of the foundation of the cloisters in Sicily and Calabria, under the Normans.

But every part of the evidence relating to the first Crusade needs to be received with the greatest caution. I have shown elsewhere that the monkish chroniclers wrote at a great interval after that event, of which they desire to represent their Order as the prime movers. If this be not the fact, then those references of the Rabbins of the sixteenth century to the Christian Messiah and the Baptism, and again to the offices of St. Bernard, which they have derived from the monastic Chronicles, cannot be received. In fact, the evidence as a whole shows that the Crusade was originally an anti-Semitic rather than a theological movement, a popular rather than an ecclesiastical war, and that the members of the synagogues were not yet the victims of the hatred of the monks.

It is entirely vain to seek for definite geographical, and therefore historical, information from the mediæval Rabbins. It seems that about the end of the twelfth century they were beginning to grope after sites of ancient greatness of which they had long been patrioti-

thirteenth century, to a pupil of R. Akiba, who is placed in Hadrian's reign. The book *Jezirah*, perhaps of the eleventh century, is put down to Abraham *or* to R. Akiba. All that the elder Disraeli wrote in the *Genius of Judaism* is well worth comparing with the *Alroy* of his son.

cally dreaming It may be that by the siege of Ariel
or of Jerusalem they mean the siege of the Holy Place
in Syria, but it is not certain.   The evidence that ecclesiastical geography has been largely derived from
poetry lies in the mediæval geographies and maps of
the Benedictines.   And it will save the student great
waste of labour if he will attentively study these documents of ignorance.

   In the map, *e.g.*, ascribed to a prebendary of Hereford
at the end of the thirteenth or the beginning of the
fourteenth century, which stands in the King's Library,
the earth is made a circle, in the centre of which stands
Jerusalem, because the monk has found the city so
described in Ezekiel.   The childish ignorance shown
in the details and the monstrous fancies would not
be contemptible if they were not associated with dishonesty.   The important Christian centres seem to
be the Temple of St. James in Galicia and the seat of
St. Augustine at Hippo.   Another map in the Cotton
Library, erroneously assigned to the tenth century,
shows that the monk who contrived it knew next to
nothing of Europe, thought of Arabia as a small strip
of land in the farthest East, while the Jews were a
great territorial power occupying with their tribes a
vast tract on both sides of the Jordan, from Cilicia on
the north to Egypt on the south.   Maps of the fourteenth century and later reveal how slowly men were
emerging out of fairyland and beginning to discover the
world as it is.

CHAPTER IX.

THE SYSTEM OF CHURCH LITERATURE.

THE earliest Church literature is a Græco-Latin or Latin-Greek literature, and it is founded, by means of an artificial connection, upon the Law and the Prophets of the Synagogue, and upon the Oral Tradition of the Rabbins. The problem is to ascertain when and where, and by whom, this literature was constructed.

It has been shown that the Hebrew literature from the eleventh and the twelfth century is not a revival, but a beginning. The problem is, therefore—When did the revival of Greek and Latin by the monastic orders begin? What data are there, independent of the monkish fictions, by which that epoch may be determined?

With regard to the Hebrew literature : the Law and the Prophets substantially as we now possess them probably began to be well known in the synagogues about the middle of the twelfth century, when the Rabbins were dispersed from Spain, eastward with Maimonides, to the north with other emigrants, who became strong especially in Southern France.

No sooner was the canon of the Synagogue laid down than the exposition of the Scriptures begins : allegorically, Eli is succeeded by Samuel, or the second Moses takes the place of the first. The stream of oral teaching flows probably from the lips of Doctors who are inspired with the same ideas and sentiments with those of the canonical psalmists and prophets. The *Guide of the Perplexed* and the short *Mishna* or Commentary on the Law, which have been ascribed to the son of Maimun, mark this epoch. The only difficulty is the chronological one; for the exact dates of Maimonides' birth and death are unknown. We have also to take into account the fact that after his death his authority was still a subject of dispute, and that it is doubtful whether he was not outwardly a Mohammedan to the end of his days. Using the data, therefore, with the utmost caution, it appears that at some time during the thirteenth century the Rabbins of the West, in reflecting on the history of the synagogues, learned to revere the memory of the Rabbin of Cairo as if he had been a new Plato or Pythagoras.

Let us say, then, that the great Mishnic period extends, in round numbers, over the century 1150–1250. It is the period of the Scribes The Mishnic period. and Pharisees. It is the period of the Princes and of the Sanhedrin. It is the period of the union of Shem and Japheth, when the Masters of the Law began to enlarge their intellect by the study of Greek, when Aristotle was called in to aid in cultivating the vineyards of the Lord. In modern phraseology, it is the period of the Jewish High Schools, the very name of which was probably borrowed from the Greek. There is something entertaining in Rabbinical grandiloquence. These kings and priests, these sages and great ones of Cordova and Toledo, are revealed, on a steady application of the historic telescope, as humble tradesmen, —" tent-makers, sandal-makers, weavers, carpenters, tanners, bakers, or cooks." We begin to understand from what sources the ideal of the Rabbinical St. Paul has been derived. Apart from their tendency to dream and mythopœia, they are healthy and admirable men, full of sagacity and morality, as all their proverbial wisdom shows ; in fact, the John Bunyans of their time.

Emanuel Deutsch, in the *Quarterly Review* of October 1867, pointed out that the period of Mishnic development is the period in which Christianity arose. He further pointed out once more the striking parallels of dogma and parable, of allegory and proverb, between the Gospel and the Talmud. He showed that the Pharisees were the very pith of Rabbindom, and that their hypocritical counterfeits were even more bitterly denounced in the Talmud than in the Gospel. But, unfortunately, Deutsch did not rescue the subject from its anachronistic confusion. He did not perceive, for example, that the story of Hillel is an allegory of Spanish Rabbindom, as Jerusalem is a poetic name for the Schools. His statement that the period of the Mishna coincides with the rise of Christianity means that the time of the historical teachers of the synagogues coincides with the time of the uprise of Benedictines, Dominicans, and Franciscans.

To turn our attention now to Greek literature. The age during which we *know* that it was being revived in Italy is that of Petrarch and his friend Barlaam, the Calabrian bishop—in other words, during the fourteenth century. How long before that age did Greek literature begin to flourish in the quiet and reserve of the cloisters ? The fact is, that before the fourteenth century there were no libraries but the closets of the Benedictine cloisters, and that in these there were to be found, so far as we know, in the middle of the thirteenth century and later, little or nothing but

Bibles, Service-books, Rituals, Gospels, and Epistles. Greek literature was not revived at Constantinople or any city of the East during that age, as the facts collected by the Benedictine fathers, Mabillon and Montfaucon, decisively prove. It began in Italy, and spread through France and the West by the agency of the Benedictines.

The facts are similar in reference to the Latin literature. The name of Petrarch is again a landmark for its flourishing time. But in reference to Petrarch himself we have to ask, What became of the costly library which he is said to have bequeathed to Venice (1374)? How much did he know of the *Divine Comedy* or of the Fathers and Doctors of the Church named in the poem? Again, Petrarch was a great lover of the Latin classics. What measure does his Latin afford of the attainment of his time or of the dark ages which had gone before? To ask such questions fairly is at once to admit how great a difficulty the advocates of the genuineness of Church literature labour under when they would maintain that in the eleventh and the twelfth centuries a considerable mass of excellent Latin writing had been produced. The great mediæval handbook of theology was the *Sentences* of Peter Lombard, who is said to have been Bishop of Paris in the latter half of the twelfth century. And yet so late as the year 1279, in a catalogue of books bequeathed to the Church of Paris by the Bishop Tempier, there is no mention of the Master of *Sentences* or of any other Father or Doctor. It could not have been until late in that age, or at the beginning of the next, that such a book could have been known and used in the schools. He is first named among ecclesiastical writers by Henry of Ghent 1290.

In the light of these indications, we cannot assume that the primitive Orders could have begun their literature, or even could have been formed, until some time in the latter half of the twelfth century. And it is with great difficulty that we can collect what was occurring in any part of Italy or of the West during that important age, 1150–1250. All that we can do is to follow the Chronicles, and rejecting from them what is prodigious, receive what is not in itself improbable, because it coincides with evidence from other sources.

Let us keep our gaze steadily fixed upon Tusculum, which during that age was the seat of a powerful family of nobles who had much to do with the formation of the Catholic Church. There was still, probably, a numerous body of Mohammedans in the neighbourhood. The name Saracinesco reminds of the fact. Southern Italy abounded with Mohammedans, Jews, and other Orientals. The feeling of resentment against their domination had long been growing, and was now perhaps at its height. The only way in which they could be overcome was by the organisation of a corporation in imitation of their own, and which united secular and spiritual authority in the hands of the same persons.

The infancy of the Catholic Church is the infancy of the primitive Orders, or, to speak more accurately, of the one primitive Order of Greek and Latin monks, which in the fourteenth century split asunder into the two Orders of St. Basil and St. Benedict. According to the general tenor of their traditions, the Basilians were the teachers of the Benedictines, their patrons. But the origins have been enveloped in a haze of mythology. That Basil and the two Gregories flourished in Cappadocia during the fourth century is a myth which was rendered plausible by the fact or the belief that Greek letters had flourished in that land during Roman times. No one in the West was likely to contradict the story. But the fact is, that the Greek monks went out from Italy to the East, and the myth of their coming to Italy from Cappadocia is a case of "reversed or double wandering." Equally mythical is the tale of St. Benedict in the sixth century. This part of the tradition is flimsy enough, and may be dismissed without further examination. Apart from other reasons, when we come to the year ten hundred, we are still in the mythological atmosphere.

Yet the legend of St. Nilus contains some important facts, in an anachronistic form. He is said Legend of St. Nilus. to have been born at Rossano in Calabria, which was an important centre of Greek Monachism in the fourteenth century and later. He is said to have known Jewish scholars of Otranto ; but the fact is, that a Greek abbot could not have known the work of Domnolo or any other Jewish scholar on the Creation until some time in the twelfth century. Then, but not till then, a Rabbin might talk of the Word of the Lord going forth from Bari and His Law from Otranto ; then there may have been a Jerusalem in those towns. The rise of the legend of St. Nilus may therefore be traced to that or the following age, and it serves to connect together the haunts of Greek Monachism in Calabria and Apulia with the famous cloister of Grotta Ferrata at Tusculum.

Coming now to about the year 1163, the tradition runs that the cloister was then in existence, but that the monks abandoned it in consequence of the civil war which broke out between Rome and Tusculum ; that they fled to Subiaco, and remained under the

Y

roof of the Benedictines for near thirty years.   The
tale of the flight may be regarded as a conventional
fiction; but the sojourn of Greeks and Latins under
one roof for a long period at the beginning of the
activity may be regarded as a certain fact, and one
that explains the rise of Church literature.   The
history of Subiaco itself has never been critically
written, but the Art of the Sagro Speco points to the
thirteenth century, and it may with caution be assumed
that the cloister dates from the preceding age.   In
memory of the hospitality of the Benedictines, it is
said that the Basilians presented them with the
Capuccio of St. Basil himself.

About the year 1191 Tusculum is said to have been
destroyed, and the name Frascati came into use.   The
Monastery of Grotta Ferrata has been imagined to rest
on the site of Cicero's villa.   From this time it is said
to have been under the powerful protection of the
Counts of Tusculum, and to have acquired great
territorial possessions.   The Greek monks were also
influential in the early times of Monte Cassino, as the
legend of St. Nilus and other particulars clearly show.
In short, the critical history of the early Catholic
Church is the critical history of the three cloisters.

It is said that Innocent III. resided at Tusculum,
and that he was connected with the Counts.
Innocent III.
Materials for the writing of a critical bio-
graphy of this Pontiff do not, however, exist, and we
must content ourselves with the bare indication that the
headship of the Church as a secular organisation was
in the family of the Counts.   According to one story,
Innocent was Count of Segni, and his birthplace was
Anagni.   On the other hand, he has been described as
a man of the lowest plebeian extraction.   But the facts

about Anagni in connection with Boniface VIII. and the year 1303, when he is said to have been imprisoned by the French in concert with a Colonna, have probably cast their reflection on the earlier time. Significant, also, is the statement that Innocent studied at Paris, and that he wrote many volumes. We are at least not very far from the time when there was a theological school at Paris.

The tradition that Innocent wrote on the office of the Mass and on Baptism cannot be accepted as equivalent to fact. But the statement that the visible head of the Church died at Perugia in 1214, on his way to reconcile the Genoese and Pisans, is one of many indications that the Church was at the time more a political military league than a religious institution. What had the Greek and Latin monks been doing during this half-century that lay between their junction at Subiaco and the death of Innocent? Let us assume that they had laid the foundations of their system, that they had agreed upon their *Kerugma* or Preaching, and that they had sent forth their missionary bands into the West. The assumption must still be cautious and provisional.

They formed part of the great league of nobles and priests, the League of the Cross. Their mission was to proclaim the virtues of that sign, of the "Victorious Tree, protection of the true," and to denounce destruction against Mahometry and Jewry. The helmet was often exchanged for the cowl, but the cowl as frequently for the helmet. Wherever the Benedictines came in their early campaigns, there must have been scenes of violence and bloodshed; and their martyrs must have been, in opposition to those of the Muslim under the Crescent, men who fell in defence of the Cross, and all the traditions of the West with which it was associated. Little could have been heard at this time, as we suppose, of the dogma of the Crucifixion. Nor is it possible to represent too strongly the dense ignorance that must have prevailed in the whole rank and file of the militant monks. They called themselves slaves of God, and in effect they were servile of origin, and servile in the terrible discipline to which they were subjected. But the organisation which the Lord Abbots controlled was more perfect, and more adapted to conquest than any the world had known since the Roman legion or the hosts of the Commander of the Faithful.

But to return to Tusculum. In the time of Gregory IX., who is said to have been of Anagni and of Innocent's house, we begin to emerge into the light. It may perhaps be believed that during his session, 1225–1240, a picture ascribed to St. Luke was carried to Grotta Ferrata, in consequence, they say, of a revelation from the Blessed Virgin herself. It may be believed that this Pontiff gave his name to the Chants and other parts of the Church service, which must have been undergoing great development during this period. It may also be believed that with the Franciscans and the Dominicans and the Hermits a fresh wave of enthusiasm rolled over the world, and that the mystery of the Crucifixion began to be unfolded to the popular mind. Yet the tumultuous Romans have not been overcome, and the Apostolic College has found a determined foe in the Emperor Frederic. Gregory himself is said to have died of grief. And certainly when, by the aid of the Chronicles, we endeavour to form an idea of the situation of the Church, it seems to have been well-nigh desperate. Yet organisation prevailed, in spite of the captivity of the Cardinals and a vacancy of twenty-one months in the Apostolic See.

It is perfectly certain that during this time the monks could not have been writing much Church history or dogmatic theology. Not until calmer days supervened, and the mere struggle for existence had come to an end, was there either motive or possibility for the construction of an ambitious literary system. The most significant thing in this relation is the tradition that Nicolas IV. (1276–1282), of the Ursini family, a Franciscan, and formerly named Jerome, was a peaceful and learned man who wrote many tractates on the Old and New Testament, and who favoured learned Cardinals. Certainly it cannot have been much earlier that the New Law or Testament could have been compiled ; and there are strong links of connection between the Mendicants and the teaching of the book. The good Nicolas is supposed to have come to a premature end, in sorrow, after enduring the rivalry of an ignorant Saint, Celestine, who in turn is deposed by the violent Boniface. The latter " came in like a fox, lived like a lion, and died like a dog " (1291–1300).

The coins inscribed with the name of this Pontiff may possibly be genuine, but scant indeed are any authentic monuments of this age. Not a portrait of any thirteenth century Pope, for example, has come down to us. We may seek wistfully, but vainly, in the original Holy Land of the Campagna for sepulchres of the founders. Aquino is associated with the name of the Angelic Doctor, but neither there nor at Monte Cassino, which claims him as a pupil, can authentic memorials of St. Thomas be found.

The age was one of organisation, of aggression, of fortification. It was an age of extravagant oral fiction, which rooted itself at the shrines of saints, and in the recurrent festivals in their honour. One of the most interesting events in this relation was the establishment of the shrine of St. James of Compostella in the very land of the infidels, a rival to Cordova, the Mecca of Spain. Possibly the militant Order may date from late in the preceding century. Until the establishment of the Knights of St. John in Rhodes early in the next century we cannot think of much Christian progress in the East. There can be no doubt that, from the Moslem point of view, the Nazaraeans were a sect of the West, and of the West alone.

Let us suppose that in the latter part of the thirteenth century the need was felt of a fixed literary Tradition, so to be called, and that the monks of St. Basil, with their Latin patrons, were the pioneers of the revival of Greek letters. Any clearer knowledge of what was done from that time must depend on the study of the Catalogues of Church writers which were produced from the Western monasteries from about a century before the invention of printing. These Catalogues show, beyond doubt, that Church history, so called, was first schemed and then written. It was deduced from a theological and ecclesiastical theory, viz., that the Incarnation of the Word had occurred at the beginning of the Roman Empire, and that a series of historical witnesses could be adduced in support of Christianity from the times of the Apostles down to the dark times in which the Church was in reality founded. It is impossible to deny on the evidence that until the thirteenth century the very names of these writers had not been heard of in the wide world, and that not until the following age was there a reading public of any extent ready to receive the writings ascribed to them.

In the study of the following Catalogues the student will find the whole system of Church literature laid bare.

Apparently the first Basilian Catalogue is the so-called *Library* of Photius, dated 892. Photius is an imaginary patriarch, and the date of the Catalogue is false. It contains 280 names, and is nothing but a scheme of Greek theological literature partly compiled, partly in course of compilation, in the monasteries of the West. The contents prove that the Christian theory of the past is still in its inception. The MSS. are Cardinal Bessarion's of Venice, and those of Paris. Cardinal Bessarion became commendatory abbot of Grotta Ferrata about 1469, and probably enough the early history of this compilation may be connected with that monastery. The safest way to arrive at a probable conjecture of the date is by comparison with the Ecclesiastical History ascribed to Nicephorus Callistus, with which it often corresponds. The latter work has never been dated before the early fourteenth century. The *Library* of Photius cannot have been constructed long before.

It offers at first sight a formidable mass of learning to the reader, but proves, on examination, to be of very shallow content. It will be only necessary briefly to indicate its character.

This Catalogue first names Josephus and Philo, whose works are entirely the fabrication of the Greek monks, with the aid, very probably, of some Jewish apostate, such as the author of the corresponding work of Josippon. Again, the intention of the forger is apparent in introducing the name of Justus of Tiberias. He must have known of the Rabbinical school at that place, and he pretends that this Justus wrote a history from Moses to

the third year of Trajan. Then he goes on to say that
this writer, being a Jew and labouring under Jewish
disease, makes no mention of the advent of Christ, His
deeds or miracles. There can be no stronger evidence
that the Basilian monk is well aware that the Jews had
no knowledge whatever of an advent of God to Syria in
human form, and that he is one of a conspiracy who
are resolved upon forcing that theory upon the world.

Nor had the existence of Essenes or Therapeutæ
ever been revealed to the consciousness of the world
outside the cloisters. It is needless to refer to the
passages relating to Christ and to St. James in Josephus.
Let us hasten from the distasteful subject with the
remark that Jewish critical scholars should long ago
have detected the false origin of these writers, who have
been so long used as instruments of injustice against
the race. Another curiosity in this monastic *Library*
is the so-called *Book of the Christians*, or *Exposition
of the Octateuch*, falsely ascribed to the reign of the
Emperor Justin. It is said that the writer of the
book makes mention in passing of Genesis and of
Exodus. He dwells in his narrative and theory on the
Tabernacle. He runs through the Prophets, and thence
the Apostles. He says that the sun has the magnitude
of two climates; that angels are not in heaven, but
only above (or under) the firmament and with us; that
Christ, ascending from the earth, entered the inter-
mediate region between heaven and the firmament,
and that this is alone the kingdom of heaven. He
states other absurdities.[1]

By such a notice as this the monk contrives to
represent that some crude form of Christianity was in
existence during the reign of Justin, and to call atten-

---

[1] Cod. 36. There are similar things in "Basil" and "Ambrose."

tion to a theory which he intends to adopt in some amended form.   In another article he calls attention to " Anonymous testimonies of Christ from Anonymous Gentiles,"[1] which he does not produce.   He Testimonies. himself has no articles on Jesus Christ, Peter, Paul, or any New Testament writer.   He mentions " Justin Martyr's " *Apology*, the sophistries of which are nothing but the productions of these false Basilian philosophers. The Basilians, to do them justice, avow in their works a literary morality which justifies their enormous mendacities.   Lies are useful, and truth may be suppressed in the interests of the Church.[2]

We are in search of Church history.   The first Church historian is named by the Basilians Eusebius Eusebius Pamphili, and he is planted in the Pamphili time of Constantine the Great.   The information about him is given in a halting and confused manner, and is distributed under different numbers in different parts of the Catalogue.[3]   To him is ascribed the *Evangelical Preparation*, the *Evangelical Demonstration*, the *Confutation* and *Apology*, the *Ecclesiastical History*, and the *Life of Constantine*; also the *Brief Confutation* of Hierocles on Apollonius of Tyana. The compiler of the Catalogue denounces this Eusebius as a blasphemer, because he calls the Son the Second Cause, and the General-in-Chief of the hosts of heaven. There are other signs of " Arian madness " in him.

A significant name in the Catalogue is that of the monk St. Nilus, a mystic prototype of the St. Nilus. Abbot of Grotta Ferrata.   We may dismiss Cod. 276. the work with the remark that the student who subjects

---

[1] Cod. 170.
[2] Eus., H. E. viii. 2.   Cf. P. E. xii. 5, on education by fables.
Cod. 9, 13, 27, 39, 118, 127.

it to a thorough examination will discover the ground-plan, so to say, of the Church literary structure, and all his studies will thenceforward be simplified.

We pass on to the second Catalogue, which is con-Catalogue II. tained in the Lexicon of Suidas. We have
Suidas. none but internal indications as to the date of this Lexicon. Scholars have assigned it, from such evidence, to the period 900–1300. We will assume it to have acquired its present form not earlier than the end of that period. It consists of a series of notices on ancient authors and subjects, with which has been incorporated a number of Church notices, by a monk of the Order of St. Basil. These notices abound in curiosities, nay, in revelations of the most startling kind when the student first comes upon them. The Old Testament books appear to be quite novel and imperfectly known ; so also the New Testament books. Moreover, the New Testament narrative is not followed in the accounts given of the rise of Christianity.

The interpolator is strong in theology, but in place Fables in of history he offers nothing but the most
Suidas. audacious conflated myths. There is nothing to be met with in all ecclesiastical literature more circumstantial than the tale under the title " Jesus the Christ and our God." It is here related with prolixity how, in the time of the Emperor Justinian, one Philip, a silversmith, persuaded one Theodosius, chief of the Jews, that Jesus had been enrolled in the Jewish priesthood. The Jew is made to say that he is convinced of the truth of this, but dare not avow it for fear of his people. Another long circumstantial tale relates how Dionysius the Areopagite, from Athens, witnessed the eclipse at the time of the Passion, in

Egypt, and felt assured that some momentous event had taken place. There are no articles on Peter or Paul, but under another title a very rhetorical description is given of the career of the latter apostle. Under the articles "Apostle" and "Evangel" other strange things may be read. This Lexicon is undoubtedly a source anterior to any *plenary* New Testament or Service Book. From it may be collected an account of the early forms of Christian legend and dogma very different from that in the canonical sources.

Upon the work of Eusebius Pamphili are made to depend a string of so-called historians— Socrates, Sozomen, Theodoret—who proceed with their theological inventions down to the year 439; Evagrius advances to the year 593. Nicephorus Callistus, who is admitted to have written in the fourteenth century, carries us to the year 610. A continuator goes on till 911. One of the constant devices of the monks is to multiply writers by the system of continuators, who are often betrayed by identity of style to the writers whom they are supposed to continue.

The System of Historians.

The reader may consult either the work of Eusebius Pamphili, ascribed to the fourth century, or that of Nicephorus, ascribed to the fourteenth, for the theory of Church origin. It is substantially the same thing, except that the later mythologist knows more than the earlier. Neither of them derives his ideas from the New Testament; but while Eusebius appears to have little more than the bare scheme of the books before him, Nicephorus appears to have the complete text. The most important part of these histories is the Introduction, which announces the great Christological theory from which the history

The First Ecclesiastical History.

is to be deduced. It is a dogma of the Advent of
"Christ our God." It is substantially the theory of
the prologue to the fourth Gospel. The rest is sheer
fable, and that of the most impudent kind, designed in
order to make good the pretension of the Church to
have been founded by the Incarnation, at the beginning
of the Roman Empire. It is a monument of literary
disgrace, and the fact that ecclesiastics have gone on
editing such flimsy lies in the interests of the Church
cannot be reflected on without pain. Kestner, early
in this century, saw that Eusebius had practically no
historical sources, but Kestner did not push his discoveries further. The list of bishops and priests is a
list and nothing more. The wonderful library of the
martyr Pamphilus at Cæsarea in the third century is
a library in Utopia; and when we have gazed long
enough at the great Origen, with his corps of girl
amanuenses busy constructing Church literature, the
scene melts, and we find ourselves in the Scriptorium
of Grotta Ferrata or Monte Cassino.

It gives us a clear idea of the kind of audience before
whom this history was first recited when we
read that the Emperor Philip about the year
247 was converted to Christianity, and when
a Latin monk says he cannot conceive *why*
he was converted unless that the thousandth year of
the City must be dedicated to Christ rather than to
idols.[1] It is sufficient to study the prologues referred
to, in order to be convinced, beyond possibility of
doubt, that the Church theory of the connection with
the Roman Empire is a dogma, and nothing but a
dogma, a transcendental theory, represented and set
forth in the guise of fact.

The Audience of the Ecclesiastical History.

[1] Anon. Vales. xxxiii.

Equally clear is the dogma of Jesus Christ and the explanation of the sources whence His tran- *The Dogma* scendent ideal was derived.   His name Jesus *of Jesus Christ.* is from the Hebrew *Jeshua*, and there is no other account of its origin.   His name *Christus* is from the epithet of the Jewish high-priest, "the Anointed One."   He is conceived as an Archangelic Being, as the Word of God ; and a variety of other epithets are lavished upon Him expressive of His majesty.   It stands beyond all question fast in these sources that the Divine Founder, the *homo manifestus ex homine virgine, deus occultus ex deo patre*, with His Apostolic College, is the creation of the Church, as are all of the sacerdotal series which link that College with later times.

The Basilians, imitating the Arabians and Jews, also produce Chronicles wherein the course of *The System* the world is deduced from the Creation and the *of Chroni-* first man Adam.   The Chronicle of Eusebius *cles.* is brought down to Constantine, and is followed by that of Syncellus to Diocletian, by that of Theophanes the Isaurian to the year 813.   Malelas fills up the space between Adam and the year 566.   Then comes Theophanes, "the father of many a lie," in Gibbon's phrase, who continues to 811 ; Scylitza, whose *Epitome* covers the period 811–1081, Leo the Grammarian, George the Monk, follow.   The Paschal Chronicle by three hands begins with the Creation and ends with the year 1042.   Cedrenus ends his Compendium with the year 1057 ; S. Metaphrastes carries his Chronicle to 963 and is continued to 1059.   M. Glycas ends with the year 1118, and C. Manasses is supposed to flourish about 1150.   But the evidence, both external and internal, points steadily to the conclusion that these writers were contemporaries and of the same cloister, or system of cloisters.

The Chronicle of Zonaras begins with the Creation and finishes with the year 1118. Nicetas continues to 1203, Nicephorus Gregoras to 1359, and L. Chalcondylas deals with the period 1297–1462. The influence of Homer and Herodotus has been observed in these later writers of the " Nazaræans."

It is not probable that any of these chroniclers began writing much before the year 1300. There are important particulars in Nicetas showing that Byzantium was still in the thirteenth century an old Roman city in appearance. Gregoras is a good witness for the fact that the Mohammedans were the critics of the Christians, and, we must add, the unanswerable critics ; while Chalcondylas shows the greatest respect for the Mohammedans, and gives a close account of their belief and their rites. He does not speak of Christians, but of Nazaræans and of the religion of Jesus, which he knows to be in some way connected with Islam. He confuses Isa with Jesus, saying that Mohammed honoured Jesus as the Apostle of God.

Another series of biographic fictions links the interval between the Emperor Justinian and the time of the first Crusade by the names of Menander, Simocatta, Constantine Porphyrogenitus, Leo Diaconus, Psellus, and Anna Comnena. The *Alexiad*, 1069–1118, was written in a cloister, as was the work of John Cinnamus, 1118–1176. These works appear to date from after the separation of the Greeks and Latins.

The period 1204–1261 is covered by George Acropolita, who is continued by G. Pachymeres to 1308. The work ascribed to John VI. Cantacuzene, but written by a monk, covers the period 1320–1357; that of M.

Ducas the period 1341–1462, and that of George Phranzes the period 1261–1477. These later writers still describe their objects in so vague and dreamy a manner that it is doubtful whether they have not been ante-dated. It seems part of the system of the monks not to sit down to write their story until they are safe from contradiction and criticism.

It is impossible to speak too strongly of the tedium and the disgust which the reading of the so-called Byzantine writers inspires. They are nearly all of them infected by the monkish vices—unblushing mendacity, boastfulness, delight in images of violence and obscenity, hatred of the wedded life, contempt of all that passes for virtue outside the cloister. As historic sources they are all but valueless, unless their method be narrowly studied, and we draw the opposite inference from their statements to that which they intend to convey to the mind of the reader. Nothing is more convincing of the fabulous character of their system than the discovery of the ignorance of Chalcondylas in his late time. The following are some of his statements :—

John Cantacuzene is said to have been made a Nazaræne under the name Matthew, and Rhodes was the headquarters of the Nazaræans at the time. The Sarmatians or Russians are said to follow the laws of Jesus under a Greek Pontiff, rather than the Pontiff of the Romans. Sarmatia is said to extend toward the ocean as far as Prussia, and to the white-robed Nazaræi and the Sanctuary in this land. They seem to be Germans, and they have a Sanctuary to be compared with that in Rhodes and that in Spain. These three Sanctuaries all know to have been founded for the religion of

Chalcondylas, c. 1460, and the Nazaræi.

Jesus against the Barbarians. Many at Prague, on the other hand, have been till lately fire and sun worshippers; and they only, as far as the author knows, are outside the two religions known to him, viz., that of Jesus, and that of Mechmet and Moses. Is he referring to the Jews? He speaks as if, in the prevailing darkness, there were but the two religions at all distinctly known.

He speaks of Calabria as formerly called Hellas, and he has heard a strange tale of the prophetic powers of Joachim. He speaks of him as doorkeeper in a monastery of the Nazaræans in Italy. In the same connection he has a lively passage on the mode of election of the High-priest or Pontiff of the Romans, and bears witness to the immense influence of the Colonna and Ursini families in the Cardinalate. He repeats the strange tale of the female Pope and the ceremony at the election connected with the belief. He shows how the Italian princes are interested in the Pope. If there are two sons in a family, one receives civil and the other ecclesiastical preferment. Ambition makes the High-priest an object of great affection and honour in the families of the nobles.

He knows the monastery of St. Phocas in Asia Minor called Cordyla. He knows of Monothelites and Jacobites in Egypt, who are "great nations." He thinks of them vaguely as belonging to the religion of Jesus the God, but adds that they hold neither the Greek nor the Roman dogma. There are also a large number of Manichaeans. He calls the Caliph king of Memphis, who is High-priest of the Mohammedans in Asia, Libya, and Europe. It is they who have custody of the Sepulchre of Jesus in Palestine, from which they derive great gain. Palestine extends from

Alexandria to Cœle-Syria, and here, at ruined Jerusalem, is the Tomb of Jesus.

In his intelligent account of the rise of Mohammed and the customs of the Turks, he says that the followers of Islam believe Jesus to be an The Muslim. Apostle of God, and that Jesus sprang from an angel Gabriel and from Mary, who was a virgin. Jesus was a superhuman Hero, and He will come at the end to judge the world. He describes the pilgrimage to Mecca to the Tomb of the Prophet, in which Europe still takes part. It is manifest that Chalcondylas, a man of rank under the Duke of Athens in the fifteenth century, is neither Mohammedan nor Christian, and that he is unable to distinguish critically between the two systems. He does not know the bare name of Christian. He thinks of the military monks as Nazaræns of Rhodes, and fails to recognise their presence in Greece. And so vague is his knowledge of Roman history, he says that, after Alexander the Great, the Romans by fortune and valour came to great power. They handed over Rome to the supreme Pontiff, crossed into Thrace under the Emperor, and made Byzantium their metropolis; Emperors of the Romans the rulers of Byzantium still called themselves. But the people of Rome and the Pontiff quarrelled with the Greeks and set up a Gallic or German Emperor of the Romans. Religious dissension led to the expedition of the Westerns against Byzantium. The Greek seat of empire was removed to Nicæa. Byzantium was recovered. At last John, Emperor of the Greeks, took with him the Pontiff of the Greeks and went to Italy in order to put an end to religious disputes, and gave aid against the Turks. He came to an agreement with the Roman Pontiff in the Italian Synod; but on his return the

Greeks of Byzantium refused to abide by its terms, and
the discord became perpetual. This writer is thought
to have been living so late as 1490, yet to him the
wonderful story of the translation of empire is still
fresh and but vaguely known.

To resume on this part of the subject. It seems
that the Greek and Latin monks remained in union
from the latter part of the twelfth century during
nearly the whole of the following age. The seats of
literary activity were the Italian and French cloisters;
and it was by their consent that the idea of a Holy
Catholic Church, "the beginnings of all things," but
rooted temporally in the old Roman Empire, was fixed.
They had, perhaps by the end of the thirteenth century,
contrived a great consensus of opinion on the part of
imaginary Fathers in the East and West. They had
claimed Asia Minor and Syria under the names of
Justin, Eusebius, Basil, the Gregories, Chrysostom;
Egypt under the names of Origen, Clement, Atha-
nasius, Cyril; Italy under the names of Ambrose,
Leo, Gregory; Africa under the names of Tertullian,
Cyprian, Optatus, Augustine. They had planted Epiphanius in Cyprus. They had begun to do what they
often accuse imaginary sects of heretics of doing. By
the time the printing-press came into operation, they
had written "*a great number of spurious books, under
false titles, with the view of terrifying fools.*" [1] Indeed,
the shameless audacity with which they presumed on
their power, or on the ignorance of the public, is
apparent through the whole of their writings.

They indulged well-known propensities of the human
mind. They argued that, if a theory of the world were
only proclaimed loudly and long enough by a great

---

[1] Theodoret, *Haer. Fab.* i. 19, cited by Hardouin, *Prolegg.* 31.

chorus of consentient voices, if it could be shown that it had been opposed by a multitude of sects in distant times and places, all of which had been refuted and overthrown, the world would at last be forced into assent. But it is these very imaginary heretics who condemn the authors of their being, because the opinions ascribed to them are nothing but a strange revelation of the absolute unbelief of the monks themselves in the stories they were forcing on the imagination of the world.

By that time they had rendered the Bible, or parts of it, into Greek and Latin; they had perverted it into a repository of types and allegories in favour of their theory; they had begun, in pursuance of the same method, but they had probably not completed, the *Apostle* and the *Book of the Gospels*. Probably they had written the so-called apocryphal books of the Old Testament, which are still held in high esteem by the Catholic Church. They deliberately cast doubt upon writings which they themselves produced, so that in sheer bewilderment men's minds might be thrown upon the authority of the Church alone.

The events which led to the flight of the Popes to Avignon, and to the schism between the Greeks and Latins, produced a fresh effort of literary activity. Under the flimsy pretext of a dispute concerning the Procession of the Holy Ghost, the Greek monks disguise their jealousy of their Latin colleagues. They began the construction of a fresh theological and liturgical literature. They wrote the series of monkish tales which pass under the name of the Byzantine History, with all its imaginary councils and heresies and theological emperors; while the Latins were contriving their corresponding tales of supreme Pontiffs in the

West. From the fabulous habit of ante-dating the dispute into the ninth century, and again to the time of the first Crusade, it is difficult to fix upon the exact epoch when the two orders became irreconcileable. It is not probable that the general public ever heard of two Catholic Churches, and of an old rivalry between Patriarchs and Popes, until the fifteenth century.

However, the important fact in reference to the present investigation is, that long before their separation the Greek and Latin monks had consented to that theory of the Church which is laid down in the writings ascribed to Eusebius Pamphili, and that these writings cannot be dated far from the time when the centre of the Christian world was in the South of France.

The Latin Catalogues of Illustrious Men present analogous features to those of the Greeks. Greek influence is still observable in the name Eusebius Hieronymus, commonly called St. Jerome, who links his Catalogue with the work of his namesake, Eusebius Pamphili. The Catalogue is falsely dated in the fourteenth year of Theodosius (392). The Greek version by Sophronius links it to the productions of the Greek monks. It contains 135 names, from Simon Peter to Jerome, and has an impudent preface, in the worst manner of the monk, in which he pretends to address an ex-Praefect Dexter, alludes to a Catalogue in the Brutus of Cicero, which he prays the Lord Jesus Christ that he may be enabled to imitate; he launches out against Celsus, Porphyry, and Julian, as "mad dogs against Christ," as if he were their contemporary; is petulantly conscious of a taunt that the Church had no philosophers and doctors; and brandishes this list in the face of his public as a triumphant proof to the contrary.

On examination, the Catalogue proves to be based on those of Suidas and Photius   The notices in Suidas are often translated word for word.   But the significant circumstance is that neither of those Greek Catalogues give a single name of Latin ecclesiastical writers.   These illustrious of the Latin monasteries are, then, the product of Benedictine imagination at some time not before the thirteenth century.   The plenary New Testament is still unrecognised, and fables are introduced about Peter, James, John, and Paul, from other sources. Peter went to Rome to conquer Simon Magus in the second year of Claudius, and held the priestly *cathedra* till the last year of Nero.   He was crucified head downwards.   Of James, Bishop of Jerusalem, stories are told similar to those in Eusebius Pamphili; also a story of the appearance of the risen Lord to him, with circumstantial details.   For the first time we learn that Paul had been called Saul; Eusebius knows nothing of this.   We learn also for the first time that he was of the tribe of Benjamin, and of the town Giscalis in Judæa.   Sentences are furnished from his epistles with a view to make out his relation to Nero's time.   In connection with the statements in Eusebius Pamphili, it is clear that the scheme of the Pauline epistles was first laid down, and that it was but gradually filled in, a fact which accounts for the difficulty of these writings.

But not to detain the reader with these particulars. Once more we confirm our view of the origin of Christendom in this source.   There is no history in our sense; it is the great romance of the Church unveiled.   Theology and christology inspire everything. There is polemic against Mages, Manichees, Jews, and other Unitarians.   There is dogmatic writing on the Incarnation and the Trinity, the manifestoes of an Order, the thoughts of a corporation, never of the independent thinker. The whole object is to make out that the system of the Church had been handed down from the days of the first Bishop in Rome; that at the end of the fourth century she could count her scholars by scores from Cæsarea in Cappadocia to Barcelona in Spain; that the East was linked with the West in the person of Jerome, who is merely made to say of himself that he was born at Stridon, on the borders of Pannonia and Dalmatia.

This reference affords no clue to the place and time Gennadius' of the composition of the Catalogue. But a Appendix further list is appended, nominally by Gennadius, a priest of Marseilles, and falsely dated at the end of the fifth century. It contains ninety-nine more illustrious names, among which may be mentioned Vincent, priest at the monastery on the isle of Lérins opposite Marseilles, also an ex-abbot of the same cloister, and other writers at Marseilles and at Arles. Now, it is absolutely certain that there were no Church foundations at either of these places in the fifth century, and not probable that they existed there long before the Popes came to Avignon.

Although, then, the names of all the great fathers and doctors of Church glitter on these Catalogues, they prove, on examination, to be no more than names and shadows which haunted the imagination of the French cloisters in the first periods of Church literary activity. It is impossible to affix them to any known personality. The reader may take any one, or all of these names, and inquire into the extraction, the date of birth and death, the previous history of the writer. He is referred to the writer's own works. He finds some incoherent, rambling story, written as if in a dream.   He is dissatisfied.   He asks for particulars from a contemporary.   He meets with a member of the same Order, or he consults Father Mabillon, who refers him back to the writings of the doctor himself.   No one outside the cloisters was ever acquainted with these personalities.

The facts to which we are referring account for that peculiar immobility and rigidity in Church literature which must often have struck the mind of the student with an impression of the prodigious.   The writers ascribed to the fifth century have the same style, the same thoughts, as those who are admitted to have written in the fourteenth.   There is no development, no progress.   Phenomena offer themselves which are impossibilities to those who have studied the nature of the human mind.   Even Benedictine rule could not defeat nature.   A monk of that Order will not write in the present day precisely as a William of Malmesbury or an Orderic wrote.   The discrepancy of times will make itself felt.   It is the want of discrepancy between such a writer as St. Bernard and such a writer as Jerome or Augustine which betrays that they belonged to the same age, and were produced in the same forges.

The Basilian and Benedictine patrologic mythology is laid bare in the contrivance of these lists. Patrologic The great literary heroes of the Basilians are mythology. St. Basil and the two Gregories, who it is pretended were contemporaries of the Emperor Julian.   The tale of his apostasy is part of the same system of fiction. The student may plant himself at Athens, and may persuade himself, since there is no evidence to the contrary, that the embers of old philosophy were kept alive in that glorious city down to the end of the eighth century. He may transplant himself to Cæsarea or Mazaca in Cappadocia, contemplate the ruins of a mediæval city, and allow the Basilian heroes to vanish into their transcendent sphere. He may visit Cyprus, and convince himself that the name of St. Epiphanius was not heard of until the time of the Crusaders' kingdom in the East. He may make pilgrimage to the Holy Mountain of Athos, find himself in Middle Age scenes, at the heart of Middle Age religion, and in the midst of ignorant monks exert undisturbed his critical faculty in drawing a sharp line between the luxuriance of fables about Constantine and Helena and the epoch at which the Coenobites carried them thither, which was probably early in the fourteenth century.

The Benedictines mythically link themselves to the Basilians in the person of St. Jerome, who is St. Jerome made to say that Gregory of Nazianzus was his preceptor. But they give the name of no convent as the scene of these instructions. In the rambling and loosely dated life of Jerome, he is made to travel from Aquileia to Rome, and from Rome to Bethlehem and to Egypt. He settles at Bethlehem, is followed by Roman ladies, who found there a nunnery, and there he dies. This again is a reflection of something that was happening during the later Crusades. Again, Rufinus of Aquileia is said to have been the great translator of the works of the Greeks into Latin, as well as to have been the great expounder of the symbol and creed of the Apostles. The general fact is patent, from the letters ascribed to Jerome, that correspondence was actively kept up by means of the post and of travelling monks between the cloisters of the West and of the East.

The Catalogue of Jerome and Gennadius must early have been copied and passed round to the Western monasteries.   The Benedictines then proceeded to build other Catalogues upon the same basis.   These we now proceed to notice.

To the ominous name of Isidore of Seville is attached a Catalogue of Illustrious Men, which continues that of Gennadius.   It begins with the second century, and the name of Xystus or Sixtus, A.D. 129.   It extends, with forty-seven names, to the supposed time of Isidore himself in the seventh century.   Here for the first time it is discovered that the famous preacher, John of Constantinople, bore the surname of Chrysostom, or Golden Mouth.

Catalogue II Isidore. Migne, Patrol. lxxxiv. 1081

Now, as for San Isidoro, he was not heard of in Seville until there was a religious congregation settled there to honour him as tutelar, to relate his miracles, and to write Church fiction under the patronage of his name.   The history of Seville is one of the most decisive contradictions of the monkish story that can be conceived.   In the seventh century it was old Roman.   Not a Moor, much less a Jew, was there.   It was a Moslem city from the eighth to the end of the twelfth century.   It is Moslem in appearance still.   The giralda or belfry was built about 1196, by Abu Jusuf Yacub, for a mueddin. There are arches of Norman Saracenic, which carry us back in thought to Apulia and Sicily.   The present imposing cathedral, standing on the site of the mosque, once more sends forth its voice of testimony to the fact that the Church reposes on the foundation of Islam. The Isidorian monks could not have been here till about the time of St. Ferdinand.   They may perhaps have been at Leon, of which city San Isidoro is also

San Isidoro

lord, as early as the twelfth century. But it is not in the least probable that this Catalogue was compiled before the latter part of that age. An important particular in confirmation of this is the fact that the compiler is the first to discover that the Emperor Justinian was a Church author. To him he ascribes, not works of codification, but a treatise on the incarnation of the Lord, which he sent into diverse provinces![1]

Justinian discovered a Churchman and Theologian.

The next Catalogue is that of Hildefonso, Bishop of Toledo, and *protégé* of Isidore. This list also depends on that of Jerome and Gennadius. It stretches from Pope Gregory to Archbishop Eugenius II., and contains fourteen names.

Catalogue III. Hildefonso. Migne, xcvi. 196.

At Toledo the cathedral is ascribed to St. Ferdinand, about 1226. It stands on the site of a mosque. There are, of course, myths about the descent of the Virgin, with St. Peter, St. Paul, and St. James, to an earlier church. The Jewry, with its synagogues of Moorish architecture, bears its silent evidence to the religious history of the city. The Jews were here probably later than the Moors. There is no reason to identify them with the figurative "Amalekites" whom the Moors found in the city. The oldest synagogue does not probably carry us to a higher point than the eleventh or twelfth century. Toledo bears still a Moorish face, and the earliest Christian buildings of this "Durham of a once golden hierarchy," the churches and convents, now silent as tombs, fall in the period after Alonso VI., 1085, the Emperor of Toledo, and not long before St. Ferdinand.

Toledo.

[1] C. 18.

The next Catalogue is that ascribed to Dom Sigebert of Gemblours. He has 171 ecclesiastical writers— beginning with Marcellinus, an ex-disciple of Simon Magus, and then disciple of Simon Peter in Rome, who wrote an account of the great conflict between the two Simons, which is essential to Christian legend. It is symbolic of the war waged by the Church against all the Oriental sects connected with the Moslems that preceded her rise, and was earlier told in a manner markedly different and less refined than in the canonical Acts of the Apostles.

Catalogue IV. Sigebert. Migne, clx.

This compiler follows Jerome and Gennadius, and supplies some gaps in their list from his own invention. He too has the fable of the Basilians concerning Dionysius the Areopagite, and how he witnessed the eclipse at the time of the Passion at Heliopolis.[1] Again he produces Justinian as an ecclesiastical writer, and perhaps for the first time ascribes to him the *Codex*, as well as the *Institutions* and the *Digest*. Here we find the names of Bede and Alcuin and Einhard, biographer of Charlemagne. The authority for Bede is simply Bede's own words, and nothing more. The names are merely disguises of unknown monks of the Order, contemporaries and collaborators of Sigebert himself. His own name stands last; and the particulars given teach us nothing but what we knew before, viz., that we are in the company of an imitator of Eusebius, a confederate of the Basilian and Benedictine authors and founders of the faith. The date of his death is given as 1112, but in reality we know not his exact epoch, which must depend on the probable date of the foundation at Gemblours, and the rise of

[1] C. 4. The myths sprang up at St. Denis.

the Paris Academy.   R. de Monte is said to continue
Sigebert's *Chronicle* to 1186.

The next Catalogue bears the name of Honorius of
Catalogue v.
Honorius.
Migne,
clxxii. 197. Autun, supposed to have flourished *c.* 1112–
1137. The date joins to that of Sigebert.
Again we have to do with an obscure member of the Order. He has four books, " On the
Luminaries of the Church." His first book is taken
from Jerome's catalogue, his second from Gennadius',
his third from Isidore, his fourth contains seventeen
names from various sources, Bede, Alcuin, Honorius,
and others of his contemporaries. He has an amus-
ing preface, in the thoroughly florid Benedictine
style.

The next Catalogue carries us back to the Benedictine
Catalogue
VI. The
Illustrious
of Monte
Cassino. head-quarters at Monte Cassino. It is a list
of the illustrious of that cœnobium, and
depends on the lists of Jerome, Gennadius,
and Isidore. The first name is that of St.
Benedict, the forty-seventh and last is that of Peter,
the deacon and librarian, who is supposed to say that
in 1128, at the age of twenty-one, he went into exile.
The Chronicle of this monastery ascribed to Leo of
Ostia is brought down to 1115. There are strong
evidences of fraud in connection with the history of
the Chronicle.

A Supplement by Dom Placidus begins with Abbot
Supplement. Richard, *c.* 1256, names Abbot Bernard, 1272,
then goes on to Ignatius, who died in 1514,
and ends with Gregory, cardinal, who died in 1584.
How is the strange hiatus in the series to be accounted
for ? Many of the names of the later abbots remind
of the Greek influence on the cloister ; among them
are Justin, Chrysostom, Jerome.

To Peter the Deacon is ascribed another list of the just men of the cœnobium, wherein is described how they lived and died, from St. Benedict himself to a monk of the same name under Desiderius. These are edifying fictions. Catalogue VII. Migne, clxxiii. 1010.

The anonymus of the monastery of Melk in Austria (in later times a great literary centre), who is supposed to be writing in 1215, depends also on Gennadius. His list extends from Pope Telesphorus, A. 128, down to Radpertus Magnus, who is said to have begun writing in 1111, the date when Sigebert ceases. There are 117 names. Catalogue VIII. Migne, ccx111. 965.

Then we come to the "Anonymus Zwetlensis," equally unknown, who produces a History of the Roman Pontiffs, from St. Peter down to Celestine III., A. 1191. And this book is probably the first attempt that was made to construct a complete list of the Popes before his epoch. The first article contains a remarkable address of St. Peter to his successor Clement, which throws light on the passages in the New Testament relating to the Prince of the Apostles. Linus and Cletus were merely his coadjutors, they had not the pontifical power of binding or loosing which was solemnly conferred on Clement in the words uttered by Peter before his passion. There are 179 names. The notice of Celestine III. is very slight, consisting of the statement that he crowned Henry, son of the Emperor Frederic, when he came to claim the kingdom of Apulia. Catalogue IX. Migne ib 987.

To Ralph de Diceto, Dean of St. Paul's, London, according to tradition, early in the thirteenth century, there has been ascribed the meagre *Imagines Historiarum*, and the poor list of illustrious men, among whom Pompeius Trogus is found. Catalogue X. Ralph de Diceto, c. 1210.

But the industry of the present Bishop of Oxford has not been rewarded by the discovery of the personality of this ecclesiastic. Any Dean of St. Paul's at that date must, however, have stood in the bare dawn of Christianity, when Paul was but beginning to be heard of as tutelar of the city of London. It may be observed that the so-called ten writers of English history, of whom De Diceto is one, who are supposed to sit down at the end of the twelfth century, or during the next age, to continue the History of Bede, represent the like system of contrivance that we have detected in the chronicles of the Order on the Continent. It is only when we come to the reign of John that we begin to move toward historic ground. But English history needs to be re-written.

The next Catalogue is that ascribed to Henry of Ghent, playfully called "the solemn doctor" of the Sorbonne. He continues the list of ecclesiastical writers from Sigebert down to the year 1280. But nothing is really known of the personality of "Henry of Ghent," the Archdeacon of Tournay. The beginnings of monastic life in the Low Countries must have been but faint at that epoch. This list contains sixty names. The first is that of "Foulcher of Chartres," to whom has been ascribed a History of the First Crusade, 1095–1127. There is not a word about this work, however, in "Henry of Ghent," and it is certain that not a line of it was penned during the twelfth century.

The fifth name is that of Anselm, ex-Abbot of Bec, and Archbishop of Canterbury: so that not earlier than 1280 did men begin to speak of his *Cur Deus Homo*, which develops the incarnation from an *à priori*. The ninth name is that of St. Bernard, founder of Clairvaux; but the catalogist adopts the device which is noticeable in the case of St. Augustine and others: he pretends that the works of St. Bernard are so well known, it would be an impertinence to give a list of them! A notice of Peter Abailard shows that the fable of his relations with St. Bernard, illustrative of orthodoxy and heresy, had been devised at the date of this Catalogue. The author is connected with the rising School of Paris. He names Hugo of St. Victor as expositor of the *Hierarchy* of St. Denis and author of a book of *Sentences*. It is this Hugo who was later called the "Tongue of St. Augustine," because his matter and manner so closely resembled those of the saint. With good reason, since the works of St. Augustine may have been begun in the Victorine cœnobium, late in the thirteenth century. Richard of St. Victor is also extolled as a great genius, for his rationalist work on the Trinity. Peter, Abbot of Cluny, wrote Epistles, Visions, and Revelations; but not a word is said of his translation of the Koran, either in the notice or in the scholium which adds the title Venerable to his name.

Peter Lombard is named as President of the Theological School of Paris and author of the "great and arduous work," the *Sentences*, which could not have come into general use till the fourteenth century. In 1280 it has not yet been discovered that Peter had died in the bishopric of Paris, 1159.

He is followed by Peter the Eater (Comestor or Manducator) author of a School History, abbreviated from the Testament. Pope Alexander III. is named, followed by Innocent III., but no dates or other particulars of their personality are given.

The thirty-seventh name is that of Jacobus de Vitreio, Bishop of Acco in Syria. He is said to have written an Oriental History, relating to the time of the Crusades, a word not used by the catalogist. The same Jacobus exposed the errors of the abandoned Mahomas, in which the unhappy Arabs obstinately persevere to the present day. This is perhaps the first Church allusion to the Mohammedans, the first indication of the design to garble the Koran, and represent Mohammed as the disciple of Jews and Christians.

Our author names the great Dominican and Franciscan doctors, but in such a way as to show that the bare ideas or eidola of them are merely present to his mind. Thus Hugo, the first Dominican professor of theology, Vincent, author of the *Speculum*, Albert of Cologne, are produced; but nothing is known of Hugo de S. Caro, of Vincent of Beauvais, of Albert the Great. These surnames are later discoveries, as are most of the works ascribed to the bearers of them. Thomas, however, is known already as De Aquino, and William, the invective opponent of the two orders of friars, is known as St. Amor. But a very subtle *opuscle* on this controversy is all that is set down to the credit of Thomas, who is not yet discovered as Angelic Doctor. The humour of " Henry of Ghent" is shown when he says of Albert, that "while he too much follows the subtilty of secular philosophy, he over-clouds to a certain extent the splendour of theological purity."

Alexander of Hales is named, but the compiler has not read any of his writings. Bonaventura, we are told, was an Italian of the Order of Minores, and he wrote an *opuscle* on the *Sentences* of his master Peter. In like manner Remund, the General Prior of the Dominicans, is simply so called. He has not yet culminated as St. Raymond Pennafort of Barcelona.

But the design of ascribing a work of fictitious jurisprudence to him is apparent. His name is followed by that of Gratian, the Bologna monk, whose name is equally an invention with the "Decrees" connected with it

An Appendix, of uncertain date, shows that, as usual a later writer has more clearly discovered the persons of Anselm, Abailard, Bernard, and others.   It contains eleven names.

Appendix.

If at this point of the investigation the reader turns to the massive quartos in which Dom Mabillon has collected the Acts of the Saints of the Order of St. Benedict, from the founder himself to St. Bernard, he will see that not a line of these Acts could have been written down until late in the thirteenth century, and that when they began to be written the materials were solely drawn from ideal sources, analogous to those from which the Church painters draw.

It may be convenient here to introduce the poet of the *Divine Comedy*, whose mind is filled with imagery drawn from the Greek and Latin poets and from the new secular and ecclesiastical romances.   The date of the poem is uncertain ; but the references to Church matters are fairly consistent with the tradition that the poet studied at Bologna and perhaps at Paris. He has no very clear historic perspective. He appears to confound, *e.g.*, the time of Justinian with that of Charlemagne. The Fathers, in his view, belong to an indistinct and unascertained past. Thomas d'Aquino is eminent in the fourth heaven, and with him are Albert of Cologne, Gratian, Peter, not named as Lombard, but as writer of the opening lines of the *Sentences ;* Solomon the sage incongruously follows, to be succeeded by St. Denis,

Fathers and Doctors in Dante, c. 1320?

as author of the *Hierarchia*, and by the Advocate of Christian Times, the teacher of Augustine—probably Orosius. He thinks of the bones of Boëtius laid at Cieldauro in Pavia; he passes on to Isidore and Bede, with whom Richard, the superhuman genius of St. Victor, is named in the same breath. Then we have a picture of Sigieri, or Sigebert, reading in a street _{Par., canto X.} of Paris. The poet's praise is fulsome; and one wonders how much of the writings of these musical-voiced doctors he had perused.

In the next canto St. Thomas discourses the praises of St. Francis and his bride, the Evangelical Poverty. The poet certainly imagines that before the coming of St. Francis the precepts of the Gospel had never been obeyed since primitive times. He names some of his followers. St. Francis and St. Dominic are the seraphic and cherubic doctors of the Church, her two chief escorts. They are the nearest and dearest friends of Christ. Bonaventura in turn recounts the self-denying and apostolic life of St. Dominic, and the torrent-like impetus of his enthusiasm. And with the Franciscans are joined Hugo of St. Victor, Peter the Eater, Peter of Spain; Nathan the prophet, the Metropolitan Chrysostom, Anselm, Donatus, Raban, Joachim the Calabrian abbot.

Then, again, we find King David and King Hezekiah with the Emperor Trajan and the Emperor Constantine, and Virgil's Ripheus, "most just of the Trojans," who is said to have had anticipatory faith in Christ. They are all in Paradise. In the seventh heaven's contemplation we are introduced to no earlier exemplar of the contemplative life than the Benedictine St. Pier Damiano, eremite and cardinal. The poet takes occasion to censure the cardinals of his time, who have departed from the example of the great mendicants, St. Peter and St. Paul. But no allusion is made to the writings of Damiano. The poet refers to the legends of Monte Cassino and other Benedictine cloisters, concerning their ideal founder, and concerning Macarius and Romuald. To St. James of Compostella he appears to ascribe the canonical epistle. With St. Peter and St. John, St. James assumes the place of a leading doctor of the Church.

A further invective against Boniface VIII. and other Popes is put in the mouth of St. Peter, who wears the aspect of Jove or Mars; Linus, Cletus, Sextus, Pius, Callixtus, and Urban are named as martyr-Popes. Significant is the censure of the keys as a military ensign, and of the seal attached to "sold and lying privileges." The poet denounces the fables concerning the eclipse at the Passion which were to be heard in the pulpits of Florence, and the jocularities of Easter sermons; he calls the friars of St. Antony swine. But the time of primitive purity to which he looks back is the time of the mendicants, or beyond them, in an aoristic past.

Hardly can he have perused the writings ascribed to St. Bernard, for St. Bernard is represented as gazing with exceeding enthusiasm on the Blessed Virgin, whose faithful servant he professes himself to be. Interesting is the picture of the Croatian peasant viewing the handkerchief of Veronica. It reminds us that for many decades pictorial art had been impressing the Christian legend on the minds of the multitude, with whom to see is to believe. The absence of all chronological taste is again observable when Eve is seen at the feet of Mary, and beneath, Rachel, Beatrice, Sarah, Judith, Rebecca, Ruth. Then with John Baptist are associated Augustine, Francis, and Benedict.

It is remarkable how little use the poet makes of the
New Testament, seeing that he contrasts so strongly
evangelical simplicity and purity with the pride and
depravity of the papal court.   He appears to have derived his ideas of the Gospel from the contemplation
of the lives of the mendicants and from the tenor of
their preaching.   His knowledge of fathers and doctors is about on a level with that revealed in the work
of Henry of Ghent; and on the whole his work is
decisive witness that the revival of classical literature
and the beginning of Church literature fell in nearly
the same period.   The evidence as to the date of the
Divine Comedy is, however, by no means so clear as
could be desired.[1]

The Canterbury Tales are a still more valuable source
The Canter-   of knowledge than the Divine Comedy.   If
bury Tales.   they were written down not far from the
year 1480, they reflect light upon perhaps a century
before that date.

The author is well acquainted with the Roman poets,
and with sentences of the Benedictine "Fathers."   He
appears to be peculiarly fond of Seneca, whom he often
quotes, and whose works were now more fully known.
There is the same want of perspective in his view of
the past that we have noted in Dante.   In one place
he says, while enforcing a moral lesson, "Read David
in his Psalms, and read Senec."   Chaucer would
perhaps have been perplexed by the question, from
what age of the world these works had respectively
come down?   He reads the books for the good in

[1] I would ask the reader to consider all that Mr. Symonds and other
contemporary critics have written on the chronicles of the Italian cities,
and the uncertainty about their date and authenticity.   He will see that
the Church chronicles cannot be separated, in this respect, from the secular
chronicles.

them, not to ascertain their chronological relations or differences of style.

The Rules of St. Benedict and St. Maur had grown old in Chaucer's time, as the picture of the hunting abbot reminds us; possibly they had been in existence for some 200 years. He is incidentally a witness to the early enthusiasm of the friars, and to the ill-repute which they have now largely incurred: "Friars and fiends be but little asunder." There is a passage which tends to confirm what has been said of the relation of the friars to the New Testament.

> " Our sweet Lord Jesus
> Spake this of friars, when he saide thus,
> *Blessed be they that poor in spirit be.*
> And so forth all the Gospel may ye see
> Whether it be liken our profession,
> Or theirs that swimmen in possession."

But still more important is the view given in Chaucer of the forms of Christian belief and practice among the common people, because they aid to define our ideas of what the preaching and teaching had been before the "Fathers" had been written, and before there existed any considerable body of readers to receive them.

In popular belief, Christ is certainly both God and man; but the greater emphasis is laid upon the idea of his Godhead. He is regarded as Governor of the course of nature; and, in fact, has assumed, like another Apollo, the attributes of the Supreme himself. His name is taken in vain with what would now be considered an offensive profanity; he is thought of as a Being who bestows temporal blessings or curses. He is "the highe God on whom that we believe," "the highe God who all this world hath wrought," and who has uttered the words recorded

Popular Christology.

in the Gospel. The violent contrast between one who is conceived as Heaven's King, yet a portion of whose blood is preserved in the Abbey of Hales, is most revolting. The Virgin is described as both mother and daughter of Christ.

The great object of popular devout contemplation is the Passion, which had long been dramatically represented, and was perhaps beginning to be figured upon devotional tablets. The Lord's Prayer is recited as a charm against evil spirits. A new superstition has been introduced into the minds of the people, or old superstitions have been christened. It cannot be denied that we are brought nearer to original Christianity in the following lines than in either the canonical books or the Fathers—

> " Awake and think on Christe's passioun,
> I crouche thee from elves, and from wights.
> Therewith the night-spell said he anon rights
> On the four halves of the house about,
> And on the threshold of the door without.
> *Lord Jesus Christ and Sainte Benedicte,*
> *Blesse this house from every wicked wight,*
> *From the nightmare, the white Paternoster ;*
> *Where wonnest thou now, Sainte Peter's sister ?*"

The Christianity of the people has been derived from oral marvellous tales of unknown origin, supported by the gross evidence of relics carried about by pardoners from Rome : rags, shoulder-bones of holy Jews' sheep, the veil of our Lady, a gobbet from the sail of St. Peter's boat. These are the imaginary means of securing physical weal. The whole representation of Church belief and practice, as given in these extraordinary revelations, shows that neither had sprung from any source but that of worldly ambition, greed, and lust. The noblest ideals of the New Testament stand in ironical contradiction with the actual system of the ecclesiastics. The few who lead blameless and gentle lives are driven to the wall by the men of violence, of blood, and extortion. The life that had been lived in the synagogues in England must have been incomparably purer and sweeter.

Yet we find the hideous conventional tales against the Jews of their murdering children in theo- *The Jews.* logical animosity. It is represented that the serpent Satan, who had "his wasps' nest in the Jewish heart," inspired them to put an innocent boy out of the world, who had gone through an Asian Jewry singing the *Ave Maria*. Such inhumanities of thought against the unhappy people were the direct fruit of the teaching of those who contrived the tale of Herod's massacre of the babes, which was repeated each Advent-tide.

With regard to the Mohammedans, the poet is incidentally a witness to their intense faith in *The Muslim.* the Koran and the Prophet, and to the fact that they regarded Christianity as a younger system. The mother of the Sultan, who is willing to be christened that he may wed the daughter of an Emperor of Rome with the aid of the Pope of Rome, exclaims—

> " Life shall rather out of my body start
> Than Mahomet's law go out of mine heart.
> What should we tiden of this newe law
> But thraldom to our bodies and penance,
> And afterward to hell to be y-draw,
> For we renied Mahound our creance?"

At the time of this tale, the time of King Ella, the poet thinks of all Northumberland as pagan; Wales has become the refuge of Christianity, and the Book of the Gospels produced is Briton. But there is not the slightest indication that the poet, who seems master of all the learning of his time, could have given any chronological account of the beginnings of the Church in this island. Beyond the fourteenth century his glance plunges into the fabulous obscure. One may well suppose that, had he fully possessed the romances of Arthur, the monkish tales of Saxon and Norman kings, we should have found greater wealth of allusion to them. His knowledge of the old Roman time, if so it can be called, appears derived from the allegories of the *Gesta Romanorum*, and from some passages in Lucan. If Dante had no distinct view of historic changes in the Western world, the English poet has not acquired it.[1]

We pass on to the year 1492, when the Benedictine Abbot of Spanheim, John of Trittenheim, addresses himself to the compilation of another list of ecclesiastical writers. It is still based on those of Eusebius, Jerome, Gennadius, Isidore, Honorius, and Sigebert. But the astonished reader observes that in the interval of two centuries a vast mass of books has been brought to light quite unknown to any of the previous Catalogues. The fact is a decisive proof that the fourteenth and the fifteenth centuries were above all the ages for Church forgery. Jerome, Chrysostom, Augustine, and others, have now that bulky appearance which age in the Church confers. In regard to Augustine especially the contrast is amazing between Jerome, who can only name the work on the Trinity, and the Abbot of Spanheim, who

Catalogue XII. Trithemius.

---

[1] See the illustrations of the state of thought in this period, in Buckle's *Hist. of Civilisation*, I. c. vi. It is needless to observe that Geoffrey of Monmouth did not write in the twelfth century.

produces more than 200 works, and declares the man to be a liar who says he has found the whole of Augustine.

It is a curious fact that the Abbot, who ascribes seven works to Henry of Ghent, makes no mention at all of his work on ecclesiastical writers. It would seem as if that Catalogue were being compiled near the same time. The good Abbot ends his long list of 963 names with the modest insertion of his own, after the precedents of Sigebert and the others. There are some additional lists to this work, which found a continuator in Aubert Miræus, Dean of Antwerp, whose *Ecclesiastical Library* was published in 1649.[1]

But if we are led, by the study of the imposing Catalogue of the Abbot of Spanheim, to draw favourable inferences as to the state of culture in that cloister during the fifteenth century, his own words will correct us. In a homily he addresses his monks, telling them that their predecessors had so sold and scattered the library that he had only found fourteen volumes. In 1469 five dissolute monks had been cast out, with their abbot, Otto de Colonna. His successor, John de Colenhausen, is well spoken of. When De Trittenheim succeeded to the abbey, he made great exertions for the furnishing of a library, which was without rival in Germany. He had collected more than 2000 volumes from different parts of the world, MSS. and printed books. But there had been no such learned abbot, men said, since the time of St. Bernard.

If we glance at the contemporary library of Cardinal Bessarion, and at that of the Vatican, we shall be reminded how great a stimulus had been applied by the invention of printing to the production and the

[1] See Fabricius, *Bibl. Eccles.*, 1718.

study of ecclesiastical literature. Nicholas V. is said to have collected 6000 volumes.

It is, as we have said, in the study of the Catalogues The Missal. thus briefly reviewed that the whole system The Apostle and structure of the Church literature may be and the Gospels. approached. The history of the New Testament, for example, lies implicit in the history of the Service Book. The history of the words *Missa, Missal*, point back to corresponding synagogue use, and their rise may be traced in the pseudo-Fathers, Ambrose and others. It is convenient to think of the epoch of Gregory IX., 1225–1240, as that in which the formation of the books called the *Apostle* and the *Gospels* was incipient.

From Photius, the Eusebii, and from Suidas and the rest, it can be clearly collected how gradually the scheme of these books—the one to contain sentences of Apostolic authority, the other narratives of the "sufferings, wonders, and teachings" of the Saviour— was executed. From Tertullian we learn how the device of making imaginary heretics bear witness to some form of these sacred books was adopted. But these matters belong to the details of the subject. The important thing is to observe the epoch at which the work began, and the fact that the friars, as well as the primitive monks, had their part in it.

The Epistles, when analysed, fall asunder into a number of lections, or small epistles, and correspondingly the Gospels into a number of small gospels. Each forms in the Missal an independent whole, illustrative of the observance of the day. Perused in that light, most of the difficulties of interpretation vanish. For example, the Gospel in John xiii. 1–15, illustrates the act of lavation, or washing of feet, still practised at

Rome and Vienna on Maundy Thursday. It gives a dramatic scene in which Christ prototypically performs the act, with the most solemn sacramental injunctions for its continued observance. The passage is a dead letter to Protestants and to English Catholics, yet is valuable as showing how Church literature bases itself on custom, and how with the vitality or decline of custom the idea flourishes or decays.

The lection John v. 1-4, is in like manner explained by reference to the dogma concerning St. Raphael, archangel, one of the seven angels _{St. Raphael} who stand before the Lord, of whom we read also in the book of Tobias as deliverer from evil demons. He goes down at certain seasons to wash in the pool. Raphael came into the Church from Islam, as did Michael.

The passages relating to the blessed Virgin Mary can only be understood when they are compared with the ideas and sentiments awakened by the great feasts in her honour, such as the Assumption, and with the lessons from the Old Testament, which have contributed to form her ideal in the conscience of the Church.

The canonical Acts of the Apostles can only be understood in the light of the origin of Whitsuntide, the dogma of the third Person of the Trinity, and of the mission to the Gentiles.

But the most important part of the New Testament consists of the legenda of the Pascha. They should be carried into the light of the *Ludi* _{Legenda at the Pascha.} *Paschales*, the passion plays, of which we hear only in the thirteenth century, in the Coliseum. It was by an appeal *oculis fidelibus* of the multitude, as well as by preaching, that the great drama of the Passion became impressed on their mind, with all the antipathy thereby excited against the Jews. It stands fast in all the writings of the Greek and Latin doctors of the Catalogues that the Passion was purely a dogma derived from mystical exegesis of the Old Testament, and represented as fact by sacred dramatic art.

In general it must be insisted upon, after all our long aberrations in the study of the Epistles and Gospels, that these books were from the first and still remain sacerdotal in their origin, mystical and dogmatic in their character. They were monastic, they were written in the cloister and for the cloister, in sympathy with the life of the religious of the cloister can alone be understood and obeyed. When the reforming monk broke his vows, and wedded a nun, he should have known that the New Testament was no longer a book for him. The book is also Roman, Pontifical and Petrine; it contains not the first but one of the most memorable assertions of the primacy of Peter, as the holder of the keys, and the first Vicar of Jesus Christ.

The New Testament monastic.

Roman, Pontifical and Petrine.

Now, with regard to the period of the composition of the Epistles and Gospels, there are several lines of evidence which conduct us toward a tolerably safe conclusion. In the first place, the Basilians and Benedictines teach that the New Testament is based on the Old. In a saying ascribed to St. Jerome, he declares that everything in the Old Testament is a type of something in the New, everything in the New Testament is a fulfilment of some prophecy in the Old. If those Orders were not in possession of the lessons of the Synagogue in some version until some time in the twelfth century, the New Testament could not have been begun till that age.

Date of the New Testament.

Again the Service Books, whether of Rome or Sarum, cannot be dated earlier than that age. The Roman

Missal, as we now have it, shows a long history of elaboration in the hands of the monks and the friars.

Another fact in this connection is that the writers of the New Testament show great acquaintance with the Talmud, as scholars have recognised since Lightfoot. It was not until the thirteenth century that the Talmud became the object of jealous denunciation and violence on the part of the churchmen; it could not have been known to them at least until late in the preceding age. Nor is it irrelevant to this subject to bear in mind that the Benedictines of Cluny do not give an earlier date for their Latin mistranslation of the Koran than 1143, which is proleptic. Their debt to the Koran and to the Talmud probably commences at nearly the same epoch.

Another aid to the determination of the period lies in the Ritual Book, the *Ordo Romanus I.* of the Benedictines. The legends of the Passion lie implicit in this book. In the next age we may conceive the Easter stations beginning to be held, on Sunday in S. Maria Major, on Monday in S. Peter, on Wednesday in S. Laurence, and on Thursday in S. Paul. *The Ordo Romanus. Mabillon, Mus. It. ii.*

Again: there is a strong affinity of the legends of the Franciscans to many most significant passages of the New Testament. And if these passages are historic reflections of the Franciscan ideal, the New Testament could not have been *completed* until the thirteenth century. *The Franciscans and the New Testament.* The case stands thus: Either the Franciscans copied the miracles of Christ into the life of their founder, or they saw in their founder qualities which served to fix their ideal of the Christ. And there are many ideals of the Christ in the New Testament.

It was in the time of the Franciscan enthusiasm that the following words first acquired that spirit and life which has long deserted them, at least for the mass of our lay people, who nevertheless profess to obey them :—

"Provide neither gold, nor silver, nor brass, in your purses ; nor scrip for your journey, neither two coats, neither shoes, nor yet staves : for the workman is worthy of his meat."

"If thou wilt be perfect, go and sell that thou hast, and give to the poor, and thou shalt have treasure in heaven; and come and follow Me."

"Every one that hath forsaken houses, or brethren, or sisters, or father, or mother, or wife, or children, or lands, for My name's sake, shall receive a hundredfold, ˙ and shall inherit everlasting life."

"Having food and raiment, let us be therewith content."

To St. Francis is ascribed the saying, "Poverty is Christ's bride and friend; she is root and foundation and queen of all virtues. If the friars forsake her, the whole covenant is dissolved; if they hold fast to her, and give the world a pattern and example, the world will nourish them."

"Go two and two, and preach peace to all, keeping it in your own hearts. Be not led astray to hate and wrath ; be not misled from the path you have entered. We are called to guide wanderers, to heal the wounded, and raise up the bowed down."

Passages like this would prove little, inasmuch as similar passages are known to and commented on by Cassian of the Benedictines, who, however, had not precisely *our* New Testament in his hands. But there are other passages which correspond more exactly to the ideal of the saint, who for example is described as so greatly the object of reverence in Bologna in the year 1220, that men and women rushed upon him in crowds, and he thought himself blessed who could but touch the hem of the saint's garment. When he preached it is said that men of letters wondered greatly at his discourse, for he was an unlettered man.

It has even been said that the Franciscans endeavoured to exalt their founder over Christ Himself in respect of his holiness and perfection. He hungered forty days, changed vinegar into wine, cast out devils, and raised the dead. Often he spoke with Christ; and at last Christ Himself pressed upon him the marks of the nails on his hands and feet. It is true that the Dominicans jealously denied this, themselves having prolific or analogous miracles. The legend, however, obtained its sanction, and the seventeenth day of September recalls the memory of the stigmas of St. Francis Confessor. The prayer recites how, when the world was growing cold, Christ renewed the sacred marks of His Passion in the flesh of the blessed Francis; the Epistle, Gal. vi. 14–18, speaks of glorying in the cross, and of the bearing of the marks of the Lord Jesus in the body; while the Gospel teaches self-denial and the taking up the cross to follow Christ.

These passages are also remarkable as showing that at the time they were composed the cross—at the time of the first Crusade solely the sign of victory and triumph—has become confused with the crucifix, and is now the centre of wonderful mysteries, shown forth especially by Divine revelation in the blessed Francis.

Similarly, when it is said that St. Dominic, as head of the Preaching Order, began to teach pub- The Dominilicly in his thirtieth year after the example cans. of Christ, it is that the example of Christ, as that of the

Baptist, prince of monks, has been found to illustrate and dignify the preacher's rule and calling. All these things can be understood in the light of that time when every important institution, from the foundation of Monte Cassino onwards, was traced to the inspiration of the Divine human founder of the Church. In general, our inquiries in this department of Church literature point steadily to the conclusion to which we have been led again and again, that it was not till the time of Innocent III., or later, the foundations were finally laid, and that the canon of the New Testament could have been fixed.

It may be added that the geography of the New Testament is the incorrect geography of the time of the third Crusade, while Syria was yet a dreamland in the conception of the West. Its historical geography, before and after the Crusades, sorely needs to be written. Such a work would dispel many a lingering delusion.

Geography of the New Testament.

It is not yet clear whether the book was first written in Latin or in Greek. Perhaps the opinion may be ventured that it reads better in the Vulgate than in other versions, and that the Greek corresponds nearly to that of Cedrenus and writers of the Basilian Order in general.

Perfectly correct is the remark of Professors Pierson and Naber, in their work, *Verisimilia*, that the oldest foundation of Church ideas is not to be found in the New Testament. We may dig and dig again, they say, but there is always an earlier stratum, as in the cities of Asia Minor or of Greece. To this earlier stratum of Church tradition the attention of the reader may presently be invited. It will reveal great crudities, and suggest through what a long process of refinement the canonical Gospels and Epistles have passed.

The Book of the Popes shows the same kind of structure with the rest of the biographic literature. Not a line of any such book could have been penned till late in the thirteenth century, if even then. The terms *pontiff* and *papa* were of late introduction; in the early Catalogues the Bishop of the City of Rome is still spoken of.

The Book of the Popes.

Passing over for the moment the monstrous tales of the Popes of the tenth century—the obscure age of the mythologists—the notices referring to the next or "Hildebrandine Age," consist merely of crude official lists in barbarous style and various hands. There is a poor Life of Hildebrand, falsely dated 1128; there is a pamphlet on the same subject by Cardinal Benno. A Life of Paschal II. introduces the first description of the Consecration and the Procession in the Sacred Way. Various writers, as Peter of Pisa, Pandulf, Cardinal Boso, continue the Papal succession for the next age. But there are significant gaps. With Innocent III. begins a new series of Lives, still broken. A laudation of Innocent IV. has been ascribed to his chaplain, N. de Curbio. As we have no genuine portrait in painting, so neither have we in literature of any thirteenth century Pope.

After that time the biographic department appears to have fallen into the hands of the Dominicans. The name of Martin the Pole marks another tedious tale of falsification in connection with his *Chronicle*, said to have been written about 1270. Then we have Ptolomæus of Lucca, who produces a Church History to the year 1313; Augerius, who brings us to 1321; and Henry of Diessenhoven, to 1361. The Lives of the

Avignon Popes, written in the French cloisters, have been edited by Muratori.

Convenient compilations are those of Platina, and of Joannes Stella, from the fifteenth or sixteenth century. The latter makes free use of the Canons in Gratian.

With regard to Gratian's collection of Canons, it will be remembered that Poggio attacked the author, exposed the Latin of the compilation, and denounced it as a system of forgery. A warning—too long neglected—to inquire into the quality of the Papal archives.

The Decre- tum of Gratian.

A second collection has been ascribed to Innocent III., a third to Honorius III., and the complete Code to Raimund the Dominican, 1234. But as we have seen, the author was gradually discovered at a later date. Another book is said to have been added by Boniface VIII. It is more probable that the system of fabrication was begun in the time of that ambitious Pope.

On the Gratianic collection of Canons, Gregorovius remarks:—"This famous Code of the Middle Age stands before us to-day, when criticism has long unmmasked its inventions and lies, the legal Colossus of the barbarism and darkness in which mankind for so many centuries lay exiled. It rested on them with oppressive weight, falsified the constitutional ideas of Church and State, and obscured the judgment of long periods simply in order to secure to the priesthood, and above all, to the Papacy, the rule of the world."

This collection contains the false Donation of Constantine and the Isidorian Decretals. But it is not probable that any part of this literature was compiled till the fourteenth century, as attention to other parts of the evidence will show.

It may be regarded as certain that the pseudo-Decretals do not date before the time of Boniface VIII. at the earliest.   They reflect the desire of the Papal lawyers to prove the right of the Popes to universal dominion, both as temporal and spiritual lords.   Not till that time could the Church boldly assert herself as the kingdom of this world, of which Christ was the Head, the Pope being Vicar of Christ-God, so that whoso had not the Pope for his head had not Christ.   The like proud pretensions are no doubt connected with the name of Innocent III., but according to all indications, his time was that of the very infancy of the system.

Pseudo-Decretals of Isidore.

Formerly the Book of the Popes, like the Decretals, was assigned to the ninth century, and to the hand of Anastasius the Librarian.   But attention to the facts about libraries and librarians is sufficient entirely to dispel this illusion.   Moreover, the contents of the Lives referred to that age are wholly incredible, as the example of the female and maternal Pope reminds us—a tale that certainly did not spring up until the thirteenth century, as Döllinger has shown.   That the tale should have been suggested to fancy by the sight of some statue of a woman with a child in the Lateran Way, if so it was, reminds us how obscure and fabulous the distant ninth century must have appeared to the later age.   There is a number of other violent tales, emanations from the Benedictine cloisters; the discrepancies in dates betray the mendacity of them, as for example in the horrible tale concerning Pope Formosus.   In the next age we have the strange romance about Theodora, the new Semiramis and magnificent patroness of the Apostolic Chair.   Again the tale helps us to estimate the great distance at which the writers must have lived from that age. If it be asked, Why did the Papal romancers venture on these astounding fictions ? our answer is that they were to the taste of their times. And the more romantic the story of the Papacy was conceived to have been, the more wickedly the Popes were believed to have lived, the greater the Divine marvel in the perpetuation of the institution. But enough of these details. The question is, When did the Benedictines and Dominicans begin this series of fables ?

There have been the usual wild conjectures as to the date of the MSS. But the opinion of the specialist Giesebrecht coincides with the general results of the study of the Catalogue literature. The parent MS. comes from La Cava of the Benedictines. Folio 1–171 has been written in one hand from St. Peter to Honorius II., 1126. Folio 172–185 has been written in one hand from Innocent II. to Hadrian V., 1131–1275. Now this last hand is of the *fourteenth* century. It is a weighty fact.

Giesebrecht remarks that the Book of the Popes reflects throughout the spiritual movement of the whole West—that of the Benedictines as well as of Rome. It is clearly revealed here, as in their other sources, how determined they were to make Church heroes of Pipin and Charlemagne, who stand out from the desolation of following times even as Constantine stands out from the sterility of the period between him and Islam. The monks have laboured at this idea of an alliance between the Popes and the Frankish kings, but it falls baseless so soon as the epoch of their first literary activity is discovered. The Catalogue of the Popes is later than the Catalogues of the illustrious writers of the Church. It is simply another camera from which Church portraits have been cast upon the artificial screen of earlier ages.

To turn for a moment to the contents of the book. They are a clumsy miscellany of notices of buildings, votive offerings, Church usages, and the like, hung, so to speak, as on pegs, on the names of the Popes. Simon Peter comes to Rome to take his seat in the *cathedra*, because the city, as head of the whole world, was suitable for the pontifical seat. He overcame Simon Magus. He was crucified head downwards. His canonical deeds are recited, and it is claimed that he was elected by Christ to the supreme pontificate, with the power of the keys. His prototype is Moses. He instituted the fast of Quadragesima, as is clear from Canon XCIII. He appointed Linus and Cletus as his suffragans, also Clemens.

But we will not pursue the extraordinary tale of inventions and anachronisms. It would be tedious and useless, after all that has been said on the subject. There are many curiosities of structure : in particular it may be seen how certain ideals are duplicated ; how the wicked Damasus II. finds a mythic fore-type in the violent Damasus I. and the like in other cases. It is only when we reach Popes the *third* of their name that we approach the actual historic time.

Such a profound impression of system and of mass is made upon the unwary reader who wades through the literature we have reviewed, so is he affected by the constant tone of piety prevading the whole imaginary retrospect, that he is still liable to fall back into illusion, and to mistake a dream-world for reality ; and he needs to turn renewed attention to the actual state of things during all the twelfth century. He wakes to discover the striking poverty of all literature.

He finds that our English chroniclers dated in that age appear to know more of Rome than the Romans themselves. He finds Jews and Manichees swarming everywhere, Peter Lombard's text-book unknown as yet in the Cathedral Schools, the academies of Paris, Bologna, Padua, Naples, and Rome not yet able to make themselves felt. There was, in short, no public in any part of the world in whose ears the historic and theologic declamation of the Papal army could have been intelligible until late in the next century.

Let us assemble in one representation all that can be known of other branches of Church art—sculpture, where the epochal name is Nicolas of Pisa; painting, where Cimabue furnishes a landmark; Gregorian music, developed in Cluny and Citeaux; every indication is of the thirteenth century as that in which progress in these departments began to be made.

Note.

I have referred in my Preface to the surprise with which I recently found that Father Hardouin had in 1690–1692, when he was of the mature age of forty-five, arrived at results almost identical with those set forth in these pages. In case his *Prolegomena*, London 1766, should not be readily accessible to the reader, I give a brief statement of his opinions. The ecclesiastical history of the first twelve centuries is absolutely fabulous. The series of Popes is no more authentic then the series of Jewish high-priests. The theory of a succession of Fathers down to St. Bernard is analogous to the theory of the Rabbins of a succession of prophets to Ezra, and after him of a succession of wise men. The monks said, "The Fathers were until Bernard, the Scholastics to Thomas Aquinas, after him all were infants." Their frauds must have been begun long after the stated time of Bernard. The agreement, often verbatim, of the monastic chronicles, *e.g.*, for the year 1215, show that they came from one workshop. Not one was written by a contemporary of the events described. The opportune time for the forgers was from some epoch in the thirteenth century onwards, until past the epoch of printing. They had among them astronomers, physicians, poets, savants in Hebrew and Arabic. The name of Planudes, 1350, translator of Augustine on the Trinity into Greek, marks an epoch a little later than the production of that work in Latin. During about 1350–1480 were written the works which have been ascribed to the eleventh and following ages, especially the Decretals of the Popes. Charters, diplomata, false privileges, were concocted during the same period in the cloisters of Italy, France, and Germany. The books were written on parchment rather than paper, that they might appear older and last longer. The oldest MSS. contain both the works of the Fathers, still considered genuine, and those which have been reckoned false from disparity of style and other reasons.

The forgers had the measure and form of letters for different centuries, and corresponding parchments and inks, by which they simulated a seventh, eighth, or ninth century style. Cf. e.g., Montfaucon, *Palæographia*, p. 326, where a fourteenth century scribe imitates the eleventh century character. Copies which have been supposed to date from the eighth century on the credit of the statement of the writers show the same form of writing, the same character, because the copyists had the same alphabet before their eyes. In the year 1712 was edited the Epitome of Lactantius from the MS. of the Turin Library. The editor gave a specimen of the letters; it is the same character as that of the Royal MS. of St. Paul's Epistles (see Montfaucon, *Palæographia*, p. 217), and that of the St. Germain MS. of the same Epistles (p. 218), and the Paris MS. of the four Gospels. So similar is the character that you might swear that these MSS. were not only from one workshop, but from one hand, or if from many hands, certainly from those who had the same alphabet before their eyes, or same form of letters. Cf. Mabillon, *De Re Diplom.*, p. 233.

A MS. of St. Jerome in the Royal Library of Paris bears a Greek epigraph stating that it was written in the eleventh century. Experts would say that it dates from the fifteenth century. No Hebrew MSS. in our libraries are believed to be older than the fourteenth century. In Hebrew character the forgers could not, as in Latin, pretend a Merovingic, Lombardic, Saxon form.

There are no Biblical MSS. in the libraries not elegantly written and finished, because there are none incorrupt. Of the Vulgate there are no copies, because such were written only for use, and when worn out were cast away. There was no Royal Library in France till Charles V., the Wise, 1364–1380. So late as 1304, Simon, Bishop of Paris, had no books to bequeath to his Church except books for the use of the Church of Paris. In 1279 the legacy of Simon Tempier, Bishop of Paris, consisted of two Missals, one Gospel and Epistles, three Graduals, one Episcopal Ordinary, a Breviary in large letters, and two others, a Collectarium, and a Troperium or hymn-book. Mention is also made of a Bible in two volumes, which he bought for £200. No Greek or Latin Father, no Peter Lombard even, is mentioned. Yet Peter Lombard is supposed to have lived a hundred years before, to have been Bishop of Paris, and to have been a great Patristic scholar !

In 1271 the Archdeacon of Canterbury bequeaths all his theological books to the Chancellor of Paris. There is not a Father nor a Scholastic among them. In C. Hemeræus' work on the Academy of Paris, a catalogue of books from the Armarium of St. Mary of Paris is given. It dates from the fourteenth century. There are thirty-eight volumes with Biblical matter. Two more volumes contain the *Sentences* of Peter Lombard, and the *Questions* of Peter of Poitiers. There is no Father, no ecclesiastical historian.

At the capture of Constantinople, 1453, there are said to have been only fifty MSS. in the Patriarchium, only 180 in the whole city. In the West, Montfaucon numbers 20,000. The Greek MSS. were first written in the West.

F. Hardouin says of the Acts of Martyrs, that it was necessary they should be written equally with the Ecclesiastical History and the Lives of Saints, so that it might appear that in every age of the Church the doctrine contained in the writings of the Fathers had been approved and handed down by holy men, and that numberless martyrs had poured forth their blood in defence of the same. With strange irony he adds that these fictitious stories of martyrs had given rise to *true* martyrs in his own time, in Japan, Brazil, amd elsewhere. So the Almighty had brought good even out of lies. The good Jesuits, reading those stories, had been inspired to devote their lives and labours, and to undergo cruel tortures like unto their God. They say that J. Gerson wrote that it was right to invent Lives of Saints, with the view of fostering piety.

The age which saw the rise of the Romance in Western literature, witnessed also the compilation of the Ecclesiastical Histories and Lives of the Saints. The Church was deceived when she believed the writings of the Fathers to be genuine without examination, and when she suffered lies to be inserted in the Breviary and the public prayers, with stories of Honorius, George, Catherine, and others.

F. Hardouin dates the first design of the forgers in France from Philip Augustus, 1180–1229. Much more was done under Philip the Fair, 1285–1314, and under Philip of Valois, 1328–1350; and the construction of literature went on to an immense extent during the next 150 years.

The evidence, however, does not seem clear as to the priority, as he maintains, of the Latin Church, the Latin Bible and Service Books, over the Greek. The books, while the Greeks and Latins remained in union, appear to have been written in both tongues.

CHAPTER X.

EARLY FORMS OF THE CHRISTIAN LEGEND.

AND now once more it is necessary to tread again old ground, and to place before the reader the brief outline of the story published to the world at the opening of the Universities by the members of the Orders.

They, at the end of the twelfth century, can produce no testimony of "folk who had seen length of days, and had talked much anent sic matters," to borrow the phrase of our Walter Scott. They can refer to none whose memory in a green old age might carry them back to an epoch where links might again be formed with a dim past. No! they talk much of Paradosis or tradition; but this is found to consist of paper links, of dogmatic notes, of chips from the literary workshops where the whole work of theological construction is going on. There is no simple intelligible account of a martyrdom on behalf of a popular cause, not a line which proceeds from one who had his eye fixed on historic objects. All smells of the scriptorium, the parchment, and the lamp.

All is deduced from Theology and Christology. Christ is more divine than the mass of men suppose. Christology. The dignified name of Christians has been derived from Him. His mode is twofold. As God, He may be compared with the head of the body; and He may be compared with the feet, in so far as He put on man of like passions with us for the sake of our salvation.[1]

The Christians are of great antiquity, although there are men who suspect them to be a new and foreign sect, of yesterday and not before. For the Hebrew prophet asks, *Who shall declare His generation?* None knows the Father except the Son, nor could any authority know the Son except the Father who begat Him. Our author is not citing the New Testament.

The epithets or titles of Christ are—

1. The Light before the World.

            The Titles of Christ.

2. The intelligent and substantial Wisdom before the Ages.

3. The living God-Word, in the beginning with the Father existent.

4. The first and only Offspring of God before all Creation and Workmanship, seen and unseen.

5. The Arch-General of the celestial, rational, and immortal Host.

6. The Angel of the Great Council.

7. The Minister of the unutterable designs of the Father.

8. The Demiurge or Creator of all things together with the Father.

9. The Second Cause of all things after the Father.

10. The genuine and only-begotten Son of God.

11. The Lord and God and King of all begotten things, who has received the rank and might with Divinity itself, and power and honour from the Father.

The "mystic theologies of Scriptures" declare that— "In the beginning was the Word, and the Word was toward God, and the Word was God. All things

---

[1] Euseb., *H. E.*, i. 1, 9.

became through Him, and apart from Him nothing became." [1]

It is maintained that Moses, the most ancient of the Prophets, bears witness to Him in the words, "Let *us* make man," and that the Psalmist, xxxiii. 9, alludes to a second Divine Being, the Word. The Word appeared to Abraham as an ordinary man, also to Jacob. Joshua or Jesus, the successor of Moses, called the Word the Arch-General of the power of the Lord, having beheld Him in human form and shape. It was He with whom Joshua-Jesus conversed at Jericho, He who spoke to Moses from the bush. Personified Sophia or Wisdom in the book of Proverbs is identified with the Word as one pre-mundane essence which ministered to the Father from the creation of the world.

Christ was not early preached to the nations, because their savage state would not admit of it. War was made on God, and there were battles of giants against heaven. Dire punishments fell on the race, until at the last pitch of its wickedness, "the first-born and first-created Sophia of God, and very pre-existent Logos by excess of philanthropy, appeared in visions of angels or in His own person." So the seeds of piety were scattered; and the whole nation derived from the Hebrews was devoted to the worship of God. This new people received through Moses images and symbols of a certain mystical Sabbath and circumcision, and initiation into other mystical theorems, though not the absolutely plain mystagogies. Such was the origin of the nation of Christians, or of the Catholic Church.

We are now invited to make a great leap in historic

Mystical Origin of the Christians.

---

[1] John i. 1, is slightly fuller in expression.

contemplation, from Moses to the Emperor Augustus. The New Law spread through the world like a fragrant breeze, men's manners were The Reign of Augustus. softened and prepared, until at the beginning of the Roman Empire the Teacher of Virtues Himself in human form appeared, died, and suffered such things as followed from the prophecies. For they had foretold that Man at once and God should sojourn in life, a doer of strange deeds, and that to all nations a Teacher of the pity of the Father should be shown; they had foretold the strangeness of His generation, and the new teaching and the marvels of the works; the manner of the death, the resurrection from the dead, and finally, the Divine restitution into heaven.

Here is one of the earliest statements of the Credo, the manifesto or symbol of the primitive Orders. We have not arrived at the time when it is represented as the joint constructive work of the College of Apostles, as in the treatise of Rufinus, the monk of Aquileia. One prophecy is here cited in support of the argument, it is that in Daniel concerning the throne of the Ancient of Days, and the eternal authority of the Son of Man.[1]

It is then shown that the names Jesus and Christ have been also derived from the Hebrew Scriptures. Christus is the rendering, however The Names Jesus and Christ. inexact, of the Hebrew epithet of the high-priest, *Ha-Mashich*, the Anointed. The successor of Moses was not at first called Jesus, but Navé, by his parents. Moses gave him the name Jesus as a high distinction much greater than that of royalty, for it typified the Saviour. This argument rests on the fact that in the Septuagint Joshua son of Nun becomes Jesus son of Navé, Nauses, or Auses.[2] One of the

[1] vii. 9 ff.   [2] Cf. Eus. *D. E.* iv. 17.

Latin monks says that Osee was the earlier name, and
that it means Saviour.   Later than them, the canonical
writer in Matthew says that Jesus means Saviour.

It was thus that Moses bestowed the appellation of
Jesus Christ upon the two most distinguished men of
his time, the high-priest, and the destined leader after
himself.   After Moses, the Prophets name the Christ,
and foretell the plots of the Jews against Him, and the
calling of the nations through Him.   Two references
are then given, both of them utterly false in their interpretation, as the merest tyro in Biblical criticism is
aware.[1]

The anointed Jewish kings were shadowy, eikonic
Typical Christs, images of a royal authority.   Some
Christs. of the Prophets also became Christs in type,
through the chrism or anointing.   They bore relation
to the true Christ, the supreme High-priest, King, and
Prophet.   But these shadowy Christs of old never
called their subjects Christians, nor received reverence
from them.   Nor were men disposed to die for them
after their death.   Shadows they were, and symbols
only; they could stir up no excitement among the
nations of the world.   They could not vie with the
reality exhibited by the Head of the Christians.

He received no symbols and types of high-priesthood;
He derived not His blood from priestly men; He was
not raised to empire by human guards; He was not a
prophet like those of old; He attained no dignity nor
precedence among the Jews.   Yet in preference to all
He is called Christ, the only true Christ of God who
has filled the world with the truly august and sacred
appellation of Christian.   He has handed down no
longer types and images, but the mere virtues them-

[1] Lam. iv. 20; Ps. ii. 7.

selves, and a celestial life with the very dogmata of truth, to His Thiasotes, the members of His secret communion.

He has received the Divine chrism by the Divine Spirit, by participation of the unbegotten and paternal Godhead, as Esaias taught, and also the Psalmist.[1] He was not bodily anointed among the Jews, He was not of the tribe of priests, but He held an immortal and undecaying priesthood to endless ages from God Himself before the Morning Star.[2]

The monk of the Basilian Order closes his Christology with the remarkable words, " Let these things be my necessary premises before the History, that no one may think that our Saviour the Lord Jesus the Christ is a new-comer because of the times of His incarnate polity. That no one may think the teaching of Him new and strange, as if we should suspect that by a new man, and one in no respect differing from the rest of men, it had been contrived."

It is with fresh interest, in the light of this great transcendental theory, that the incident of the anointing by the woman with the alabaster box of ointment, the ascription of kingship to Christ in the mouth of Pilate, and the predictions of Christ in the canonical narratives, may be read. The incident of the two swords has also reference to the pretensions, both spiritual and temporal, of the rising Christian empire. Its head is revered both as Cæsar and Supreme Pontiff, the rival of the old wearers of the purple, whose memory was a distant dream at the time of the composition of the Christology. As old Roman poets had sung of

---

[1] Esa. lxi ; Ps. xliv. 6 ; 109.

[2] The legend in Suidas, s. v. Ἰησοῦς, must therefore have been earlier than the *Eccl. History*

Deus Cæsar, the first and only salvation of the world,[1]
so now the monks chant the praises of Christus Deus
as sole Ruler of mankind.

The monks, like old Roman conspirators, were dazzled
with the vision of the purple, as the charming legend
of St. Martin may remind us. But not until an epoch
when the old Imperium had become a name and a
shadow, not until the sinews of its strength had utterly
failed, could these extraordinary claims of the Thiasos
of Christus to world-empire have been put forward,
even in the most veiled and allegorical form, without
being promptly extinguished in blood. Nor were they
actually asserted in mediæval Rome without bloodshed.

The Basilian historian continues to turn the leaves
The New
Nation.
of his Septuagint version in search of traces
of the New Nation existent in fact, though
not in name. He traces them in Esaias lxvi. 8, finds
them in the time before Abraham ; nay, their mode of
life was laid down at the creation. They who lived
between Adam and Abraham, as they did not observe
circumcision, Sabbaths, abstinence, certainly fore-
shadowed the Christians ; and they in the Patriarchal
time clearly knew and conversed with the Christ of
God. In his uncircumcised state Abraham received
the great promise of a posterity. All this has been
written down, be it remembered, before the great
canonical saying ascribed to Christ Himself, "Before
Abraham was, I am."

It may relieve the subject if we recall the fact that
Allegorical
Treatment of
Homer and
of the Bible.
in this attempt to convert the Hebrew Scriptures into a repository of allegories and symbols
of Christianity, the monks were to some extent
copying the example of some of the later Greek

---

[1] Martial, ix. 66, viii. 66, v. 3, ix. 27, 87 ; Statius, *Silv.*, v. 1, 37.

philosophers in dealing with Homer. Homer had once been the Bible of the Græco-Roman schools. He was used in the interests of moral edification. Maximus of Tyre compares his poetry to the painting of a Polygnotus or a Zeuxis. The painter will aim both at art and at virtue. He will seek to reproduce the truth of form and substance, yet his lines will be drawn in imitation of beauty. So in Homer's writing there is the poetic element, which assumes the form of fable, and the philosophic element, which commends and teaches virtue. Achilles and Agamemnon present images of the passions of youth and of authority. In contrast stands Nestor, the image of age, prudence, and eloquence. Thersites represents the ugliness of the disorderly multitude. In the brave gentleman and perfect leader, who restrains the fleeing noble with gentle words, and who strikes the noisy plebeians with his sceptre, you have the image of Socrates in his converse with a Timæus, a Parmenides, or a Thrasymachus.

Paris opposed to Hector is intemperance and cowardice opposed to bravery and temperance. And so with the other heroes. Athena is understood as the principle of virtue, and Aphrodite as the principle of love. In the Odyssey, Homer mirrors the perfect state; and the *moly* of Circe is allegorical of heroic and invincible valour.[1] Homer, in short, is the Prince of Philosophers, and sound morality and life-wisdom is to be extracted from his pages. Maximus, who disdains the Greek sophists from Thrace or Cilicia, certainly did not dream of the invasion of the schools by Orientals or Orientalised sophists, who should cast aside Homer altogether in favour of writings

[1] *Diss.* xvi.

out of which they were to extract ambitious theories of government rather than incentives to personal improvement. He converts poetic persons into general forms of thought; the monks of St. Basil convert ideas into poetic persons. The contrast of the books, the method, and the intention, marks the great chasm that lies between the old and the new philosophy.

The extraordinary value attached to the Hebrew books witnesses both to the great ascendancy of the Rabbins from the twelfth century, and still more to that of the Muslim, who had for many ages been appealing as the warrant for Islam to "the books of old, the books of Ibrahim and Musa.[1] It is useful to remind ourselves at this point that the Christology of the Church is ignored or denounced by the unanimous voice of the Mosque and the Synagogues.

But to return. Eusebius proceeds to deal in the same theological manner with the Incarnate Epiphany of the Saviour as a journey. There are in him and his *confreres* discrepancies in the date of the Nativity, which is said to have fallen some time in the period 749–753 of the city of Rome. There are also discrepancies about the census under Augustus. Of more importance is the revelation of the manner in which the legend of the Advent was constructed. The first Adam was formed on the sixth day. Now, since one day is with the Lord as a thousand years, it follows that on the sixth day of a millenary Jesus Christ appeared on earth. The millenary was the sixth from Adam, or the 5500th year, according to the general opinion. Some said more, some less; but at all events, the appearance must have been in the last times, according to Scripture.

The Epiphany.

[1] *Surah*, lxxxvii. 10.

Then again, according to the Scriptures, Christ must be born at the time when the ancient rulers of the Jewish nation ceased.   The Basilians accordingly make their Josephus state that Herod the Idumæan was their first foreign ruler.   The chronological argument is also supported from David.   It is needless, after all that has been said of the origin and date of the writings of "Josephus," to explore these contrivances further.

It has before been noticed that the first ecclesiastical historian has nothing but the bare scheme of   The Genea-
the Gospels in his hands.   He labours to   logies.
reconcile the discrepancies of the two genealogies of Christ by pointing out that one is calculated according to nature, the other according to law.   Both the real and reputed fathers of Joseph have been recorded, in agreement with the Levirate law.   Then he pretends that Herod the Great came from Ascalon, and that, humiliated by the sense of his lowly birth, he committed the archives of the great Jewish families to the flames. A few persons had copies, and among them were the Desposyni, or relatives of the Lord.   They came from Nazaroi and Kochaba, Judaic villages, and they recalled the genealogy of Christ.

It appears that He becomes heir of David through His legal or adopted father Joseph, while Mary as an heiress is assumed to be of the same tribe with Joseph. But the legend of the Holy Family carries us back through the little or apocryphal Gospels to the Koran. The Gospel of the Birth of Mary says that she was sprung of the royal race of David, born at Nazareth, and educated at Jerusalem.   Her father was Joachim, her mother Anna, the former of Nazareth, the latter of Bethlehem.   The *Protevangelium of James* elaborates the legend of Joachim and Anna, and Mary is ascer-

tained by the high-priest to be of the tribe of David.
This Gospel is the true link between the New Testament and the Koran.   The monks here for once desert
the Old Testament, for the Miriam of its pages could
not supply the ideal of Mary in the New.

The exaltation of Mary in the cult of the Church
The Cult of the Blessed Virgin. was a direct consequence of the exaltation
of Christ.   The Basilians, who follow Eusebius
as historian, denounce his theology as too
low when he describes Christ as the Second Cause.
If Christ became God absolutely in the dogma, then
necessarily Mary must become Mother of God.   But
this worship was cautiously introduced, or it was
forced upon the Church by the feeling of the peoples
of the South, so long impregnated with the Arabian
tradition.   At first the origin of the worship is set
down to the Gnostics, which name veils sectarians who
followed the knowledge revealed in the Koran.   Then
it is ascribed to the Collyridians by the monk of
Cyprus who writes under the name of St. Epiphanius;[1]
and Collyridians is another term of monkish invention
for followers of the Arabian tradition.   Again, the
term Nestorians is another veil for the same tradition.
They are said to have maintained that the child of
Mary was not born Divine, just as the Mohammedans
maintain.

Another tedious record of literary forgery here intervenes.   Books were ascribed late in the twelfth
or in the thirteenth century to St. John and to St.
Melito, describing the transit of the Blessed Virgin
into heaven.   Again, Pope Gelasius is made in the
fifth century to mention an apocryphal, that is, a popular
book on the same subject.   The dogma of the Assump-

[1] *Haer.* 89.

tion is also ascribed to Gregory of Tours, to Andrew of Crete, and to St. John of Damascus, who is supposed to describe her burial in Gethsemane, and the discovery of the empty coffin.[1] The interpolation in Eusebius' Chronicle, A. 48, has long been recognised as such. In the illustrious Doctors, both Greek and Latin, of the great Catalogue of Jerome and Gennadius, there are many passages which seem studiously to disparage Mary as guilty of unbelief, vain-glory, and the like; nor can it be denied that she is the object of rebuke in the canonical Gospels.

The Augustinians, writing probably late in the thirteenth century, speak of her as under original sin. The doctrine of Peter Lombard and others is that she was cleansed from original sin before her birth, like the Baptist. It is not until the fourteenth century that Duns Scotus broaches the idea of an Immaculate Conception. The final triumph of the dogma in our own times is one of the most remarkable proofs that after all the Church is not so rigid and immobile in her opinions as is commonly supposed. Church doctors still launch a theoretical anathema against those who would render *latreia* to Mary, but the fine distinction between this and other kinds of worship can hardly be appreciated except by the professional theologian.

The Basilians committed themselves from the beginning to the dogma that Christ was born of the Virgin Mary, and their proof is the mistaken passage in Isaiah, "Behold, a young woman shall conceive and bear a son." As usual, they give emphasis to the dogma by calling into existence a sect of Ebionites, who are made to maintain that Christ sprang from ordinary generation. These things are repeated several

[1] Cf. Necephorus Callistus, *H. E.*, dated 1305.

times in the first Ecclesiastical History, and have created the intended impression that heretics united with Catholics in acknowledging a Christ, a St. Joseph, and a St. Mary. Between that work and the completion of the Missal there has been a development of the ideal of the Holy Family, in accordance with the principles of Church construction.

St. Joseph is prefigured in the "just man" of Ps. xci., who also offers the ideal of the Abbot; also in the fine description of one beloved of God and men in Ecclesiasticus xlv. 1–6. To this the Gospel for the Feast of St. Joseph corresponds, Matt. i. 18–21. Another Old Testament passage which has been drawn upon is Genesis xlix. 22–26, where blessings are invoked on the head of the Patriarch Joseph, and on the crown of the Nazarite among his brethren. This is read on the Feast of the Patronage of St. Joseph; and the Gospel for the same day, Luke iii. 21–28, describes Jesus as the beloved Son of God, but reputed son of Joseph, the spouse of the Holy Mother.

On the Feasts of the Conception and the Nativity of the Blessed Virgin, a source for her ideal is found in the fine description of Sophia or impersonated wisdom in the book of Proverbs viii. 22–35. The Gospel is the genealogy in Matt. i. 1–16. On the Feast of the Annunciation, her ideal is sought in Ps. xliv., also in Isa. vii. 10–15. But the Gospel narrating the visit of the Angel Gabriel, which points to the Arabian tradition, is Luke i. 26–38. On the Feast of the Visitation, the book of Canticles supplies the poetic lesson, ii. 8–14, and the Gospel is Luke i. 39–47. In the Mass of the Blessed Virgin from Candlemas, the Feast of her Purification, to Easter, the lesson consists of the praise of Sophia, Eccles. xxiv. 14–16, and the Gospel is Luke xi. 27–28, containing the words, "Blessed is the womb that bare Thee." From Easter to Pentecost the Gospel is John xix. 25–27, containing the words, "Behold thy Son," "Behold Thy Mother!"

In no passage is Mary regarded as the anti-type of the Miriam of the Old Testament. On the ^{St. Joachim.} Feast of St. Joachim, her father, the genea- ^{and St. Ann.} logy is read from Matt. i. 1–16. St. Ann is commemorated as mother of Mary, as in the Mass for Holy Women, or as a martyr, not a virgin. The parents of Mary, for whom no prototypes have been found in the Old Testament, come from the Arabian tradition. So also do Zacharias and John Baptist. The story of the dumbness of the former has been preserved in Luke i. 5–17, 57–68. The ideal of John has been taken from Isa. xlix. and Jer. i. 4–10. Elizabeth is traced to the priestly stock of Aaron.

It is a very curious circumstance that the Gospel referring to Martha and Mary (the contrast in personal forms of the active and the contemplative life), is read not only on the Commemoration of St. Martha, virgin, but also on the Feast of the Assumption. Here it is the Blessed Virgin who chooses the good part which shall not be taken from her.

The Order of Mount Carmel appears to have been instituted at nearly the same time with the ^{The Carme-} Franciscans and the Dominicans. They are ^{lites.} honoured with the particular patronage of the Blessed Virgin; and it is probable that the propagation of the cult from the thirteenth century was in great part due to the exertions of that Order. A Day of Solemn Commemoration of the Blessed Virgin Mary of Mount

Carmel is recognised in the Service Book. It is another illustration of the manner in which the four great Orders of friars, the Franciscans, the Dominicans, the Augustinians, and the Carmelites, entered into the labours of the two primitive Orders, and largely contributed to enrich the great treasury of Church ideals.

The popular love towards the Holy Family—Jesus, Mary, Joseph—is one of the chief features of Catholic religion. But few are aware that, with the exception in one respect of Joseph, the original of the Holy Family may be found in the Surah of the Koran, which recites the Divine Word concerning the family of Imram.

The birthplace of Christ is discovered in the prophet Birthplace of Christ Micah v. 2. The Mages from the East inquired of Herod where the infant King of the Jews was, because they had seen His star in the East, and had made the journey in their zeal to worship Him as a God. Herod, thinking his rule endangered, was greatly moved ; and having ascertained that Bethlehem was the predicted birthplace, issued an order that boys at the breast in Bethlehem and all its mountains, from two years and downwards—according to the precise time stated by the Mages—should be destroyed, thinking certainly that Jesus would share the fate of his equals. The Boy, however, anticipated the snare, and was conveyed to Egypt, owing to the epiphany of an angel who had informed His parents of what was to happen.

The historian refers from this narrative to "the sacred writing of the Evangel." But had the canonical Gospel been in the hands of his readers, his narrative would have been unnecessary, which does not depend on the canonical Gospel. The origin of the Magi is to be found, again, in the Old Testament.   The Basilian who writes under the name of Justin Martyr gives a variant of the tale, and points to the passage in the prophet, "Before the Boy shall have knowledge to any father or mother, He shall receive the power of Damascus and spoils of Samaria." This was fulfilled, he says, in "our Christ." The Mages are frequently called the Mages from Arabia.[1] The monk Malelas speaks of them as coming from Persia to bring gifts to Christ as to a great king and conqueror.   In mediæval geography, Arabia and Persia are confounded, and in the fourteenth century Mohammed is still spoken of as a rich Persian. There are other variations.

All these details are understood when they are read in the light of the Feasts of the Nativity and of the Holy Innocents on the 28th of December, and are compared with the passages in Esaias, cc. ix., lx. The delight which the chronographers find in portraying the sufferings of Herod, in their Josephus and elsewhere, is delight in inflicting vengeance on the persecutor of the infant Church in the person of its Head.

The place Nazaret is also discovered in the prophet,[2] who is assumed to say, "Nazaræus He shall be called." It is almost needless to observe that the Hebrew of the text has been grossly misunderstood. It means, He shall be called Shoot, Branch (*Nēzar*). This is converted into an epithet of Christ, *Nazaræus*, and a place is then called into being to correspond with the epithet.[3] The history of the word,

Nazaret and Nazaræus.

---

[1] Dial. lxxvii. ; cf. Tertull., *Adv. Marc.* iii. 13, *Adv. Jud.* c. ix.

[2] Isa. xi. 1.

[3] Cf. Matt. ii. 23. But the Gospel for the Last Vigil of the Epiphany, Matt. ii. 19-23, has, *He shall be called a Nazarite.*

and of the imaginative edifice built upon it, is sufficient to illustrate the mystical method by which the whole canonical narrative was constructed.

An important, though uncanonical legend of the Augustus and monks of St. Basil—to be found in the the Pythia. Chronicle of Eusebius, in Malelas, Cedrenus, and Nicephorus Callistus—is that of Augustus, who made a hecatomb and consulted the Pythian Oracle in the fifty-fifth year of his reign. "Who, after me, shall rule over the Roman state?" There was given him no answer from the Pythia. Again he made a sacrifice, and inquired of the Pythia why the Oracle was silent. And this answer was at last given him: "A Hebrew Boy, the Ruler of Olympus, bids me depart from this abode, and return to Hades. Go, then, and visit our altar no more."

Παῖς Ἑβραῖος κέλεταί με Θεὸς μακάρεσσιν ἀνάσσων,
Τόνδε δόμον προλιπεῖν, καὶ ἄιδος αὖθις ἱκέσθαι
Καὶ λοιπὸν ἄπιθι ἐκ πρόμων ἡμετέρων.

Then Augustus, departing from the Oracle, went to the Capitol, built there a great altar and lofty, on which he wrote in Roman letters, *This altar is of the First-begotten of God*. And this altar is on the Capitol unto this day, as the wise Timotheus narrated.

The Franciscans were not to be found on the Capitol until about 1250; and certainly it could not have been long before their time that this legend was first published.

The *Gospel of the Infancy* is important, as throwing Gospel of light upon ideas that became current during the Infancy. the thirteenth century in the Church. They have been derived by the Benedictines and Basilians from the Mohammedans, in common with other matters of so-called apocryphal, *i.e.*, præ-canonical books.

Here Jesus addresses His mother from the cradle, and declares that He is the Word of God, according to the Annunciation by Gabriel, and sent for the salvation of the world.   Joseph and Mary come to Bethlehem, and the Child is born in a cave, which is filled with the splendour of light.   A Hebrew midwife lays her hands on the Child, and is cured of disease. Shepherds come, and there is an apparition of the heavenly host, who render praises to God.   On the eighth day the Child is circumcised, and the Hebrew midwife preserves a memorial of the event in an alabaster box, of which Mary the sinner later became possessed, and used for the anointing of our Lord.

The incident of the appearance in the Temple on the fortieth day is told much as in the canonical Gospel.

The Mages are said to come to Jerusalem in accord with a prophecy of Zoroaster.   Herod hears the tidings, and Joseph and Mary take the Child to Egypt. Their arrival produces great consternation among the priests, and an idol announces to them that an unknown and true God has come hither, and falls in the same hour.   Demons come forth from the mouth of the priest's son in the form of birds and serpents.   So the prophecy, *Out of Egypt I have called My Son*, was fulfilled.

A number of romantic tales follow.   A dumb bride recovers her speech as she kisses the Lord in the arms of Mary.   A woman afflicted with an incubus (Satan in form of a serpent) is in like manner delivered.   A leprous girl is cleansed by washing in water which

---

[1] See the service for July 22, in the Missal.

had been used for the bath of Jesus, and the leprous son of a great lady, who exclaims, Blessed is the mother who begat Thee, O Jesus! A young man, who has been turned into a mule by evil arts, recovers his form when Jesus is placed upon his back.

The Holy Family come in a desert place upon a band of thieves. One of them, Titus, begs his comrade Dumachus to let them go. Dumachus refuses. St. Mary promises that Titus shall be received to the right hand of God, and Jesus prophesies to St. Mary that in thirty years' time the two thieves shall be crucified with him, and Titus shall precede Him into Paradise. She replies, "God forbid, my son!"

On the return to Bethlehem, similar miracles are again wrought in the cave. Judas Iscariot, possessed by Satan, strikes the side of Jesus, but in the same hour Satan comes forth from him in the form of a mad dog. Where Judas (the personification of the Jews) struck Him, the Jews later pierced Him with a lance. The boy Jesus makes birds of clay and animates them. Passing by a dyer's shop, whose name was Salem, He enters and casts the clothes into the vat. The dyer on his return complains to Jesus, but the clothes are brought out, each with the desired colour. The story points to the Moslem legend of Isa, son of Mariam, as patron of dyers, Kessæus (Abu-Mohammed Abd-Allah), in H. Sike, *Evang. Infantiæ*, 1697, notes, p. 55.

Other fables follow which will be found again in the works of the Basilians ascribed to Justin Martyr, St. Basil, St. Chrysostom. Jesus did carpenter's work along with St. Joseph. He works a miracle by which He shows Himself prototypically the Good Shepherd of Israel. He learns Hebrew letters of Zacchæus, who so wonders at His knowledge, he thinks He must have been born before Noah. Another master struck Him; his hand withered, and he died. He is found in the Temple among the Doctors, teaching them literature, science, physics and metaphysics, hyperphysics and hypophysics. Comparison shows what a process of refinement our canonical narratives of the Infancy have undergone.

We come to the twelfth year of Tiberius's reign, when Pilate is said to be appointed Praeses of Syria, or Epitropos, Procurator of Judæa. Eusebius declaims against certain forged "Memorabilia against our Saviour," because they have falsely set down the date of the Passion in the seventh year of Tiberius's reign.[1] This is but a figurative way of making a correction. No Memorabilia, no Acts of Pilate, have ever been discovered. It is also observable that he passes over the Circumcision, Fasting, and Temptation, and proceeds to the Baptism, which is fixed in the fifteenth year of Tiberius, and the fourth of the Hegemony of Pontius Pilate, when Herod and Lysanias and Philip were Tetrarchs of the rest of Judæa.[2]

Eusebius, relying on his monk Josephus, calculates that the whole time of the teaching was not four whole years, since four high-priests in four years, from Annas to the appointment of Caiaphas, discharged each a year's ministry. Caiaphas was probably high-priest in the year of the Passion. Again he shows that he has naught but the bare scheme of the canonical narratives before his mind.

He further has the theory of twelve Apostles by

[1] *H. E.* i. 9.
[2] i. 10; cf. the much fuller and later canonical account in Luke iii. 1.

eminence, and of other seventy sent two and two before the face of Christ into every place and city whither He was to come. But he falters when he attempts to produce a list of their names. Nor has a list of the Apostles, simple and unconfused, ever been produced to this day.

He calls in his Josephus to confirm the tradition that John the Baptist was beheaded by the younger Herod. The passage in Josephus is wretchedly written, and describes in a rambling manner the *baptismus* or *baptisis* of John and its nature.[1] It is needless to say more about the Josephus passage on Jesus, except that it proceeds from the Basilian forge, and has been flourished in the face of the world as historic evidence by a long series of Basilians and Benedictines. The student may trace in it the same style that appears in other notorious forgeries.[2]

John Baptist.

The Feasts of the Nativity and the Beheading of St. John the Baptist show that his ideal has been derived from Jeremiah i., and from Isaiah xlix., though ultimately he is traceable to the Yahia in the Arabian tradition of the family of Imram.

Eusebius passes over the Passion without the slightest effort at details, such as we find in the canonical narratives. On the other hand, he occupies himself at length with the elaborate fable of the interchange of letters between Abgarus, king of Edessa, and Jesus, and the mission of Thaddæus, said to be one of the seventy, to Abgarus. Embedded, however, in this long story, is the *Credo* of the Church. Abgarus is reported to have said to Thaddæus—" Relate

Jesus and Abgarus.

---

[1] *Antt.*, xviii. 5. 2.

[2] *Antt.* xviii. 33; cf. Eus., *H. E.* iii. 33, *D. E.* iii. 5, Hieron, *De Vir. Ill.* xiii., and many others collected in Whiston.

to me concerning the coming of Jesus, how it came
to pass, and concerning His power, and in what power
He did the things which I have heard of." And Thaddæus: "Now I will be content," he said, "since to
preach the Word I was sent. But to-morrow assemble
me all thy citizens, and in their presence I will preach
and scatter among them the Word of Life, concerning
the coming of Jesus, as it came to pass, and concerning
His mission, and for what cause He was sent by the
Father, and concerning the power of His works, and
mysteries of which He spake in the world, and with
what power He did these things, and concerning His
new preaching, and concerning His littleness and
humiliation, and how He humbled Himself and died,
and belittled His Godhead, and was crucified, and descended into Hades, and split asunder the barrier from
eternity not split, and brought up the dead; for, descending alone, He raised up many, then went up to
His Father." "And Abgarus commanded on the morrow
his citizens to gather together to hear the preaching of
Thaddæus, and after these things he ordered gold and
silver to be given him. But he would not receive it,
saying, *If we have left our own things, how shall we
receive the things of others?* These things were done
in the 340th year, which, usefully for reading from the
Syrian translated, may here seasonably lie."

Between the baldness of Eusebius and the elaboration of the canonical accounts of the Passion, The Passion.
a considerable interval must lie, which is
partly filled up by recitals to be found in all the
leading Greek and Latin writers of the Catalogue of
Jerome and Gennadius, commonly called the Fathers.
These recitals are all based on the *Credo*, but not on
the New Testament. There are variations in them;

they show inequality of style; they are all representations of what may be called the Ecclesiastical Epic of Redemption, and they prepare the way for more chaste and finished canonical narratives.

It is observable that, in many of the Basilians, Pilate is styled the Hegemon or Præses of Syria, rather than the Epitropos or Procurator of Judæa. A name is also given to his wife, Procla, who warns him, "Let there be naught between thee and this just man, for many things I suffered to-day in a dream because of Him."

It stands fast, and is beyond all contradiction, that The Passion, the Passion is in Church teaching a dogma, a Dogma. a mystery, or sacrament, the evidence of which lies solely in the sentiment of the believing mind which is taught to discover the dogma in the pages of Psalmists and Prophets. It is nowhere aught but a theological necessity. And when the orthodox ascribe to the heretics the opinion that the Passion was an ecclesiastical dream, they complete the proof against themselves by calling forth a voluminous echo from the Doctors of the Mosque and the Synagogue. A few illustrations may be given.

It behoved Jesus to preach for one year only, in accord with Isa. lxi. 1. Some say that He suffered in the sixteenth year of Tiberius, on the 25th Phamenoth, or the 25th Pharmuthi, or the 19th of the same month.[1] The same writer finds the Passion foretold in the *Republic* of Plato. Another adduces a great mass of proof from the Prophets in support of the legend. He finds Judas and the conspiracy against Christ in the Psalms, in Zechariah, and in Jeremiah, who is said to

---

[1] Clem. Alex., *Strom.* i. 21 ; cf. Cotelerius, *Ad Constt. App.* v. 13, on these discrepancies.

name Him as Judah, xvii. 1–4.   In Amos is found the eclipse at the Passion.[1]   Another insists with emphasis on the verity of the Birth and Passion; and passionately points to Golgothas in proof, declaring that the whole world has been filled with fragments of the wood of the Cross.   Christ was judged at night, when it was cold and a fire of coals had been laid, as we read in Zechariah, who speaks of a day that was neither day nor night (xiv. 7), and in Amos, who speaks of the sun going down at noon.   Another certain proof of the Passion is the partition of the coat, and the casting of lots for the tunic, in Ps. xxii., and the red garments of one coming from Bosor, Isa. lxiii. 1, 2.   Golgotha is the centre of the earth, Ps. lxxiii. 12; thence Christ spreads out His hands to grasp the world, Isa. lxv. 2.   The wine mixed with myrrh is found in Ps. lxix. 21, the thieves are reproduced from Isa. liii. 12, the mockers from Ps. cviii. 25.[2]

The Gregories declaim against the Oriental heretics in like manner who assert the phantasmal nature of the Birth and Passion.   Chrysostom is haunted by Marcion and the Gnostics.   He argues on the sign of Jonah, that this figure was brought forward that the truth might be believed.   If Jonah in the whale's belly was not a phantasy, neither was it phantasy that Christ was three days in the heart of the earth.   The Marcionites were children of the devil, because they consider the Cross and Passion phantasies.[3]   The same writer labours to show that Christ confessed to Pilate that He was a celestial King of a kingdom not of this world.   His taciturnity before Pilate was in accord

[1] Euseb. *D. E.* lib. iv., 6, 10
[2] Cyril of Jerus. *Catech.* xiii., 24, 25, &c.
[3] Hom. 43 (44).

with Isa. lviii. 8.[1]   The orator, preaching on the
Vesper of the Pascha, declaims, with studied malevo-
lence, against the Jews who preferred Barabbas to the
Saviour of the world; he would lash his audience into
fury against them.   Then he turns his invective against
the audience themselves, whom he denounces as filthy
in their vices, and in their language to one another in
church.   It is a most repulsive scene from the Dark
Ages and the turbulent formation of a new world.
There is no sweet reasonableness here.   Against the
dark background, filled with Oriental deniers of the
dogma, St. Peter stands out gloriously as the champion
of consubstantiality, and the monks are the true
philosophers, who lead the life that is obnoxious to
no decay.[2]

The Latins are quite equal in audacity to their
Greek brethren.   It is saddening to observe that under
the name Tertullian some writing of a man of genius
is to be found who has prostituted his gifts to the
service of the most unprincipled sophistry.   He seeks
for and finds the Nativity and Passion in the book of
Daniel, c. ix.   The Passion was consummated in the time
of the seventieth Hebdomad, at the Feast of the Pascha,
on the first day of unleavened bread, when they slew
the Lamb at evening.   The Synagogue slew Him with
maledictions, that they might fulfil the prophecies.
He asserts that the Sacrament of the Passion must be
figured in predictions.   The incredible must be fully
foretold, otherwise great would be the scandal.   The
magnificent event is shrouded in the obscure, that the
intellect in its difficulty may seek for the grace of
God.[3]   He puts into the mouth of his imaginary

---

[1] Hom. 86 (87) and 87 (88).   [2] Hom. 54 (55).
[3] Tert., *Ad Nationes.*

Marcion the statement that in the fifteenth year of
Tiberius Christ descended to a town of Galilee,
Capharnaum, from the heaven of the Creator.   The
object is to represent the Orientals as bearing witness
in another manner to the Church legend.   He dis-
covers, with his brethren, the old Roman Cross, symbol
of power and victory, in the Old Testament.[1]   This
was the sign made on the door-posts in the blood of
the Pascha; this was the unicorn in the blessing of
Joseph, the stake on which the healing serpent was
raised.   He is none the less assured that the Cross
belongs to the victoriæ and trophies of the Romans.

He speaks of Pilate as Procurator of Syria, asserts
that the Jews bore away the body of Christ to the
sepulchre, and sat around with a guard of soldiers.[2]
He refers to pretended arcana or archives of the
Romans.   He thinks of Galilee as part of Judæa.   He
deduces the details of the Passion from Ps. ii., from
Hosea x. 6, from Isa. liii. 7, l. 4, from Ps. xxii. 10, 16.
The whole event, indeed, is in that psalm.   The veil
of the Temple is rent by the breaking forth of the
angel who deserts the daughter of Zion, Ezek. xi. 23.
The writer of Ps. xxxi. 6, labours to render Christ
himself.   It is passionately insisted on that only flesh
could be said to expire.   Joseph of Arimathæa knew
this; he was the "blessed man" of Ps. i.   In Hosea v.
15, vi. 1, is to be found an allusion to the women who
went early to the tomb.   The body was missing, according to Isa. lvii. 2, and in the same prophet are to be
found the women who look on, xxvii. 11, LXX.   It
is shown why the disciples are rebuked for supposing
they saw a ghost after the Resurrection, Lc. xxiv. 37–39.
They were tempted to the Marcionite heresy.

[1] *Adv. Jud.* 10; *Adv. Marc.* iii. 18.   [2] Apol. xxi.

The texts ascribed to St. Cyprian were probably written at a time when there was a cloister at Carthage in the thirteenth century. They contain the same dogmatic theory, attacking the Jews.[1] Pilate is again said to be Procurator of Syria. The *Credo* is set forth with beauty and eloquence of language, as a poem of the Church, and it is shown that the noble army of martyrs is a necessity, as witnesses and imitators of Christ. In an elaborate Christology, the writer once more shows from the prophets that the Jews were bound to fix Christ to the Cross, that in the Passion and the sign of the Cross is all virtue and power, and salvation for them that are marked with the sign on the brow, and so on.[2]

The excellent stylist, who writes under the name of Lactantius, not earlier than the fourteenth century, follows the same method. He draws upon the second chapter of the Wisdom of Solomon in his account of the Passion. He speaks of Pontius Pilate as Legate of Syria.[3] He refers to Kings and Chronicles even for proofs of the Passion. Yet he is uneasy in the consciousness that the dogma of the assumption by God of a natal and suffering body is felt to be inconvenient and unreasonable. He meets the objection by an *à priori* theological argument.

These illustrations will enable the reader to understand how absolutely certain it is that the New Testament was constructed on the sole basis of dogmatic theory and poetry. The dictum of the monk who writes under the name of St. Jerome is unexceptionably confirmed :—

"Whatsoever we read in the Old Testament, we

---

[1] *De Idol. Van.* xiii.   [2] *Testimon.* ii. 20.
[3] *Epit. ad Pentad.* xlv.

find again in the Gospel; and what has become a lection in the Gospel is deduced from the authority of the Old Testament; there is nothing dissonant, nothing diverse in them." [1]

The Augustinian of the fourteenth or fifteenth century, who writes the romantic *Confessions*, says that he had been a Manichæan, and that their saints and elect had told the Catholics in private that the New Testament Scriptures had been forged by some writers unknown, who desired to insert the law of the Jews in the Christian faith. [2] The object of this confession must be to represent that the heretics did acknowledge *some* form of the legend, as in the similar declaration about Marcion and the Gnostics. Remove the Manichæan veil, and the Arabian or Persian critics of the Church stand revealed. The great prominence given to Faustus, the eloquent, pious, and dangerous Manichee, is due to the same motive; the historic precursors of the Church became in dogmatic thought dissenters from it.

This able rhetorician is clearly aware of the artificial nature of the legend. He says, "If these writings had been false, all things would be exposed to the risk of falsehood. . . . Because the writings were true, I acknowledge the whole man in Christ, not the body only, or a spirit with body without mind, but very man." He explains also why the Church delights in calling up swarms of heretics from the silence. It is that the sentiment of the Church and the dogma may be made to stand out in relief. It behoved that there should be heresies, that the approved might be made manifest among the weak.

The author of the *De Civitate Dei* betrays the same consciousness of a public who looked upon the works

----

[1] *Ep. ad Damas.* on Isa. vi.   [2] *Confess.* v. 11.

of the monks and friars as fictions. He says that the
dispersion of the Jews is described in the Prophets,
and that if Catholic writers had contained such things,
they might have been thought forged.[1] Apparently
aware that they have no character for veracity to lose,
he indulges himself in the wildest fables about the
Goths, and about the bones of St. Stephen, and other
matters. The work is an elaborate attack on reason
and the common-sense perceptions of the world. It is
intimately connected with the rise of the Papacy and
of the Pauline theology.

His theory of the Passion is that Christ as High-
priest offered Himself in the Passion for us, that we
might be the body of so great a Head. He is Mediator,
Priest, and Sacrifice. This is the sacrifice of the Christians : many, one body in Christ. The Church offers
herself in the oblation she presents.[2] A great development of the dogma is here observable, correspondent
to the development in the ritual of the Mass. The
writer does not rely on the canonical Scriptures in his
argument ; he refers to them as if quite recent, as of
eminent authority, in which we have faith concerning
those things which it is not expedient we should ignore,
nor by ourselves are fit to know.[3]

Those who are content to live in the world of dogma,
and to defy the teaching of fact, may take delight in
this work. But it is impossible for those who know
and prize the facts to peruse it without strong feelings
of repugnance. Here is a man who calmly transplants
himself into the beginning of the fifth century, and
makes free with the name and the verses of Claudian
for Church purposes. He concocts a wonderful fable,
according to which the Church ought to have come to

[1] *C. D.* iv. 34.   [2] x. 6.   [3] ix. 3.

an end in the year 399, knowing, as he does, that the
Church had not then been heard of. Between Claudian
and this Augustinian there has passed not merely an
interval of many centuries, there has been a great
lapse and fall of the virtue of mankind.

So well he knows the temper of the time, or so conscious is he of the power at his back, he offers the
incredible for belief with the most cynical effrontery.
Yet we wrong the old Cynics by employing that adjec-
tive. He speaks of the ignorant fishermen whom
Christ sent with the nets of faith to the sea of this
world, so few in number, and who took so many fishes
out of the whole race. He declares that the incredible
has come to pass. The Resurrection and Ascension
are incredible; the belief of the world in a thing so
incredible is incredible; and incredible is it that ig-
noble, lowly, and ignorant men should have persuaded
the world effectually of a thing so incredible.[1] He
discloses the secret of the offensive operations of the
Church against human reason, when he says that testimonies of many incredible things are heaped together
in order that one incredible thing—the resurrection in
the flesh—may be believed. So are the obstinately
incredulous bent to belief.

The strange was made familiar, the marvellous common, the unwonted customary to the fancy of the people,
until taste and relish for the fact was corrupted and
spoiled, and the spread of science became impossible.
This monk does not himself believe in the dogma; he
delights in it as the flag of a great conquering host,
he glories in the Cross as the adopted symbol of the
prevailing City and Church of God, the Christian
Empire which sees the world at its feet. He has

[1] *C. D.* xxii. 5.

entered into the labours of the Basilians and Benedictines, and rears his imposing structure on their foundations. But now to return to the Basilians.

In Suidas' Lexicon we read of Dionysius the Areopagite, that he was a hearer of Paul, by him brought to Christianism, and made Bishop of Athens. He was at Heliopolis at the time of the Passion, and saw the moon falling on the sun, though it was not the time of the solar and lunar conjunction ; and again, the same opposed, contrary to nature, to the diameter of the sun from the sixth hour till evening. Christ, the Author of all created things, alone could cause this marvel. Dionysius is said to have written these things in an epistle to Polycarp ; and a fulsome eulogy is passed on the learning and genius of Dionysius. It is pretended that he was put to death at the same time with Ignatius, the God-bearer, in the reign of Trajan.

The Eclipse at the Passion.

The tale of Beronice, Bernice, or Veronica, is also anterior to the canonical narrative of the woman with the issue of blood. She is of Paneas, where Herod II. dwelt. She desires to erect a statue in honour of Jesus, because she had been cured by Him. But she dared not do this without the king's permission, so she presented a supplication to that effect, the contents of which are given at length. Herod is here addressed as August, Toparch, Legislator both of Jews and Greeks, King of the land of Trachonitis. He gives permission, and the statue, made of bronze, with an admixture of gold and silver, is erected. It may be still seen, say the monks, in an Oratory at Paneas, in the house of one Bassus, a Christian, formerly a Jew.[1]

Veronica.

[1] See the literature on this subject in Gregorovius, *Gesch. d. Stadt Rom* ii. 189.

In Suidas, again, is to be found the elaborate fable, of which mention has already been made, The Election of Jesus Christ to the Priesthood. concerning the enrolment of Jesus in the Jewish priesthood. Philip, a Christian silver- smith in the reign of Justinian, seeks to persuade Theodosius, chief of the Jews, to his faith. Theodosius confesses that he believes in the advent of Him fore- told by Law and Prophets, but that human reasons stand in the way of his becoming a Christian. Were he to become Patriarch of the Catholic Church, he doubts whether he should enjoy greater observance and respect than that which now falls to his lot. He then confides to his friend a literary and secret mystery of the Hebrews.

There are twenty-two letters in the language, twenty- two inspired books, and there were in ancient times twenty-two priests in the Temple. A book was then laid up, containing their names and those of their parents. When one died the rest met, and chose another in his room. A priest died at the time Jesus was in Judæa, and before He had made Himself known. After many nominations had been rejected, a priest proposed the name of Jesus, son of Joseph the car- penter, with a high eulogy on His character. Some objected that He was not of the tribe of Levi, but of the tribe of Judah; but the priest answered that the two tribes had formerly been intermixed. Hence sprang the stock of Joseph. It was finally resolved that Jesus should be elected to the place of the defunct priest.

On inquiring for the parents, it was found that Joseph was dead, and that the mother only was living. Mary was called to the Council, and confessed that Jesus was her son, and that He had no father upon earth.

She then narrated the Annunciation. The midwives were sent for, and her report confirmed. The priests then entered in their book that the Priest Jesus, Son of the living God and of Mary the Virgin, had been elected in place of the defunct. The book, at the time when the city and Temple were taken, was preserved and laid up at Tiberias, and the mystery was known to very few.

The Christian proposes to inform the faithful Emperor Justinian, and to have the book fetched from Tiberias. But, in deference to the timid remonstrances of the Jew, he desists from the project. The story ends with a reference to the unfailing Josephus and Eusebius Pamphili. It is pretended that Josephus, in his *Memoirs of the Captivity*, says plainly that Jesus performed sacred rites in the Temple along with the priests. The scene in St. Luke's Gospel, where Jesus enters the synagogue at Capernaum, and reads out of the prophet Esaias, is also referred to in proof of the statement. Had not Jesus, says the monk, held some sacerdotal office among the Jews, a book would not have been given to Him to read in the synagogue. For among Christians, laics have not the like permission, unless they have been co-optated into the clerics.

The Basilian maintains that he has shown from Josephus and from Luke that Theodosius the Jew did *not* forge the above story. It is of importance, as showing the manner in which the passage in Luke was written as prototypical of priestly functions. It must have been penned at some time during a late century, when the Rabbinical school at Tiberias was known. It may be mentioned by the way, in regard to Josephus, the oft-quoted "Jew and lover of truth," that a comparison of Photius' and Suidas' Catalogues seems to show that the mass of fiction under his name was slowly compiled, and catalogued before it was fully complete.   In Suidas we read that he wrote the *Antiquities*, from the beginning of the world to the fourteenth year of Domitian.   This is repeated in Jerome's Catalogue.   But the work actually extends only to the twelfth year of Nero.   The great object in this work was to create antiquity for the Jewish people, as ancestors of the Christians, and to give currency to the fictions concerning Jesus, the Baptist, St. James, which are cited again and again *ad nauseam*.

The student may be left further to explore for himself the monkish curiosities in Suidas, which bring before him the time when both the Old and the New Testaments are writings that have the charm of novelty for the world of the cloister, on the eve of the opening of the Universities.

The Basilians say that the fame of the Resurrection and Ascension was noised abroad, and that Pontius Pilate transmitted a report to Tiberius of the circumstances, declaring that Christ was believed to be a God by the mass of the people. *Tiberius consults the Senate on the Deification of Christ.* That Tiberius referred the matter to the Senate, who rejected the report because they had not first examined the question—the old law being in force that none should be deified among the Romans except by the vote and dogma of the Senate.   The Roman jurist Tertullian, destined to give a name to a doctor of the Church, is cited in support of this audacious fable.   It is made out that Tiberius was a convert to the dogma and a friend of the Christians.[1]

The next reign is decorated with various fables, and

---

[1] Eus., *H. E.* ii. 2.

especially with the story of the embassy of Philo to
Caius
Caligula. Rome on behalf of the Jews. The monks
quote their own forgeries under the names
of Josephus and Philo as evidence.

The reign of Claudius is again epochal in Church
legend. In the beginning of it Evodius is
Reign of
Claudius.
Rise of the
Name Chris-
tiani. said to have succeeded St. Peter in the
Bishopric of Antioch; and under him they
who had been called Nazaræi and Galilæi
were now called Christiani. The canonical Acts of the
Apostles, however, date the rise of the name in the
time of Peter.

The monks of St. Basil pretend that the fatal times
for the Jews began in the eighteenth year after the
Ascension, when a voice was heard from the Holy of
Holies on the Day of Pentecost, *Let us depart hence.*
They cite their Josephus, but do not preserve a consensus of dates. They cite their Philo in evidence of
the existence of the ascetic Therapeutæ in Egypt, as
precursors of the monks.

The Basilians say that, when Nero began to reign,
Reign of
Nero. he inquired concerning Jesus, of whom he
had heard that He was a great philosopher
and a worker of wonders. Not knowing that He had
been crucified, he desired that He should be brought
to Rome, that he might question Him, Nero himself
being an Epicurean. But when Nero learned that
Jesus had been crucified by the Jews in their hatred,
though He had done no wrong, he was moved with
anger, and sent Maximus into Judæa, and ordered
Annas, Caiaphas, and Pontius Pilate to be brought to
Rome. The party of Annas and Caiaphas made many
charges against Pilate, but admitted that Jesus had
been given up to the laws. They managed their

affairs prosperously by means of bribery, and so departed.

The arrival of St. Paul at Athens during this reign was remarkable for his encounter with Dio- St. Paul at Athens. nysius the Areopagite philosopher, in whom the Basilians take so great delight. When St. Paul addresses him, Dionysius replies, "What God dost thou preach, babbler?" But having listened to his teaching, Dionysius fell at his feet and begged that he might be illuminated, *i.e.*, baptized, and become a Christian. St. Paul baptized him, and made him Bishop of that region.

The Basilians differ among themselves as to whether Simon Magus (and Simon Peter) came to The Two Simons at Rome. Rome in the reign of Claudius or of Nero. They say that he pretended to be Christ, true in this to the method of representing that all heretics recognise and counterfeit the Catholic dogma. Simon Magus kept a huge shepherd's dog before his lodging in Rome, bound by a chain, which would not suffer any to enter, except at a sign from Simon. But Peter, on arriving, loosed the chain, and bade the dog go in to Simon and announce in a human voice that Peter, the servant of the most high God, desired to come in. The dog delivers the message, and Simon Magus, not to be outdone by his rival, bids the dog in turn deliver an invitation to Peter in a human voice. Peter enters, works miracles, in all surpassing the Mage.

A tumult in the city follows, and the matter is reported by the Præfect Agrippa to Nero. The Emperor causes the two Simons to be brought before him, also Pontius Pilate to be brought from prison. And Nero said to Simon, "Art thou he whom men call Christ?" He answered, "Yea." Then Nero asked Peter, "Is

he indeed the Christ?" And Peter answered, "He
is not, for I am of Christ's disciples, and with these
eyes I saw Him taken up into heaven." Then Nero
questioned Pilate, and said, "Is this he whom thou
gavest up to be crucified?" Pilate, fixing his eyes on
him, said, "It is not he; for this man is long-haired
and obese." And concerning Peter he asked him,
"Dost thou recognise this man as a disciple of Christ?"
And he answered, "Yea, for I brought him into the
Prætorium as Christ's disciple, and when he denied
this I dismissed him." Then Nero ordered both Simon
and Peter to be cast out of the palace; Simon because
he falsely declared himself to be Christ, and Peter
because he had been convicted by Pilate of having
denied Christ.

Contests followed between the two Simons in the
working of miracles. A great bull was brought out.
Simon Magus whispered into its ear, and the bull died.
But Peter after prayer recalled the bull to life. And
all praised Peter, saying, "To make the dead to live
is the greater miracle." They wrought many other
signs in the presence of one another, which are written,
says Joannes Malelas, in the Acts of the Holy Apostles.
He means the Acts which were put forward in the
name of St. Clement, who, in the Photian Library, is
said to have been second Bishop of Rome after Peter;
in the Catalogue of Jerome, the fourth.[1] Clement is,
in fact, a more important name in early Church
literature than Peter or Paul. To him are ascribed
Canons of Synods, under the name of Apostolic Constitutions, the Acts of Peter and his Dispute with Simon
Magus, and the Recognitions.

But the Apostle Peter slew his antagonist, who was

---

[1] Cod. 112, *De Vir. Ill.* 15.

minded to ascend to heaven, by prayer.   For Simon Magus said to Peter, "Thou didst say that Christ thy God was taken up.   Lo! I also will be taken up." And Peter saw him rising, lightened by magic art, into the air, in the midst of the city of Rome.   And Peter prayed, and Simon Magus was borne down from the air to the earth upon the street, and was dashed to pieces.   His remains lie there to this day where they fell, surrounded by a stone chancel.   The place from that day has been called the Simonium.

A considerable interval evidently has elapsed between the barbarous writings of Eusebius or Malelas and the dignified canonical account of the conflict of St. Peter with Simon Magus in the Acts of the Apostles.   The father of the sin of simony is overthrown in his seat, Samaria, and is brought to repentance, without being suffered to come to Rome at all.   It is in the light of writings ascribed to St. Peter Damiani, Glaber Rudolfus, and dated in the eleventh century, though really composed at a later time, that the canonical legend can be thoroughly understood.   It is the monks who from the first complain that this disease of *Simony* has spread through the Church, so that ecclesiastical offices are as venal as merchandise in the market.   The fact is one of the strong incidental proofs that the Church depended from the first on the patronage of the wealthy, and was made an instrument of temporal ambition.

Connection of Simony with the Legend.

When Nero heard that Simon Magus had been slain, he was moved with wrath, and ordered that Peter should be seized and slain.   When St. Peter was seized, he handed over the episcopal robes to Lenus or Linus, his disciple, who had followed him.   A description of Peter's personal appearance is given, which, with similar descriptions, suggests that the time is in the dawn of Church pictorial art. His character, on which the canonical representations have been based, is the following: "Prudent, swift to wrath, changeable, timid, speaking under the influence of the Holy Ghost, and working wonders."

He suffered martyrdom, crucified head downwards, for he had bound the Præfect by an oath that he should not be put to death as the Lord had been put to death. This occurred in the consulship of Apronianus and Capito, says Malelas, but there are discrepancies between him and the Chronicle of Eusebius. Nero also caused Pilate to be beheaded,[1] saying, "Why did he give up the Lord Christ to the Jews—a man blameless, and doing works of power? For if His disciple did such wondrous things, how mighty must He have been?" In the same reign St. Paul arrived in Rome, sent from the land of the Jews to plead his cause, and he also became a martyr by beheading, on the third before the Kalends of July, in the consulship of Nero and Lentulus. Nero ordered the bodies of the holy Apostles to be cast forth unburied. A personal description of St. Paul is given. He was prudent, moral, affable, sweet, an enthusiast under the influence of the Holy Spirit, and endued with the power of healing.

The Festival of SS. Peter and Paul, on June 29, is one of the greatest in Church history. In reading the Lesson and the Gospel for that day, also those for the Feast of St. Peter's Chair at Antioch and at Rome, and again those for the Commemoration of St. Paul, we understand the spirit

The Feast of SS. Peter and Paul.

---

[1] Malelas, and *Chron. Alex.* But Eusebius, Cedrenus, Zonaras, make him commit suicide in the time of Caligula. Glycas beheads him in Tiberius' reign.

and purpose of the great Petrine and Pauline passages in the New Testament. Taking our stand in the quarter of the Vatican about the year 1280 by the first Church of St. Peter, and looking toward the Janiculum, we hear the rumour of the Apostolic pair, as tutelar saints of the city of the Cæsars, beginning to fill the air. Our glance presently falls on Jewish faces, perhaps on those of other Orientals, Arabs, Moors, Persians, followers of the Manichæan creed, disowners alike of the Scriptures of the Synagogue and of the Church. It is then we begin to understand how old Oriental dogma assumes to the imagination of the Churchman the loathed form of heresy; how the nearest critics of the Church—the Jews—must be branded with the mark of ancestral crime; how all other Oriental critics of her system must be condensed into the person of Simon the Mage, the pretender to Divine honours, the rival and the vanquished victim of the first Vicar of Jesus Christ. We learn also how the great pretension of the Church to teach and rule the nations of mankind is becoming embodied in the personal legend of the Apostle of the Gentiles.

CHAPTER XI.

THE INTERPOLATIONS IN THE LITERATURE OF THE ROMAN EMPIRE.

THE literature of the old Roman Empire has come down to us from the cloisters mutilated, interpolated, and glossed by the hands of the Benedictines. The men who were responsible for the composition of the works ascribed to Josephus have inserted a mass of absurdities relating to Jews, Samaritans, Egyptians, Christians, &c., into the pages of the Romans. The ecclesiastical theory of the geography and history of Judæa has been here embodied—a geography and history which date perhaps from about the time when the Hospice of St. John of Jerusalem was established, when Monte Cassino monks had founded there the Abbey of Our Lady of Latina, and were to be found also at Bethlehem and Mount Sinai, at Cæsarea and Gaza. I do not pretend to offer an exhaustive list of the interpolations, but merely to cite some of the most striking, with a view to show that we have not in our hands a pure edition of the Greek and Latin classics of the Empire.

How visionary mediæval geography was may be seen by the study, *e.g.*, of the works ascribed to the Benedictine " Orosius," and still better, after examination of a mediæval map of the world like that in the Cotton Library, "Tiberius, B. 5." This MS. in Latin and Anglo-Saxon cannot be of earlier time than the thirteenth century, and it shows, among other things, what astonishing representations the monks had formed to themselves of the territory of the Jews. The tribes of Israel occupy the territory between Tharso, in Cilicia, and Cæsarea Philippi on the north, to Alexandria on the south; from the Mediterranean on the west to the Euphrates on the east. Syria, Arabia, and Mount Sinai in the desert lie still further east beyond the Tigris. It is easy to understand, in the light of this witness, how they could persuade themselves that the Jews had exercised a great warlike dominion in the time of Alexander the Great and of the Roman Emperors.

Such ideas were originally derived from the Rabbinical dreamers and Cabbalists of the thirteenth century. From the *Sepher Juchasim*, and other such dream-histories, the tale about Jaddua, Iddo, or Jaddus, and his reception of Alexander the Great, passed from A. ben David to Josephus Gorionides and the other Josephus, and so to Paulus Diaconus, Freculphus, and others of the same confederacy. But the monks have far outdone their Rabbinical preceptors. Their object was to represent the Jews as extremely ancient and powerful, because they themselves, the Christiani, were to be represented as a sect of them. And at the same time the object was to represent the Jews as the object of the greatest hatred and spite to the Roman people, so that they might justify their system of persecution against the unhappy people. The modern reader has only to examine with strictness the Roman geography, and then the Arabian geography, to compare with these the Rabbinical geography, in order to be convinced of the baselessness of all the tales concerning the relations of Romans to Jews during the old Empire.[1]

Cicero, in a speech delivered a few years after the pretended triumph of Pompey over the unfortunate Jews, is made to allude, as if with bated breath, to their great numbers and influence in Rome. One absurdity is supported by another. The orator is made also to allude to the *Ituræans* as archers and brigands.

Cicero, B.C. 106–43.

Pro Flacoo, B.C. 58. Phil. ii. 44.

Virgil, in his Georgics, is made to sing of bearing *Idumæan* palms to Mantua.[2] There is no reason to suppose he had ever heard of *Idumæa* or Judæa. The epithet, moreover, is otiose where it stands. But more important is the fourth Eclogue in the present relation. Here the forged Sibylline verses, spoken of by the Basilian who writes under the name of Justin Martyr, occur at once to memory. They have been also cited in a forged *Concio ad Clerum*, in the name of Constantine, and the monks pretend that Cicero had rendered them into Latin. The Emperor is made to sanction the Messianic interpretation of Virgil, and the monk who writes a Commentary on Romans, in the name of Augustine, puts his finger decisively on the line—

Virgil, B.C. 70–19.

Ultima Cumæi jam venit carminis ætas.

But the Cumæan Sibyl herself seems to be the invention of the monks. It is "Lactantius" who talks of her. We need but remind the reader of the forged acrostic oracle in the *De Civitate Dei*,

Acrostic. Oracle.

---

[1] See also the Hereford Map in the King's Library, and the *Polychronicon*, ascribed to the Benedictine Higden.

[2] iii. 12 V. Probus, *in loc*, says the Idumæans are Jews of Palestine. Cf. also Æl., *H. A.* vi. 17.

on the words Ιησοῦς Χρειστὸς Θεοῦ υἱὸς σώτηρ, which pseudo-Augustine pretends that the Proconsul Placidianus had shown him.[1]

But Virgil became a great Middle Age prophet in the age immediately preceding that of Dante, and to that age the forgery possibly belongs. The feeling about the Sibyls may be illustrated from early Italian engravings.[2]

Most of our MSS. of Horace come from the Benedictine monasteries of France, where his writings were copied industriously from the thirteenth or fourteenth century. His text has been interpolated with clumsy places relating to "the Jews." He is made, like Cicero, to allude to their great numbers in Rome, and overwhelming influence,[3] and their credulity.[4] A Roman is supposed to talk of their "thirtieth Sabbath," and to be afraid of offending the *curti Judæi !*[5]

Horace, B.C. 64-7.

And Horace, like his friend of Mantua, and like following poets, is made to introduce the palms of Idumæa, as if they grew only there—

" Herodis palmetis pinguibus."[6]

Ovid, in the *De Arte Amandi*, is made to allude to the Sabbath as kept by the Syrian Jew, in another place by the Syrian Palestinian.

---

[1] *C. D.* xviii. c. 23.

[2] See the treatise of F. Piper on Virgil as Prophet, 1862, and Th. Creizenach on the Æneid, the fourth Eclogue, and the Pharsalia in the Middle Ages, 1864. The fables about him in the *Gesta Romanorum*, cc. lvii. cxx., appear to date from the thirteenth century. Further, in Teuffel's *History of Latin Lit.*, § 226, Virgil and Lucan are also made to allude to Ituræan archers, like Cicero, *Georg.* ii. 448, *Phars.* vii. 230.

[3] *Sat.* i. 4, 143.   [4] v. 100.   [5] ix. 70.

[6] *Ep.* ii. 2, 184.

Strabo in his description of Syria is made to utter absurdities about the Libanus and the Jordan and Gennesaritis; about Joppé and the myth of Andromeda, Jerusalem, the "metropolis of the Jews;" about Gadaris, Azotus, Ascalon, and Gaza.[1] The reader will find the mediæval sources of these notions in Josephus, the first book of Maccabees, and Stephanus of Byzantium; in Sozomen, v. 3; in Marcus Diaconus' Life of St. Porphyry, c. 8.[2]

Strabo, c B.C. 54–A.D. 24.

Then Strabo is supposed to speak of *Judæa* in a very singular way. The western parts are held by the *Idumæans* or *Nabatæans*, who went over to the Jews and joined in their customs.[3] Most of the country is said to be inhabited by mixed tribes of Egyptians, Arabians, and Phœnicians. Such are those who dwell in Galilee and Jericho, and Philadelphia and Samaria, which Herod called Sebaste. There being such a mixture of population, the prevailing report of those connected with the Temple in Jerusalem says that "*the ancestors of those now called Jews were Egyptians.*"

The whole history of the "land of Jehuda" in the Old Testament, or of *Judæa* in the writings of the monks, shows that at the time of the Crusades the name was but coming into use to denote an undefined tract of land like Syria, of which the churchmen intended to take possession, as "promised to the son of David."[4] Nothing is plainer than that Rabbins and monks first dreamed of Judæa and Jerusalem as the heritage of

---

[1] xvi. 755, 759.

[2] Cf. in general Reland, *Pal.* 778; Bunbury, *Hist. of Ancient Geog.,* II. 270.

[3] See the source of this story in Josephus, *Ant.* xii. 8, 6, xiii. 9, 1; I Macc. v. 65; also in the false Joseph ben Gorion.

[4] Stephanus, *s. vv.* Εθνικοῖ, Ιουδαία, actually derives from *Judæa* and *Idumæa*, sons of Semiramis, or from one Judæus, son of Sparton !

David, and then sought to discover them to the senses of men.[1] Strabo knew of Syria, but nothing is more certain than that he was wholly ignorant of any geographical tract called *Judæa*, or the land of the Jews.

And then Strabo is supposed to tell us that Moses was an Egyptian priest, and that he had a part of the land Egypt, and removed thence, being displeased with the customs, and many who honoured the Deity removed with him.   Then we have a theological disquisition on the error of Egyptian and Libyan and Hellenic religion.   Moses is said to have declared that *"the element which surrounds us all, the land and sea, was God alone, which we call heaven and world, and the nature of existing things."* There is more of this kind of writing, much in the same windy style that characterises the mock Josephus. Moses led a large number of men to the spot where the building in Jerusalem now stands.   Then we have an attack on the *superstitions* of the Jews, their abstinences and circumcisions.   Nothwithstanding their dissensions and troubles, they preserved their Acropolis intact.   More disquisition on religious rites follows, the object of which is to prove that the Jews had institutions like the Greeks, oracles and diviners. Moses is compared to Amphiaraos, Trophonios, Orpheus, Musæus, Zamolxis ; to the Gymnosophists of the Indians, the Mages and Necromancers of the Persians, the Chaldæans of the Assyrians, the Etruscan Haruspices among the Romans. "Thus the Jews had a good beginning, but turned aside to the worse."

Judæa being ruled by tyrants, Alexander first proclaimed himself king instead of priest. His sons were Hyrcanus and Aristobulus, who disputed about the

[1] See the Basilian Cyril, *In Jesaiam.*, lib. i. or. ii., on the *sensible* Judæa,

government, and were overcome by Pompey, and so forth. In short, we are in the hands of the men who compiled Josephus and other mediæval fictions.

No one acquainted with the sober and accurate manner of the Roman geographer will believe that he wrote this passage. It is equally certain that no Rabbin of Tiberias, or of any other school, wrote it. When the old question, *Cui bono?* is once fairly asked, no other answer can be given than that the writers interested in inserting the passage were those who were stirring up Europe to rescue the "Holy Land" from the Moslem infidels, and who represented Christians as the true successors to the temporal glories of David.

The reader may compare what Laurence Valla has said in reference to the Latin monk's Commentary on Jonah,[1] and may further trace these geographical ideas in other ecclesiastical sources.[2]

The shortest way to the detection of the forgery is perhaps through Josephus Gorionides, once confounded with the other Josephus, but now known to be an Italian mediæval Jew. He quotes as authorities Strabo, Nicolas of Damascus, and Titus Livius.

Mela places Azotus in Arabia. He divides Syria into Coele, Mesopotamia, Damascene, Adiabene, Babylonia, *Judæa*, Sophene. Palestine touches Arabia, Phœnice extends to Cilicia. Then Antiochia is named.

Pomponius Mela.

---

[1] *Elegant.* v. 6.

[2] Joseph., B. J. 3, 9, 2; Egesipp. *De Ec. Hieros.* iii. 20; Hieron. *In Jonam.* An anonymous monk of Ravenna, whose writings have been attached to P. Mela, has written, probably in the thirteenth century, a dreamy theological geography in his study, in which he gives *Joppis, Azoton, Ascalon, Gasis,* as towns of Judæa. He cites as his authority one Castorius, and mentions the *Jeromisus* among the "very many rivers" of Judæa, ii. 14. Similarly, Pliny and Ptolemæus give in the same order *Gaza, Ascalon, Azotus.*

In Palestine is the great fortress of Gaza, also Ascalon, and Joppè; in Phœnicia is Tyre.

With Mela may be compared Pliny, lib. v., and Ptolemæus, who defines *Judæa* as Syria Palestina, as does the interpolator of Dion Cassius in chapter 37, and others, whether they interpolate or write under the names of Eusebius and Jerome.

Diodorus, who in his first book is made to allude to the leading rite of the Jews as similar to that of the Egyptians, has ascribed to him also an absurd tale concerning Antiochus Epiphanes. *Diodorus Siculus, c. 30 B.C.*
He made war upon them, and went into the sanctuary of God, which it is not lawful to enter, except for the priest. He found in it a stone statue of a man with a thick beard, sitting on an ass, holding in his hands a book, which he suspected to be the book of Moses, who founded Jerusalem, and the nation, and who was the author of the misanthropic and evil laws to the Jews. It is further pretended that Antiochus insulted the statue and the sacred books, and that he extinguished "their undying candlestick, which burned without ceasing in the Temple," and so forth.[1]

It is monks of the fourteenth or fifteenth century who call attention to the history of this writer: Roger Wendover, Matthew of Westminster, Radulfus de Diceto. The work is known to us through the corrupt abridgment *Pompeius Trogus, said to be a contemporary of Livy.*
of Justinus, a much-read Middle Age book of the cloisters.[2]

It contains, in a crude form, a fantastic theory of the monks concerning Jewish history. The origin of the Jews is said to be from Damascus, and Damascus took its name from a King Damacus. After him, Azelus,

---

[1] *Ecl.* xxxiv. 1.   [2] Cf. Hieron. *In Daniel.*; Orosius i. 8, &c.

Adores, Abraham and Israhel reigned. Israhel divided the people into ten kingdoms, and handed them to his sons. The story of Joseph is told, and his son is said to be Moses. When the people are expelled from Egypt, Moses, repairing to Damascus, his old fatherland, occupies Mount Syna. The institute of the Sabbath is termed a fast, as in Suetonius.[1] Moses is succeeded by his son Arruas, who is made king. We are told that Xerxes first subdued the Jews; they later came under the sway of Alexander the Great; they revolted from Demetrius, and obtained friendship and liberty from the Romans.[2] But the reduction of Syria to a Roman province by Pompey is told in a line; it is "Syria of the Jews and Arabs." [3]

The source of these tales will be found in the writings of the forgers of a late century: in "Josephus against Appion," in the Benedictine "Orosius" i. 8; in "Rufinus," "Julius Firmicus," &c. They pretend that Joseph was worshipped as Serapis, or Osiris, or Arsaph. So also "Clement of Alexandria," and "Augustine." When Moses is said to inherit paternal science, the meaning is that he was a Mage. Pliny, xxx. 2, is made to say that there was in his time a magical faction derived from Moses and Jochabel his mother; while Apuleius joins Moses with Jannes as very celebrated Mages. Diogenes Laërtius is made to witness to the connection of Jews and Mages.

Another source of absurdities is the interpolator of Suidas' Lexicon, to whom reference has been elsewhere made. Alexander, surnamed Polyhistor, of the time of Sulla, is said to have written that there was a *Hebrew woman named Moso, who had written down the Law of the Hebrews.*

---

[1] The Saturday fast at Rome is meant. [2] xxxvi. 2. [3] xl. 2.

The story that the Jews were driven out of Egypt as lepers is in Justin, xxxvi. 2, repeated in Orosius, and in the forged passage, Tacitus v. 3.   On Mount Sina compare the Benedictine Sulp. Severus, *Dial.* i. 11, Gal. iv. 25.

With the foolish story in Justin that the Sabbath was consecrated for ever as a fast, in memory of the end of hunger and wandering, may be compared the passages in Dion Cassius, chap. 37, that in pseudo-Augustine, *C. D.* vi. 11, where the humane Seneca is made to bitterly attack the Jews as *sceleratissima gens,* and to pretend that the Sabbath has become an universal custom. Compare the canonical Gospel, Luke xviii. 12.

The talk of the Jews deriving their income from *opobalsamum,* found only in Judæa, Justin xxxvi. 3, may be compared with passages in Pliny, xii. 25 (54), Strabo, xvii. 2, 41, Solinus, xlviii., and with the talk of Herod's palm-trees.   The forgers were acquainted with the trade of mediæval Jews, but their idea of Oriental geography was vague as a dream.

This writer, who is animated by the old Romish spirit, and a great lover of the Roman name, _{Velleius} simply says that Syria and Pontus were _{Paterculus, B C. 19,–A D.} monuments of Pompey's valour.   He ap-_{31.} pears to have escaped the hand of the interpolator.

In the *Epitomæ* of Livy, Pompey, after reducing Pontus to a province, is said to have subdued the Jews, and to have taken their fane in Hierosolyma, inviolate up to that time.[1]

In Lucan's *Pharsalia,* Pompey is made to say—"Cappadoces mea signa timent, et *dedita sacris Incerti Judæa Dei, mollisque Sophene.*"[2] _{Lucan, 39-65.}

Here again the same theological colour is apparent,

[1] *Epit.* cii.   [2] ii. 593.

and even obtrusive. The *incertus deus* reminds of the
passages in Strabo and in Tacitus; and the anxious
desire to fix in the reader's mind an association between
Pompey and the Jews is again to be recognised, as
also in a couplet inserted in Claudian, doubtless from
the same hand.[1]

Again, in Lucan we read—in the same Pompeian
interest—

> Accedunt Syriæ populi, desertus Orontes,
> Et felix, sic fama, Ninos; ventosa *Damascus*,
> *Gazaque*, et arbusto palmarum dives *Idume*
> Et Tyros instabilis, pretiosaque murice Sidon.[2]

The historian of Alexander's conquest is made to
tell how the *Samaritans* burned a Præfect
of Syria, Andromachus, alive.[3] The source is
again the Basilians Eusebius and Cedrenus,
Josephus and Epiphanius.

Q. Curtius,
temp. Ves-
pasian.

In the Supplement of Freinshem to Book ii. 11, will
be found further illustrations of this point.

Most of the MSS. of Juvenal have been greatly
corrupted. The passages in him relating to
Jews in Rome in the first century have attracted attention by their strangeness. We must decide
against them on the same ground. It is hardly necessary to discuss them in detail; that in the fourteenth
Satire most clearly betrays the hand of one of the same
class of forgers who have tried to emend Strabo. Juvenal
is made to enumerate, among the bad examples set by
parents, the superstitious feeling about the Sabbath.
The son of such a father *adores nothing but the clouds
and the spirit of the sky. He thinks swine's flesh to
be the same as human flesh, and presently practises*

Juvenal.

---

[1] *In Eutrop.* i. 220.   [2] iii. 215; cf. vii. 230.   [3] iv. 8.

circumcision. Accustomed to contemn the Roman laws, they learn and keep and fear the Judaic jus: whatever Moses handed down in a secret volume, which teaches you not to show the way except to a fellow-worshipper, and to lead verpi *alone* (an obscene term) *to the sought fountain.*[1]

The Latin is bad, the animus shown still worse. The scholiast betrays the origin of the interpolation by talking of baptism; and the mention of the "Secret Roll" reminds us of the legends of the Jewish Cabbala.

In the sixth Satire a clumsy "aside" is thrust in, alluding to a land where kings "*observe festal Sabbaths with bare feet, and ancient clemency indulges old pigs.*"[2] Just so Tacitus is made to say that pigs grow old among the Jews. Josephus and Hegesippus also described Berenice coming with bare feet to Jerusalem.

The bad Latin in the line—

"*Arcanam Judæa tremens mendicat in aurem,*"[3]

again attracts attention. Juvenal could not have written it. But the picture of the stealth of Jewish prophesying, and their readiness to sell you any sort of dreams for a small bit of money, is only too characteristic of that period of the Middle Age when such things were done. In this and in some other places the attempt is made to thrust in the Jewish religion in connection with that of Isis and Osiris.[4]

Another picture of Jewish beggars living in the temple of the Camœnæ, according to the scholiast, betrays the same hand and repeats the same phrase, *cophinus fænumque supellex.*[5]

---

[1] *Sat.* xiv. 96, *seq.*; cf. the learned notes in Mr. Mayor's edition.
[2] vi. 155, *seq.*   [3] vi. 542.
[4] It is more like a description of the Gipsies.   [5] iii. 14.

Again, *Idumæan* is used for *Jewish* in the phrase,
" Idumæae Syrophœnix incola portæ." [1]

The interest of the Western monks in Seneca con-
Seneca *c* 3   sists in their desire to make him out a friend
B.C.-65 A.D.   of their St. Paul. They have forged a series
of foolish letters with this object in view; and they
have moreover inserted a passage ironically allusive to
the Jews in the Epistles to Lucilius :—

" I have taught how the gods are to be worshipped.
*Let us forbid any one to kindle a lamp on the Sabbaths ;
since neither do the gods need light, nor do even men
delight in smoke. Let us forbid the offering of morning salutation, and sitting at the doors of temples.
Human ambition is taken by such offices as these. He
worships God who knows him." [2]

There is also an allusion to certain rites of foreign
nations, and arguments of superstition in favour of
abstinence from certain animals, which are probably
from the same hand. [3]

The source of the forgery may be seen in the false
Augustine, *C. D.*, vi. 11.

The Epigrams of Martial have been interpolated with
Martial, c.   several spiteful and obscene passages relating
42-102   to the Jews ; and he also is made to use the
word Idumæan as equivalent to Jewish. Titus with
his father merited an Idumæan triumph,[4] and we hear
once more of the Idumæan palms.[5] We hear of the
" fasts of the Sabbatarians " as causing bad breath ;[6]
and in a picture of the streets of Rome, the Jew who
has been taught by his mother to beg (rogare) is introduced.[7] We hear of " circumcised Jews," [8] and of a

---

[1] viii. 160.　　　　　　　[2] *Ep.* i. 95.
[3] *Ep.* i. 108 ; cf. Tacit. *A.* ii 83 ; Suet. Tib. xxxvi.
[4] ii. 2.　　[5] x. 50.　　[6] iv. 4.　　[7] xii. 57.　　[8] vii. 29.

pretended Jewish slave who has come from "burnt Solyma," and is subject to tribute.[1]

In Valerius Flaccus also we find *Idumé* and *Solymus* used in the same allusive manner. He is sup-posed to say, in his address to Vespasian— Val. Flaccus, temp. Vespasian.

> "versam proles tua pandet *Idumen*
> (Namque potest) *Solymo* nigrantem pulvere fratrem.
> Spargentemque faces et in omni turre furentem." [2]

The MS. of this poem, which has not been recognised by ancient writers except Quintilian, was discovered at the Benedictine convent of St. Gall by Poggio in 1417.

Another hint of the manner in which the Latin monks fabricated evidence in favour of their theory about the Jews is furnished by the A. Julianus. Latin monk who writes under the name "Minucius Felix," and who pretends to cite one Antonius Julianus, of the reign of Vespasian, as having said that "*the Jews deserved their ill fate by their own iniquity.*" [3] With him is made to join Josephus, or the Basilian monk who writes under his name, and who calls this Julian Procurator of Judæa.[4] Bernays has justly conjectured[5] that Tacitus' story in the *Histories* was derived from this source—in other words, wholly from a monkish source.

Another of the discoveries of Poggio or Politian at the Benedictine cloisters of St. Gall, was the MS. of the *Punica* of this poet, which C. Silius Italicus, 25-101. was subsequently lost.   Silius has been made, like other Latin poets, to sing of the "race of Palestine," meaning the Jews (iii. 600 *seq.*)—

> "hic fera gentis
> Bella *Palæstinæ* primo delebit in ævo."

---

[1] vii. 54 ; cf. xi. 95.   [2] *Argonaut.* i. 12.   [3] *Oct.* xxxiii. 4.
[4] B. J. 6, 4, 3. .   [5] *Sulp. Severus,* p. 56.

That bold interpolations were made in the text of this poet in the Juntine edition of 1515 has been already recognised.

Another of Poggio's discoveries was the MS. of Statius 45-96. Statius. In the *Silvæ* we find the lines—

"Latius cui ductor Eoa
Signa, *Palæstinasque* dedit frenare cohortes." [1]

And again—

" An *Solymum* cinerem, palmetaque capta subibis,
Non sibi felices silvas ponentis *Idumes*." [2]

And again—

" Quidquid nobile Ponticis nucetis,
Fecundis cadit aut jugis *Idumes*." [3]

This poet was a favourite of the Middle Age, as readers of Dante may recall. He is made in the *Purgatorio* to say—

" In that time
When the good Titus, with Heaven's King to help,
Aveng'd those piteous gashes, whence the blood
By Judas sold did issue, with the name
Most lasting and most honour'd, there was I
Abundantly renown'd." [4]

Then in Persius we have the strange description of Persius, c. the "days of Herod," when the "lanterns 34-62. pour out their fat mist," and again, as in Horace, his auditor is supposed to stand in dread of the "circumcised Sabbaths" of the Jews—

" Labra moves tacitus, *recutitaque sabbata* palles." [5]

Here, too, the rites of Isis are brought into close connection with those of the Jews.

[1] iii. 2, 104; cf. 138 *seq*   [2] v. 2, 138.
[3] i. 6, 12.   [4] *Purg.* xxi.   [5] *Sat.* v. 188, *seq.*

To Quintilian, the arbiter of taste, some of the monks of the West have had the audacity Quintilian, to ascribe their own paltry declamations.[1] 35-95. There are no other witnesses to the *Declamations* ascribed to that author. In addition to this, he is made to censure the unsocial nature of the Jews in his *Institutes.* [2]

We come now to the strange story which Tacitus is supposed to tell about the Jews in the fifth Tacitus, c book of his *Histories*, which should have 54-119. contained the account of what happened in the Roman Empire during the years 69 and 70.

After all that has been said about the Benedictines and their literary activity, we may now certainly affirm that this strange piece of mythology was their production. The principal MS. is the Mediceus II., incorrectly supposed to have been written between 1053–1087. And it is the monks who write under the notorious names of Tertullian[3] and of Jerome[4] who direct our attention to the work. The passage instructs us, in connection with other evidence, how entirely fantastic were the notions about the Jews at the time of their settlement as a schola in Rome.

Here *Judæi* are said to be derived from *Idæi*, because they were once, in the days of good King Saturn, settled in Crete! Some say that in the reign of Isis, the overflowing multitude of them in Egypt was disburdened upon the neighbouring lands, under the leadership of *Hierosolymus* and *Judas*. Others talk of Assyrian settlers who gained possession of a part of Egypt and then of Hebrew lands. Others trace the name *Hierosolyma* to the *Solymi* of Homer's song.

---

[1] See Jerome, *In Esai.* viii. præf. ; Lactant. i. 21, v. 7, vi. 23.
[2] iii. 7, 21.   [3] *Apol* xvi.   [4] On Zach. lib. iii. c. 14.

2 F

Then we have the strange story of Moyses and the herd of wild asses which conducts him to the waters; and the description of Jewish customs. The object of the whole is to create the impression on the minds of students that Tacitus thought the people of immense antiquity, that he looked upon their rites with contempt, and yet that he was aware of features in their life which resembled the life of the monks. He is made to blow hot and cold, because the monks hate the orthodox Jews, and at the same time desire to represent the Jews as their ancestors.

When we name Sulpicius Severus, the monk of Aquitaine, we name a monk of the same Benedictine confederacy, who wrote about the same time with his brother monk of Monte Cassino, and who is a fellow-forger of tales about the Jews in his *Historia Sacra*.

The same MS. contains the Annals, xi.–xvi., in which occurs the notorious passage concerning *Christus* and the *Christiani*. Here the writer is thinking in Catholic phrases. He renders confessors by *qui fatebantur*, and talks obscurely of *flagitia* in connection with the Christian name.

In the Annals, ii. 85, we have the absurd passage corresponding to one in Suetonius, Tib. 36, in which several thousand Jews are said to have been enrolled as soldiers and sent to Sardinia.

The supposed correspondence of Pliny with the
Pliny the Emperor Trajan is not to be found in any
Younger, extant MS. It was added to the collection
62–113. by Aldus.

The fraud should have long ago been discovered. One cannot read the first two sentences without feeling that this is the writing of a man unaccustomed to think in classical Latin. He probably thought in French.

What can grate more harshly on the ear than such phrases as *cunctationem meam regere* and *ignorantiam instruere*? Other expressions reveal the hand of the forger in Tacitus. We have the talk about *flagitia, faterentur* used in an obscure sense, *sacramento* in the Catholic sense, and the like. Pliny was neither a Catholic, nor was he the man to employ expressions which he did not understand. So long used as an evidence of Christianity, the letter is in fact one of the most glaring and impudent fabrications in the long series.

The theory of Pompey's triumph over the Jews will be found inserted in the writings of Appian;[1] also of Trajan's war upon the Jews in Egypt.[2]

Second Century. Appian.

Similar things will be found in Herodian; and Irmisch has pointed out many passages in which Herodian appears to be an "imitator of Josephus." In other words, he has been tampered with by the Basilians and Benedictines.

Herodian.

The fragments of Dion Cassius' work have come to us from the hands of the same men who wrote the flatulent nonsense that passes under the name of Josephus. Zonaras, a monk of the Order of St. Basil, has been good enough to make an abstract for us of the first twenty books; another monk of the same Order, Xiphilinus, has made an epitome of the later books. They have taken care to insert their theories about the Jews in many places in the text, of which it may suffice to give the mere list,[3] after all that has been said.

Dion Cassius.

---

[1] *De Bell. Mithrid.* 106, 114, 117.
[2] *De Bell. Civ.* ii. 90.
[3] xxxvii. 16, xxxix. 56, xlvii. 28, lxvi. 4–7, lxvii. 14, lxviii. 1, 32.

In the Life of Julius Cæsar we read that at the public mourning on his death, the Jews were conspicuous among a great multitude of foreigners. They frequented the pyre " for nights running," *noctibus continuis !* In Josephus, *Ant.* xiv. 14, will be found the explanation of this remarkable behaviour.

Suetonius, 75-160.

Augustus is made to allude, in a pretended letter, to a " fast of the Sabbath," the ecclesiastical Saturday fast. He praised Caius because, in passing by Judæa, he had not prayed at Jerusalem. Claudius expelled from Rome Jews who rioted on the instigation of one Chrestus. Christiani are a race of men of new and malefic superstition. There are the fables about Vespasian, and his triumph over the Jews. Titus is said to reduce Tarichæa and Gamala, " very strong cities of Judæa." Domitian was present at the Jewish triumph of his father and brother. And then there is the indecent talk of the Jewish *fiscus* and its oppression, of which there are echoes in Martial.

In Florus we find again the fable of Pompey entering Jerusalem, where he sees that "*great Arcanum of the impious race.*"[1]

Florus, c. 138.

In Arrian's Lectures of Epictetus another allusion to the Jews and abstinence from swine's flesh is impertinently thrust in. In the discussion on *Notions*, the philosopher asks, "Who does not lay down that the just is the fair and the becoming ? When, therefore, does conflict arise ? In the accommodation of notions to particular things, when one says, 'He did well, he is brave, or otherwise.' Hence strife arises among men. *This is the conflict of Jews, Syrians, Egyptians, and Romans, not as to the question whether the holy and right is above all to be*

Epictetus.

[1] iii. 6, 30 ; cf. Aug. *C. D.* xviii. 45, Idatius, and other Benedictines.

*preferred and pursued, but whether this is right or
wrong, to live on pork.* This you will find to be the
quarrel of Agamemnon and Achilles," &c. The interpolated patch upon the text is most glaring. And the
offence is great against a writer so distinguished by
the best Roman and philosophic feeling.

Again, the philosopher nobly chides those who would
take up the profession of philosophy, when they cannot
fulfil the calling and duty of a man. He contrasts the
doctrine of the lip and the truth that has been digested
by the mind.

"What is the difference whether you discourse on
the principles of this or that school, of Epicurus or
the Stoics? Why do you deceive the people? *Why
do you pretend, being a Jew, to be a Greek? Do you
not see how each is said to be a Jew? how each a
Syrian? how each an Egyptian? And when we see
one taking two sides, we are wont to say, 'He is not a
Jew, but a hypocrite.' But when he takes up the
affection of one who has been baptized and has professed, then he is indeed and is called a Jew. So also
we Parabaptists in word indeed are Jews, but in fact
something else.*" [1]

Here canonical echoes strike upon the ear. Not
only have the monks put these startling observations
into the mouth of Epictetus, but they have been in-
debted to him in more than one place in the compilation of the New Testament. However, the object
here is to confound Jews with Christians, as in other
interpolations.

The clumsy hand of the monks is again most em-
phatic in another passage, where the philosopher is
discoursing on fearlessness of mind. He dwells upon

[1] ii. 9.

the usual counteractions to fear, contempt of the body and of riches. But he is made to say something quite contrary to the spirit of philosophy : " If any one is so affected towards wealth and towards the body, towards children and wife—*if, in fine, by a certain madness and despair he is affected so that it makes no difference to him whether he has those things or not,* what tyrant will be dreaded, &c. ? *Then, if one may be affected by madness towards these things, and by habit the Galilæans,* can none know by reason and demonstration that God has made all things in the world, and the whole world free and perfect?" [1] The incoherence introduced by the interpolator, and the injury done to the calm argument of Epictetus, is nothing less than revolting.

The *Manual* was introduced by the monks, with alterations, into their schools.

It appears that the Latin monks were interested in the tales of magic and miracle to be found in Apuleius, and they have inserted some things into his text which have led unwary readers to suppose that he was acquainted with Judaism and Christianity. The references to him are frequent in works ascribed to Augustine.[2]

Apuleius. Time of Ant. Pius and M. Aurelius.

Among the jurists of the second century, Papinian and others, there was actually a Roman lawyer of the name of Tertullian, who wrote eight books of *Questions.* Nothing better illustrates the effrontery of the monks than the fact that in the first Ecclesiastical History [3] they have borrowed the name of

The Jurists. Tertullian.

---

[1] *Diss.* iv. 7.

[2] *C. D.* viii. 12, 14, 19 ; *Epp.* 136, 138 ; Lactant. *D. I.* v. 3, vii. 18. Cf. the foolish invective in Apul. *Met.* xi. 14. The subject has been further treated by Hildebrand, 1842, 1. p. xlix.

[3] Eus. *H. E.* ii. 2.

this lawyer as a mask for one of their own apologetic writers.   It is indeed probable enough that some of the numerous Tertullianic tracts[1] produced in the Western monasteries were the work of a man of legal training, as well as of shrewd, though dishonest wit.

Pausanias, who probably knew little of Syria, is also forced to witness to an imaginary territory   of the Jews : " In the *land of the Hebrews* Pausanias. there is a tomb of Silenus, &c."[2] And then again, " *the Hebrews who dwell above Palestine* have enrolled a soothsaying woman named Sabbé."[3] And Hadrian subdued "*the Hebrews who dwell above the Syrians.*"[4] Here again the forgers are detected by means of their Josephus.[5]   Pausanias is also supposed to be acquainted with the *silk* of the Hebrews.[6]

Nor are the monks who contrived the fable of Helena and Constantine content without making this author witness to a tomb "*among the Hebrews of a native lady Helené, in the city Solymi, built by the emperor of the Romans.*"[7]

In his account of Pompey, Plutarch is made to enumerate, as the nations over which the   general triumphed, Pontus, Armenia, Cappa- Plutarch. docia, Paphlagonia, Media, Colchis, Iberes, Albani, *Syria*, Cilicia, Mesopotamia, the parts about *Phœnice*, and *Palæstine, Judæa*, Arabia, and all the pirates by land and sea.   Among his captives was the *king of the Jews, Aristobulus.*[8]

The tractate on Isis and Osiris ascribed to Plutarch is, we think, also of doubtful genuineness.   In the

---

[1] See *Apol.* 1-6, 28-44 ; *De An.* 6.   [2] vi. 24.   [3] x. 12.
[4] i. 6.   [5] *Ant.* vii. 9, 11, viii. 7, "land of the Hebrews."
[6] v. 5.   [7] viii. 16.   [8] Chap. xlv. ; cf. chap. xxxii.

Symposium the God of the Jews is identified with Bacchus, and the Sabbath is derived from Sabbo.

In his tractate, *On Superstition*, the following passage is clumsily thrust in:—"The Jews on the Sabbath sitting rigidly, when the enemy put up ladders, and took the walls, did not rise, but remained as in a net, being bound by superstition." And again, "See how the Jews and Syrians think about the gods; look at the works of the poets, how full they are of superstition."[1]

Upon Lucian the Basilians make a violent attack, pretending that he blasphemed the name of Christ. Gesner and Niebuhr, however, exposed the forgery of the *Philopatris;* and equally the *Pereginus*, in which the monks level their satire both against Christians and against Cynics, must be rejected. In another spurious piece a satirical allusion to the Jews occurs.[2] The *Alexandros* or *False Prophet* has been written or interpolated in the same interest.

Lucian.

It will be noticed that in the *Peregrinus* the same system is pursued by the monks of representing the *Christiani* as a poor and despicable sect, related in some way to the Jews. They cast out Peregrinus for eating of some forbidden food.

The story about Philo of Byblus and Sanchoniathon emanates from the fancy of the Basilians. They talk of Hierombalus, the priest of the god *Jeuo;* also of the Jews and other matters which show that they have not yet the canonical text of the Hebrew Scriptures in their hands.[3] Jeoud, the mythic ancestor of the Jews, is made son of Kronos; the

Philo of Byblus.

---

[1] *De Stoic Repugn.* 38.   [2] *Tragodo-podagra,* 173.
[3] Eus. *P. E.* i. 9, *seq.*

Phœnicians call him Israel. The name of Chna was changed to Phœnix, and so on.

Not content with representing Aurelius as a persecutor of the Christians, the monks have borrowed from him, as from Epictetus, in the composition of the Sermon on the Mount.[1]

Marcus Aurelius.

Numenius is made a contemporary of Plutarch by the monks of St. Basil, and a mouthpiece of their dogma of the Logos. To him also is ascribed the absurd saying, that "Plato was Moses talking Attic Greek."[2]

Numenius.

The Basilians also link themselves to the neo-Platonists in the persons of Ammonius, and Hermes Trismegistus, and again that of Amelius, who, it is pretended, was acquainted with the definition of the Logos in the fourth Gospel.[3]

The mediævalists resolved to force an echo from the celebrated neo-Platonist to their dogma, and even to make him a witness to their existence in the fourth century. Not content with this, they insert into his treatise on abstinence, where he so nobly teaches the spirituality of true religion, and the uselessness of sacrifices, a notice of the Jews.

Third Century. Porphyry, c. 233-305.

"And yet among the Syrians, the Jews, because of sacrifice from the beginning, still sacrifice animals; as Theophrastus says, 'They do not feast on the victims, but burning them whole by night, pouring much wine and honey over them, they consume the sacrifice quickly, lest the All-seer should be spectator of the deed.'"[4]

We need cite no more of this absurd passage. There is another in which the abstinence from swine is men-

---

[1] See Gataker, *Index Locorum S. Scripturæ.*   [2] Suidas, *s. v.*
[3] Eus. *P. E.* xi. 19.   [4] *De Abst.* ii. 26.

tioned, and Porphyry is supposed to learn from Josephus of the three sects of the Pharisees, Sadducees,
and Essæi. He digresses into a description of the
latter, who are none other than the mystic ancestors of
the mediæval monks, and wholly their creation.[1] Thus,
although the monks have never produced the treatise
that they pretend Porphyry wrote against the Christians,
they have inserted a very neat account of Monachism
into his treatise. There is yet another passage, in
which the neo-Platonist is supposed to recognise Gymnosophists, Brahmans, and Shamans of India ; also
Bardesanes, the Oriental heretic. This, too, is monkish,
and serves to remind us of the conditions of Oriental
influence under which the Catholic Church arose.[2]

Interesting in its way is the attempt to make
Porphyry cite the book of Genesis in connection with
the old folk-idea of the birth of souls from water.
He says that the Naiad Nymphs signify the virtues
that preside over the waters, or in general all souls that
come to birth. "Souls haunt the divinely-breathed
water," as Numenius says, *"for this reason declaring
that the Prophet said, the Spirit of God was borne
on the waters."* [3]

It will now be apparent from whose hand proceeded

D. Longinus.

the remarkable passage wherein Longinus is
supposed to be vaguely acquainted with the
writings of the Jewish legislator, and to quote from
them an example of the sublime.[4]

In the Lives of Hadrian and Antoninus Pius there

The *Historia,*
Augusta.

are incidental references to risings of the
Jews, but no recognition of the existence of
Christiani till we come to the Life of Sept. Severus

[1] *De Abst.* iv. 11–13.
[2] Ibid. iv. 17.
[3] *De Antro Nymph.*
[4] ix. 22.

ascribed to Spartianus. Here we read that the Emperor, on his way from Antioch to Alexandria, A. 202, laid the foundation of many laws for the Palestinians.

" He forbade men to become Jews under heavy penalty. He laid down the same sanction concerning the Christiani." [1]

In the first Ecclesiastical History it is indeed this year that is signalised by the story of Origen and the persecution.[2]

Again, by a law of Hadrian emasculation is forbidden as a species of murder. It seems that our interpolator has striven to create the impression that the Romans confounded the act with circumcision.[3] The reader will again recall the story of Origen, and the desire of the ecclesiastics to represent themselves as a sect of the Jews.

In the strange Life of Heliogabalus—a disgraceful lampoon—there is the following strange story :—

" He consecrated Heliogabalus on the Palatine Mount by the imperial dwelling, and made him a temple, desiring to transfer the type (or effigy) of the Great Mother, and the fire of Vesta, and the Palladium, and the Ancilia, and all the venerable objects of Roman affection, to that temple, with the purpose that no god should be worshipped at Rome except Heliogabalus. *He said, moreover, that the religion of the Jews and the Samaritans, and the Christian devotion, should be transferred thither, that the priesthood of Heliogabalus might hold the secretum of all cultures.*" [4]

---

[1] C. xvii.   [2] *H. E.* vi. 2.

[3] *Vit. Hadr.* c. xiv. ; cf. *Digest.* xlviii. 8, 4, 2 ; Paulus, *Sent.* v. 22, 3, 4 ; Modestinus, *Dig.* xlviii. 8, 11.

[4] C. iii. The expressions *secretum* and *cultura* are ecclesiastical. Eus. *H. E.* vii. 30, 9 ; Lactant. v. 7 ; Tert. *Apol.* xxi. ; *Cod. Theod.* xv. 4, 1.

In the Life of Alex. Severus we read that he reserved
privileges to the Jews, and suffered the Christiani to
exist.[1] And the same intention is shown by this interpolator to represent the cult of Christ as recognised
along with that of other gods. A picture is drawn of
this Emperor performing divine service in his lararium
or chapel, honouring the departed elect, among whom
were Apollonius, Christ, Abraham, Orpheus, and others.[2]
It is also represented that he observed the Roman
Saturday by going up to the Capitol ; and that he
desired to build a temple to Christ, and to receive Him
among the gods, which Hadrian had meditated to do.
Hadrian had ordered temples in all states to be made
without images,[3] and so had favoured the opinions of
the Christiani.

Then we have allusions to the custom among Christians and Jews, of publishing the names of priests to
be ordained, put into the mouth of this Emperor.[4]

Another interpolation seems to be connected with
the Church of Ara Coeli. Certain Popinarii complained
that the Christiani had seized a site which belonged to
them, and the Emperor replied in favour of the religionists.[5] He is supposed to have learned the " Golden
Rule " from Jews or Christiani, and to have had it
written up on the Palatium and public works.[6]

In the Life of Aurelian we find that an Epistle on
the Sibylline Books is ascribed to him, and he is made
to allude to a Church of the Christiani.[7]

---

[1] C. xxii.   [2] C. xxxii.

[3] C. xliii. The talk of *simulacra* betrays the ecclesiastical hand. See the
Vulgate of Osee, xi. 2 ; Acts vii. 41 ; 1 Thess. i. 9 ; 1 Jo. v. 21 ; Apoc. ix.
20 ; Col. iii. 5.

[4] C. xlv. The verb *ordino* is ecclesiastical. Cf. Dionysius Exiguus, *Cod.
Conc. Ancyr.* xxix. 37.

[5] C. xlix.   [6] C. li.   [7] C. xx.

In the Life of Saturninus we come upon an extra-ordinary passage in which an attack is made upon the "Egyptians," and they are mixed up with Christians and Samaritans. An epistle from Hadrian is produced, in which he writes of Christiani, Jews, and Samaritans as worshipping Serapis.

The reader will find the origin of these strange tales in the Josephus of the monks, and again in their Eusebius, their Socrates, and their Sozomen. Though they are of quite another kind than the tales of the emperors in the *Gesta Romanorum*, they are equally devoid of all historical foundation, and were doubtless conficted near to the same epoch.

Other forgeries in the *Historia Augusta* were ex-posed by Father Hardouin, in his examination of the coins of the period.

There was a genuine F. Maternus in the time of Constantine, who wrote an astrological work.   Fourth Cen-The true old Roman morality and religion is tury. Fir-micus Mater-to be found in it. The man who speaks nus. Time of daily of the gods and with the gods should Constantine. form his mind and heart for the imitation of Divinity. "Seek all the ornaments of virtue. Be modest even among the sober, be content with low living and little wealth." And so forth. Nothing can be more amus-ing than to contrast the poetical, distant, and vague conceptions of the highest beings in this writer with the pretended definitions of the Council of Nicæa. A gulf of some 1000 years, in fact, separates this Maternus from his rival, set up by the Western monks to pour out a stream of declamation against old reli-gion and old philosophy.

We need touch but briefly on Eutropius, the friend of the house of Constantine, and other chroniclers of the fourth century.   Buddeus has remarked, in

The His-
torians of
the Fourth
Century.—
A. Victor,
Eutropius,
S. Rufus.
a note, on the strange silence of Eutropius in reference to the conversion of Constantine and the rise of the Christian religion. Was spite the cause?   No: it was simply that Eutropius and his contemporaries knew nothing whatever of any change in the religious conditions of the empire.   Apart from this, one of the most unpardonable offences of the Basilians and the Benedictines is that they have conspired to deface and to caricature the bright image of Julian, one of the purest and noblest of spirits, according to the testimony of his comrades and intimates, that ever adorned the purple.   He died fighting for our Western culture, and has been rewarded by the title of apostate from a semi-Oriental religion of which he never heard.   Monte Cassino monks are again the offenders here.[1]

The Basilians continue to represent their party as in relation to the philosophers of the fourth century. Basil and Chrysostom, it is pretended, were pupils of Libanius, and other imaginary monks corresponded with him.   Gregory of Nazianzus is linked with Himerius, and with Julian at the school of Athens.

It is certain that none of the works ascribed to Julian are genuine: it is the monks who insist upon making him reflect their theories about the religious condition of the empire in the fourteenth century. Especially noteworthy is the frequent insertion of the name *Galilæi* in the Epistles; it is one of the names which the monks have fixed upon as those of imaginary Jewish ancestors of the Christiani.   The whole series

[1] On Jerusalem and the Jews see Eutrop. vi. 14, vii. 19, *seq.*—the story of the Josephi again.

of fables relating to the Emperor's desire to rebuild the temple at Jerusalem, and so forth, will be seen, in the light of our investigations, to be a historic absurdity.

One of the most valuable of our too scanty documents from the Roman Empire is the *Res Gestæ* of A. Marcellinus. Ammian, the officer and friend of Julian. The first part of the work has been destroyed, the remainder has been fearfully garbled. The principal MS. was brought from the Benedictine cloister at Fulda by Poggio.

Here again the theological geography and history has been inserted into the text. Pompey is said to have formed the "regions of Palestine" into a province, after the conquest of the Jews and the capture of Jerusalem.[1] The series of lies about Julian, the source of which will be found in the Basilian who writes under the name of Gregory Nazianzenus—is also duly inserted. Then we have the usual explosion of spite against "stinking and riotous Jews," in an ancedote about Vespasian. Nor are the Christiani spared. In a ridiculous scene their bishops come with a ragged mob into the palace, and the imperial preacher gives them civil admonition. He had found that the Christiani were fiercer than wild beasts towards one another.[2]

There is a long list of extraordinary passages, in which allusions are made to Christian priests, bishops, and deacons mixing in some unaccountable way with the affairs of the world. They are members of con- spiracies ; they are employed as ambassadors. A rebel Roman general is slain on his way to a Christian conventicle at Cologne.

According to the conjecture of Gutschmid, after

[1] xiv. 8.   [2] xxii. 5.

a description of Egyptian culture the author is supposed to say, "From these sources I H S., advancing through sublime discourses, in amplitude the rival of Jove, though He saw not Egypt, served with glorious wisdom" (xxii. 16, 22).

In the monkish tract called *Excerpta Valesiana*, appended to this work, the reader will find the clue to these curious interpolations. It is indeed hard to say, in particular parts of the work, how much is Roman and how much Catholic. The death-bed scene of the great Julian has, however, been spared, and the work, compared with that of Eutropius and other annalists, contains complete materials for the exoneration of that Emperor from the foolish charges made against him. To enter into a full examination of this subject would carry us too far from our present purpose. Let it suffice to observe that neither Julian nor his contemporaries had, or could have, the slightest knowledge of ecclesiastical affairs.[1]

With regard to the term *Galilæi*, so constantly occurring in the pretended work of Julian, it is traceable solely to the canonical and other sources of the Basilians and the Benedictines. The like observation applies to the *Nazoræi* or *Nazaræi*, which the monks who write under the names of Epiphanius and of Tertullian declare was one of the early names of the *Christiani*. It is probably taken from the Arabic and Jewish Nozara, Nozarim, as a general term for heretics. How entirely ignorant the monks must have been of the geography of Syria at the time they began this activity may be seen from the work, *Cyril against Julian*, where Galilæi are thought of as a people "in

---

[1] To Eutropius add A. Victor and S. Rufus Festus, as sources for the character of Julian.

Judæa," and then as all the Gentiles! The idea of them as Christians has been derived from the passage in Isaiah.

The rise of the denomination Galilæi, for the ancestors of the Christiani, may be dated from about the time of William of Tyre,[1] after the foundation of the principality of Antioch by the Normans.

Claudian, one of the finest of old Romans, has not only had Christian hymns, long admitted to be spurious, ascribed to him, but he is made, with Lucan, to re-echo the tale about Pompey and the Jews— Claudian.

> " In mercem veniunt Cilices, Judæa, Sophene,
> Romanusque labor, Pompeianique triumphi." [2]

The sentence, " *Judaicis* quæ pingitur India velis," [3] has also given rise to speculation. *Lydiacis* and *Niliacis* have been suggested as emendations.

The *Epitoma* of this author deals with military affairs. He is an old Roman, but an attempt has been made to impart a Christian colour to his writing, in the same way that Firmicus or Ammian have been dealt with. For example, he makes Roman soldiers swear " *by God, and Christ, and the Holy Spirit, and by the majesty of the Emperor, which, according to God, should be loved and worshipped by the human race.*" [4] F. Vegetius Renatus, *temp.* Theodosius I.

The monks have disfigured the *Itinerary* of Rutilius, a poem inspired by genuine old Roman feeling, with another spiteful explosion against the Jews— P. Rutilius Numatianus.

> " *Humanis animal dissociabile cibis.*" [5]

---

[1] vii. 1. [2] *Eutrop.* i. 220. [3] Ibid. 357.
[4] ii. 5. [5] v. 384

Then we have a declamation against the "frigid Sabbaths" and circumcision—a wish that they had never been subdued by Pompey and Titus, and the absurd assertion once more renewed that the victorious Romans stand in dread of the Jews.

Here also we find the first of a series of satires upon the *monks*, with a pun upon their name ; the isle Capraria is said to be full of them.[1] The passage is amusingly characteristic of the sly forgers of Monte Cassino.

There is also a line about Osiris unsuitable to the mouth of a Roman præfect.[2]

The original Boetius is a popular eclectic philo-
Fifth Century. Boetius.
sopher; he follows Plato and Aristotle, Cicero and Seneca. Though innocent of any but old Roman piety, he has been converted by the monks into a Christian, and his treatise, *De Consolatione*, has been used in their interest.

The same system of interpolation has been applied
Zosimu, c. 430–491.
to the work of Zosimus, who was a Roman *Comes*. He is made to tell a strange story of the conversion of Constantine by a certain *Egyptian*, who persuaded him that the opinion of the Christiani was destructive of all sin. The crime-stained Emperor received the story, and renounced the mantic art. The reader will find the source of such stories again in writings composed in the Basilian monasteries.[3]

There are other interpolations, favouring Church theories of history.[4]

---

[1] v. 439, *seq.*   [2] v. 375.

[3] See the Homily ascribed to Chrysostom, *In Ep. ad Phil.* c. iv. hom. xv. 5, where Fausta is exposed to wild beasts. Cf G. Codinus, *De Origg.*, who says Constantine had been made a Christian by Euphrates, his Accubitor.

[4] See iv. 2, 36 ; contrast the inscription in Gruter, p. 160, which contradicts the story. The Roman emperors remained pontiffs to the end.

A great object of the interpolations in Ammian and Zosimus has been to represent Churches as asyla in those times.[1]

Then we find a long fable about Theodosius the Great, and how he endeavoured to persuade the Senate to become Christian.[2] Then we have the story about John (Chrysostom), bishop of the Christiani, inserted (A. 401), and the anger of the Empress against him. "The fellow was a clever hand at managing the senseless mob." One of the curiosities of the monkish imagination is its delight in representing monks and their heroes as prominent in turbulent scenes. Nor is it possible to avoid a smile when we come upon a picture of the monks drawn by the hand of one of their own number. So strong was their craving for notoriety, or their fear of detection, they have not scrupled to launch a stray invective against the Orders. It is said of them that celibates are useless for war or other necessary political service, that they have appropriated the greater part of the land, and under pretext of charity to the poor, have reduced all to poverty. *When* could this passage have been written down?[3]

An analogous passage inserted in Eunapius, and the notorious story of the murder of Hypatia, belong to the same category, and betray the same effort after false notoriety.

Again, a good monk plays the part of intercessor with Alaric; and Zosimus the old Roman chimes with Sozomen the Basilian monk as representing the Bishop of Rome as ambassador to the Emperor in 409.[4] An interesting tale relates how the prohibition of the

[1] Zos. iv. 40, v. 8, 18, 29, 35, 45, 50.   [2] iv. 59.
[3] v. 23; cf. Socr. *H. E.* vi. 18; Sozom. viii. 21, Eunapius, *Vit. Ædesii*, s. f.
[4] ix. 6, 7.

Christiani from wearing the belt of service in the palace had been withdrawn.[1]

Zosimus also is made to repeat some of the Basilian tales about Julian.

Macrobius is a valuable source for old Roman religious ideas of his time. He is absolutely ignorant of Jews, yet he is made in one passage to relate a joke of Augustus, when he heard that Herod in Syria had ordered boys within two years old to be slain, and that he had also killed his son—

Macrobius.

> "'Tis better to be Herod's pig than his son." [2]

After all that has been said elsewhere, I need only advert to the mass of fraudulent writing which has been put forth under the name of the Emperor Justinian and the scholars who flourished in his reign. The remains of the treatise of John the Lydian on monks bear witness to the fact that the institutions of the old Roman state religion remained unchanged. Yet, when John is discoursing on sacrifices, a monk has thought proper to insert a text from Isaiah, "To what purpose is the multitude of your sacrifices unto Me?" &c. As if the Imperialist were a Jew.

I hope I may excuse myself from discharging any more of monkish falsehood and nonsense into these pages. The above specimens will have shown their animus and their method. It was well calculated to deceive, and it has deceived that large class of persons who find the lies of an individual detestable, but who respect and believe the lies of a confederacy. By means of tales which encourage popular odium of the Jews, and which magnify alike the virtues and the vices of Christiani or Monachi, with their mysterious

---

[1] v. 46.   [2] Sat. ii. 4; cf the original in Ael. *Var. H.* xii. 56.

and polyonymous ancestry, the authors have certainly flattered many persons of their time and obtained a strong hold of the credulity of the world.

At what time were these interpolations made? When we consider the great poverty of books in the monasteries and the schools, and the smallness of the reading class at any time before the great revival of learning, it seems almost certain that much of the work was not attempted until just before that revival, when the monks must have felt that their day of judgment was at hand. Some have suspected Poggio himself of a part in the nefarious work. At all events, many of these forgeries have been executed with sufficient cleverness by the mercenary servants of the Pope to deceive generations of scholars, otherwise acute, who have approached the literature under the stupor of ecclesiastical prepossession. The renewed study of the subject will convince the educated world how young and recent are many of those ideas in respect of the origin of Christendom which have prevailed among us since the invention of printing and the diffusion of books.

CHAPTER XII.

SUMMARY AND CONCLUSION.

AND now to bring these inquiries for the present to a term. Let me invite the reader to recall, in one rapid survey, the course of events in our European world since the conquests of the Arabians, from the seventh to the ninth century. In the ninth century the prevalence of the creed of Islam, from the Indus to the Straits of Gibraltar, is the great, the imposing, the never-to-be-forgotten fact in the history of our culture. The next century is the darkest of all the ages: we can know little or nothing of what was occurring in our world, except from the slight deposit of fact contained in later chronicles. It may, perhaps, be regarded on the whole as an age of repose. The Arabians were advancing in culture, and the Western world was slowly recovering from its long dismay. The beginning of the age is marked in literature by the production of the great Chronicle of Al Tabari at Bagdad, and its close by the infancy of the Hebrew language and literature at Cordova.

The eleventh century shows us again the world in strong commotion. The Turkish hosts, fresh champions of the religion of Allah and His Apostle, are the terror of the Roman Empire in the East as the Normans in the West. When we arrive at the last decade of this age, we stand at the greatest epoch in European history since the rise of Islam. It is the epoch of those expeditions to the East commonly called the Crusades, or Sacred Wars.

Now there is a considerable mediæval literature relating to the first of these wars, which should be closely and much more critically examined than hitherto it has been. But I may, in closing, offer upon this subject a few general observations. In the first place, this literature partly belongs to the synagogues, partly to the cloisters of the great Orders, and partly to the Arabians. All, therefore, who were concerned in the making of our mediæval culture were interested in this event, and have recorded their impressions of it. It is from a comparison of these impressions that we can alone hope to approach the actual occurrence. For the facts have been, as usual, enveloped in interested fable.

With regard to the Jews, it may be said generally that their historic memory begins with that war, and their impressions have been written down as if with pens dipped in blood. The synagogues in Germany were attacked by the rabble of the host, and the devotees of the Law were massacred, or they themselves chose death rather than life under circumstances that cannot now be thought of without horror and profound pity. These things have been written down in the language of the Bible, and in the style of the Bible, by men of the same Rabbinical class with those who produced the Biblical writings, and who were well aware that the lamentations of psalmists and prophets were the expression of hearts that had suffered sorely in that terrible time. It was the time when the people seemed forsaken of the Eternal.

If my argument in these pages has borne hardly

against the Orders, I am the more glad to state my own opinion that they had no share, direct or indirect, in these atrocities. The monks, as usual, represent one of their fraternity as the prime lever of the whole movement. Yet the tale about Peter the Hermit of Amiens is not only grossly improbable in itself, it stands in contradiction with other statements of the Papal writers. This has been noticed by M. de Montalembert, the great fautor and defender of the monks, who deprives Peter of the credit of the origination, and is disposed to assign the same to Urban II. The utterances, however, which have been put in the mouth of that Pope, were in all probability coolly written down more than a century after the event.

Of the work written in a Basilian cloister and ascribed to the Princess Anna Comnena, all that need here be said is that it was written at some time after 1148, and probably long after, when the liberty taken with her name and house was not likely to be censured. Similarly the work ascribed to Zonaras was written in the cloisters of Mount Athos at some undefined time after 1118. The Chronicle of Glycas, which ends at the same year, was written in the fifteenth century.

There is a mass of writing, equally dubious in date, from the Latin cloisters. Curious, for example, is the story of the Chronicle of Monte Cassino, ascribed to Leo of Ostia and Peter the Deacon in the twelfth century. About 1439 Ambrose Traversarius is said to have made an epitome of it, and in 1513 this epitome is edited at Venice by another monk of the Order as if it were the genuine work of Leo. Yet another monk of Monte Casino alters and mutilates the same MS., and edits it at Naples in 1616. What can be said for the genuineness of the longer Chronicle in the face

of facts like these?   Another epitome, for the period
496–857, has been designated by Wattenbach a "por-
tentous Chronicle."   The same epithet may perhaps
be applied to a mass of other writing from the same
page, including the "History" from the pens of
anonymi of Monte Cassino, covering the periods 1000–
1212, 1000–1154.   When we arrive at the handwriting
of the period 1191–98, 1209, we have still no contemporary writer.   Now, if no men were from that
sacred height looking on the events of 1096, we may
well despair of discovering a monk in any part of the
world who was.

Whether we read in the historic epic poem of
William of Apulia, who probably writes at Bari, or
in the Chronicle of Lupus of the same town, or in
the romantic pages of William of Jumiège, William
of Malmesbury, or Orderic Vitalis, or Fulcherius of
Chartres, it is with the result of convincing ourselves
that these men wrote at a great distance from their
objects, and much nearer to the time of Matthew Paris
than to that of the first Crusade.   Some of them write
as good Latin as that of the monks who pretend to be
eye-witnesses of the deeds of Charles the Great, or of
the state of the world in the fifth century.   It is one
of the facts which betray them.

William of Tyre is supposed to lay down his pen in
the year 1184.   And the weak inference is drawn that
he must have died soon after.   He may have been
Chancellor of King Amalarich and Bishop of Tyre, but
the unfortunate fact is that no more is known of his
extraction, the date of his birth and death, than in the
case of any other member of his Order.   The like may
be said of his continuator, Bernard the Treasurer, who
is supposed to lay down his pen in the year 1275, some

sixteen years later than the Benedictines of St. Albans. But there are other important indications of the true epoch of the chroniclers of the first Crusade.

The Arabians apparently do not take pen in hand to record that event until the thirteenth century; and their touch is not firm until they have advanced some decades beyond the capture of their Holy City, Ailia, called by the monks Hierosolyma, or Jerusalem. Moses Maimonides is said to have been born about forty years after the taking of that city, and perhaps during that interval the vivid descriptions in poetic and oracular form of the great event which stamped upon the brows of the Rabbin the expression of the man of sorrows, had been written down and had been recited in the synagogues. It must be repeated that the life of Maimonides, c. 1139–1205, is the strongest datum that we possess, and constitutes at present the most certain clue by which we shall be enabled to extricate ourselves from the labyrinthine paths of mediæval history.

Now the author of the *Gesta Dei*—or as Gibbon preferred, *Diaboli per Francos*—is said to have been Guibert, Abbot of St. Mary, at Nogent-sous-Conci. Whenever the writer lived, he saw a certain correspondence between the events of the war in Syria and descriptions in the book of Ezekiel, which he freely cites as prophecies. If the book could not have been known in the cloisters until some time long after Maimonides' time, and it appears certain that it could not have been so known, then the writer of the *Gesta*, with his colleagues in the Orders, may fairly be placed about the middle of the fourteenth century. This result coincides with the result of all our previous investigations.

I leave the reader to examine for himself the works

written by Spanish Rabbins in the sixteenth or seventeenth centuries, the Chronicles of R. Joseph, the *Sceptre
of Judah*, and the *Valley of Baca*. The Rabbins had
but scant materials in the Hebrew language. They
have had recourse to the monastic sources, and have
been deceived by fables respecting the existence of
Jews so early as the sixth century in Europe. When
they come to the persecutions at Granada, c. 1066–
1070, they have some indistinct traditional particulars,
handed down in the synagogues. Only when they
come to the year 1096 do they begin to give details,
which throw a flood of light upon the meaning of the
Book of Esther, and upon that infinitely pathetic
elegiac strain which we hear equally in the songs of
the Korachites and in those of the Rabbinical poets,
the forerunners or contemporaries of Maimonides. A
voice sounds still from the Biblical page, pleading with
us no longer for mere cold justice, but for love towards
a people who have indeed borne the chief burden of
the sin and sorrow of that awful time.

The more attentively we study the facts relating to
the beginning of the Chronicle literature in general, so
far as they have yet been ascertained, the state of
libraries, the extreme paucity of readers at the close
of the fourteenth century, the more difficult it will be
to admit that, for the two or three centuries following
the first Crusade, we have anything more than a system
of romantic fiction, based on dim reminiscences of
actual historic events. Only in the fourteenth century
is the Church emerging out of obscurity to be described
by poet and philosopher, her exact origin unknown to
the men of science.

And now let us use the privilege of imagination, so
habitually misused by the men of the Middle Ages, and,

before; and the last hour of our existence does not bring death, but only consummates it. We die many times; our last death is that which snatches us away.

A brave and wise man ought not to flee, but to march forth from life. And above all, we should avoid the lust of dying, which seizes upon many.[1] The prayer of Mæcenas was extremely base, on the other hand, when he longed for life, though in the absence of all that makes life a good.[2]

When that day shall come which shall separate this mixture of the divine and human, I shall leave this body where I found it; I shall restore myself to the gods; not that I am now apart from them, but an element of the grave and terrene detains me. Through these delays of mortal time there is a prelude to yonder better and longer life. This space from infancy to old age is like a preparation for a second birth of nature. Another origin expects us, another state of things. 'Tis only after an interval that we can bear heaven. I look intrepidly forward to yonder decretory hour. 'Tis the last hour for the body, not for the soul. Look upon all that lies around you as the furniture of an inn. You may not take out more than you brought in. . . . That day that you dread as your last is your eternal birthday. Lay down the burden![3]

The Better Life Beyond.

It is sometimes said that Seneca is profuse in words. Is it not to be admired that on topics so trite as life's elementary interests and duties there should be so great an abundance of expression? The stream of eloquence is always sweet and pure, and of clearness undisturbed. He accosts us never as a superior, always as a brother or a friend. A gentle and strong hand

[1] Ep. xxiv. [2] Ep. ci. [3] Ep. cii.

kingdom. A few years after the fall of Tyre, we hear of Messiahs starting up in France, in Spain, in Persia. Wandering Rabbins begin to arrive in London. R. Ben Ezra is here, a little later than the middle of the century, writing a poetical treatise in praise of the Sabbath. Like another Ulysses, he roams from city to city, from Toledo to Rome and Mantua, and again to Tiberias. He and his brethren doubtless pass in the East for faithful followers of the Prophet and the Koran. If we can trust Benjamin of Toledo, there were but a few hundreds of the sons of Jacob in the whole of Syria during this age.

The coming of the Rabbins prepared for the coming of the monks, just as the unpopularity of the Jews in general paved the way for the success of the Church polemic against the whole race. How is it possible to think of the monks in London, or any part of the island, until they had the Dogma and the Legend to proclaim, which was at the same time a proclamation of war on the part of the Abbots against the Rabbins? We hear of the Abbot of Rievaulx writing his ecclesiastical romance about King Edward the Confessor in the year 1163, a date that must be taken with great latitude for correction. We hear of the enigmatic De Diceto as Dean of St. Paul's about forty years later. On the whole, the provisional conclusion may be adopted that the Benedictines came hither during the latter half of the century, and that St. Peter and St. Paul became tutelar saints of the Thames a few years later than they became tutelars of the Tiber. Then it was that the cloud of fable began to envelop the origins of English history, and that our country became a holy land, sanctified by the footsteps of St. Joseph of Arimathea and the Apostolic pair.

The beginnings of Oxford and Cambridge can be
hardly discovered at the close of the twelfth century;
and certainly, until those schools were founded, little
or nothing could have been heard in this island concerning the Christian theory of the past. There were
the dramatic ceremonies centering upon the Mass;
there was the Missal, with its lessons, gospels, and
epistles; there was little more. It requires an effort
of imagination to conceive the paucity of Bibles through
the whole period from the first Benedictine foundations
down to the dissolution of the monasteries. Lindisfarne,
for example, has been made the object of the special
investigations of Mr. Raine. The tradition runs that
the Priory was erected about 1094, and that the island
became holy ground. It is probable that the date
must be lowered by about a century.

But Mr. Raine has shown that the little library of
the Priory could at no period boast of a classical author,
a Chronicle, or even one of the numerous treatises
ascribed to the Venerable Bede; and that it is a
positive fact, from the year 1416 to the dissolution, the
monks were frequently, and in fact generally, without
a Bible. Nothing more was necessary than the Service-
books. On Holy Island, then, as conveniently as on
any other monastic ground in the island, the line may
be drawn between the luxuriance of the dream-world
to which St. Cuthbert and Bæda belong, and the hard
prosaic fact of the origins. To such fact we must
adjust our intelligence, by such fact we must correct
our fancies, if we are ever to see clearly into the
beginnings of English history.

Suppose then that we stand in the dawn of Christian
light in England, from the last decades of the twelfth
century. The Pontifical tradition invites us to follow

the steps of an English monk, who quits the island to assume the direction of the Order—that is, of the Catholic world. Suppose that we visit on our way the cloisters of Cluny, Citeaux, and Claremont. We may find there great enthusiasm, great hopes of military glory in the East, and of spiritual victories in the West, but dense general ignorance of everything literary except the contents of the Service-book. Arriving at Monte Cassino, we find ourselves in a strong fortress, the seat of Christian orthodoxy, guarded by the sword of temporal power. We find the gaze of the monks set toward Rome, where a conflict is beginning between them and the Senate and people. Many of the fraternity are stirring up the maritime cities to furnish the material for the Oriental war. At the Greek cloister of Grotta Ferrata, dependent on Monte Cassino, the monks are perhaps busy, conjointly with their Latin brethren, in devising their ambitious literary scheme.

Visiting Rome, we witness a riot among the people, caused by the arrival of the new Pope, and a Cardinal is assailed with blows. Leaving our countrymen to persecute the people with curses bitter and dire, and with an interdict, we turn southward, and find the King of Naples and Sicily actively hostile against the Order. Suppose that we tarry in those regions for a few years, long enough to hear more futile curses launched against the king, and then withdrawn, and to receive the news of the expulsion of our countryman from Rome, and his death at Agriganum.

Then we hear of the setting up of a number of rival Popes. Intrigues against the liberties of England come to our knowledge; we hear of the flight of the chieftain of the ecclesiastical soldiery to the Continent, presently of his return and his sanguinary death on the floor of the minster at Canterbury. A few years later, and the Emperor Frederic besieges Rome. The Pope, in the disguise of a cook, flees to Venice and hides himself in that city. The next Pope is also cast out from Rome; his faction lose their eyes, and he flees to Verona. Four others rapidly follow, all ardent for the Oriental war, and determined upon making Rome the seat of a new empire. They are especially bent upon securing the alliance of Genoa and Pisa.

In the last years of the century we are in Spain, studying in the Rabbinical schools of Cordova and Toledo. We hear perhaps of the rising fame of the elder Kimchi of Narbonne, who is yet a young man. We hear much of Maimonides, and, travelling to Cairo, find him at the head of his school, in the ripeness of age and faculty. We have reached the centre of the orthodoxy that is elder than the Christian. We make the pilgrimage to Mecca, and find ourselves at last at the eldest of all the seats of orthodoxy from which Europe has been influenced. A few years later we hear of the death of Maimonides, yet a few years more of the death of Innocent III. at Perugia in the midst of Crusading business. So have affairs taken the form of a great revolution. A new spiritual empire has been created, the world has been launched upon a new course.

During the course of these travels we have paid visits to Syria, and have seen that land become the sink and gutter of all the vices of Europe, as the monks of the cloisters of England unite with those of Tyre in bearing witness. The clergy and people are given over to luxury, the whole land is sordid with crime and uncleanness, the whole world tottering beneath the burden of its sins. The Patriarch is living in open adultery. Murderers, thieves, and the off-scouring of mankind arrive in the guise of pilgrims, escaping from justice in their native lands, and return no better than they came. But amidst all this outbreak of human folly and wickedness, the one mind and spirit of the Bishops and Abbots is clearly discernible pervading the ranks of their army, and set upon establishing strongholds of their power, no matter at what cost of human life and human virtue, alike in East and West.

The argument of these pages has been that the Roman Church came into being as the rival of the greater Church of Islam, and was borne to power upon a passionate current of anti-Semitic feeling which set in from the time of the conquests of the Turks. Had we been present in the Holy City on the 3rd October 1187, when Saladin entered to the sound of trumpets, we might have listened to an eloquent oration from the lips of a doctor of Islam which would have convinced us of the truth of that proposition. Mohammed Ibn Saki read a lesson from the Koran, and thus addressed the assembly :—

"Praised be Allah, who hath exalted Islam by His favour, hath cast down the many gods by His power, rules the world after His will, divides benefits by the measure of our thanks, casts down the unbelieving by their craft, gives power to princes in His justice, promises the future life to them that fear Him. He commands, and none gainsayeth; He fulfils His counsels, and there is no delay! Allah, whom I praise, gave to His elect the victory and purified His house, that was full of the filth of idolatry. He is the one only God without associates, the Eternal who begetteth not nor was begotten.

"Mohammed, His Servant and Apostle, who in one night journeyed from Medina to the Holy City and ascended into heaven, cast down idolatry, and put lies to shame. For it is blasphemy to call the son of Mariam a god; yea, he himself will not deny that he is but the Servant of Allah. Ye had the greatest happiness; ye have delivered the dwelling of the Prophets, the home of revelation, the goal of the pilgrimage of the saints. Because of this conquest the gates of heaven opened, beams of light pierced to the deepest abysses, angels rejoiced, the powers of heaven prayed for you, the prophets and apostles of Allah wept tears of joy. Preserve this blessing of the Lord by the fear of the Lord! Beware of evil passions, disobedience, and sloth; beware lest the devil and unbelief glide into your hearts.

"Allah hath chosen you, therefore sacrifice yourselves joyfully for Him; help Him, and He will help you; think of Him, and He will think of you; show Him good, and He will show it to you. Or do ye believe that your sabres of steel, your fine horses, or your endurance has won the victory? Only with His help can ye destroy the godless, cut off the shoots of the unbelievers, and fall upon them as an easy prey. The Holy War is your best service and your noblest custom. But Thou, O Allah our Lord, preserve the Sultan, who bows himself before Thy power and owns Thy benefits; preserve Thy sharp sword, Thy shining brow, the Protector and Defender of the true faith, the Victorious Prince, the Centre of Thy faithful ones, Conqueror of the Cross, Purifier of Thy holy house, surround him with Thine angels, and exalt him for his deeds!"

Of the time immediately following Gibbon has written, that the pecuniary emolument of the Saladine tithe must have tended to increase the interest of the Popes in the recovery of Palestine. "Under Innocent III., that young and ambitious priest, the successors of St. Peter attained the full meridian of their greatness; and in a reign of eighteen years, 1198–1216, he exercised a despotic command over the emperors and kings, whom he raised and deposed; over the nations, whom an interdict of months or years deprived, for the offence of their rulers, of the exercise of Christian worship. In the Council of the Lateran he acted as the ecclesiastical, almost as the temporal, sovereign of the East and West. It was at the feet of his legate that John of England surrendered his crown; and Innocent may boast of the two most signal triumphs over sense and humanity, the establishment of Transubstantiation, and the origin of the Inquisition."

Yet the judicious Hallam observes that, as Hildebrand, Gregory VII., appears the most usurping of mankind till we read the history of Innocent III., so Innocent III. is thrown into the shade by the superior audacity of Boniface VIII. This pontiff, whose memory is darkened by the accusation of fraud and violence, celebrates in 1300 a centenary commemoration in honour of St. Peter and St. Paul, dressed in imperial robes, with the two swords borne before him. If the precedent for this jubilee in 1200 be imaginary, as Hallam admits, equally imaginary are a multitude of acts ascribed to the time of Innocent III.

The lives of the Popes during the thirteenth century are in fact allegorical of the struggles of the great Orders of monks and friars, and they may be fitly perused in the light of the antiquities of Segni, Aquino, and Monte Cassino. The striking legend of Boniface VIII., that "he came in like a fox, lived like a lion,

and died like a dog," is in fact symbolic of the first
age of the Papacy, as the ill name of Clement V. marks
the second in its seat at Avignon.

The story of the Rise of Christendom, as I have
endeavoured in these pages to discover it, is a story of
ambition and violence, disguised under the pretext of
self-devotion and philanthropy. In these late times,
the incessant declamation of the Papal advocates concerning the necessity of the temporal power to the
Vicar of Christ, plainly reveal the instinct which has
governed the great Orders from the very beginning.
They meant to make the material world their own.
These magnificent abbeys, minsters, and cathedrals that
we see around us are monuments of the Christian
Empire which tell no lying tale. It is impossible to
connect them for a moment in our thought with the
Galilæan fishermen without an ironical smile. They
speak of human pride and luxury; they witness to the
impoverishment of our kings and our people in the
interests of a self-elected class. They have been beauti-
fied by the hand of time, and the dark conditions of the
world under which they arose have been forgotten
by the multitude. But there can be no doubt that
these piles were erected, to the dismay of thoughtful
observers, upon the very ruins and wrecks of the freedom of mankind.

It is sometimes argued that the Church once held to
the text, *My kingdom is not of this world*, and that
the text is a judgment upon her pretensions to worldly
power. This argument was stated, with great wealth
of epigram and irony, in a sermon preached twenty
years ago before the University of Oxford by the
Regius Professor of Divinity, on the eve of the assem-
bling of the great Council in Rome. It seems to me

that the preacher—one of our most admirable philosophers in the surplice—was in error when he fixed that meaning on the text. For the Commentaries on the Passion show that the Church means simply to assert the celestial, the supernatural origin of the kingdom. She would prefer, doubtless, to strike her foes prostrate to the ground by the mere force of supernatural terror; and the material sword is a poor weapon to employ in her service who has legions of angels at her command, and who can wield the sword of the Spirit. None the less the Vicar of Christ has claimed the two swords from the beginning; and we see, from the exhortations of St. Bernard to the soldiers of the Temple, that the Church at her origin had unsheathed and was sharpening the temporal sword.

But it has been my task to trace analogous violences of the pen, which have too long escaped the notice of the world. Far more mischief and suffering has been caused by her misuse of this humble instrument. Monkdom passed under the censure and condemnation of the world some 400 years ago, yet the false theory of history which was dictated to an army of scribes and copyists still remains in our literature, still troubles our imagination and our conscience. It is time to say that the claim to the temporal power was from the first founded on figments of the pen, and can now be only maintained by appeals to obsolete forgeries. And apart from that, the mere claim is in itself a proof that the Church is a kingdom of this world. As the preacher before the university observed, it were vain to say that the ultimate objects of Christ's kingdom were spiritual rather than worldly, because the test is, not the nature of the objects, but the nature of the means. If she uses force for this purpose—whether of the

sword or the pen—and declares that she does this by
inherent right, the Church is by her own profession a
power of this world.

Felicitously the preacher observed that the insistance on this claim has in it "the spirit of longing for
what is lost which is so common a trait of human
nature—that desiderium and regret which magnifies
the past, even because it is past, and clings to it the
more because it can never return. When the temporal
power of Rome is over in fact, it just then exists most
rigidly and imperiously in speculation. The greater
intensity of it as a dogma compensates for the absence
of it as a possession." But the preacher did not see
that the Church was committed to this position, which
now seems so self-contradictory and suicidal, by her
original claim, not merely to have been coæval with
the old Roman Empire, but to have been the Roman
Empire itself in its divine form.

Turning to the recent utterances of another admirable countryman, a Roman ecclesiastic, I find that he
still asserts the absolute independence of the Vicar of
Christ of any power under heaven. He relies upon a
History of the Pontiffs which I have shown to be un-
historical, and asserts that from 800 to 1800 the Vicars
of Christ exerted a true, proper, and complete sovereignty over the city of Rome; that the anti-Christian
revolution of our own age crowned its sacrilege on
September 20, 1870, when by force and bloodshed it
usurped the sovereignty of the Vicar of Christ in the
Holy City. I must, on the contrary, with great respect
for the orator, but with great firmness, maintain, in the
light of the foregoing pages, that the Vicars of Christ
were the most violent usurpers of the rights of individuals, of peoples, of kings, of humanity itself, that our

world has ever seen ; that their ascent to power could only have occurred during a long eclipse of truth and justice, and that truth and justice have asserted themselves in their fall.

The same orator maintains that the history of civilisation is the history of Christianity, that the history of Christianity is the history of the Christian Church, that the history of the Christian Church is the history of the supreme Pontiffs, the greatest legislators and rulers the world has ever seen. The substance of the last two propositions cannot be disputed. But, with regard to the first proposition, it seems to me that the history of the mediæval Pontiffs is not the history of civilisation, but part of the history of a great interruption in our Western culture, of which another part is the history of the Caliphs and of the Oriental religions which flourished under their rule. I know not how any independent thinker can fail to concur with this opinion when, for example, he turns over the pages of Stobæus' *Florilegium*, perhaps compiled in Justinian's time, and glances back at the intellectual monuments of the shining thousand years which had elapsed before the death of that emperor.

What have the Dogma and the Legend done for the education of the world? What benefits have flowed to humanity from the great Church organisations? It is impossible to discover any benefits that have not been accidental to the system, nor due to the goodness of individuals who have been enlisted in the service of the Church. It is not the system which has made civilisation, but civilisation which has softened and gradually transformed the system. It has been common, for example, to say that Christianity or the Bible has made England great. On the contrary, it is the vigour

of English intellect and humanity which has been
constantly impressing itself on the spirit and teaching
of the Church from the time of the Reformation.   Since
the multitude became possessed of the Bible, they have
made the Bible echo their own sentiments, which have
become more and more humane.   The interpretation
of the Bible changes with every generation, and so
measures the progress of culture.   But the attempt to
cling, from old habit and affection, to the mediæval
literature, while it has been suffused with modern
meanings, has led at last to a great confusion of ideas.

Nominally we are Christians, but really we mean
humanity.   The creed is still recited, though not an
article remains intact in general belief.   The New
Testament is revered, yet none thinks of obeying its
plainest rules of conduct.   There is little spirit of
persecution, because no dogma commands a hearty
assent.   Experience is our master, and as experience
shows that the life of the rebel against the dogma
may be purer and nobler than that of its professional
supporter, a coldness toward all dogma has set in.
Enthusiasm for it cannot be kindled; yet the people
do not willingly hear it oppugned.   In such a time
of lukewarmness the influence of true teachers, who
know that the study of facts must precede the formation of opinions, and that in the knowledge of the
facts that concern us lies our salvation, is enfeebled.

It may yet be long before we recover that simplicity
of thought about life and duty which was reached by
antiquity after long toil.   But if it be asked, "What,
in the decay of the mediæval ideas, will be the teaching
of the future?" acceptable answers may surely be
found, none the less pertinent and fresh because they
are ancient.   What can be better than the intention

of the following: "Ariston said that of objects of philosophic inquiry some concern us, with others we are not concerned, and others are beyond us. Ethics are our concern; dialectics are not, because they do not contribute to the improvement of life. The secrets of nature are beyond us, it is impossible to know them." Or than this: "To know God is difficult, and to express Him impossible. For to signify that which is bodiless by means of the body is impossible, to apprehend the perfect by means of the imperfect is not possible. Nor is it easy to associate the unseen to that which is but of short duration. The one is for ever, the other passes away: the one is in truth, the other is but shadowed by phantasy. The weaker differs as much from the stronger, and the less from the more, as the mortal from the divine. The interval between these darkens our vision of the fair and good. By the eyes bodies are visible, and by the tongue things seen are said; but that which is bodiless, and inapparent, and most formless, and not composed of matter, cannot possibly be apprehended by our senses. I conceive, O Tât, I conceive what cannot be uttered, and this is God."

Had the Orders, with whom we have been concerned so much in these pages, been the true philosophers and the true Stoics they professed to be, they would have circulated such simple life-wisdom in the world as current coin, and we should now be blessing their memory instead of deploring the enormous waste of human heart and brain which their effort to extirpate that wisdom from the world has caused. And what will be the future of the great teaching Orders of the Church? It is impossible to contemplate them in this day without interest and affection, partly because they link us to a distant time, partly because there have been found in their ranks many of the very flower of mankind. What records of unstinted devotion and courage and patience in the cause of the Christian Empire are to be found, *e.g.*, in the annals of the great Society of Jesus! Who can think without admiration of the extraordinary ardour with which these modern Crusaders went on their missions to far-distant barbarians, that they might print the Dogma and the Legend on those rude imaginations—nay, upon the very marks of animals and the flowers of the field? Yet their lives were no less vainly squandered than those of the mediæval enthusiasts.

How long will successive generations of religious men be ordered, like so many forlorn hopes, to assault the slowly recovering conscience of the world? For surely no clear-sighted churchman can expect that the Church will regain her old power and prestige, unless the conditions of her rise were to recur. Were the European states to exhaust one another in internecine war, were the Orientals again to rush in upon us, the organisation of the Church might enable her to triumph again amidst the ruins of our culture. But *absit omen*, none but fanatics could desire an event like this. On the other hand, with the defeat of the claim to temporal power, the Church must surely undergo a change in her constitution. Her conscience also will awaken, and she will confess that the claim deserved to fail because it was from the first fraudulent and unjust.

Why should we acquiesce in the notion of the rigidity and immobility of the Church? It is not a fact, it is no law of Nature. What art has done, art may undo. Persistence in her great dogmatic dream has brought her into collision with the facts of the world; so soon as she adjusts herself to the facts of the world her dream will change. Were a new spirit to be breathed upon the Orders, it would be as life from the dead for the mass of mankind. Were the priesthood to discern clearly that the founders did not build for eternity, but for time, not with far-reaching views for human good, but in short-sighted selfishness, they might renounce their principles. They might resolve to be philosophers in reality and in truth; they might call men to wisdom, virtue, and freedom with greater joy than they have ever called them to servility; they might at last establish a spiritual empire founded on truth and love. They might replace the forged links with antiquity by a genuine connection; they might restore culture, and bring it to a nobler pitch than ever antiquity knew.

During the last twenty years it may seem at first sight as if the bark of St. Peter had been deliberately steered toward the breakers and the rocks. But we can hardly ascribe such infatuation to the ruling spirits in the Church. Either their policy is a mechanical necessity, the result of her past history, or it is a policy of calculation. If it be the latter, then the rulers of the Church either contemplate a state of political anarchy and the decay of culture, or they contemplate changes in the Church organisation itself. Let us hopefully assume the latter alternative. Were the Pope, for example, to become in fact a subject of the British Empire, he would prove a powerful defender of our law and order. Gradually we should cease to hear of his claims to an *imperium in imperio*, and the Church under his rule, being in fact subject to the state, would in time be so recognised in dogma. Gradually also theology would be subordinated to ethics, and the teaching influence of the Church would be exerted in favour of science and humanity. Should other ecclesiastical heads arise in other empires, the results would then be analogous. It would be the interest of the teachers to move with, no longer against the current of the interests of their fellow-citizens.

The requirement of celibacy in the clergy would in due course be dispensed with, and the gain would be great to the strength and harmony of society and the state. Slowly, in short, the clergy would be transformed into a body of philosophers, mixing freely with all classes of society, imparting the best knowledge, and inculcating the noblest moral ideals of the time. They would be a mighty leverage for good, they would no longer be warring against principles that the most enlightened of mankind approve and love. Such in outline must be the form of our desires for the future, who wish well both to the Church and to mankind. There seems to be no reason why we should despair of their realisation, so soon as the Church herself admits and faces the facts of her historic origin.

Euripides, in some lines of great simplicity and beauty, sings of the three virtues which all should be taught to practise from childhood : to honour the powers above, the parents that begat us, and the common laws of our country. If we do these things, we shall enjoy the fairest crown of glory for ever. The words are equally adapted to our times as to his, they may be applied to England and the Empire no less than to Hellas. Church organisations were never needed to teach these lessons, and it is because of the Church organisations that they still remain untaught as the elements of conduct, and that our moral condition is confused and weak. We are a house divided against itself.

So soon as the teaching classes recover a distinct conception of virtue, which is but a name for the essential strength of humanity, so soon as they see clearly that the love of truth for truth's sake is the highest object and the fairest result of culture, a great reformation must set in. No nobler rule of teaching can guide our schools and universities than the *Sola bona quæ honesta* of the Stoics. In our time the old universities have undergone great changes, and new universities are being formed. If the teachers do their duty, they will deliver the facts, and no longer the dogma, concerning these past 1800 years of the world's history. They will explain that the dogma has less relevance to the terrestrial scene than the dogma had to the celestial scene before the time of Galileo. They will restore the broken continuity of culture, and bring the world once more into communion with its true spiritual masters.

With great interest I have perused the eloquent sermon of Archbishop Ireland preached at Baltimore on the occasion of the centenary celebration of Catholicism in America. His text was from Ecclesiasticus iv. 33, "For thy soul fight for justice," &c. The orator hailed the "new century" with all the enthusiasm of a philosopher and a philanthropist. Among his remarkable sentences were these :—

"I love my age. I love its aspirations and its resolves. I revel in its feats of valour, its industries and its discoveries. I thank it for its many benefactions to my fellow-men, to the people rather than the princes and rulers. I seek no backward voyage across the sea of time. I will ever press forward. I believe that God intends the present to be better than the past, and the future to be better. We should live in our age, know it, be in touch with it. Our work is in the present, and not in the past. It will not do to understand the thirteenth better than the nineteenth century."

There was much more to the same effect. But even in America, and in this late nineteenth century, the clergy must be unable to carry out the noble ideas of intellectual and social reform sketched by the Archbishop so long as they are fettered by the traditions of that dark age which still casts its shadow on us all. It is full freedom of conscience that the Church needs; and freedom of conscience she cannot gain until she has sat in judgment upon the deeds of her founders, and has renounced for ever the ideas which have failed to save the world.

It is time to lay down my pen. I have shown that the Church was founded in a time of darkness, wrath, and dismay, and that the sole apology for the misdeeds of her founders lies in the fact that it was a time when violence alone prevailed on the earth. In these gentler days it surely is not too much to hope that she may resolve to turn down her falsified and iniquitous pages, and begin the chronicle of a new era, inscribed with the records of her endeavours in the cause of knowledge, of truth, of human love—records at the same time of the admiration and gratitude of the world. May these things be!

INDEX.

PRINTED BY BALLANTYNE, HANSON AND CO.
EDINBURGH AND LONDON.

Milton Keynes UK
Ingram Content Group UK Ltd.
UKHW020939201024
2274UKWH00035B/329